Fictions of Authority

Fictions of Authority

WOMEN WRITERS AND NARRATIVE VOICE

Susan Sniader Lanser

Cornell University Press

ITHACA AND LONDON

First published 1992 by Cornell University Press.

International Standard Book Number 0-8014-2377-5 (cloth)
International Standard Book Number 0-8014-9921-6 (paper)
Library of Congress Catalog Card Number 91-55537

Printed in the United States of America

Librarians: Library of Congress cataloging information appears on the last page of the book.

⊗ The paper in this book meets the minimum requirements of the American National Standard for Information Sciences— Permanence of Paper for Printed Library Materials, ANSI Z39.48-1984.

in memory of my mother
Mildred Gerstein Sniader

Contents

Acknowledgments   ix

Introduction

1 Toward a Feminist Poetics of Narrative Voice   3
2 The Rise of the Novel, the Fall of the Voice: Juliette
   Catesby's Silencing   25

Part I. Authorial Voice

3 In a Class by Herself: Self-Silencing in Riccoboni's
   Abeille   45
4 Sense and Reticence: Jane Austen's "Indirections"   61
5 Woman of Maxims: George Eliot and the Realist
   Imperative   81
6 Fictions of Absence: Feminism, Modernism,
   Virginia Woolf   102

7   Unspeakable Voice: Toni Morrison's Postmodern
     Authority   120

Part II.   Personal Voice

8   Dying for Publicity: *Mistriss Henley*'s Self-Silencing   141

9   Romantic Voice: The Hero's Text   155

10   *Jane Eyre*'s Legacy: The Powers and Dangers of
     Singularity   176

11   African-American Personal Voice: "Her Hungriest
     Lack"   194

Part III.   Communal Voice

12   Solidarity and Silence: *Millenium Hall* and *The Wrongs
     of Woman*   223

13   Single Resistances: The Communal "I" in Gaskell,
     Jewett, and Audoux   239

14   (Dif)fusions: Modern Fiction and Communal Form   255

15   Full Circle: *Les Guérillères*   267

     Index   281

Acknowledgments

As I hope this book makes evident, writing is not an isolated act. The collective imagination of my students and colleagues has shaped my thinking in ways no longer traceable. Grants from the American Council of Learned Societies, the National Endowment for the Humanities, Georgetown University, and the University of Maryland at College Park enabled vital spaces of unfettered time. Bernhard Kendler and Kay Scheuer at Cornell University Press, and Lauren Oppenheim provided crucial editorial support.

The project would have faltered long ago without the intelligence and generosity of those who read individual chapters or the entire manuscript, sometimes in several forms. Evelyn Torton Beck was the book's earliest mentor and continues to inspire me professionally and personally. Mary Wilson Carpenter's astute and thorough reading of a later version was immeasurably helpful in revising the manuscript. Maria Lima turned her quick mind to assistance both critical and editorial. Sharon Groves, Leona Fisher, Annette Oxindine, Jo Radner, and Mary Helen Washington read and advised. Joyce Kornblatt heard the questions beneath my questions. Jack Undank and Alan Wilde were demanding readers and loving mentors throughout these several years. My deepest gratitude is reserved for Michael Ragussis, whose brilliant and tireless readings of several versions, and whose often daily engagement with problems both momentous and minuscule, far surpassed the mutual attentiveness of close relationship. The distance this book has traveled over the years of its composition is in large measure his gift.

I am not the only one who has dwelt with this work and been subjected to its claims on time, space, and energy. Jo Radner has been lovingly present and steadily responsive to my questions and concerns. My sons, Steve, Tom, and Chris, who became adults as this project developed, remained good-natured enthusiasts who have learned that a book is never finished until it is in print.

I have sometimes said that I wrote *The Narrative Act*, with its structures and diagrams, because my father was an engineer. This book is for my mother, who hoped to be a writer and whose life ended before she could find a public voice.

An early version of part of Chapter 2 was published as "Courting Death: *Roman, romantisme*, and *Mistriss Henley*'s Narrative Practices," *Eighteenth Century Life* 13 (February 1989). An early version of part of Chapter 2 appeared as "Plot, Voice, and Narrative *Oubli: Juliette Catesby*'s Twice-Told Tale," in *Eighteenth Century Women and the Arts*, ed. Frederick M. Keener and Susan E. Lorsch (Westport, Conn.: Greenwood Press, 1988), copyright © 1988 by Hofstra University. I am grateful to the John Hopkins University Press and to Greenwood Publishing Group, Inc. for permission to make use of this material.

S. S. L.

INTRODUCTION

1

Toward a Feminist Poetics
of Narrative Voice

> Why this privileged relationship with the voice?
> —HÉLÈNE CIXOUS, "The Laugh of the Medusa"

Few words are as resonant to contemporary feminists as "voice." The
term appears in history and philosophy, in sociology, literature, and
psychology, spanning disciplinary and theoretical differences. Book
titles announce "another voice," a "different voice," or resurrect the
"lost voices" of women poets and pioneers; fictional figures ancient
and modern, actual women famous and obscure, are honored for
speaking up and speaking out.[1] Other silenced communities—peoples
of color, peoples struggling against colonial rule, gay men and lesbians—have also written and spoken about the urgency of "coming
to voice." Despite compelling interrogations of "voice" as a humanist
fiction, for the collectively and personally silenced the term has become a trope of identity and power: as Luce Irigaray suggests, to find
a voice (*voix*) is to find a way (*voie*).[2]

1. A few titles: *In a Different Voice; American Women, American Voices; The Sound of Our Own
Voices; The Other Voice: Scottish Women's Writing since 1808; Finding a Voice: Asian Women in
Britain; Territories of the Voice: Contemporary Stories by Irish Women Writers; Radical Voices: A
Decade of Resistance from "Women's Studies International Forum"; The Indigenous Voice: Visions and
Realities.*
2. Luce Irigaray, *This Sex Which is Not One*, trans. Catherine Porter with Carolyn Burke
(Ithaca: Cornell University Press, 1985), 209. As my references to Cixous and Irigaray em-
phasize, even "poststructuralist" feminists have been unwilling to abandon the word *voice* as
a signifier of female power, for women have not *as a body* (in both senses) possessed the logos
that deconstruction deconstructs.

3

In narrative poetics ("narratology"), voice is an equally crucial though more circumscribed term, designating tellers—as distinct from both authors and nonnarrating characters—of narrative. Although many critics acknowledge the bald inaccuracy of "voice" and "teller" to signify something written, these terms persist even among structuralists: according to Gérard Genette, "in the most unobtrusive narrative, someone is speaking to me, is telling me a story, is inviting me to listen to it as he tells it."[3] Narration entails social relationships and thus involves far more than the technical imperatives for getting a story told. The narrative voice and the narrated world are mutually constitutive; if there is no tale without a teller, there is no teller without a tale. This interdependence gives the narrator a liminal position that is at once contingent and privileged: the narrator has no existence "outside" the text yet brings the text into existence; narrative speech acts cannot be said to be mere "imitations," like the acts of characters, because they are the acts that make the "imitations" possible.

Despite their shared recognition of the power of "voice," the two concepts I have been describing—the feminist and the narratological—have entailed separate inquiries of antithetical tendency: the one general, mimetic, and political, the other specific, semiotic, and technical. When feminists talk about voice, we are usually referring to the behavior of actual or fictional persons and groups who assert woman-centered points of view. Thus feminists may speak of a literary character who refuses patriarchal pressures as "finding a voice" whether or not that voice is represented textually. When narrative theorists talk about voice, we are usually concerned with formal structures and not with the causes, ideologies, or social implications of particular narrative practices. With a few exceptions, feminist criticism does not ordinarily consider the technical aspects of narration, and narrative poetics does not ordinarily consider the social properties and political implications of narrative voice.[4] Formalist poetics may seem to fem-

3. Gérard Genette, *Narrative Discourse Revisited*, trans. Jane E. Lewin (Ithaca: Cornell University Press, 1988), 101. I consider this distinction not essential but conventional: narratives have narrators because Western literature has continued to construct reading and listening in speakerly terms. The convention may already be disappearing in an age of mechanical reproduction, bureaucratic discourse, and computer-generated texts. For an opposing viewpoint, see Jonathan Culler, "Problems in the Theory of Fiction," *Diacritics* 14 (Spring 1984): 5–11.

4. On the tension between feminism and narrative poetics see Robyn Warhol, *Gendered Interventions: Narrative Discourse in the Victorian Novel* (New Brunswick, N.J.: Rutgers University Press, 1989), 12–20; my essay "Toward a Feminist Narratology," *Style* 20 (1986): 341–63; and my subsequent exchange with Nilli Diengott in *Style* 22 (1988): 40–60.

inists naively empiricist, masking ideology as objective truth, sacrificing significance for precision, incapable of producing distinctions that are politically meaningful. Feminist criticism may seem to narratologists naively subjectivist, sacrificing precision for ideology, incapable of producing distinctions that are textually meaningful.

These incompatible tendencies, which I have overstated here, can offer fruitful counterpoints. As a narratological term, "voice" attends to the specific forms of textual practice and avoids the essentializing tendencies of its more casual feminist usages. As a political term, "voice" rescues textual study from a formalist isolation that often treats literary events as if they were inconsequential to human history. When these two approaches to "voice" converge in what Mikhail Bakhtin has called a "sociological poetics,"[5] it becomes possible to see narrative technique not simply as a product of ideology but as ideology itself: narrative voice, situated at the juncture of "social position and literary practice,"[6] embodies the social, economic, and literary conditions under which it has been produced.[7] Such a sociological or materialist poetics refuses the idealism to which both narrative poetics and some forms of feminist theory have been prone, an idealism that has led in the first case to a reading of textual properties as universal, inevitable, or random phenomena, and in the second to the assumption of a panhistorical "women's language" or "female form." I maintain that both narrative structures and women's writing are determined not by essential properties or isolated aesthetic imperatives but by complex and changing conventions that are themselves produced in and by the relations of power that implicate writer, reader, and text. In modern Western societies during the centuries of "print culture" with which I am concerned, these constituents of power must include, at the very least, race, gender, class, nationality, education, sexuality

---

5. A "sociological poetics" is described in P. N. Medvedev and M. M. Bakhtin, *The Formal Method in Literary Scholarship: A Critical Introduction to Sociological Poetics*, trans. Albert J. Wehrle (Baltimore: Johns Hopkins University Press, 1978), 30. The feminist attention to voice generated by Bakhtinian theory is a welcome new inquiry; see especially Dale M. Bauer, *Feminist Dialogics: A Theory of Failed Community* (Albany: SUNY Press, 1988). On the whole, however, "feminist dialogics" have not focused on the close formal distinctions found, for example, in Bakhtin's "Discourse on the Novel," but have followed Bakhtin's tendency elsewhere to equate "voice" with discourse in the Foucauldian sense.

6. Raymond Williams, *Marxism and Literature* (Oxford: Oxford University Press, 1977), 179.

7. I am using "ideology" throughout to describe the discourses and signifying systems through which a culture constitutes its beliefs about itself, structures the relationships of individuals and groups to one another, to social institutions, and to belief systems, and legitimates and perpetuates its values and practices. This definition does not address the question of whether there is a "real" outside ideology that is not itself ideological.

and marital status, interacting with and within a given social for-
mation.

So long as it acknowledges its own status as theory rather than
claiming to trade in neutral, uninterpreted facts, a historically-situated
structuralist poetics may offer a valuable differential framework for
examining specific narrative patterns and practices. The exploration
of narrative structures in women's writings may, in turn, challenge
the categories and postulates of narratology, since the canon on which
narrative theory is grounded has been relentlessly if not intentionally
man-made.[8] As one contribution to such a feminist poetics of narrative, this book explores certain configurations of textual voice in
fictions by women of Britain, France, and the United States writing
from the mid-eighteenth century to the mid-twentieth—the period
that coincides with the hegemony of the novel and its attendant notions of individual(ist) authorship. Recognizing that the "author-
function" that grounds Western literary authority is constructed in
white, privileged-class male terms,[9] I take as a point of departure the
hypothesis that female voice—a term used here simply to designate
the narrator's grammatical gender—is a site of ideological tension
made visible in textual practices.

In thus linking social identity and narrative form, I am postulating
that the authority of a given voice or text is produced from a conjunction of social and rhetorical properties. Discursive authority—by
which I mean here the intellectual credibility, ideological validity, and
aesthetic value claimed by or conferred upon a work, author, narrator,
character, or textual practice—is produced interactively; it must therefore be characterized with respect to specific receiving communities.
In Western literary systems for the past two centuries, however, discursive authority has, with varying degrees of intensity, attached itself
most readily to white, educated men of hegemonic ideology. One
major constituent of narrative authority, therefore, is the extent to
which a narrator's status conforms to this dominant social power. At
the same time, narrative authority is also constituted through (historically changing) textual strategies that even socially unauthorized

8. Nor is this true only of formalist critics like Genette, Shlomith Rimmon-Kenan, Wolfgang
Iser, and (less egregiously) Seymour Chatman. The work of materialists like Fredric Jameson
and even Bakhtin, which has been so enthusiastically embraced by critics working with "marginal" discourses, is androcentric in both its textual canon and its assumptions about literature.

9. On the "author-function" see Michel Foucault, "What Is an Author?" in *Language,
Counter-Memory, Practice: Selected Essays and Interviews*, ed. Donald F. Bouchard (Ithaca: Cornell
University Press, 1977), 113–38.

writers can appropriate. Since such appropriations may of course backfire, nonhegemonic writers and narrators may need to strike a delicate balance in accommodating and subverting dominant rhetorical practices.

Although I have been speaking about authority as if it were universally desirable, some women writers have of course questioned not only those who hold authority and the mechanisms by which they are authorized, but the value of authority as modern Western cultures have constructed it. I believe, however, that even novelists who challenge this authority are constrained to adopt the authorizing conventions of narrative voice in order, paradoxically, to mount an authoritative critique of the authority that the text therefore also perpetuates. Carrying out such an Archimedean project, which seems to me particularly hazardous for texts seeking canonical status, necessitates standing on the very ground one is attempting to deconstruct. While I will acknowledge ways in which women writers continue to challenge even their own authoritative standing, the emphasis of this book is on the project of self-authorization, which, I argue, is implicit in the very act of authorship. In other words, I assume that regardless of any woman writer's ambivalence toward authoritative institutions and ideologies, the act of writing a novel and seeking to publish it—like my own act of writing a scholarly book and seeking to publish it—is implicitly a quest for discursive authority: a quest to be heard, respected, and believed, a hope of influence. I assume, that is, that every writer who publishes a novel wants it to be authoritative for her readers, even if authoritatively antiauthoritarian, within the sphere and for the receiving community that the work carves out. In making this assumption I am not denying what Edward Said calls the "molésted" or "sham" nature of textual authority in general and of fictional authority in particular, but I am also reading the novel as a cultural enterprise that has historically claimed and received a truth value beyond the fictional.[10]

I have chosen to examine texts that engage questions of authority specifically through their production of narrative voice. In each case, narrative voice is a site of crisis, contradiction, or challenge that is manifested in and sometimes resolved through ideologically charged

10. See Edward Said, "Molestation and Authority in Narrative Fiction," in *Aspects of Narrative: Selected Papers from the English Institute*, ed. J. Hillis Miller (New York: Columbia University Press, 1971), 47–68. On the status of fiction see also Peter J. McCormick, *Fictions, Philosophies, and the Problems of Poetics* (Ithaca: Cornell University Press, 1988).

technical practices. The texts I explore construct narrative voices that seek to write themselves into Literature without leaving Literature the same. These narrators, skeptical of the authoritative aura of the male pen and often critical of male dominance in general, are nonetheless pressed by social and textual convention to reproduce the very structures they would reformulate. Such narrators often call into question the very authority they endorse or, conversely, endorse the authority they seem to be questioning. That is, as they strive to create fictions of *authority*, these narrators expose *fictions* of authority as the Western novel has constructed it—and in exposing the fictions, they may end up re-establishing the authority. Some of these texts work out such dilemmas on their thematic surfaces, constructing fictions *of*—that is, *about*—authority, as well.

When I describe these complexities in some women's writings I am not, however, suggesting any kind of "authentic" female voice or arguing that women necessarily write differently from men. Rather, I believe that disavowed writers of both sexes have engaged in various strategies of adaptation and critique that make their work "dialogical" in ways that Bakhtin's formulation, which posits heteroglossia as a general modern condition, may obscure.[11] It is possible, for example, that women privileged enough to write literature are particularly susceptible to what Margaret Homans describes as "a specific gender-based alienation from language" born of the "simultaneous participation in and exclusion from a hegemonic group."[12] My reading suggests that different communities of women have had different degrees of access to particular narrative forms. I am especially interested in those female narrators who claim public authority, since within the historical period I am studying it has not been voice in general so much as public voice that women have been denied. As I will suggest further on in this chapter, these concerns lead me less to a new narrative poetics than to a poetics attentive to issues that conventional narratology has devalued or ignored.

11. Bakhtin's formulation that all novelistic discourse, if not all discourse, is irreducibly double-voiced makes more difficult the differentiating of specific ways in which the words of a disauthorized community are "entangled, shot through with shared thoughts, points of view, alien value judgments and accents," and dwell in "a dialogically agitated and tension-filled environment of alien words" (*The Dialogic Imagination*, trans. Caryl Emerson and Michael Holquist [Austin: University of Texas Press, 1981], 276).

12. Margaret Homans, "'Her Very Own Howl': The Ambiguities of Representation in Recent Women's Fiction," *Signs* (1983): 205. Homans's suggestion that this ambiguity characterizes all women's discourse seems to me problematic insofar as it presumes that all women are simultaneously inside and outside a hegemony.

Before describing more fully the focus of this book, I want to illustrate the complex dynamics that may govern a specific production of female voice by turning to a curious document that appeared in *Atkinson's Casket* in April 1832:[13]

FEMALE INGENUITY.

Secret Correspondence.—A young Lady, newly married, being obliged to show her husband, all the letters she wrote, sent the following to an intimate friend.

> I cannot be satisfied, my Dearest Friend!
> blest as I am in the matrimonial state,
> unless I pour into your friendly bosom,
> which has ever been in unison with mine,
> the various deep sensations which swell
> with the liveliest emotions of pleasure
> my almost bursting heart. I tell you my dear
> husband is one of the most amiable of men,
> I have been married seven weeks, and
> have never found the least reason to
> repent the day that joined us, my husband is
> in person and manners far from resembling
> ugly, crass, old, disagreeable, and jealous
> monsters, who think by confining to secure;
> a wife, it is his maxim to treat as a
> bosom-friend and confidant, and not as a
> play thing or menial slave, the woman
> chosen to be his companion. Neither party
> he says ought to obey implicitly;—
> but each yield to the other by turns—
> An ancient maiden aunt, near seventy,
> a cheerful, venerable, and pleasant old lady,
> lives in the house with us—she is the de-
> light of both young and old—she is ci-
> vil to all the neighbourhood round,
> generous and charitable to the poor—
> I know my husband loves nothing more
> than he does me; he flatters me more
> than the glass, and his intoxication
> (for so I must call the excess of his love,)

13. I discovered this letter accidentally some years ago in *The Genteel Female*, ed. Clifton Furness (New York: Knopf, 1931). On that book's endpaper is reproduced the page from *Atkinson's Casket* that includes this letter, sandwiched between a commentary on angels and directions for calisthenic exercise. For a discussion of other aspects of the letter, including its "plot," see my essay "Toward a Feminist Narratology," 346–57.

often makes me blush for the unworthiness
of its object, and I wish I could be more deserving
of the man whose name I bear. To
say all in one word, my dear, ____, and to
crown the whole, my former gallant lover
is now my indulgent husband, my fondness
is returned, and I might have had
a Prince, without the felicity I find with
him. Adieu! May you be as blest as I am unable to wish that I could be more
happy.

For those who believe in a "women's language" that is "polite, emo-tional, enthusiastic, gossipy, talkative, uncertain, dull, and chatty,"[14] or "weak, trivial, ineffectual, tentative, hesitant, hyperpolite, euphe-mistic, and . . . marked by gossip and gibberish,"[15] this text might be hailed as perfect evidence. Its self-effacing writer, who blushes at her own "unworthiness," nonetheless cannot "say all in one word"; rep-etition, hyperbole, convolution, and grammatical anomaly are the per-vasive structures of her text. It has been argued that such self-deprecating, uncertain, and verbose discourse, which women in cer-tain circumstances have supposedly been encouraged to adopt, also undermines its own authority.[16]

But let us recall that this bride was obliged to show the letter to her husband; a note at the bottom of the *Casket* entry tells us that "the key to the above letter, is to read the first and then every alternate line":

I cannot be satisfied, my dearest Friend!
unless I pour into your friendly bosom,
the various deep sensations which swell
my almost bursting heart. I tell you my dear
I have been married seven weeks, and
repent the day that joined us, my husband is
ugly, crass, old, disagreeable, and jealous[;]
a wife, it is his maxim to treat as a
play thing or menial slave, the woman
he says ought to obey implicitly;—

14. Cheris Kramarae, "Proprietors of Language," in *Women and Language in Literature and Society*, ed. Sally McConnell-Ginet, Ruth Borker, and Nelly Furman (New York: Praeger, 1980), 58.
15. Dale Spender, *Man Made Language* (London: Routledge, 1980), 33.
16. Robin Lakoff, *Language and Woman's Place* (New York: Harper and Row, 1975), 7.

> An ancient maiden aunt, near seventy,
> lives in the house with us—she is the de-
> vil to all the neighbourhood round,
> I know my husband loves nothing more
> than the glass, and his intoxication
> often makes me blush for the unworthiness
> of the man whose name I bear. To
> crown the whole, my former gallant lover
> is returned, and I might have had
> him. Adieu! may you be as blest as I am un-
> happy.

If the surface letter is virtually a sampler of what has passed for "women's language," this "subtext" is an equally striking example of what might stereotypically be called "men's language": it is "capable, direct, rational," "strong,"[17] "forceful, efficient, blunt, authoritative, serious, effective, sparing and masterful."[18] This narrator, writing for a sister's eye, shows herself angry, decisive, judgmental, acutely aware of her husband's deficiencies and her own lost opportunities. Beneath the putatively feminine voice of effusive self-effacement lies the putatively masculine voice of indignant self-assertion, which the writer cannot inscribe in the more public version of her text. These formal differences between the letters, which share the same originating female voice, are clearly not differences in the sex of the narrator, though they may be attributable to differences in the sex of the narratee. The "feminine style" of the surface text, that "powerless," non-authoritative form called "women's language," here becomes a powerfully subversive mask for telling secrets to a woman under the watchful eyes of a man. In Irigaray's terms, the surface letter is a "disruptive excess," a "mimicry": it deliberately adopts a "feminine" position that is exaggerated into subversion by exposing the mechanisms of its own abjection (thereby revealing at the same time its dependence upon "the words of the powerful").[19] The female voice conforms in order to "con" form: "women's language" becomes a calculated response to alienation and censorship, an evasion of material threat.

I will argue, however, that this discourse is not simply "women's language"—or even, as some linguists would have it, a universal "lan-

---

17. Kramarae, "Proprietors of Language," 58.
18. Spender, *Man Made Language*, 33.
19. Irigaray, *This Sex Which Is Not One*, 76–78; Sheila Rowbotham, *Woman's Consciousness, Man's World* (Harmondsworth, England: Penguin, 1973), 32.

guage of the powerless"—but the product of a particular set of stereotypes that become codified in Victorian gender ideologies. This language is associated specifically with the "lady" who maintains her position through a conscious or unconscious discourse of devotion to the men who control her life. It is less the language of *women* than the language of *wives*: the *woman* in this text—the independent human of female sex—is in fact represented by the voice whose language would be called "masculine." In other words, in this blatantly dialogized discourse, both voices are female; "female voice" is not an "essence" but a variable subject position whose "I" is grammatically feminine. The particular characteristics of any "female voice," then, are a function of the context in which that voice operates.

This context, moreover, is less simple than it appears. Because the letter is deliberately coded, the subtext makes the surface letter seem only a fiction and the hidden message all the "truth." In this case "women's language" becomes a code adopted to confuse a male "public," as if privately— that is, to another woman—a woman can simply say what she means. But this opposition deconstructs itself when one asks how two such disparate narratives can produce a continuous text. The articulation between surface and subtext, the syntactic hinge that binds and finally transforms the whole, is a set of negative constructions that the decoding process pares away:

> I [... have *never* found the least reason to] repent
> my husband is ... [*far from* resembling] ugly, crass, old ...
> a wife, it is his maxim to treat ... [*not*] as a plaything
> [*Neither* party], he says, ought to obey implicitly
> I am *un*[able to wish that I could be more] happy—

This negativity turns out to be more than the link between texts; it makes the surface text not simply a proclamation of one woman's marital happiness but an indirect indictment of marriage itself. In its negations, the surface letter written "for" the husband describes as normative the kind of marriage the writer claims to have escaped; each statement about the speaker's good fortune implies a norm in which brides repent their marriages, husbands are monstrous, and women are "playthings" or "slaves." Thus, by saying what one marriage is not, the surface text shows what its narrator expected marriage to be. While the subtext condemns one husband and laments one bride's fate—suggesting that the writer has merely married the "wrong" man—the surface letter condemns marriage itself, presenting as typical the conditions that seem in the subtext to be individual. The subtext, with its portrait of a miserable bride, thus becomes an illustration of the surface text rather than its antithesis, and it is fitting that the two versions meet only in a shared dissatisfaction, in the single line that does not change: "I cannot be satisfied, my dearest Friend!"

Even without the subtext, then, the surface letter is already double-voiced, representing in one discourse both the uncritical acceptance of one marriage and a critical rejection of marriage itself. This doubleness also means that the surface letter is at least as authoritative as the hidden undertext, that authority resides not simply in "men's language" (which in this case is asserting only an individual, experiential "truth"), but also in the indirection of a censored and stereotypically "feminine" form. Nor is this letter simply a "palimpsest" in which "surface designs conceal or obscure deeper, less accessible (and less socially acceptable) levels of meaning,"[20] for this "surface design" turns out to carry meanings at least as disturbing as the subtext it purports to protect.

I have explored this letter in some detail not to reinforce notions of discursive sexual difference but, on the contrary, to suggest the complexity and specificity of (women's) narrative practices even in obviously coded texts. Underscoring crucial differences of function and form between "private" and "public" discourse, the letter represents its own formal practices as neither arbitrary nor simply representational, but as responses to situational imperatives produced by the relations of power that acts of telling entail. Narrative status, contact, and stance are revealed to be mutually constitutive: the ways in which narrators represent themselves, the relationships they construct with narratees, and the ideological and affective positions they take are dynamic and interdependent elements. In illustrating the intricacies of narrative strategy in a culture that censors female voice, and the specificity of different narrative constructions for different audiences and purposes, the letter asks those who would not be deceived "husbands" not only to read beneath surfaces but to read surfaces anew, not only to read manifest "content" but to read the content of manifest "form." And if the letter as private correspondence seems to figure the male as the duped reader and the female as the ideal

---

20. Sandra Gilbert and Susan Gubar, *The Madwoman in the Attic: The Woman Writer and the Nineteenth-Century Literary Imagination* (New Haven: Yale University Press, 1979), 73.

one, the letter as a public document has as its audience the unidentified reader of either sex who, presented with the text as it appeared in *Atkinson's Casket,* can read beyond the immediate context of the letter-writer's circumstances to understand "female ingenuity" as cultural critique.

Finally, the publication of this letter in 1832, in a city where African-American and white women were becoming involved in abolitionist activity (the Philadelphia Female Anti-Slavery Society was founded in 1833), suggests that the relationship between patriarchy and slavery implicit in the reference to the wife as a "menial slave" may be more than casual: it both raises the problematic history of white women's appropriation of slavery by analogy[21] and reminds us that American slaves also made extensive use of coding in order to evade censorship. It seems doubly appropriate, then, that "ingenuity" means not only a paradoxical blend of skillful design and apparent openness but also, according to the *OED,* "the quality or condition of being a free-born man." In theory, writing becomes a powerful site of transformation to this "condition" of freedom insofar as writing may be detached from its producing subject. The public circulation of texts by women has thus posed a pervasive threat to patriarchy, as the public circulation of slave writings posed a pervasive threat to slavery, and these threats may explain why the forms and performances of women and peoples of color have often been devalued as mere "ingenuity."

Atkinson's Casket presents the bride's letter without revealing the circumstances of its composition, the identity of its composer, or the process by which it came to be a public text. If, as I suspect, the letter is apocryphal (that is, not an actual bride's correspondence), it is double-voiced in yet another sense: it has represented fiction as history. The voice that introduces the letter becomes its authorizing agent and the letter-writer a fictional narrator created to perform a politically motivated exercise in "ingenuity." Fiction becomes a set of strategies for mitigating the audacity of opposition, and the very fact of the fiction becomes evidence of a censorship subtler but no less significant than that imposed on the young bride. Private voice (here,

---

21. I mean here the use of analogies with slavery not as a way of combating slavery but as a way of legitimating women's rights. Although I do not doubt the conscious intentions of those Americans and Europeans who made such analogies in the eighteenth and nineteenth centuries, I believe they tended to work more to the benefit of white women than to that of slaves. The same holds for contemporary analogies between "women" and "blacks," which also risk erasing black women because "women" comes to imply white women, and "blacks," black men.

the voice of the bride addressing only her closest female friend) becomes an enabling strategy for writing what is manifestly forbidden as "public" narrative. To other compelling explanations for women's historical association with the novel—its formal and thematic pliability at the time when women began writing in significant numbers; its ambiguous status as literature; its feasibility as a source of both income and discursive power—one must surely add the opportunities the novel affords for creating voices on the margins of fiction and history that both mask and enable the most challenging fictions of authority.

This book begins with the simultaneous "rise" of the novel and emergence of modern gender identity in the mid-eighteenth century, and moves toward what may well be the twilight of both. As I situate narrative practices in relation to literary production and social ideology, I will be asking what forms of voice have been available to women, and to which women, at particular moments. My intention is to explore through specifically formal evidence the intersection of social identity and textual form, reading certain aspects of narrative voice as a critical locus of ideology.

I have organized the book to focus on changing problems and patterns in the articulation of three narrative modes which I call, respectively, authorial, personal, and communal voice. Each mode represents not simply a set of technical distinctions but a particular kind of narrative consciousness and hence a particular nexus of powers, dangers, prohibitions, and possibilities. Across all three modes, however, I will be concerned with two aspects of narration that I consider of greater significance in the construction of textual authority than narrative poetics has traditionally allowed. The first is the distinction between private voice (narration directed toward a narratee who is a fictional character) and public voice (narration directed toward a narratee "outside" the fiction who is analogous to the historical reader). The second is the distinction between narrative situations that do and those that do not permit narrative self-reference, by which I mean explicit attention to the act of narration itself. It is my hypothesis that gendered conventions of public voice and of narrative self-reference serve important roles in regulating women's access to discursive authority.

I use the term *authorial voice* to identify narrative situations that are heterodiegetic, public, and potentially self-referential. (Gérard Genette, observing that every narrator is potentially an enunciating "I,"

suggests the more precise term *heterodiegetic* for what is traditionally
called "third-person" narration in which the narrator is not a participant in the fictional world and exists on a separate ontological plane
from the characters.[22]) The mode I am calling authorial is also "extradiegetic" and public, directed to a narratee who is analogous to a
reading audience.[23] I have chosen the term "authorial" not to imply
an ontological equivalence between narrator and author but to suggest
that such a voice (re)produces the structural and functional situation
of authorship. In other words, where a distinction between the (implied) author and a public, heterodiegetic narrator is not textually
marked, readers are invited to equate the narrator with the author
and the narratee with themselves (or their historical equivalents). This
conventional equation gives authorial voice a privileged status among
narrative forms; as Bakhtin states, while the discourse of a character
or a stylized narrator is always a contingent "object of authorial understanding," authorial discourse is "directed toward its own straight-
forward referential meaning."[24] Moreover, since authorial narrators
exist outside narrative time (indeed, "outside" fiction) and are not
"humanized" by events, they conventionally carry an authority superior to that conferred on characters, even on narrating characters.
In using the term "authorial" I mean as well to evoke Franz Stanzel's
distinction in *Narrative Situations in the Novel* between "authorial" and
"figural" modes: while authorial narrative permits what I am calling
narrative self-reference, in the "figural" mode all narration is focalized
through the perspectives of characters, and thus no reference to the
narrator or the narrative situation is feasible.

I want to suggest as a major element of authorial status a distinction
between narrators who engage exclusively in acts of representation—
that is, who simply predicate the words and actions of fictional characters—and those who undertake "extrarepresentational" acts: reflections, judgments, generalizations about the world "beyond" the fiction,
direct addresses to the narratee, comments on the narrative process,

---

22. Gérard Genette, *Narrative Discourse: An Essay in Method*, trans. Jane E. Lewin (Ithaca: Cornell University Press, 1980), 244–45.

23. On the concept of diegetic levels, see ibid., 227–31. On the distinction between private and public voice, which is not identical to Genette's distinction between primary and inserted narrative, see my book *The Narrative Act: Point of View in Prose Fiction* (Princeton: Princeton University Press, 1981), 133–48, and "Toward a Feminist Narratology," 350–55.

24. Mikhail Bakhtin, *Problems of Dostoevsky's Poetics*, ed. and trans. Caryl Emerson (Minneapolis: University of Minnesota Press, 1984), 187.

allusions to other writers and texts.[25] I will be using the term *overt authoriality* or simply *authoriality*, to refer to practices by which heterodiegetic, public, self-referential narrators perform these "extrarepresentational" functions not strictly required for telling a tale. I am speculating that acts of representation make a more limited claim to discursive authority than extrarepresentational acts, which expand the sphere of fictional authority to "nonfictional" referents and allow the writer to engage, from "within" the fiction, in a culture's literary, social, and intellectual debates. On the other hand, as Shlomith Rimmon-Kenan has observed, when a narrator "becomes more overt, his chances of being fully reliable are diminished, since his interpretations, judgements, generalizations are not always compatible with the norms of the implied author."[26]

Extrarepresentational acts are especially critical to a polyglossic genre like the novel because they enable the narrator to construct the "maxims" that Genette describes as the foundation of verisimilitude.[27] In other words, the reception of a novel rests on an implicit set of principles by which textual events (for example, characters' behaviors) are rendered plausible. To the degree that a text's values deviate from cultural givens (as they will to some degree in all but the most formulaic of fictions), they must be established (or inferred) for each narrative instance so that readers can construct the story as "plausible" and embed it in a "world view."[28] Ideologically oppositional writers might wish, therefore, to "maxim-ize" their narratives in order either to posit alternative textual ideologies or to establish the writer, through her authorial narrator-equivalent, as a significant participant in contemporary debates—all the more during those periods when the novel was one of the few accepted means for women to intervene in public life.

It should not be difficult to understand why, with differences in kind and intensity according to time, place, and circumstance, women writers' adoption of overt authoriality has usually meant transgressing

25. Each of these "extrarepresentational" acts may of course be embedded in sentences of representation; the two activities are sometimes simultaneous.
26. Shlomith Rimmon-Kenan, *Narrative Fiction: Contemporary Poetics* (London: Methuen, 1983), 103.
27. Gérard Genette, *Figures II* (Paris: Seuil, 1968).
28. On the importance of "maxim" see Nancy Miller, "Emphasis Added: Plots and Plausibilities in Women's Fiction," *PMLA* 96 (1981): 36–48; reprinted in *The New Feminist Criticism*, ed. Elaine Showalter (New York: Pantheon, 1985), 339–60.

gendered rhetorical codes. In cultures such as the ones I am examining, where women's access to public discourse has been curtailed,
it has been one thing for women simply to tell stories and another
for their narrators to set themselves forth as authorities. Indeed, authorial voice has been so conventionally masculine that female authorship does not necessarily establish female voice: a startling
number of critics have referred in the generic masculine to the narrators of such novels as *La Princesse de Clèves* and *Pride and Prejudice*.[29]
Thus, on the one hand, since a heterodiegetic narrator need not be
identified by sex, the authorial mode has allowed women access to
"male" authority by separating the narrating "I" from the female
body; it is of course in the exploitation of this possibility that women
writers have used male narrators and pseudonyms (acts that may have
profited individual writers or texts, but that have surely also reinforced
the androcentrism of narrative authority). On the other hand, when
an authorial voice has represented itself as female, it has risked being
(dis)qualified. It is possible that women's writing has carried fuller
public authority when its voice has not been marked as female.

The narrators I discuss in Part I of this book have sought not simply
to tell stories, but through overtly authorial practices to make themselves (and, I presume, their authors) significant literary presences.
After examining an eighteenth-century text that proclaims the difficulty of achieving authoriality, Part I focuses on four canonical writers
(Jane Austen, George Eliot, Virginia Woolf, and Toni Morrison) in
order to explore the means by which each has constructed authorial
voice within and against the narrative and social conventions of her
time and place. In the work of all four writers I see a reaching for
narrative hegemony, for what Wayne Booth has called "direct and
authoritative rhetoric,"[30] that is obscured both by the writers' own
disclaimers and by a tendency in contemporary feminist criticism to
valorize "refusals" of authority in ways that seem to me ahistorical.

I use the term *personal voice* to refer to narrators who are self-
consciously telling their own histories. I do not intend this term to

29. For example, in *The Dual Voice: Free Indirect Speech and Its Functioning in the Nineteenth-
Century European Novel* (Manchester: Manchester University Press, 1977), Roy Pascal insists
that Jane Austen's narrator be called by the "generic" masculine; Laurence Gregorio makes
a similar insistence "for the sake of clarity" about *La Princesse de Clèves* in *Order in the Court:
History and Society in "La Princesse de Clèves"* (Stanford French and Italian Studies 47, 1986),
1. For the argument that the unmarked narrative voice is neither gendered nor necessarily
human, see Culler, "Problems in the Theory of Fiction."
30. Wayne Booth, *The Rhetoric of Fiction* (Chicago: University of Chicago Press, 1961), 6.

designate all "homodiegetic" or "first-person" narratives—that is, all those in which the voice that speaks is a participant in the fictional world—but only those Genette calls "autodiegetic," in which the "I" who tells the story is also the story's protagonist (or an older version of the protagonist).[31] In my exploration of personal voice I will exclude forms such as the interior monologue, which are not self-consciously narrative and which, like figural narration, cannot construct a situation of narrative self-reference.

The authority of personal voice is contingent in ways that the authority of authorial voice is not: while the autodiegetic "I" remains a structurally "superior" voice mediating the voices of other characters, it does not carry the superhuman privileges that attach to authorial voice, and its status is dependent on a reader's response not only to the narrator's acts but to the character's actions, just as the authority of the representation is dependent in turn on the successful construction of a credible voice. These differences make personal voice in some ways less formidable for women than authorial voice, since an authorial narrator claims broad powers of knowledge and judgment, while a personal narrator claims only the validity of one person's right to interpret her experience.

At the same time, personal narration offers no gender-neutral mask or distancing "third person," no refuge in a generic voice that may pass as masculine.[32] A female personal narrator risks the reader's resistance if the act of telling, the story she tells, or the self she constructs through telling it transgresses the limits of the acceptably feminine. If women are encouraged to write only of themselves because they are not supposed to claim knowledge of men or "the world," when women *have* written only of themselves they have been labeled immodest and narcissistic, and criticized for displaying either their virtues or their faults. Moreover, because male writers have created female voices, the arena of personal narration may also involve a struggle over which representations of female voice are to be authorized.

Although authorial narration, with its omniscient privilege, is usually understood to be fictional, fiction in the personal voice is usually

31. See Genette, *Narrative Discourse*, 227–47.
32. Obviously, a woman writer may choose an explicitly male "I"-narrator, as dozens of women writers from Hannah More to the Brontës to Willa Cather and Marguerite Yourcenar have done. When I speak of the teller here, I am speaking of the female *narrator*, not the female writer.

formally indistinguishable from autobiography. Given the precarious position of women in patriarchal societies, woman novelists may have avoided personal voice when they feared their work would be taken for autobiography. The use of personal voice also risks reinforcing the convenient ideology of women's writing as "self-expression," the product of "intuition" rather than of art;[33] perhaps this is why Maxine Hong Kingston stated recently that she did not believe she would be a "real" novelist until she had written a book in the authorial voice.[34] In view of these constraints, my discussion of personal voice is especially concerned with variations in the accessibility of public and private forms of personal voice to particular communities of women at particular moments in history. Part II attempts to interpret patterns of personal voice respectively in European women's writings from the late eighteenth to the mid-nineteenth century and in African-American women's writings from the nineteenth century to the contemporary period.

Conventional narrative poetics has often viewed authorial and personal voices as formal antitheses, the one constituting the "diegetic" voice of a fictional author, the other constituting the "mimetic" voice of a character. Indeed, the two modes carry different forms of rhetorical authority: paradoxically, authorial narrative is understood as fictive and yet its voice is accorded a superior reliability, while personal narrative may pass for autobiography but the authority of its voice is always qualified. But the opposition is far from definite: the eyewitness narrator used, for example, in Aphra Behn's *Oronooko* (1688) and George Eliot's *Scenes of Clerical Life* transgresses the polarities of "third-person" and "first-person" narration that are usually assumed to be formally unbridgeable.

The tendency to oppose these modes also conceals similarities between them. Both forms bear the potential for public, self-referential narration and thus for enacting a relationship between "writer" and audience and indeed an entire "story" that is the story of the narration itself. Moreover, the narratological tendency to oppose authorial and

33. See, for example, Jean Larnac's argument that women's literary power resides in their ability to "feel vividly and immediately to release from themselves feelings they have just experienced, without waiting for the fruitful germinations that come from slow meditation," in *Histoire de la littérature féminine en France* (Paris: Kra, 1929), 111.

34. Maxine Hong Kingston, in a reading given at Georgetown University, April 1989. Kingston was referring to *Tripmaster Monkey—His Fake Book* (New York: Knopf, 1989), whose authorial voice, she says, is absolutely—and to her, unmistakably—female even though it is never marked as such.

personal voices conceals the degree to which both forms are invested in singularity—in the presupposition that narration is individual. This narrative individualism that European cultures take for granted explains why authorial and personal voices have been so commonly practiced and so thoroughly analyzed, while so little attention has been given to intermediate forms such as that of Christa Wolf's *Nachdenken über Christa T.* (1967), in which the narrator is reconstructing the life of another woman but is also in some sense a protagonist herself, not simply an eyewitness or biographer.

This individualization of narrative also explains why my third mode, *communal voice*, is likewise a category of underdeveloped possibilities that has not even been named in contemporary narratology. By communal voice I mean a spectrum of practices that articulate either a collective voice or a collective of voices that share narrative authority. Because the dominant culture has not employed communal voice to any perceptible degree, and because distinctions about voice have been based primarily on the features of this dominant literature, there has been no narratological terminology for communal voice or for its various technical possibilities.

By communal narration I do not mean simply the use of an authorial voice that resorts to an inclusive "we" (as George Eliot's narrators sometimes do), nor the multiple narration Faulkner adopts in a novel like *As I Lay Dying*, nor the presentation of divergent and antithetical perspectives on the same events that characterizes epistolary novels such as *Lady Susan* and *Les Liaisons dangereuses*. I refer, rather, to a practice in which narrative authority is invested in a definable community and textually inscribed either through multiple, mutually authorizing voices or through the voice of a single individual who is manifestly authorized by a community. In Part III, I will distinguish three such possibilities that result from various confluences of social ideology with changing conventions of narrative technique: a *singular* form in which one narrator speaks for a collective, a *simultaneous* form in which a plural "we" narrates, and a *sequential* form in which individual members of a group narrate in turn. Unlike authorial and personal voices, the communal mode seems to be primarily a phenomenon of marginal or suppressed communities; I have not observed it in fiction by white, ruling-class men perhaps because such an "I" is already in some sense speaking with the authority of a hegemonic "we." My survey of communal voice in Part III moves from an exploration of constraints on communal voice in the eighteenth century, through "singular" manifestations in the nineteenth, to a range of formal possibilities available to modern and postmodern narratives.

Because the structures of both narration and plot in the Western novel are individualist and androcentric, the articulation of a communal female voice is not simply a question of discourse but almost always one of story as well. Although it is possible to represent female community without communal voice, it is difficult to construct communal voice without constructing female community. Communal voice thus shifts the text away from individual protagonists and personal plots, calling into question the heterosocial contract that has defined woman's place in Western fiction. My examination of more and less realized communal forms in the singular, sequential, and simultaneous modes suggests the political possibilities of constituting a collectice female voice through narrative. At the same time, communal voice might be the most insidious fiction of authority, for in Western cultures it is nearly always the creation of a single author appropriating the power of a plurality.

The three modes of narrative voice on which this book concentrates seem to me to represent three distinct kinds of authority that women have needed to constitute in order to make their place in Western literary history: respectively, the authority, to establish alternative "worlds" and the "maxims" by which they will operate, to construct and publicly represent female subjectivity and redefine the "feminine," and to constitute as a discursive subject a female body politic. Each form creates its own fictions of authority, making certain meanings and not others articulable. Although I begin with authorial voice because it is the oldest and most basic mode and end with communal voice because it is the newest and least conventional, I refrain from any absolute evaluation of the three modes. I will speculate briefly in my final chapter about the value of each of these narrative "tools" for dismantling, to use Audre Lorde's now-famous metaphor, the "master's house."[35]

A book with a title as general as this one owes its readers some explanation of what it is and is not meant to be. In no way does it embraces the range of techniques and questions that are subsumed in the concept of "narrative voice." By choosing certain general cat-

---

35. Audre Lorde, "The Master's Tools Will Never Dismantle the Master's House," in *Sister/ Outsider* (Freedom, Calif.: Crossing Press, 1984), 110–13.

egories and distinctions, I hope to demonstrate that even the broadest, most obvious elements of narration are ideologically charged and socially variable, sensitive to gender differences in ways that have not been recognized. Because I have written this book for a general scholarly readership rather than for specialists in narratology, I have tried to keep technical terms to a minimum. Although I have introduced a few new concepts here, my earlier book, *The Narrative Act: Point of View in Prose Fiction*, describes in more detail most of the aspects of narrative voice on which this work relies.

In several ways this is a preliminary and speculative project. Because I focus on moments of crisis or breakthrough at which certain narrative practices become (im)possible, many important writers and literary events do not figure here. Nor do I mean to imply a linear growth in women's narrative authority: the history of voice in women's writings reflects what Mary Poovey affirms are "uneven developments."[36] At the same time, narrative authority—like many other possibilities for women—is currently wider and deeper both for individuals and for previously silenced groups of women than it was two centuries ago, despite historical lapses and contemporary absences that remind us not to see any gains as inevitable, universal, or permanent.

The broad scope of the book makes my work preliminary in still other ways. Although the narrative poetics I envision is fully embedded in material-historical analysis, carrying out such a project would require engaging the conditions of cultural production for each individual text to an impossible degree given the broad historical and geographic arena that this book encompasses. In attempting to illuminate large patterns of voice in Western fiction, I have had to rely more on general developments in literary history than on particular developments in social and material life.

Because literary form has a far more uncertain relation to social history than does representational content, even a fully materialist poetics would be hard-pressed to establish definitive correspondences between social ideology and narrative form. I have nonetheless considered it fruitful to venture speculations about causal relationships that others may be able to establish or refute. Having learned from my biochemist friend Ellen Henderson that "how?" is a scientific ques-

36. Mary Poovey, *Uneven Developments: The Ideological Work of Gender in Mid-Victorian England* (Chicago: University of Chicago Press, 1988).

tion but "why?" is not, I have sought through this project to show how particular writers and texts may have come to use particular narrative strategies.

Finally, this project remains rooted in Western theory and history. I am concerned that my "inclusion" of African-American novels places these texts in a eurocentric framework and thereby imposes the risk of perpetuating the distortions for which I fault literary history. My study does not explore the emerging novelistic traditions by women of Asia, Africa, and Latin America, and I mention only briefly some of the rich new fiction by Asian-American, Latina, Chicana, Arab, and Native American women in the United States. There remains a great deal to learn by studying narrative voice as it has been developing in countries and communities where women are just beginning to write, or where the novel is a relatively new genre produced through complex interactions between native and colonial forms. For this reason, especially, feminist criticism will need many more studies of women's fictions, studies focusing on many different cultures and from many different vantage points, before anyone can speak with authority about women writers and narrative voice.

2

The Rise of the Novel,
the Fall of the Voice:
Juliette Catesby's Silencing

We can only grasp silence in the moment in which it is
breaking.

.   .   .

As soon as we learn words, we find ourselves outside them.

—SHEILA ROWBOTHAM, *Woman's Consciousness,
Man's World*

It has become a critical commonplace to associate the "rise of the
novel" in the eighteenth century with a parallel "rise" of woman's
place in literature. Certainly no period in Western history saw a more
dramatic increase in the number of writing women.[1] And certainly
female voice emerged in this same period as a significant feature of
fictional narrative: the most canonical titles of eighteenth-century English and French novels (*Moll Flanders, Roxana, Pamela, Clarissa, La
Vie de Marianne, Fanny Hill, Julie, ou La Nouvelle Héloise, La Religieuse*)
bear witness to the dominance of the female figure not only as "heroine" but as a narrator of the text that bears her name.[2] Since by mid-

1. For some empirical data, see Judith Phillips Stanton, "Statistical Profile of Women
Writing in English from 1660 to 1800," in *Eighteenth-Century Women and the Arts*, ed. Frederick
M. Keener and Susan E. Lorsch (New York: Greenwood Press, 1988), 247–54. One should
not forget that Japanese women had written prolifically a millennium earlier, during the
Heian period.

2. See Nancy K. Miller, *The Heroine's Text: Readings in the French and English Novel 1722–
1782* (New York: Columbia University Press, 1980), x.

century women were routinely writing novels and novels were routinely writing female voice, it would seem that, as Nancy Armstrong has suggested, "the rise of the novel and the emergence of female authority" are "elements of a single historical event."[3]

In theory, the entry of women into writing seriously threatens prevailing patriarchal hegemonies, just as the emergence of "print culture" challenges other hierarchies of caste and class by providing an oppositional vehicle for (literate) persons without other access to power. Not only does print allow women publicly to challenge the terms of their own domination, but once they are identified as discursive "I's," such women become "individuals," occupying the position of privileged-class men. In the discourse of "Enlightenment," in other words, individual voice paradoxically offers a potential mediating ground for transforming "the sex"—a caste—into a "we," a body politic.[4]

Given the numbers of women writing in the eighteenth century and the popularity of female narrative voice, the novel might have become an early site for such a transformation in authority. I want to argue, however, that the form that female voice came to assume in the period usually associated with the modern novel's consolidation as a genre worked more effectively to reconcile patriarchy with "democracy" than to expose contradictions between the two. The narrative mode that dominated the novel by mid-century, in which the heroine tells her personal, usually amorous history to a private, usually epistolary narratee, channeled female voice into forms that contained and defused it, minimizing the power of "free speech" to destabilize patriarchal culture and undermining the potential even for white, privileged-class women to maintain an enduring literary authority. I am speculating that narrative voice provided an outlet for discharging a female discursive "excess" that never had to be opposed openly, limiting the "sphere" of female discourse and making its authority conditional and ultimately co-optible. Negotiating the tension between patriarchal imperatives and Enlightenment politics, between individual desire and collective control, the narrating voice became a fiction

3. Nancy Armstrong, "The Rise of Feminine Authority in the Novel," *Novel* 15 (Winter 1982): 129. See also Armstrong, *Desire and Domestic Fiction: A Political History of the Novel* (New York: Oxford University Press, 1987).

4. Mary Poovey's *The Proper Lady and the Woman Writer* (Chicago: University of Chicago Press, 1984), chap. 1, describes more fully this conflict between individualism and the status of women as an undifferentiated caste.

of authority beneath which historical women and their public power could be erased. The mechanisms by which female voice was encouraged, regulated, and dissipated are vividly represented in Marie-Jeanne Riccoboni's *Lettres de Milady Juliette Catesby à Milady Henriette Campley, son amie* (1759), a book of enormous popularity that offers one of the strongest critiques of sexual politics written during the period of propriety that bridges the more outspoken moments of Mary Astell and Mary Woll-stonecraft. Juliette Catesby's "free" voice opposes the conventional plot in which a heroine moves, as Rachel Brownstein has put it, "toward her inevitable end, death or marriage, along lines her body generates."[5] In this struggle, *Juliette Catesby*'s overt movement toward marriage is undercut by a covert movement toward death, a death prefigured in the novel's subplot and refigured in the silencing of Juliette's voice. Because the courtship depends upon the rise and fall of its narrator's authority, *Juliette Catesby*'s "resolution" exposes the gender arrangements that construct the place of female voice—and also, I argue, of the woman writer—in the body of literature that Nancy Miller has labeled the "heroine's text."

The novel begins by giving its epistolary narrator every advantage: Juliette's is the dominant voice, her confidante Henriette but a silent recipient, and the voices of other characters subordinate discourses inserted into Juliette's own. This narrative posture must stabilize the divided identity of a character who is struggling against her own desires: as the novel opens, Juliette is fleeing Lord Ossery, to whom she had been secretly engaged two years earlier, but who had unac-countably abandoned her to marry someone else. Ossery is now pur-suing Juliette again, his wife having died and left behind a child tellingly named Juliette. Because Juliette Catesby's flight from London to Winchester is also a flight from Ossery's desire to explain himself, narration becomes the ground on which the marriage plot must be resolved. In a revision of the "amorous" epistolary tradition begun by the *Lettres portuguaises* in which a female narrator is imprisoned in an endless, insatiable heterosexual desire for which writing becomes

---

5. Rachel Brownstein, *Becoming a Heroine: Reading about Women in Novels* (New York: Viking, 1982), 81. To my knowledge the only mid-eighteenth-century novel in which the heroine unequivocally chooses independence to marriage is Françoise de Grafigny's *Lettres d'une péruvienne* (1747). The man Zilia refuses, however, is not her beloved Aza, who has betrayed her, but a French "benefactor" whom she esteems but does not love. Zilia's resistance to Déterville seems to me inseparable from her status as colonized subject.

the substitute,[6] Juliette Catesby uses her letters to resist heterosexual love and the male dominance that she believes inevitably attends it.

Juliette authorizes her resistance by writing Ossery's betrayal as a generic plot of male treachery and usurping men's power to reduce the Other to "the sex." Women love and men lust; women are faithful and men betray; women are generous and men self-interested. Except for a paragon pointedly named Sir Manly, virtually all male characters are treated with irony or contempt, their actions probed for inconsistency and insincerity, their words filtered through her judging and ironizing voice. When a new suitor declares his love, for example, Juliette turns the avowal to parody:

> Sir James wrote to me. His letter is tender. He *will love* me, but *silently*. He *will not dare to ask me* the reason for *my tears*[. . .]He ends by swearing eternal love . . . Eternal, my dear, they all promise *eternal* love.

> [Sir James m'a écrit. Sa lettre est tendre. Il *aimera*, il se *taira*. Il *n'ose me demander* le sujet de *mes pleurs*[. . .]Il finit en m'assurant d'un amour éternel . . . Eternel ma chère, ils promettent tous un amour *éternel*.][7]

Each supplicating letter from Ossery is subjected to similar nullifying mimicry; even his near-fatal illness is ridiculed after the news of it has momentarily weakened Juliette's resolve: "Oh these men! these men! See how they take advantage of events: when the means of subjugating us seem lacking, an unforeseen incident, chance, an *illness* leads them toward their goal . . . Are their wrongs diminished? no, but . . . he was *ill*" (31.125–26).

The vulnerability to male discourse implicit in Juliette's need to mock it—what Sheila Rowbotham would call her "dependence on the words of the powerful"[8]—provides the basis for Ossery's counterstrategy: if he is to win her over he must enter Juliette's text, displace her voice, and turn her from narrator to narratee. The long written confession that Ossery finally sends her, and which she inserts into her correspondence with Henriette, becomes the test of discursive authority: only if Juliette can dismantle or rewrite his narrative—

---

6. See Linda S. Kauffman, *Discourses of Desire: Gender, Genre, and Epistolary Fictions* (Ithaca: Cornell University Press, 1986).

7. Marie-Jeanne Riccoboni, *Lettres de Milady Juliette Catesby à Milady Henriette Campley, son amie* (Paris: Desjonquères, 1983), Letter 19, p. 86. All further references will appear in the text. English translations are mine.

8. Sheila Rowbotham, *Woman's Consciousness, Man's World* (Harmondsworth, England: Penguin, 1973), 32.

dialogize it into parody—can she sustain her vision of Ossery and of his sex.

What Juliette learns from this confession is certainly amenable to a feminist reading: in a moment of drunken "forgetfulness," Ossery has raped Jenny Montfort, the young sister of a schoolmate, who seemed in that instant "only a woman offered up to my desires" (35.149)—only, that is, the member of an unindividuated caste. When Jenny became pregnant and threatened suicide Ossery married her, but two years later she has succumbed to an illness brought on, ironically, by unrequited love for her own seducer-husband. Her death, which she hoped would free Ossery from a "chain that weighs you down" (35.160), is thus virtually the suicide she once threatened. Now Ossery swears to Juliette that in his heart he has never betrayed her, that his only sins are those of momentary sexual indiscretion and fear of telling her the truth.

Because Juliette has generalized Ossery's acts as "male" behavior to which she has opposed a female superiority, what is at stake in her response to this confession-by-letter is far more than her judgment of a single man or even of men in general. If, as Ruth Perry says, "it is the adamant protection of individuality which stands at the heart of most of the sexual refusals in epistolary fiction,"[9] then there is nothing less at stake in Ossery's penetration of Juliette's narrative than her identity as "individual." Voice becomes the site of Juliette's resistance to being "only a woman offered up to [Ossery's] desires"; narrative authority becomes the barricade between male desire and the fall into sexual anonymity; and "individuality" becomes the condition of female authority just as it is the escape from the caste status implicit in Ossery's rape of Juliette. A conventional (androcentric) reading could well make the episode with Jenny a peccadillo for which Ossery has already paid dearly and from which Jenny's death has mercifully delivered him. In this case the tragedy becomes Ossery's; he is a victim not only of circumstance but of his own honorable decision to marry a woman he does not love.[10] If Juliette accepts this

9. Ruth Perry, *Women, Letters, and the Novel* (New York: AMS Press, 1980), 131.

10. Sylvain Menant gives just this reading: "however justified [Juliette's] complaints against men may be," he says, "they do not really apply to Lord Ossery," who, despite his "lapse," "merits esteem and even pushes fidelity too far," so that the novel "actually strengthens the value and confidence one can place in human nature and in men in particular" (preface to *Juliette Catesby*, vii–viii, translation mine). Contrast Joan Hinde Stewart's "grave doubt that the delicate and introspective" Juliette will "find an authentic partner in the man she knows Ossery to be" (*The Novels of Madame Riccoboni* [Chapel Hill: North Carolina Studies in the Romance Languages and Literatures, 1976], 119).

reading, her analysis of men is trivialized and negated, she replaces Jenny as the desired object, and the "happy" ending can ensue. But the textual ideology already constructed by Juliette's voice opens up another reading with Jenny as the tragic subject for whose irreversible fate Ossery is wholly responsible. Indeed, Jenny Montfort's story already dissolves the opposition in which the heroine takes one of two paths—in Brownstein's words, to "get virtue's earthly reward, a rich husband, or be seduced and die of it."[11] The virtuous Jenny does get the rich husband, but she has also been seduced and ultimately she dies of it.

The question, then, is which narrative Juliette will authorize. Her initial response enacts her usual ironizing appropriation of male discourse: mocking Ossery's excuse that he "forgot" his love when he seduced Jenny—"Ah, yes, men have these *oublis*" (36.167)—she blames herself for having hated a woman who was as miserable as she. She even imagines herself Jenny's rescuer by proclaiming that if Ossery had told the truth earlier, the two women could have been friends and Jenny "might be living still" (36.169). Her language at this juncture suggests that Ossery's crimes are crimes virtually against herself: when she expresses pity for "poor Lady Ossery" (36.166) she is naming Jenny with the title that would have been (and soon will be) her own, and her exclamation that "her fate touches me! [que son destin me touche!]" (35.166) might suggest that what Ossery has done to Jenny he can do to her.

And so, figuratively speaking, he does: in ceding narrative voice to Ossery, Juliette opens the path for her own marital "death." In a process of reversal made visible on the surface of the narrative, Juliette resolves her doubts and confusions—"oh, I don't know what to decide" (36.169)—by erasing Jenny's tragedy beneath Ossery's, praising his "probity" and "generosity" (36.168), and proclaiming that "all is forgiven; all is forgotten!" (37.170). This forgiveness that she once warned she could never grant him "or I hardly know myself [ou je me connais mal]" (7.22), achieved within the gap between Saturday's letter and the announcement at the beginning of Sunday's that she is off to meet Ossery, nullifies her criticisms of men and authorizes Ossery as one who knows her better than she knows herself. In capitulating to Ossery's narrative, then, Juliette "falls" from a subject whose analysis created the basis for a feminist politics into membership

11. Brownstein, *Becoming a Heroine*, 81.

in a sexual class—and in a movement so rapid that the angry discourse comes to seem almost self-parody, an exaggeration of the conventional comedy in which a woman's protests demonstrate the degree to which she must be "tamed." Paradoxically, in other words, Juliette's "fall" is fostered by her "individuality": because no textual voice corroborates her positions (all the women, including the silent Henriette, seem to be rooting for Ossery), her words can be dismissed as a temporary lapse. The individual voice that I have identified as extricating the woman from caste status becomes, ironically, the condition of her failure as well—necessary, but insufficient, for effecting change.

Indeed, it is when Juliette forgets that she "is" Jenny that the implications of Jenny's death insinuate themselves into her own narrative, and she loses control not only of her story but of the correspondence through which she tells it. While Juliette has authored every previous letter in the novel—even Ossery's confession is but an inserted text—the final letter creates a new narrative structure exposing an agenda of co-optation that I associate with the entire tradition of the "heroine's text." In this last letter, Ossery and Juliette's matchmaking cousin, Lady Ormond, take up Juliette's pen to compete with her for the textual last word. Although this letter has been seen as a "communal effort" mirroring the "excitement and confusion of the occasion,"[12] its language suggests a darker design: the erasure of Juliette's voice and with it the opposition between marriage and death that has already collapsed in the "subplot" of Jenny Montfort.

While Juliette resorted to a mimicking dependence on the words of the powerful, Ossery in this letter engages in a more overt appropriation by simply speaking in Juliette's stead: having earlier turned her from narrator into narratee, he now turns her from narrator into text. As he announces Juliette's "demise," Ossery's appropriation of her correspondence virtually defines marriage as a woman's silencing: "You write, lovely Henriette, to Lady Catesby; one can recognize your hand, your seal; but to whom can your letter be delivered? Is there still a Lady Catesby in the world? You won't find her at Hereford in any case. If in place of this friend so dear to your heart you'll accept a new one, then Lady Ossery is ready to receive your warm congratulations" (37.172–73) This new creation is unmistakably one of a class whose destiny is precisely to be owned: "She is mine, forever mine. No more Lady Catesby; she's my wife, my friend, my mistress [Elle

12. See Stewart, *The Novels of Madame Riccoboni*, 47.

est à moi, pour jamais à moi! Plus de Milady Catesby; c'est ma femme, mon amie, ma maîtresse]" (37.173). As he proclaims Juliette's new status with conspicuous redundancy, Ossery is announcing the death-by-marriage of the individualized letter-writer and title figure of the text. In this appropriation of Juliette's narrative identity, *Les Lettres de Milady Juliette Catesby* ceases to match its name, and the stories of Jenny and Juliette fuse: there is no more a Juliette Catesby than there is a Jenny Montfort.

Juliette's own ostensibly playful version of the finale only reinforces this confluence of marriage and death by implying that the marriage was imposed against her will: "Oh, my dear Henriette, they were all united against me; they only brought me here to lead me into the trap they had prepared. My cousin directed the conspiracy; they didn't give me time to breathe" (37.173). This passage recapitulates previous references to men who entrap (9.29) and stifle—as, for example, when Sir Henry attempts to "stuff" Juliette into a closed carriage until she succeeds in lowering the window and can "breathe again" (2.10–11). There is a similar negative pressure in Juliette's announcement that "*they* married me [on m'a mariée]"—as if she has not made the choice—and "so quickly, so quickly, that I honestly believe the marriage is worthless [ne vaut rien]" (37.173–74). Even Lady Ormond, who insists that "the marriage is good" and that "neither of the contracting parties wants to break it off" (37.174) emphasizes in her denial the damning terms: "a *trap*, a *conspiracy*, a *worthless marriage*" (37.174).

If *Juliette Catesby*'s marriage plot succeeds at the expense of the voice that tells it, then Riccoboni's novel exposes as a fiction the liberty of female voice in the conventional "heroine's text": whatever it proclaims, this voice is confined from the beginning in a predetermined (hetero)sexual plot that takes on the powerfully conservative mission of limiting the consequences of voice, rendering "free" speech a kind of silence already made impotent by the novel's teleology. This narrative contract in which plot curtails voice and voice gives plot the illusion of openness reconciles heterosexual patriarchy with democratic individualism by representing a woman's silencing as the product of her own desire—precisely the strategy by which philosophers such as Rousseau, Kant, and Fichte resolved their own contradictory needs to acknowledge individual rights while preserving patriarchal rule.[13]

13. In *The Science of Rights*, for example, Fichte performs the following sleight of hand:

This conflict between "democratic" and patriarchal imperatives is also what makes forms such as the epistolary novel so suitable for the "heroine's text": the letter-writer's voice operates in a discursive arena that is circumscribed by privacy, minimized by marriage-or-death closure, and masked by fictionality, so that male discursive hegemony in a manifestly public arena is at least titularly maintained. While the epistolary novel is not literally a private discourse, in other words, what it models for women is private voice. The threat posed by increasing numbers of writing women may be precisely the reason why, although women like Aphra Behn created in the 1680s and 1690s female authorial voices that openly addressed a public readership, what came by the 1750s to stand for female voice—to be, indeed, among the novel's most marketable commodities—was a voice that modeled not public proclamation but private confidence. The eighteenth-century attraction to epistolarity through which the reader becomes the (privileged and permitted) voyeur may have as one of its agendas the restriction of oppositional voices to discourses privatized in both content and form and the simultaneous resexualization of the woman (and by implication the woman writer) as a secret to penetrate. Certainly taboos against women's public writing, along with the practice by which novels were presented as the "true" histories of their narrating protagonists, discouraged the presence of the author's name on a novel's title page. In this way, just when, according to Foucault, individual authorship is becoming the ground of textual validity, the dominant female identity in eighteenth-century fiction becomes not the author's but the character's.

Implicitly this privatization of discourse suggests private solutions just where a redressing of grievances might require publicity. Thus the narrator of Riccoboni's *Lettres de Mistriss Fanni Butlerd* (1757) retaliates for her abandonment by the socially superior Alfred by publishing (anonymously) the letters that document his transgressions and her sufferings: "It's in the public press that I'll address you. You'll recognize me: a style that was so familiar to you, that so often flattered your vanity . . . but your eyes will never see again the handwriting [ces caractères] that you used to call *sacred*, that you kissed with such ardor,

---

"The question whether the female sex really has a claim to all the rights of man and of male citizens could be raised only by persons who doubt whether women are complete human beings. . . . But the question may certainly be asked whether and how far the female sex can desire to exercise all her rights" (London, 1889), 440–42. Rousseau makes similar arguments in *Emile*, and Kant in the *Philosophy of Law*.

that was *so dear* to you." Private writing, like the woman's body, can be seduced; the printed words may seem the same—"you will recognize me"—but the public text, separated from the body, escapes the man's control. Print permits Fanni to circulate to a male public the kind of angry messages Juliette Catesby confides only to one female friend: "Ah, men, who are you? What gives you the right to treat a woman as you would not dare treat a man? What law of nature, what social code ever authorized this insulting distinction? So, you live up to your word when it comes to even the least of your kind [vos semblables], but your repeated vows don't bind you to the woman [amie] you yourself choose! Ferocious monsters...on what do you base your alleged superiority? On the right of the strongest?"[14] Yet even Fanni's breach of epistolary privacy is revenge without improvement, for in *Fanni Butlerd* as in *Juliette Catesby*, change in this social arrangement is never marked as a possibility. Juliette's power (like the power of a Clarissa, a Pamela, a Julie) is a moral and emotional power without guarantee of political—which is to say public—force. In this light a "playful" comment Ossery makes when he takes over Juliette's correspondence becomes insidious: Juliette has opened Henriette's letter, he says, "with a freedom [liberté] that will perhaps surprise you; but what rights [droits] does this charming woman not have!" (37.172–73). By applying Enlightenment discourse to so trivial an act, and one that Juliette has of course been "freely" performing all along, Ossery underscores the degree to which her "droits" and "liberté" have been reduced: as wife, her rights come not from her humanity but from her "charms." And just as Juliette becomes transformed here from a writer to a text, so mid-eighteenth-century literature, as John Sitter observes, becomes committed to a notion of woman as the inspirer rather than the inspired, a notion that a few decades later will yield a Romanticism that refigures narrative voice as masculine and woman as its muse.[15]

By representing patriarchal marriage—the making of the female body into private property—as a (complicitous) subjugation of female voice, by making the character's survival contingent on the narrator's demise, *Juliette Catesby* unmasks more than one fiction of authority. For the best-known works in the heroine's tradition within and against

---

14. Marie-Jeanne Riccoboni, *Lettres de Mistress Fanni Butlerd*, ed. Joan Hinde Stewart (Geneva: Droz, 1979), 182, 186 (my translation).

15. John Sitter, *Literary Loneliness in Mid-Eighteenth-Century England* (Ithaca: Cornell University Press, 1982), 134. See also my Chapter 9.

which Riccoboni writes are also a kind of marriage, usually of male author to female narrator-character; to underscore the pervasiveness of this heterosexual writing plot, we need only place the list of title characters I mentioned at the beginning of the chapter—Moll, Roxana, Pamela, Clarissa, Marianne, Fanny, Suzanne, Julie—against their authorial counterparts: Daniel (Defoe), Samuel (Richardson), Pierre (de Marivaux), John (Cleland), Denis (Diderot), Jean-Jacques (Rousseau). Figuratively, then, Ossery's appropriation of Juliette's correspondence evokes a larger tradition, already established by 1759, in which female subjects are constructed by male pens. Like the union of Catesby to Ossery, this ostensible union of male author and female narrator risks becoming metaphorically the man's marriage and the woman's death, not simply because the novel gives male authors an unprecedented opportunity to construct "woman" according to men's desires, but because these desires and the voices that speak them are represented as a woman's own, giving the illusion that it is in fact women who have been heard. I am suggesting that the best-intended fiction of the Other, even from one who is himself or herself Other in some different way, remains theoretically equivocal, empowering the writer beneath a pretense of relinquishment: one is reminded that it seems always to have been more convenient for a society to speak on behalf of the Other than to let the Other speak. If Ellen Moers is right to suggest that gender is a figure for class in the writings of Richardson and Defoe,[16] past and present efforts at coalition among differently marginalized communities (black, Jewish, gay and lesbian) carry painful lessons about assuming commonalities.

I am not positing here an essential connection between gender and perspective or denying the ability of a writer empathically to represent an identity that is not his or her own. Nor am I suggesting that female voice in fiction "belonged" to women and was appropriated by men: probably its first modern representations are to be found in Spanish picaresque novels such as Francisco Delicado's *La Lozana Andaluza* (1528), Francisco López de Ubeda's *La Pícara Justina* (1605), Alonso Jerónimo de Salas Barbadillo's *La Hija de Celestina* (1612), and Alonso de Castillo Solórzano's *Teresa de Manzanares* (1632).[17] But in England

---

16. Ellen Moers, *Literary Women* (New York: Doubleday, 1976), 175.

17. See Edward Friedman, *The Antiheroine's Voice: Narrative Discourse and Transformations of the Picaresque* (Columbia: University of Missouri Press, 1987). Friedman shows that narrating *pícaras* have a "dubious authority": they are invariably silenced by being reinterpreted, interrupted, or "killed off" (xii).

and France female voice did emerge in the novel primarily through the writings of such women as Behn, Marie d'Aulnoy, Delariviere Manley, and Eliza Haywood rather than through men such as Defoe, Crébillon *fils*, Marivaux, and Richardson, who are represented as its originators in the distorting mirror of literary history. What is at issue, here, is the material production and representation of authority: whose versions of female voice will stand as authoritative, and under whose agency. I am reminded of a fictional autobiography published in 1983, *Famous All Over Town* by Danny Santiago, which was hailed as the first voice of an adolescent from the Los Angeles barrio; though no one doubted the book's fidelity to that experience, but there was a furious outcry when "Danny Santiago" was revealed to be Daniel James, an elderly white man who had lived and worked for many years in the *barrio*. At stake was not the validity of the representation but the politics of the masquerade.

The erasure of women from eighteenth-century literary history is similarly problematic; the woman writer disappears behind the man, and through the same gesture that structures *Juliette Catesby*'s narrative turn: a woman asserts herself as individual voice and ends up being reduced to caste status in a process signified by the erasure of her name. At a moment when the primary determinant of literary value (and, by definition, of the novel) is becoming "originality" (which I take to be the aesthetic equivalent of individualism), literary history is made androcentric through the very discourse in which such novelists as Riccoboni are named (and which even feminist studies such as this risk repeating): the representation of women writers as a class. Early discussions of the novel like Clara Reeve's *The Progress of Romance* (1785) and Anna Barbauld's preface to *The British Novelists* (1810) already reveal the tension between studying "Lady Authors" (Reeve's term) as individuals and as a group; this tension may explain why both critics, even as they identify women who wrote letter-novels, name Richardson the "original" epistolary novelist.[18] By the time David Masson writes *British Novelists and Their Styles* (1859), Scott has become the central organizing figure in the novel's history; modern British fiction is said to have begun with Jonathan Swift and Daniel

18. See Anna Barbauld, introduction to *The Correspondence of Samuel Richardson* (London: Richard Phillips, 1804), xxvi; and Clara Reeve, *The Progress of Romance* (Colchester: W. Keymer, 1785), 1.136. In Robert Adams Day's listing of English epistolary works before 1740, virtually all the novels in which a female voice is dominant are written by women (or by "Anon"). See *Told in Letters: Epistolary Fiction Before Richardson* (Ann Arbor: University of Michigan Press, 1966), Appendix A.

Defoe; the fact that Aphra Behn "alone is now usually named as representing the Novel of the Restoration shows how little of the real talent of the time took that particular direction"; eighteenth-century fiction is represented by eighty pages on six men, with Fanny Burney and Clara Reeve the only women in a brief discussion of "other novelists"; and Jane Austen merits but a mention in the long chapter on Sir Walter Scott.[19] In this way the history of the novel's origins funnels down to a book like Ian Watt's *The Rise of the Novel*, which detaches a small group of famous men from their literary roots, obscuring causal relationships between gender and genre and imagining male novelists as articulating women's "distinctive literary interests" as if women were not expressing these interests themselves.[20] Yet it is now clear that "even innovative geniuses like Defoe, Richardson, Fielding, and Smollett" drew directly upon women's narrative practices to create books whose popularity is not wholly separable from the male authors' greater ability to promote their own work.[21] Once one recognizes what Dale Spender describes polemically as "the disappearance of more than one hundred good women novelists in favour of five men,"[22] one also realizes that the ostensible "innovative genius" of the five men—and their French counterparts (say, Prévost, Marivaux, Rousseau, Diderot, Laclos)—may have been possible, to play upon a comment of Virginia Woolf, because the "experience of the [female] mass is behind the single [male] voice."[23] Yet the history of the novel is largely an individualist narrative whose chapter titles celebrate the singularity of male authors while female names disappear into class identities ("other," "minor") within the first or last chapter framing the great tradition of men's books.[24]

19. David Masson, *British Novelists and Their Styles: Being a Critical Sketch of the History of British Prose Fiction* (Cambridge: Macmillan, 1859; reprint, Folcroft, Pa.: Folcroft Press, 1969).

20. Ian Watt, *The Rise of the Novel* (Berkeley and Los Angeles: University of California Press, 1957), 151.

21. Jerry C. Beasley, "Politics and Moral Idealism: The Achievement of Some Early Women Novelists" in *Fetter'd or Free? British Women Novelists 1670–1815*, ed. Mary Anne Schofield and Cecilia Macheski (Athens: Ohio University Press, 1986), 221. In *Told in Letters*, Day argues that the derivative *Pamela* came to overshadow more "astonishing" works such as Behn's *Love Letters between a Nobleman and His Sister* largely because of "the advertising and promotion that Richardson, as a printer and influential businessman, was able to give it, [and] the verbal puffing it received from literary friends of the author" (113, 207).

22. Dale Spender, *Mothers of the Novel* (London: Routledge and Kegan Paul, 1986), 5. The men in question are (no surprises) Defoe, Henry Fielding, Richardson, Tobias Smollett, and Laurence Sterne.

23. Virginia Woolf, *A Room of One's Own* (New York: Harcourt Brace, 1929), 69.

24. This tradition continues in the most impressive of literary histories. John Bender's *Imagining the Penitentiary* (Chicago: University of Chicago Press, 1987); Lennard Davis's *Factual Fictions: The Origins of the English Novel* (New York: Columbia University Press, 1983); and

I believe that female narrative voice—specifically the voice of the "I" who is both narrator and character—ironically laid the groundwork for this dispensation with female authorship; that in the economy of Enlightenment patriarchy, once men had mastered the female "I," women novelists, especially in a literary climate that discouraged the naming of the author on a title page, became superfluous. If, as Nancy Armstrong argues, a tradition of women writers "emerged when it did, not in spite of their sex, but because a female author could say something important in feminine terms that masculine writing could not accomplish," why were the eighteenth-century female voices that literary history revered and preserved primarily manmade, and why is it *Pamela*, rather than the writings of eighteenth-century women, through which Armstrong reads the "rise of the novel" as a rise of "female authority"?[25]

Riccoboni herself experienced the fate figured in Ossery's appropriation of Juliette's pen: although her novels were highly praised (none more so than *Juliette Catesby*) by such diverse readers as Friedrich Grimm, Jean d'Alembert, Diderot, Laclos, Marivaux, David Hume, Adam Smith, David Garrick, Germaine de Staël, Restif de la Bretonne, Marie Antoinette, and Napoleon; although her name was cited with those of French "giants" including Voltaire and Marivaux, Rousseau and Racine; although men like Goldoni and Casanova translated her and men like Laclos adapted her work for the stage, Riccoboni and her novels were soon (and by any standard, inexcusably) forgotten by literary history. Even in her own time the most authoritative creators of female voice were men; Elie Fréron's review of *Juliette Catesby* ends with a triumphant snipe at Rousseau ("what will you say when you learn that the author of this Novel is a woman?") that assumes the male writer to be a likely source of female narrative voice.[26] Riccoboni's career originated in precisely the paradoxical dependence on the male word that I have been describing: her first book, the 1751 *Suite* to Marivaux's *La Vie de Marianne*, constructs a female voice that imitates a man's imitation of a female voice. By the 1750s, in other words,

Michael McKeon's encyclopedic *The Origins of the English Novel 1600–1740* (Baltimore: Johns Hopkins University Press, 1987) all identify in chapter titles the usual male novelists and texts. Thirteen of the sixteen essays in *Eighteenth-Century British Fiction*, ed. Harold Bloom (New York: Chelsea House, 1988), focus on the same seven men.

25. Armstrong, "The Rise of Feminine Authority in the Novel," 129, and *Desire and Domestic Fiction*. In the book, Armstrong mentions only a few women novelists writing before Austen (Fanny Burney, Maria Edgeworth, Anne Radcliffe), and these only in passing.

26. Cited in Stewart, *The Novels of Madame Riccoboni*, 19 (my translation).

female voice is coming back to women through the agency of men, as "Milady Catesby" is returned as "Milady d'Ossery" when her husband appropriates her correspondence with Henriette. It seems no coincidence that in both England and France highly praised writers such as Riccoboni, Françoise de Grafigny, Charlotte Lennox, and Sarah Fielding, writing precisely during these decades of a "feminization" of personal voice, disappeared from literary history in what might well be seen as a patriarchal anxiety at once of authorship and influence.

But Juliette Catesby recovers her pen from Ossery, and in the process she not only reappropriates her narrative but gives it a powerful if momentary swerve. Conventionally, marriage displaces the female friendship that has sustained an epistolary structure, and surely Ossery's appropriation of Juliette and Henriette's correspondence attempts precisely that. Yet the last avowal of love in *Juliette Catesby* is not for the new husband but for the female friend: "We await you impatiently here: no parties, no balls, without my dear Henriette; I would say no pleasures, if the person [la personne] who is following my pen with his eyes were not already a little jealous of my tender *amitié*" (35.175). Here it is the husband who gets (symbolically) abandoned, the friend whose absence mars Juliette's happiness. Not only does this text slide past the wedding night,[27] but on the very day after the marriage it is Henriette without whom there will be "no pleasures," and it is to express her desire for a woman that Juliette recaptures her pen. Riccoboni thus writes "beyond the ending" of the traditional courtship plot to reveal the kind of moment Rachel DuPlessis describes in which "subtexts and repressed discourses can throw up one last flare of meaning"[28]—a meaning suggested by Juliette's repeated evocation, "O ma chère Henriette," when she is exposing men's faults.

This final paragraph of the novel restores Juliette's authority only by supplanting the heterosexual story, making the marriage not a permanent resolution but the basis for another narrative. Riccoboni writes just the beginning of this unconventional story, suggesting that for female voice to continue there must be a space beyond patriarchal control and outside the conventions of the heterosexual plot. While

27. This departure from the traditional marriage-ending is even more audacious if one agrees that it is meant to provide an "implicit erotic release" and to suggest permanent pleasure. See John Allen Stevenson, "'A Geometry of His Own': Richardson and the Marriage-Ending," in *Studies in English Literature* 26 (1986): 471–72.

28. Rachel Blau DuPlessis, *Writing beyond the Ending* (Bloomington: Indiana University Press, 1985), 3.

Riccoboni's own philosophy and indeed the resolution of her private story were openly feminist if not lesbian—she belonged for several years to an egalitarian troupe of actors, and she lived separately from her husband with a female companion, "independent and free," from 1755 until her death in 1793[29]—her position is paradigmatic of the woman whose "independence" is in fact dependent entirely on the proceeds of her pen and who is thus materially constrained to write the novel of female capitulation that is the staple of mid-eighteenth-century literary trade. I am suggesting that the change Virginia Woolf considers more important than the Crusades or the War of the Roses, when "the middle-class woman began to write," is more complex and less conclusive than *A Room of One's Own* implies.[30] At a moment when, as Armstrong says, a "cultural sleight of hand" "both granted [women] literary authority and denied [them] political power,"[31] it seems appropriate to imagine the woman writer through the final image of Juliette, writing while Ossery looks over her shoulder and follows her pen with his eyes.

The configuration of narrative voice that is at once exposed and reinscribed in *Juliette Catesby* marks more than one equivocal chapter in novelistic history, for persistent narrative patterns take root in this complicated period when both modern femininity and the modern novel are being delimited. At the crucial moment when women are being transformed from the "dangerous" to the "feminine" sex, and gender is being reconstructed to foreclose women's earlier independence in public spaces from court to street to marketplace,[32] the kind of narrative voice modeled by Juliette Catesby helps to anchor the transition by locating the space in which a woman may "speak." This is not the space of the authoritative, public subject-in-discourse but the private space of the character who exists as discursive subject only intradiegetically, within the fictional frame. The question becomes, then, not simply whether there is "female voice" in narrative, but

29. Of her life with Thérèse Biancolelli, Riccoboni wrote: "Living for twenty-five years with a friend whose intelligence, even temper, and affability diffuse a continual comfort and delight on our relationship, I enjoy a tranquil repose. We know neither quarrels nor boredom; the word *no* is banished between us. The same principles guide us, and make us naturally of like mind." Letter of 17 April 1771, in *Private Correspondence of D. Garrick*, quoted in Emily Crosby, *Une Romancière oubliée, Madame Riccoboni* (Paris, 1924; reprint, Geneva: Slatkine, 1970), 42 (my translation).

30. Woolf, *A Room of One's Own*, 68.

31. Armstrong, "The Rise of Feminine Authority in the Novel," 130.

32. I am paraphrasing here, respectively, Mary Poovey, *The Proper Lady and the Woman Writer*; and Joan B. Landes, *Women and the Public Sphere in the Age of the French Revolution* (Ithaca: Cornell University Press, 1988), 22.

whether the *forms* of such voice carry an authority that is more than private and fictional, establishing a place for women as subjects in the newly emerging public "sphere."

The forms of narration with which I am preoccupied here are precisely those that seem to resist such containment by insisting on voice that is at once public, implicitly or explicitly female, and in some sense nonfictional, by which I mean that the narrative voice is not dependent for its authority on the fictional world but brings that world into being *as text*. Such a liminal voice mediates fiction with history, becomes the voice of history within the text, and thus establishes its speaker not simply as a fictional but as a historical "presence." In the opening chapter to each part of this book, I will suggest that some of the most oppositional public voices women novelists created in the second half of the eighteenth century are strategized not simply as speech but as staged self-silencing: not the capitulation of a Juliette Catesby but a rejection of gendered conventions through a willful refusal to narrate. If *Juliette Catesby* shows how the heroine's text compromises the heroine's voice, the self-silencing narratives show what is at stake in such a compromise by refusing it.

Part I

AUTHORIAL VOICE

The male body lends credence to assertions, while the
female takes it away.
—MARY ELLMANN, *Thinking about Women*

3

In a Class by Herself: Self-Silencing in Riccoboni's *Abeille*

So behold the bottom of an author's soul; [s]he would please
even those [s]he despises.
> —DENIS DIDEROT, of Marie-Jeanne Riccoboni

Burning dinner is not incompetence but war.
> —MARGE PIERCY, "What's That Smell
> in the Kitchen?"

For reasons that I have already suggested, most of Marie-Jeanne
Riccoboni's novels, and possibly most novels by eighteenth-century
women, were epistolary in form.[1] In pretending to be a set of private
documents never meant for publication, the epistolary novel could in
spirit if not in fact evade the distinction between public and private
discourse that has, according to Dale Spender, deterred women not
from writing as such, but from writing to and for men: "The dichotomy of male/female, public/private is maintained by permitting
women to write... for themselves (for example, diaries) and for each
other in the form of letters, 'accomplished' pieces, moral treatises,
articles of interest for other women—particularly in the domestic

---

1. On women and the epistolary novel in the eighteenth century see Janet Altman, *Episto-
larity: Approaches to a Form* (Athens: Ohio State University Press, 1983); Frank G. Black, *The
Epistolary Novel in the Late Eighteenth Century* (Eugene: University of Oregon Press, 1940);
Susan Lee Carrell, *Le Soliloque de la passion féminine ou le dialogue illusoire* (Tübingen: Narr,
1982); Robert Adam Day, *Told in Letters: Epistolary Fiction Before Richardson* (Ann Arbor:
University of Michigan Press, 1966); Linda Kauffman, *Discourses of Desire: Gender, Genre, and
Epistolary Fiction* (Ithaca: Cornell University Press, 1986); and Ruth Perry, *Women, Letters, and
the Novel* (New York: AMS Press, 1980).

45

area—and even novels for women.... There is no contradiction in patriarchal order while women write for women and therefore remain within the limits of the private sphere; the contradiction arises only when women write for men."[2] Virginia Woolf implies this distinction when, speaking of Dorothy Osborne, she states that "no woman of sense and modesty could write books," but "letters did not count."[3] In a similar vein, just a year after publishing her epistolary novel *The Coquette* (1797) Hannah Foster concludes her paean to America for "unshackling" the "female mind" for "the widely extended fields of literature" by directing women nonetheless to choose private letters as the outlet for their discursive desires.[4] The book-in-letters ruptures this dichotomy of gender and genre while pretending to preserve it, masking as mere personal writing the act of public authorship that produced the text.[5]

It is no wonder, then, that eighteenth-century women made wide use of epistolary strategies to achieve what privileged-class men could write in overtly authorial forms. For the letter is defined not by its content but by its rhetorical frame; it can embrace virtually any topic and encompass virtually any discursive mode. Epistolarity thus becomes a ready refuge, what Bakhtin calls a "compositional surrogate of the author's discourse."[6] In the novel, this compositional surrogacy, by which the reader might assume an ideological equivalence between the author and the fictional letter-writer, seems best accomplished through an epistolary structure that is dominated by a single voice. When women like Haywood, Grafigny, and Riccoboni chose such a univocal structure rather than the polyphonic form of a Richardson or Laclos that incorporates multiple letter-writers with divergent points of view, they may have been motivated not simply by representational purposes but by narrational one. For example, single-

---

2. Dale Spender, *Man Made Language* (London: Routledge, 1980) 192. The split between "private" and "public" discourse, says Spender, "does not operate for men," who "may view *all* audiences and *all* forms of writing as open to them" (193). However, Spender's statement is surely applicable only to privileged-class men. One might speculate, for example, that class status conditioned the different narrative practices of Fielding and Richardson.

3. Virginia Woolf, *A Room of One's Own* (New York: Harcourt Brace, 1929), 65.

4. Hannah Webster Foster, *The Boarding School* (Boston: Thomas and Andrews, 1798), 31.

5. Significantly, where eighteenth- and nineteenth-century novels by women have used the framing device of an editor, that editor figure has almost invariably been represented as male. Thus the public voice, the "voice-over," remains masculine even when the fictional letter-writer or memoirist is female; see, for example, Frances Sheridan's *Memoirs of Miss Sidney Biddulph* (1761), Elizabeth Hamilton's *Memoirs of Modern Philosophers* (1800), Claire Duras's *Ourika* (1820), and Georgiana Fullerton's *Ellen Middleton* (1835).

6. Mikhail Bakhtin, *Problems of Dostoevsky's Poetics*, ed. Caryl Emerson (Minneapolis: University of Minnesota Press, 1984), 205.

voiced epistolary novels by women were often designed, as both Susan Carrell and Linda Kauffman have shown, to produce and prolong passion, but erotic desire does not account for all women's uses of the single letter-writing voice. At the same time, the epistolary surrogate remains a fictional figure without the historical status accorded the extradiegetic, authorial voice. An impatience with the surrogacy of epistolarity may explain why Aphra Behn's first novel, *Love Letters between a Nobleman and His Sister* (1684–87) makes a progressively smaller use of letters, from fifty-seven in the first volume to nine in the third, so that the novel virtually loses its claim to epistolarity.

On the other hand, I have already suggested that practices of overt authoriality opened women novelists to the same charges of transgression leveled at women writing in other public-voiced genres. As several scholars have shown, such charges often confounded the economic with the sexual and textual: according to Katharine Rogers, "women who aggressively competed with men" in the literary marketplace "were attacked as if they supported themselves by prostitution" (which, she notes wryly, would have been an easier means of sustenance).[7] As I suggested in Chapter 2, the explicitly female authoriality for which a writer such as Aphra Behn was paid (and paid) in the 1680s had become more elusive by the 1740s and 1750s as notions of propriety, femininity, and the new (gendered) opposition between private and public spheres were emerging and commodification threatened the old literary aristocracies. As John Sitter describes it, in England "practical success and ambition" came to be seen as "sordid, venal, or mean," cynicism about the marketplace led to a dissociation of quality from profitability, and "ambition and wit" were censured on moral grounds.[8] In France, where it was not the gentry but the nobility in whose hands literary judgment resided, success for unconnected bourgeois men was linked to a salon culture in which the favors of aristocratic women were said to control literary careers.[9]

In such a climate, which more or less prevailed in the half-century from 1730 to 1780, women writers would be unlikely to adopt the overtly authorial voice of a *Tom Jones* or a *Jacques le fataliste*—the kind of narrator Anna Barbauld described in 1804 as one "supposed to

---

7. Katharine M. Rogers, *Feminism in Eighteenth-Century England* (Urbana: University of Illinois Press, 1982), 21.

8. John Sitter, *Literary Loneliness in Mid-Eighteenth-Century England* (Ithaca: Cornell University Press, 1982), 109.

9. See, for example, Rémy G. Saisselin, *The Literary Enterprise in Eighteenth-Century France* (Detroit: Wayne State University Press, 1979).

know every thing," who "indulge[s], as Fielding has done, in digressions, and thus deliver[s] sentiments and display[s] knowledge which
would not properly belong to any of the characters."[10] I have not
found a novel written in the first half of the century that explicitly
represents an authorial narrator as female, let alone as the text's
dominant ideological voice, as Aphra Behn represented her narrators
in the 1680s, and I am speculating that this absence of authoriality,
like the presence of epistolarity, maintains the illusion of the novel as
private discourse and helps to preserve the gendered public/private
dichotomy that Dale Spender describes. French women, writing within
the class and gender system of the *ancien régime*, seem to have avoided
heterodiegetic narration almost entirely, while those British women
who used heterodiegesis generally confined ideological comments to
the voices of characters and avoided the extrafictional and extrarepresentational structures that I have identified as constituents of authoriality: substantive prefaces, generalizations in the narrator's voice,
explicit allusions by the narrator to literature or history, direct addresses to a public narratee, and explicit references to the narrating
subject or the narrative act. Barbauld herself makes an implicit gender
differentiation when she contrasts Fanny Burney's "dramatic" practices to Henry Fielding's "display."[11]

In those few instances where I have found mid-century women's
novels venturing overt authoriality—if only, as Margaret Doody says,
"in short breaths at a time,"[12] what gets inscribed is not only the
impulse toward authoriality but the difficulty of sustaining it. For
women's authorial narrators in this period are likely to reauthorize
masculinity even in their attempts at assertiveness. Lennox's *The Female Quixote* (1752) promises an authorial stance, for example, in a
chapter titled "Definition of love and beauty—The necessary qualities
of a hero and heroine" (4.3), but the "definition" gets worked out
through a polyphony of characters' voices. And the wise voice that
sermonizes through the novel's penultimate chapter is a male "doctor"
so learned that Samuel Johnson has been thought not only his
model but his creator (possible irony, given the fact that Johnson used
without attribution Lennox's 1753 *Shakespear Illustrated* for his own

10. Anna Barbauld, introduction to *The Correspondence of Samuel Richardson* (London: Richard Phillips, 1804), xxiii.
11. Ibid.
12. Margaret Doody, "George Eliot and the Eighteenth-Century Novel," *Nineteenth Century
Fiction* 35 (1980): 282–83. Doody's other examples are from the last decades of the century,
which I treat in the next chapter as a separate period.

Preface to Shakespeare).[13] Eliza Haywood's *History of Miss Betsy Thoughtless* (1751), written late in her career, does constitute an overtly authorial voice, but from the first sentence of the novel the narrative voice dissociates itself from the class "woman" by deploring "the sex" for vanity, heartlessness, cattiness and lack of self- scrutiny.[14] Such a narrator reinscribes her identity status as masculine in spirit if not in name.

The tight position of female authorial voice in the middle of the eighteenth century is sharply crystallized in the alternatives taken by Sarah Fielding's *The Countess of Dellwyn* (1759), which visibly appropriates authoriality, and Marie-Jeanne Riccoboni's *L'Abeille* (1761–65), which visibly refuses it. In using Fielding's novel as a prelude to my exploration of Riccoboni's anomalous text, I want to open the category of "women novelists" to distinctions beyond gender by associating the different narrative strategies in these works with differences of class— of education, affiliation, relation to audience, and especially material necessity—that in turn result from both national and personal differences. While Fielding's certainly seems the more authoritative text, I will argue that *The Countess of Dellwyn*'s overt appropriation of "masculine" practices cannot escape the gender-class system that produces it, while *L'Abeille*'s overt self-silencing—in which the impossibility of escape is acknowledged—stands as an equivocal rejection of that system without yet challenging its terms. Riccoboni's narrator's "failure" of voice, in other words, makes clear what constitutes a "successful" female authoriality.

The Countess of Dellwyn is to my knowledge the only mid-century woman's novel that appropriates on a grand scale the narrative practices I have associated with overt authoriality. Prefaced by a long and learned essay on literature, reading, and authorship, the novel is filled with generalizing moral, philosophical, and metafictional commentary. The narrator's most pervasive strategy of self-authorization, beginning with the novel's footnoted first sentence, is self-characterization as an accomplished scholar of classical and Renaissance letters. Even chapter titles are enlisted in displays of scholarship, as in "An Exemplification of the Truth of Montaigne's Observation,

13. See Karl Young, "Samuel Johnson on Shakespeare: One Aspect," *University of Wisconsin Studies in Language and Literature*, no. 18 (1923).
14. Eliza Haywood, *The History of Miss Betsy Thoughtless* (1751; reprint, London: Pandora/ Routledge, 1986), 3.

That we laugh and cry for the same Thing."[15] Fielding does more than cite Virgil and Shakespeare; she appropriates them to create a feminized intertext in which the characters in her own novel are validated through comparisons, often comparisons in which Fielding's women are likened to literature's great men:

> Miss Lucum started at this Summons, like the Ghost of Hamlet's Father at the Crowing of the Cock. (1.52)
>
> Lady Dellwyn had full as much Reason to call Lady Fanny her evil Genius, as ever Mark Anthony had to give that Denomination to Caesar." (2.15–16)
>
> Perhaps Lady Dellwyn had in view Juno's Speech to Venus, in the Fourth Book of the Aeneid, in which are these Lines: (1.106).
>
> [Lady Dellwyn] might well have applied to herself what Angelo, in *Measure for Measure*, says, after he had fallen from Virtue and Innocence..." (2.281)

This feminization is consistent with Fielding's use of the vernacular for her classical references; while Henry condescends to "the ladies" by citing the Latin and then translating the passage explicitly for their benefit, Sarah simply presents all her sources in English translation. If maxims found fiction and ground authority, then *The Countess of Dellwyn* effects a kind of female remaximization, turning classical allusions to new ends. At the same time, *The Countess of Dellwyn* does not challenge the conventional masculinity of narrative voice any more than it challenges the androcentric and upperclass basis of the authority it appropriates: its preface compares a writer to a "well-bred Man," it constitutes a wholly man-made literary intertext, and it never identifies the narrator as female. To my knowledge, no other woman novelist will construct so commandingly erudite a fictional voice until Staël's *Corinne, ou l'Italie* (1807).

Riccoboni's dramatic display of self-silencing punctuates a longer and less evolutionary career. Of her eight original novels, five are epistolary and one is a private memoir addressed to a confidante; the two heterodiegetic novels, the *Histoire du Marquis de Cressy* (1758) and the brief *Histoire d'Ernestine* (1765) create implicitly female narrators with none of Juliette Catesby's outspokenness who restrict themselves

---

15. Sarah Fielding, *The History of the Countess of Dellwyn* (1759; reprint, New York: Garland, 1974), 1.52. Further references will appear in the text.

almost entirely to representational acts. In Riccoboni's fiction, in other words, narrative voice is ideologically most oppositional within the constraints of a private and "feminine" form. But the price for this confinement is exposed in Riccoboni's anomalous *L'Abeille*, a collage of short pieces that claims the *Spectator* as its model.[16] Its four sections appear to have little in common: the first ("L'Abeille") exposes the narrative dilemmas of an author whose sex is suggested only through her grammatically feminine pseudonym ("the Bee"); the second ("L'Aveugle") tells of a fairy who restores a young man's sight; the third ("Suite de l'Abeille") deplores contemporary patriarchal values; and the fourth ("Lettres de la princesse Zelmaïde") laments a new-lywed husband who has gone off to war. Across such differences, however, these four pieces share a preoccupation with authority that becomes increasingly entangled with gender until an authorial voice interrupts the last, epistolary section and openly refuses to complete it.

The first section of *L'Abeille* spins out a crisis of authority that is both coy defense and aggressive attack. Her name ("the Bee"), like her refusal to acknowledge her sex so that the reader may have "the pleasure of guessing it," situates the narrator at the margins of the masculine and the feminine, nature and art, imitation and originality, evoking precisely the dilemmas that plagued Riccoboni's career.[17] Vac-illating between submissiveness and defiance, worrying that the brev-ity of her piece may cause "doubts about my intelligence" ("L'Aeille," 459) but discouraged that "all topics are worn out [épuisés]" (462), the narrator takes for her subject her own authorial malaise.[18] The effect is a profound disturbance of the narrative contract that she recognizes may make her audience "as troubled as I, by the way I get them to read me" (461) and makes the Bee herself "most uncertain in her flight" (462), an uncertainty evident in the cautious, indirect forms with which she addresses her narratee. The Bee vows to work

16. Riccoboni apparently published the first two parts of this work in *Le Monde* in 1761 and the third part in the same journal shortly thereafter. The fourth part may have been added when Riccoboni gathered some short pieces for a *Recueil de pièces détachées* (Paris: Humblot, 1765).

17. The narrator compares herself to the mute industrious bee—grammatically feminine in French—who follows her instincts, does as she pleases, and harms no one so long as she is left alone. But *L'Abeille* also carries a masculine literary weight: it is the title of numerous journals and a trope, especially common in the eighteenth century, that served writers at least as far back as Montaigne.

18. Marie-Jeanne Riccoboni, *L'Abeille*, in *Oeuvres complètes* (Paris: Foucault, 1818), vol. 3, 459, 462. All further references will appear in the text. English translations are my own.

"without subjugation," yet she also worries that her own stories will be "badly woven," and she fears innovation because to "rise against custom" would "weaken what others have said" (463). One might contrast this anxiety to the confident wit assumed by the narrator of Marivaux's *Le Spectateur français*, or by the "author" of *Tom Jones* when he proclaims his intention "to digress through this whole history as often as I see occasion; of which I am myself a better judge than any pitiful critic whatever" and refuses "jurisdiction" to critics, who should "mind their own business," and not "intermeddle" with his "affairs or works."[19]

The Bee's dilemma of authorship, while not explicitly framed in terms of gender, entails a conflict between the two extremes that Claudine Hermann says "menace" the writing woman: imitation and eccentricity.[20] By making anxiety the very subject of her text, Riccoboni's narrator achieves the authoriality that the woman writer is supposed to avoid. But her desired and feared originality comes only from writing out her inability to write; when the Bee turns to narration proper, it is to ostensible imitation that she resorts: "L'Aveugle" claims its source in the *Tatler*, and whereas the first section of *L'Abeille* focused exclusively on its narrator, "L'Aveugle" focuses exclusively on narrated events.

Yet the fiction of imitation by which the narrator introduces "L'Aveugle" also reformulates the question of authority in gendered terms. When the "fairy" Nirsa restores Zulmis' sight so that he can marry Nadine, she not only provides the cure that the "revered sage" Alibeck has been seeking for two years, but she works her miracle disguised in the "foreign form" of Alibeck, who, she alone knows, has died. The proverbial wise man becomes the empty form through which Nirsa exercises her powers "without ever forgetting that she was Nirsa" ("l'Aveugle," 467), so that afterward she reveals her own identity and instructs the community to remember it. By adopting and then discarding the masculine form in which a misguided public has vested its confidence, Nirsa exposes Alibeck's authority as a fiction and models a strategy for appropriating masculine conventions in a way that overturns rather than reinforces their authority. Here is the inversion of Ossery's appropriation of Juliette Catesby's pen and of the male use of female voice in the "heroine's text."

19. Henry Fielding, *The History of Tom Jones, a Foundling* (New York: New American Library, 1963), book 1, chap. 2.
20. Claudine Hermann, *Les Voleuses de langue* (Paris: Editions des femmes, 1976), 37–38.

This fantasy of female power yields, however, to a harsh critique of male hegemony in the "Suite de l'Abeille," which openly declares men to be unfit for the superiority the culture confers on them. In an analysis that prefigures the arguments of Mary Wollstonecraft, the narrator complains that men have "every advantage," that "the world seems created for them alone" ("Suite de l'Abeille," 475), and she demolishes several masculinist shibboleths through a series of anecdotes, giving the last word to a father of daughters who rejects the culture's "foolish preference for a son" (480). As it silences patriarchs and privileges men who articulate women's interests, the narrative makes clear that while women may need to take themselves more seriously, it is men who must be transformed.

Most of these outspokenly feminist ideas in the "Suite de l'Abeille" are represented not in the authorial voice but in the private discourses of characters: citations from a conversation with a woman-friend, a letter from a marquise, the memoirs of a count. The first three sections of *L'Abeille* thus manifest a double and contrary movement: as matters of gender become more prominent and the text's ideological stance more radical and immediate, authorial voice diminishes. The final section attempts to erase all traces of public authorship: proclaiming herself "unable to narrate," the Bee offers a set of letters that she says are translated from the Arabic, hence ostensibly neither of her own composition nor in her own voice. These "Lettres de la Princesse Zelmaïde au Prince Alamir, son époux" begin where the conventional courtship novel concludes, with the idyllic marriage of an idealized pair. What opens as a discourse of longing by a bride abandoned when her husband rushes to help an ally in battle becomes an angry critique of patriarchal practices that, like Juliette Catesby's discourse, gains its force from the appropriation of male words. From the anguished loneliness of the first letter to the reverie of the second and the fantasy of the third, Zelmaïde fills the space of Alamir's absence with revisions rather than rejections of the circumstances that led him to abandon her. It is only after she receives the longed-for letter from Alamir that her own text swerves; with the kind of mocking double voice favored by so many of Riccoboni's narrators, Zelmaïde rewrites Alamir's letter as a woman's text: "Ah! how would one who *loved* me expose me to such sharp sorrows? You *adore* me, and I spill tears: you *desire* me, and I am far from you: *glory commands you* to *aid your allies*; and to obey, you tear the heart of your *dear Zelmaïde*" ("Lettres de la Princesse Zelmaïde," 486). With harsh irony she thanks God that

women are the weaker sex, since "strength, united to beauty" would
have made them so superior that male dominance could no longer
be justified (486). Ridiculing a code of honor that requires a man to
"flee" his wife, Zelmaïde renounces her support for the enterprise of
cultural masculinity that is also arguably the enterprise of authorship:
"if, like you, to acquire an immortal reputation I had to hurt the one
I loved, O, my dear Alamir! I could not, I would not carve Zelmaïde's
name in the temple of memory" (487).

Zelmaïde's four letters uncannily recapitulate the moods and strategies of *L'Abeille* itself, moving from doubt and anxiety to fantasies
of female power to an angry recognition of man-made injustices.
Ideologically *L'Abeille* has been growing increasingly critical of patriarchal practices; formally it has been growing increasingly "feminine" and privatized. Out of these contradictory movements the Bee
and her epistolary narrator ultimately reach a shared aporia, a no-
where-to-go already signaled by their joint dependence on "the words
of the powerful."[21] Immediately after Zelmaïde rejects inscription in
the "temple of memory," her voice stops: the Bee interrupts her letter,
and indeed the whole of *L'Abeille*, with this dramatic refusal: "To
continue a work of this kind, one must never have read the admirable
pages of Mr. Addison [*sic*]. I examine myself, I judge myself and I
stop [myself]. [Pour continuer un ouvrage de ce genre, il faudroit
n'avoir jamais lu les admirables feuilles de M. Addisson. Je m'examine,
je me juge, et je m'arrête.]" (487). On a claim of incompetence, the
Bee refuses to continue this text, which was so tortuously and self-
consciously begun.

This apparently sudden act of self-silencing, surely one of the most
blatant in all of literature, emerges from the conflicts over ideology and
form, imitation and originality, gender and authority, that have preoccupied the authorial narrator from the start. The "I" who interrupts
is the authorial narrator and not Zelmaïde, yet the self-silencing occurs
in the only section of *L'Abeille* in which Riccoboni is using her characteristic form: a fiction in letters told in the solitary voice of a female
protagonist (directed in this case not toward a woman who might
support her but, more perilously, toward the man whose values she
attacks).

That this paragraph simultaneously truncates two texts—the Bee's

<hr>

21. Sheila Rowbotham, *Woman's Consciousness, Man's World* (Harmondsworth, England:
Penguin, 1973), 32.

and Zelmaïde's—makes its equivocal posturing all the more complex. It may of course be read as sheer self-deprecation, a woman's admission of her inability to compete at the genre made famous by Addison. But since the genre that is being interrupted is Riccoboni's and not Addison's stock in trade, the self-silencing narrator is also exposing the artificiality and inadequacy, the ultimate lack of authority, of female epistolary voice. In this reading "Addison" becomes the figure for a space of (imagined) discursive autonomy where it is psychologically and materially possible to create the public forms available to privileged men. In *Juliette Catesby*, the *Spectator* had already been identified as a "model" for such a humanism that "helps us profit from the germ of goodness of which the principle is within us." But either such writing belongs to men, or women must nourish their goodness differently, for Juliette ends her discussion of the *Spectator* with equivocal self-censorship: "See how dangerous it is to read these things," she tells Henriette; "I too thought of writing a book."[22]

In her evocation of Addison as the inimitable, the Bee may also be resisting the economic and literary necessity for imitation, whether of "masculine" models or "feminine" forms. Barred from achieving the Cixouian "s'écrire" (to write herself), the Bee takes the negative power available to her: "s'arrêter" (to stop [herself]). Like the mimicry of which Luce Irigaray writes, this action exaggerates a "feminine" posture—incompetence—into an assault upon a literary establishment that demands conformity from women who would write for fame and profit. Ironically, it is the very act of self-silencing that gives *L'Abeille* its originality and its authority. The anxiety about the reader already present in the opening sentence (which also warned that the end of *L'Abeille* would not correspond to the beginning) is now displaced with pure self-centered reflexivity: "I examine *myself*, I judge *myself*, and I stop *myself*." This final sentence entraps and disempowers the narratee: refusing to narrate is, after all, as much a rejection of the reader as it is a gesture of defeat. If the four parts of *L'Abeille* channel female voice into increasing privacy, then the public voice that closes *L'Abeille* erases the tyrannical reader and reinstates the author as her own critic and judge.

By interrupting the single-voiced epistolary practice that had by the

22. Marie-Jeanne Riccoboni, *Lettres de Milady Juliette Catesby à Milady Henriette Campley, son amie* (1759; reprint, Paris: Desjonquères, 1983), 80. The choice of Addison is particularly ironic since he was far from a feminist. Juliette's own "humanism" also masks her manifest anti-Semitism.

1760s become Riccoboni's stock in trade, *L'Abeille* subverts the author's
seemingly uncomplicated relationship to her other works and opens
up the "natural" equation of women with epistolarity, not only exposing private forms of voice as insufficient but protesting through
a kind of work-stoppage the dynamics of a woman writer's material
life. Throughout the 1760s, a time when the economics of literary
production in France worked brutally against the author, Riccoboni
made her living entirely and not always joyfully through her pen.
When she was writing the first section of *L'Abeille* in which she announces her plan of deliberate brevity, she was straining to draw out
to an additional volume (and thus additional revenue) her *Histoire de
Miss Jenny* (1764). Urged to provide her publisher with new work, she
faced in the "Lettres de le Princesse Zelmaïde" this same pressure to
extend a text. Riccoboni marks her resistance in the letter to her
publisher that prefaces the 1765 *Recueil de pièces détachées*; of a still
unfinished novel, she writes, "No, I assure you, my letters aren't done
or even progressing. You press me in vain."[23] Again and again Riccoboni describes her writing as toil, even drudgery. When she tells
David Garrick that "I am weary of writing novels,"[24] we are left won-
dering whether she would find other kinds of writing more challenging; when to Anne Thickness she writes, "I would rather embroider
[*broder*] or do fancy-work than take up a pen for the profit of [literary]
counterfeiters,"[25] there is no question that for Riccoboni writing was
work and she the worker deprived of the profits of her labor. Even
the capital of her reputation had been pirated; as she wrote to Diderot,
"If a rascal broke a washerwoman's windows, the police would see
that justice was done. [But] they deny that I'm the author of my own
work, they insult me, and no one says anything."[26] No such deprivation
of reputation and reward thwarted Joseph Addison.

    It is in such material circumstances that I want to locate the dif-
ference between Riccoboni's unhappy confinement to epistolary fiction and the appropriative authoriality of Sarah Fielding. These

---

23. Marie-Jeanne Riccoboni, *Recueil de pièces détachées*, iii. It is probable that the unfinished
"letters" in question were the *Lettres d'Adélaïde, comtesse de Sancerre* (1767). In her preface to
Humblot, Riccoboni uses the ironic voice adopted by Juliette and Zelmaïde to inscribe herself
as her publisher's victim: "do you think I can write exactly when it suits you to publish?
They're asking you if *I'm writing, they're* tormenting *you, they're* interrogating *you?* You're
tormenting yourself; no one but you cares about this" (ii, my translation).

24. Cited in Emily Crosby, *Une Romancière oubliée, Madame Riccoboni* (Paris, 1924; reprint,
Geneva: Slatkine, 1970), 49.

25. Ibid., 65. *"Broder"* also means to elaborate a story.

26. Letter to Diderot, cd. 5 August 1762, cited in Diderot, *Correspondance*, vol. 4, 91.

women's careers represent very different experiences of female authorship that are easily overlooked if one designates social status through large and general categories like "middle class." Although Fielding wrote for financial gain she had other material resources, and her advantages of education and class (she was one of very few women of her time to attend school and one of even fewer to learn Latin and Greek), the reputation of her brother Henry, strong support from Johnson and Richardson, and participation in a community of learned women such as Elizabeth Montagu, Sarah Scott, and Elizabeth Carter created an especially favorable context for the kind of narrative authority *The Countess of Dellwyn* inscribes.[27] As a member (like Addison) of the gentry, the social class that was able to preserve its intellectual supremacy in England well after it lost its economic power, Fielding was far more privileged than the petit-bourgeoise Riccoboni. Moreover, *The Countess of Dellwyn* appeared late in a career in which a gradual increase in authoriality is visible: Fielding's first novel, *The Adventures of David Simple* (1744), restricts most of its copious opinion and judgment (including its satire of literary critics) to the voices of its characters, while its brief sequel of 1753 ventures more authorial comment and more direct contact with the narratee.[28] After the death of her brother (who seems to have been as competitive and patronizing as he was supportive of her work), Sarah might have felt authorized to enter the authorial space that Henry had already created for a Fielding.

Riccoboni, on the other hand, may well be the only mid-eighteenth-century French woman novelist who was not a member of the aristocracy, the class still intellectually authoritative in France even though bourgeois men were beginning to forge careers in literature. Riccoboni was born to a marriage of questionable legitimacy, lacked personal fortune, married into a family of actors, remained outside the salon culture that publicly legitimated intellectual women and upwardly mobile bourgeois men, and depended for her livelihood entirely upon the sale of her novels at a time when critics were harsh and writers were routinely exploited not only by literary pirates but by their own publishers. At the same time, the French aristocracy was

27. On male support of Sarah Fielding, see Jane Spencer, *The Rise of the Woman Novelist: From Aphra Behn to Jane Austen* (Oxford: Basil Blackwell, 1986), 91–95.
28. The 1753 section also carries a preface by an enthusiastic "female friend" (probably Jane Collier with whom Fielding co-authored *The Cry*), which may be contrasted to the condescending preface Henry Fielding affixed to the second edition of *David Simple* in 1744.

her major audience; Crosby comments that her publisher liked to
bring out her novels only when the Court was in Paris and had "no
distractions stronger than reading," and she likens Riccoboni to a
boutique vendor obliged to stock what would "tempt buyers" in this
era when the selling of one's writing signified the buyer's moral superiority.[29] When Riccoboni wrote a novel, then, she was "writing up"
to her audience; her subject matter, as Andrée Demay comments,
almost always adopts an aristocratic fictional framework that masks
"her own experience of 'middle class' life."[30] Sarah Fielding, as part
of a community of literary gentlewomen who published not only novels but critical works, wrote horizontally, for her peers.

If *L'Abeille* exposes the material and psychological bondage otherwise visible only in Riccoboni's letters and prefaces, it is fitting that,
although it was neither her most popular work nor her earliest,
L'Abeille opens the first volume of the 1790 edition of her works that
claims to have been "revue et augmentée par l'Auteur."[31] This place-
ment makes *L'Abeille* a lens through which to read Riccoboni's more
conventional novels, a preface to her corpus that exposes the economic
and sexual politics of literary production. But *L'Abeille* is not a novel,
and although Riccoboni refused to finish the "Lettres de la Princesse
Zelmaïde," she went on to write other epistolary fictions and never
created another overtly authorial voice. Indeed, her one later novel
that incorporates the kinds of "philosophical and critical reflections of
the sort which she had published fifteen years earlier in *L'Abeille*"[32] is
entirely an affair between men: in the *Lettres de Milord Rivers à Sir
Charles Cardigan* narrative authority is rendered private and male
rather than public and female.

Riccoboni did have one ready opportunity to adopt a narrative voice
of overt authoriality, and her response affirms her difference from
both Fieldings. Shortly after publishing the first three sections of
L'Abeille, at the suggestion and perhaps with the assistance of her
companion Thérèse Biancolelli, with whom she was learning English,
Riccoboni undertook for financial gain a French rendition of *Amelia*.
In Riccoboni's *Amélie; sujet tiré de M. Fielding* (1762), much of the
language and plot remain Fielding's, but Riccoboni's novel differs

---

29. Crosby, *Une Romancière oubliée*, 65.
30. Andrée Demay, *Marie-Jeanne Riccoboni ou de la pensée féministe chez une romancière du XVIII' siècle* (Paris: La Pensée Universelle, 1977), 12, translation mine.
31. Marie-Jeanne Riccoboni, *Oeuvres complètes* (Paris, 1790), vol. 1, 1–36.
32. Crosby, *Une Romancière oubliée*, p. 54.

strikingly from the original in its narrative voice. Nearly all overt authoriality has been expunged—the chapter titles, the entire first chapter, virtually all the narrator's judgments, and all direct references to the narrating "I." In this way the first five chapters of *Amelia* are reduced to six pages in Riccoboni's text. For all the skill her characters display in appropriating male discourse, for all her own success in imitating a man-made female voice in the *Suite de Marianne*, Riccoboni retells Fielding's story without Fielding's authoriality or any equivalent of her own.

Against this unmarked silence that produced *Amélie*, the dramatized *self*-silencing of *L'Abeille* becomes the subversive act of a woman who can neither continue writing as she must nor find a feasible avenue for writing otherwise. In an essay on strategies of coding in women's texts, Joan N. Radner and I identify several formal devices—appropriation, juxtaposition, distraction, indirection, trivialization, and incompetence—for embedding "feminist messages."[33] We argue that an assertion of incompetence at traditionally "feminine" activities may allow a woman to escape such activities without openly refusing them, just as Marge Piercy imagines that women "all over America" are burning meals they cannot refuse to cook. Riccoboni's proclamation that Addison's superiority makes her unable to continue her epistolary enterprise seems to me a classic act of coded incompetence, as *The Countess of Dellwyn* seems a classic appropriation of masculine authority. But both gestures remain equivocal: neither authorizes female voice, and both can be read—like all coded gestures—in ways that reinforce the very structure they are challenging: knowledge and authority remain male, ignorance and incompetence female. If self-silencing is more equivocal and potentially more radical than silence, it stops short of reconstituting authority: it can point the finger at prevailing economies but cannot offer an alternative, and its very force lies in its suggestion that no alternative is available.

The four writers whose work organizes the rest of this section—Austen, Eliot, Woolf, and Morrison—also faced particular conjunctions and disjunctions between social authority and narrative voice. I will suggest that the moral authority, if not the canonical status, of

33. Joan N. Radner and Susan S. Lanser, "The Feminist Voice: Strategies of Coding in Folklore and Literature," in *Journal of American Folklore* 100 (October–December 1987): 412–25. A revised and expanded version of this essay will appear as "Strategies of Coding in Women's Cultures," in *Feminist Messages: Coding in Women's Culture*, ed. Joan N. Radner (Urbana: University of Illinois Press, forthcoming).

each of these writers has depended on her success in negotiating an authoriality that she seems to have sought both to constitute and to reject. The oeuvre of each of these writers manifests a reach for narrative authority that is signaled in innovative practices for appropriating an authoriality that these same authors also disavow. In stressing the participation of these writers in authorial hegemonies, I am arguing that despite some recent feminist efforts to represent the writers as eschewing authority and despite the writers' own demurrals, each of them has used narrative voice to consolidate the fiction of her own authority.

4

Sense and Reticence:
Jane Austen's "Indirections"

A woman especially, if she have the misfortune of knowing
any thing, should conceal it as well as she can.
— JANE AUSTEN, *Northanger Abbey*

I think I may boast myself to be, with all possible vanity,
the most unlearned and uninformed female who ever dared
to be an authoress.
— JANE AUSTEN, Letter to Rev. James Stanier Clarke

It is no small irony that *Northanger Abbey* was published after Jane
Austen's death rather than as the brilliantly oppositional inauguration
of a literary career. Literary history has "corrected" this chronology
mainly by reading *Northanger Abbey* as a precursor to Austen's implicitly superior "mature" work. Studies of Austen's narrative methods
are prone to represent *Northanger Abbey* as a flawed or crude novel in
contrast to the later works, which are said to establish free indirect
discourse as high art. While *The Rhetoric of Fiction* does not mention
Northanger Abbey by name, the novel's inferiority is implicit in Booth's
praise of Austen for having "long since parodied and outgrown" authorial "intrusions" in favor of techniques determined (he believes)
"by the needs of the novel[s]" themselves.[1] Roy Pascal, who sees Austen's work as supplying, with only rare "lapses," the "preconditions"
for "the unhampered emergence of free indirect speech," simply ig-

1. Wayne Booth, *The Rhetoric of Fiction* (Chicago: University of Chicago Press, 1961), 250–
51.

nores *Northanger Abbey* and begins his discussion with the "first published novel."[2] Some feminist critics concerned with the ways in which Austen's novels and characters renegotiate authority have likewise taken *Sense and Sensibility* as a starting point or demoted *Northanger Abbey* to juvenilia or parody.[3]

Such appraisals valorize the "reticence" they attach to various forms of "indirection" that are indeed characteristic of Austen's work: free indirect discourse, irony, ellipsis, negation, euphemism, ambiguity. Feminist critics at least since Virginia Woolf have read these practices as enabling strategies by which Austen and other "powerless" writers could accommodate contradictions between authorship and femininity, assertiveness and propriety, anger and gentility.[4] While I too see these strategies as ideological constructions, I am concerned that such descriptions celebrate "indirection" as aesthetic and political virtue and essentialize it as "feminine." If, instead of seeing Austen's narrative practices as the inevitable product of a genius advancing without struggle in a perfect coincidence of a writer with her opportunities, one scrutinizes Austen's practices of authoriality from the juvenilia to *Sanditon* in relation to those of other women in her period, then one can identify a specific material conflict in which *Northanger Abbey* takes a central place, not only as a startlingly bold entrance into literature for a young woman in 1803, as some recent feminists argue,[5] but as a venture whose commercial fate may have encouraged Austen to alter the direction of her narrative practices. In this light, the changes in narrative voice from *Northanger Abbey* to the later novels become

2. Roy Pascal, *The Dual Voice: Free Indirect Speech and Its Functioning in the Nineteenth-Century European Novel* (Manchester: Manchester University Press, 1977), 46. On Pascal's insistence that Austen's narrator is masculine, see my Chapter 1, n. 29.

3. See, for example, Mary Poovey, *The Proper Lady and the Woman Writer: Ideology as Style in the Works of Mary Wollstonecraft, Mary Shelley, and Jane Austen* (Chicago: University of Chicago Press, 1984), 45, 112, 183, passim); Deborah Kaplan, "Achieving Authority: Jane Austen's First Published Novel," *Nineteenth Century Fiction* 37 (1983): 531–51; and Sandra Gilbert and Susan Gubar, *The Madwoman in the Attic: The Woman Writer and the Nineteenth-Century Literary Imagination* (New Haven: Yale University Press, 1979), chap. 4. It is odd to see *Northanger Abbey* classed as "juvenilia" since Austen was about twenty-three when she began the novel and twenty-eight when she sold it to a publisher.

4. On feminist indirection in Austen, see, among others, Judith Lowder Newton, *Women, Power, and Subversion: Social Strategies in British Fiction, 1778–1860* (Athens: University of Georgia Press, 1981); Poovey, *The Proper Lady and the Woman Writer*; Gilbert and Gubar, *The Madwoman in the Attic*; Claudia Johnson, *Jane Austen: Women, Politics and the Novel* (Chicago: University of Chicago Press, 1988); and Joan N. Radner and Susan S. Lanser, "Strategies of Coding in Women's Cultures," in *Feminist Messages: Coding in Women's Culture*, ed. Joan N. Radner (Urbana: University of Illinois Press, forthcoming 1992).

5. See, for example, Margaret Kirkham, *Jane Austen, Feminism and Fiction* (London: Methuen, 1983), 66–73, and Johnson, *Jane Austen*, 28–47.

accommodations far more equivocal than they appear through the convergent lenses of modern aesthetics and feminist politics.

The Austen who wrote *Northanger Abbey* was privileged by a trend toward authoriality in women's novels that was emerging during the years of her literary apprenticeship, and by the education and encouragement that gave her an extraordinary knowledge of vernacular literature and some sense of her right to practice it. Many of Austen's adolescent writings create authorial narrators who engage spiritedly in extrarepresentational acts; had *Northanger Abbey* been published when it was accepted, a similar overt authoriality would have been the hallmark of Austen's literary debut. Read against *Northanger Abbey* Austen's first published novel, *Sense and Sensibility* (1811), manifests a distinct curtailment of authorial activity through strategies that in the last novels become the basis for an incipient reinstatement of authoriality on different terms. I am speculating that these changes in Austen's narrative practices result at least in part from her devastating first experience in publishing—an experience that, especially in its historical moment, might well have suggested to Austen that reticence made sense, that a woman ambitious for money and recognition in a conservative wartime economy would be wise to curtail the authority her narrators would openly claim.

The sense of reticence that I am attributing to Austen's narrative practices emerges from her location in a period that encompasses both a dramatic rise and a sharp decline in the position of women novelists. By the 1790s, the years of Austen's literary apprenticeship that culminated in the sale of *Northanger Abbey* (then called *Susan*) in 1803, women writers in general and women novelists in particular were so numerous and diverse that the fiction of a discursive "women's sphere" had become difficult to sustain. The rise of subscription libraries, advertising, copyright legislation, and a publishing industry that capitalized on the reputations of writers as distinctive identities helped women as well as men to become figures of discursive authority. The phrase "by the author of . . . " made even the anonymous novelist an individual, permitting the woman properly shy of publicity to be "named" through a chain of book titles collectively carrying what Pierre Bourdieu describes as the "symbolic capital" in which reputation consists.[6] That many women novelists saw their sex as an en-

6. See Pierre Bourdieu, *Distinction: A Social Critique of the Judgement of Taste*, trans. Richard Nice (Cambridge: Harvard Univesity Press, 1984), 291.

hancement of this symbolic capital is suggested by the frequency with which "by a lady" appears on an anonymous title page.

This construction of the novelist as "author" supported and was supported by the new currency of authorial voice, which by 1790 had overtaken the epistolary and memoir forms in England if not quite yet in France. The shift from personal to authorial voice, which I read as a sign of emerging moral and intellectual authority for the novelist (in contradistinction to the earlier pretense of novels as historical documents)[7] is evident in the careers of a striking number of women writing in the period between 1780 and 1815 in which women novelists sustained an unprecedented if short-lived visibility. In nearly all of these cases, however, women worked "up" to authoriality and employed it sparingly. Fanny Burney, Elizabeth Griffith, Clara Reeve, Stéphanie de Genlis, Mary Hays, Maria Edgeworth, and Germaine de Staël began their novelistic careers with private forms of narrative voice that seem to have served as a testing ground, since each of these writers began after her successful reception to produce almost exclusively novels written in authorial voice.

One telling reflection of women's sense of literary entitlement by the 1790s is a change in the prefaces attached to their novels. In the eighteenth century the preface had become, as Sarah Fielding put it in *The Countess of Dellwyn*, "so general a Practice" as to constitute almost "a necessary Rule."[8] While it was conventional virtually throughout the eighteenth century for women to apologize in prefaces for either their gender or their genre, and of course for their own inferior artistry, women writing after 1790 seem more likely to resist this self-abasing tapestry. Staël and Genlis, for example, proclaim their confidence that their work will be judged on its merits and not on their sex. As firmly as Burney had allied *Evelina* with the novels of Richardson and Rousseau, Wollstonecraft claims in *Mary, a Fiction* (1788) to be constructing "neither a Clarissa, a Lady G——, nor a Sophie" but "a woman, who has thinking powers." And the brash new American Susanna Rowson confronts a critical double standard head-on, castigating the "sage critic who, 'with spectacle on nose, and pouch by's side,' with lengthened visage and contemptuous smile, sits down

---

7. This authority of the novel has been associated with a retrenching consolidation of discursive power in the conservative classes. See Nicola Watson's work in progress, and John Bender, *Imagining the Penitentiary: Fiction and the Architecture of Mind in Eighteenth-Century England* (Chicago: University of Chicago Press, 1987).

8. Sarah Fielding, *The History of the Countess of Dellwyn* (1759; reprint, New York: Garland, 1974), iii.

to review the literary productions of a *woman*," and who condemns her for some gap in knowledge that she considers inevitable given the "circumscribed" education women receive.[9]

As the "sphere" for women authors widened, however, women's discursive authority began to be represented not only as defective but as threatening and dangerous. Enlightenment, as I hope my second chapter made clear, had never deconstructed patriarchy; on the contrary, the rigidification of sexual spheres and the valorization of female domesticity continued fairly relentlessly, destabilizing female authorship even as it emerged as a significant force. The political conservatism of the 1790s sharply increased these constraints: the revolutions in France and America had silenced English radical politics even before the publication of Mary Wollstonecraft's posthumous *Memoirs* in 1798 put an end to openly feminist dialogue,[10] and in France, the Terror and its aftermath effected a withdrawal of women from public literary affairs. It seems no coincidence that by the 1790s learned women in Europe were being satirized as intellectually inferior, politically dangerous, and morally weak: 1790 marks the *OED*'s first indication that "Bluestocking" has degenerated from a descriptive to a derisive term. Even women participate: Charlotte Smith's *The Old Manor House* (1793) creates a self-important, vain, and aging *salonnière*, a "modern Centlivre" named "Mrs Manby."[11]

Female authorship at the end of the century is thus fraught with a weight of power and danger that called upon women novelists especially in England to choose authorial rather than personal voice but to minimize the authority such a voice claimed. I know of no other woman who chose the confrontational path Rowson took in her bestselling "sentimental" novel *Charlotte: A Tale of Truth* (1791), in which an explicitly female narrator constructs herself as an unequivocal truth-teller, filling the text with maxims, comments about her composition, allusions to canonical works, attacks on critics, dialogues with

9. Susanna Rowson, preface to *Mentoria* (1791; reprint, Philadelphia, 1794), iii–iv.
10. On the British association of (intellectual) women with the French Revolution, see, for example, Thomas Gisborne's *Enquiry into the Duties of the Female Sex* (1797); Christopher Hibbert, *The English: A Social History 1066–1945* (New York: Norton, 1987); Derek Jarrett, *England in the Age of Hogarth* (1974); Bonnie S. Anderson and Judith P. Zinsser, *A History of Their Own* (New York: Harper and Row, 1988), vol. 2; and Alice Browne, *The Eighteenth Century Feminist Mind* (Detroit: Wayne State University Press, 1987).
11. Charlotte Smith, *The Old Manor House* (London: Routledge and Kegan Paul, 1987), 491–92. For a sampling of caricatures to which writing woman were subjected in the next quarter-century, see Alice Kahler Marshall, *Pen Names of Women Writers from 1600 to the Present* (Camp Hill, Pa.: Alice Marshall Collection, 1985), 73–94.

various narratees to whom the narrator in Shandyesque fashion also gives voice, and even interpretations of her own work. These "digressions" are defended much as Henry Fielding defends his in passages like the one I cited in Chapter 3: "I confess I have rambled strangely from my story: but what of that?"[12] Rowson could perhaps undertake this authorial stance because she stood on overdetermined moral and literary ground, producing sentimental novels ostensibly designed to warn young ladies against independence and filial disobedience; but this boldness may also have cost her a place in the literary establishment that she challenges so openly. The best known English-language women novelists—Burney, Smith, Edgeworth, Radcliffe, Reeve— were far more circumspect, sparing in the authoriality bestowed on their narrators and equivocal in distinguishing their narrators as female. Even when Burney turned to authorial voice in *Cecilia* (1782), her narrator rarely expresses an explicit stance or calls attention to herself; *Camilla* (1796) is prefaced like all of Burney's novels with a dedication that bows and scrapes to the powerful, and while it begins with a prologue that asserts (in Johnsonian fashion) the novelist's importance as "historian of human life" and "investigator of the human heart," this assertive prologue does not appear in the second edition of *Camilla*, published in 1802. Other equivocal moments in Burney's novels recall those Lennox displayed in *The Female Quixote*: for example, the "author" implied in such chapter titles as "An Author's Idea of Order" and "An Author's Opinion of Visiting" is not Burney but a fictional character named Dr. Orkborne, "one of the first scholars in the world." Similarly, Charlotte Smith will put in the mouths of male characters original sonnets that she will later publish under her own name, but she will also give to her authorial narrator political generalizations only loosely attached to the perceptions of a character and will even use footnotes as a vehicle for opinion and historical fact. Maria Edgeworth will create in *Belinda* (1801) a female character who discourses on literary convention and "finish[es] the novel" by both staging and metafictionalizing its denouement, and the narrator of *Patronage* (1814) will engage in gratuitous displays of authoriality. Staël's epistolary *Delphine* (1802) will be followed by *Corinne, ou l'Italie* (1807), a novel teeming with intellectual, moral, historical, and aesthetic discourse in the authorial voice. Indeed, overt

12. Susanna Rowson, *Charlotte Temple*, ed. Clara M. and Rudolf Kirk (New Haven, Conn.: College and University Press, 1964), 67. The novel was originally published as *Charlotte: A Tale of Truth*.

authoriality seems to have been a mark for each of these women of the writer's status as serious literary professional.

That Austen immediately allows herself the authorial liberties toward which these more seasoned writers cautiously worked makes *Northanger Abbey*'s reach for authoriality, and for the literary attention it signifies, both fragile and remarkable. The novel marks its authoriality from the first chapter with explicit comments and maxims, frequently about women (including, of course, the famous comment that serves as my first epigraph to this chapter), allusions to literature, direct and indirect addresses to the narratee, and explicit self-reference. All of these acts focus attention on the narrating subject, who constructs her status as moralist, wit, conscious artist, knowledgeable scholar, and literary judge. As much as *Joseph Andrews*, this "parody" is a declaration of independence that acknowledges the source of its originality in other people's books; the narrator is not representing herself as a " 'mere' interpreter and critic of prose fictions" who "modestly demonstrates her willingness to inhabit a house of fiction not of her own making," as Gilbert and Gubar argue,[13] but (as several more recent critics concur) rather is marking her place in literature through the "competitive [and] friendly mastery characteristic of eighteenth century confrontations with literary predecessors."[14] I emphasize the comparison to Fielding because it is finally his narrative practices more than any eighteenth-century woman writer's practice that *Northanger Abbey*'s narration resembles. But the "author" Austen constructs and the "mastery" she demonstrates is (unlike Sarah Fielding's) insistently female; as strongly as Wollstonecraft and Rowson, if less tendentiously, and with wider-reaching implications, the narrator of *Northanger Abbey* claims literature as woman's rightful sphere.

Like most of her predecessors and contemporaries, Austen moves into authorial voice from epistolarity, with the significant difference that she did not insist on beginning her public career with epistolary work.[15] Her most accomplished early piece, *Lady Susan* (probably 1793–94), makes clear its impatience with the (now waning) letter

13. Gilbert and Gubar, *The Madwoman in the Attic*, 145.

14. Jocelyn Harris, *Jane Austen's Art of Memory* (Cambridge: Cambridge University Press, 1989), 214. See also Kirkham, *Jane Austen*, 70; Park Honan, *Jane Austen: Her Life* (New York: Fawcett Columbine, 1987), 143–44; John Halperin, *The Life of Jane Austen* (Baltimore: Johns Hopkins University Press, 1984), 115; and Johnson, *Jane Austen*, 28–29.

15. Austen's father unsuccessfully offered "First Impressions," probably the prototype of *Pride and Prejudice*, to a publisher in 1797. Its narrative structure is not known.

novel in a gesture that recalls Riccoboni's abrupt truncation of the "Lettres de le Princesse Zelmaïde": after forty-one letters Austen abandons *Lady Susan* with a playful and patently lame excuse.[16] This finale to *Lady Susan* manifests one characteristic strategy of Austen's authoriality—an assertion that is also a refusal, in this case a burst of authorial "I's" that disclaim both omniscience and reliability: "Whether Lady Susan was, or was not happy in her second Choice— I do not see how it can ever be ascertained—for who would take her assurance of it, on either side of the question? The World must judge from Probability."[17] Such practices yield a message as duplicitous as the famous sentence written to the prince regent's clergyman in which Austen "boasts" her ignorance with "all possible vanity."[18] Both instances assert authority even as they claim to relinquish it.

While some of Austen's earliest fictions are works in letters, her juvenilia also construct voices that revel in the pleasures of authorship both within the stories and in elaborate dedicatory prefaces that try on the role of famous author and delight in it. Mocking both fictional convention and her own ambitions, this "Author" announces intentions, pretends to lapses of memory, and challenges the reader's authority—and never deprecates herself or her work.[19] Authoriality is most prominent in the parodic "History of England," which creates a highly judgmental, irreverent, and witty narrator-historian who speaks directly to readers, claims her sex as a basis for judgment, and generally puts herself on verbal display. In this passage on Henry VI, for example, the narrator explicitly refuses the primacy of the representational function and claims the importance of authorial stance: "I cannot say much for this Monarch's Sense—Nor would I if I could,

16. Deborah Kaplan associates the epistolarity of *Lady Susan* with female community and the movement to authorial voice with "the triumph of Austen's general, patriarchal culture perspective." See "Female Friendship and Epistolary Form: *Lady Susan* and the Development of Jane Austen's Fiction," in *Criticism* 29 (1987): 163–78.

17. Jane Austen, *Lady Susan*, in *The Oxford Illustrated Jane Austen: Minor Works*, 3d ed., ed. R. W. Chapman (Oxford: Oxford University Press, 1933; rev. ed. 1969), 313. All further references to Austen's juvenilia and miscellaneous writings are taken from this edition and will appear in the text. Page references to the six finished novels will also be taken from the six-volume Chapman edition and will appear in the text with the chapter number in Roman.

18. Letter of 11 December 1815, in *Jane Austen's Letters*, 2d ed., ed. R. W. Chapman (Oxford: Oxford University Press, 1952), 443. In both her fiction and her letters Austen refers to herself almost exclusively as "author" rather than "authoress." I have found only two exceptions: this letter to the Reverend Clarke and the letter to Crosby asking for the return of *Susan*.

19. See, respectively, "Frederic and Elfrieda," 9; "Jack and Alice," 12, 24; "Memoirs of Mr Clifford," 43; and "Jack and Alice," 18. For prefaces that mock the moral posture so many women writers hid behind, see "A Fragment," 71; and "Scraps," 170; for prefaces that openly fantasize literary success, see "The Mystery," 55; and "Catherine," 192.

for he was a Lancastrian. I suppose you know all about the Wars between him & The Duke of York who was of the right side; If you do not, you had better read some other History, for I shall not be very diffuse in this, meaning by it only to vent my Spleen *against*, & shew my Hatred *to* all those people whose parties or principles do not suit with mine, & not to give information" (139–40). This sense of the narrator's prerogative is also evident in *Northanger Abbey*, although *Northanger Abbey* moves into authoriality with greater care. For example, given both the conventional practice and Austen's own pattern in the juvenilia, it would have been logical for *Northanger Abbey* to open with a preface.[20] I read this absence—and the absence of prefaces from Austen's published novels generally—as a dialogized silence marking both an avoidance of the frontal attack practiced by a Wollstonecraft or a Rowson, and a refusal to denigrate through the expected public demurral her writing, her genre, or her sex.

The first few chapters of *Northanger Abbey*, however, embed an oppositional stance not unlike those inscribed in the more audacious prefaces. Austen's strategies are less direct: while the introduction to Wollstonecraft's *Mary, a Fiction* had explicitly announced what its heroine was not going to be, *Northanger Abbey* adopts from its opening sentence a discourse of negation (like that of the bride's letter in my Chapter 1) that proclaims a literary philosophy by enacting it: "No one . . . would have supposed [Catherine] born to be an heroine." This parody of fictional conventions is followed by a jibe not only at heroines but arguably at writers whose works "heroines must read to supply their memories with those quotations which are so serviceable and so soothing in the vicissitudes of their eventful lives" (15): Alexander Pope, Thomas Gray, James Thomson, Shakespeare (and, in a subsequent chapter, Richardson). If Sarah Fielding's narrator showed her erudition by paying allegiance to the great literary men, Austen's shows hers by making these great men participants in if not targets of a joke. Five chapters of such ironic expressions of narrative stance set the framework for the longest "digression" in any of Austen's published works—the famous defense of novels and (women) novelists. Exposing the hypocrisy by which novels are derided within novels themselves, the narrator calls together a community of abused writers in which she dares to place herself: "Let us not desert one

---

20. The 1818 version of *Northanger Abbey* does bear a brief notice concerning its belated publication. It is of course possible that the original *Susan* did have a preface.

another; we are an injured body. Although our productions have afforded more extensive and unaffected pleasure than those of any other literary corporation in the world, no species of composition has been so much decried. From pride, ignorance, or fashion, our foes are almost as many as our readers" (37). The narrator goes on to attack those imitative writers of nonfiction who are "eulogized" out of all proportion "by a thousand pens": "the nine-hundredth abridger of the History of England" or the "man who collects and publishes in a volume some dozen lines of Milton, Pope, and Prior, with a paper from the Spectator, and a chapter from Sterne" (37). This passage does not denigrate the masters directly, but it does associate them with that which is overpraised and (like Rowson, if with better humor) takes a swipe at "the Reviewers" as well. The writings produced by Austen's novelists, in contrast, have "only genius, wit, and taste to recommend them" (37), and while sex is not mentioned, the novels the narrator praises (*Cecilia, Camilla, Belinda*) are women's works. It also seems to me significant that Austen names not the most popular works by Burney and Edgeworth but works written in authorial voice. Even more important, and easy to miss in retrospect, is the boldness of Austen's self-declared membership in the best "literary corporation in the world": unless this passage was added in 1817—and no evidence suggests that it was—then Austen has dared in her very first novel to rank herself with the two best-regarded women novelists of the day.

The conclusion to this passage insists that these novels by women (including, by implication, Austen's own) are far superior to the dull, "improbable," and "coarse" writings found in the *Spectator* that Riccoboni's Bee proclaimed herself so eager to imitate. Without ever making gender an explicit issue, then, this narrator overturns the same hierarchies that Rowson's and Wollstonecraft's prefaces protest and challenges the public's unthinking adoration of the already-canonical. While Austen certainly cherished the work of individual male writers—and I agree with Jocelyn Harris that she "took what she wanted from anywhere,"[21] the narrator of *Northanger Abbey* lacks any reverence for a male tradition per se and positions herself in the female-centered space whose absence Austen had protested at thirteen, when she complained that *The Loiterer*, the journal her brothers created at Oxford, carried too many stories by and about men.[22] As

21. Harris, *Jane Austen's Art of Memory*, x.
22. See Honan, *Jane Austen*, 61.

she put it with marvelous doubleness in her letter to James Stanier Clarke, Jane Austen spoke only the "mother tongue."[23]

It may be difficult from a twentieth-century vantage point to appreciate the overt and woman-identified authorial stance Austen constructs for what she expected would be her first published narrative voice. What is now often considered one of the strongest defenses of the novel in a novel is an impressive gamble coming from a young, unpublished writer, a woman who, having just refused a proposal of marriage (thereby risking social and economic marginality), was likely to be counting on the sales of *Susan* as significant support.[24] Although scholars have traditionally assumed that Crosby's failure to publish the book was linked to its parody of the still-popular gothic, the narrator's outspokenness may have been just as responsible. Clearly Crosby's refusal either to publish or to release the manuscript distressed and angered Austen, as Margaret Kirkham underscores when she points to Austen's signing with the pseudonymous initials "M.A.D." (for "Mrs. Ashton Dennis") her indignant letter to the publisher in 1809, and I believe Austen critics have underestimated the probable effect on a young writer of having a first novel accepted but never brought out. I am speculating that the novel's fate was at least partly responsible for Austen's literary silence during the next six years, during which she must have waited for this first novel, with its spirited engagement of literary issues, to appear. And by the time Austen did begin to publish, times had changed: English fiction, in Kirkham's words, was about to find "its Great Romantic (male) novelist, and the twenty-five years in which fiction in England had been dominated by women came to an end."[25] It is a sign of this difference that probably the best-selling novel by a woman was then Hannah More's *Coelebs in Search of a Wife* (1808), in which, if I may put it crassly, a male narrator tells women how to please men. As David Musselwhite argues, *Mansfield Park* may have been an effort to cash in on this conservative trend that made *Coelebs* (and that *Coelebs* made) so popular.[26]

It is of course impossible to know how the failure of *Northanger Abbey* affected Austen's writing or whether Austen would have created similar authorial narrators had *Northanger Abbey* become her first pub-

23. Letter of 11 December 1815 in Austen, *Letters*, 443.
24. On this point see especially Halperin, *The Life of Jane Austen*, 115.
25. Kirkham, *Jane Austen*, 72.
26. David Musselwhite, *Partings Welded Together: Politics and Desire in the Nineteenth-Century English Novel* (London: Methuen, 1987).

lished book. I am speculating that the fate of *Northanger Abbey*, which
would have reinforced the new conservative climate, may have led
Austen not to write different stories but to write them differently,
changing the shape and scope of her narrative voices. Park Honan
suggests that since in *Northanger Abbey* Austen "had openly criticized
sexist bias in literary works and in reviewers, and the novel had been
suppressed by the publishing house to which she had sold it," her
"avoidance thereafter of any open statement of a similar kind is not
surprising."[27] But the novels after *Northanger Abbey* reveal more widespread differences than the suppression of explicit feminist ideology;
all overt authoriality diminishes, and narrative stance becomes embedded through what I see as compensatory textual practices. These
changes are motivated, I argue, less by the imperatives of "realism,"
which I think we impose in some measure on Austen ex post facto,
than by the imperatives of literary and commercial success. If Shlomith
Rimmon-Kenan is right to argue that a covert authorial narrator is
likely to seem more reliable than an overt one because an overt narrator risks the reader's dissent, then Austen may be attempting to
guarantee her narrators' authority by having them speak less openly.[28]

Certainly *Sense and Sensibility* returns to the more limited, primarily
representational narrative practices that characterize the novels of
Austen's female predecessors, offering from its first chapter a straight-
forward summary of the Dashwood family's history much like the
summaries that open novels by Burney and Smith. Not only does the
somberness of *Sense and Sensibility* suit it to an age that was buying
books such as More's *Coelebs*, but the novel avoids overt authoriality
almost entirely: the narrator does not use the first person, almost
never takes an explicit stance, and says virtually nothing about either
gender or literature. Nor will any subsequent novel call attention, in
the way that *Northanger Abbey* does, to its narrative voice. While the
presence of the narrative "I" is not in itself significant, there is a
significant contrast to *Northanger Abbey* in the fact that there is only
one use of the "I" in *Pride and Prejudice*, *Sense and Sensibility*, and
Persuasion respectively, none in *Emma*, and a brief flurry late in *Mansfield
Park*. Except in *Sense and Sensibility*, all these instances of authorial "I"
are located in the final chapters of the novels and, as in *Lady Susan*
(and *Northanger Abbey*), either parody fictional convention, or qualify,

27. Honan, *Jane Austen*, 162.
28. Shlomith Rimmon-Kenan, *Narrative Fiction: Contemporary Poetics* (London: Methuen,
1983), 103.

personalize, and render ambiguous the resolutions to plots. Thus each "I" is attached to some claim of inability or some refusal to speak that is also, of course, a coded proclamation of individuality and originality: each uses a formal structure of authorial assertion in order to decline to assert, and each creates as well a sense of community with characters or with audience. It is as if these narrators cannot leave their texts without some self-representation, even though—or because—these assertions are usually negative claims such as the proclamation of incompetence that Austen wrote to the Rev. James Stanier Clarke.

The diminution of narrative self-consciousness after *Northanger Abbey* is accompanied by a similar disappearance of "maximizing" comments made openly in the authorial voice. While generalizations—explicit expressions of ideological stance that refer to a "world" beyond the fictional—are quite plentiful in *Northanger Abbey*,[29] the combined pages of Austen's five later novels yield but a score of detachable maxims that can be attributed exclusively to the narrative voice. These comments embrace a wide range of topics and varying degrees of opposition to the "culture text"—from the swipe at (male) children in *Sense and Sensibility* (1.4) to the ironic opening sentence of *Pride and Prejudice* to the passage from *Mansfield Park* that rhapsodizes about the superiority of sibling relationships to conjugal ties (24.235). Some are coy, like the assertion in *Mansfield Park* that "there certainly are not so many men of large fortune in the world, as there are pretty women to deserve them" (1.3); others are qualified by syntactic conditionals: "He was not an ill-disposed young man, unless to be rather cold hearted, and rather selfish, is to be ill-disposed" (*Sense and Sensibility*, 1.5). Since little characterizes this body of maxims save their resistance to received wisdom, they serve primarily as sporadic reminders of the narrator's presence as independent thinker and judge.

But generalizations do not disappear after *Northanger Abbey*; rather, they are rendered contingent and ambiguous through Austen's use of an "indefinite" free indirect discourse that allows the narrator an equivocal participation in the thoughts of her characters.[30] Austen is

---

29. See, for example, 1.15, 4.33, 10.74, 14.111, and 29.239.

30. In free indirect discourse, a character's speech, perceptions, or thoughts are reported in the narrator's voice, usually with some "flavor" of the character's words, but without explicit tagging of the discourse as that of the character. Free indirect discourse is discussed in numerous sources, from Pascal's *The Dual Voice* and Ann Banfield's *Unspeakable Sentences: Narration and Representation in the Language of Fiction* (London: Routledge, 1982) to M. M. Bakhtin, *The Dialogic Imagination* (Austin: University of Texas Press, 1981); Henry Louis Gates, Jr., *The Signifying Monkey: A Theory of African-American Literary Criticism* (Oxford: Oxford

widely acknowledged as one of the first writers to make extensive use
of free indirect discourse—a use that Roy Pascal finds "astonishing,"
probably because he seems unaware that for over two decades the
women Austen was reading had been making fairly extensive use of
these forms. While free indirect discourse may ironize as well as authorize and does not necessarily construct an alliance between narrator
and character, I do agree with Margaret Doody that eighteenth-
century women writers used free indirect discourse to authorize intelligent and morally superior woman as critics and interpreters of
their society; such a use will be especially important for Austen in
Persuasion and for Wollstonecraft in *The Wrongs of Woman* (see Chapter
12).[31] I want to suggest, however, that in Austen's novels free indirect
discourse also serves the inverse purpose: to authorize not characters
but the narrator herself. Free indirect discourse may embed maxims
in the more contingent authority of a character's perception in which
the narrator's participation is ambiguous. Such "hybrid" discourses
that blur narrative responsibility are less frequent in but by no means
absent from the writings of these earlier women,[32] but they become
in Austen's novels a critical mechanism for suggesting a narrative
stance whose attribution cannot be verified. Such free indirect discourse is not, however, the kind of indirection that one ought to
associate with a "discourse of the powerless." If it allows the indirect
performance of certain narrative acts, it represents not a ceding of
voice but the construction of a textual surface firmly under authorial
control.[33] The judgments rendered in the narrator's voice remain in
some sense hers, whether by sympathetic agreement or by ironic dissent. To the extent that the indirect comment is presented (or accepted) as authoritative, it does of course also authorize the character
to whom it is attached, creating a narrative complicity between the

University Press, 1988); and Bender, *Imagining the Penitentiary.*

Anne Waldron Neumann defines "indefinite" free indirect discourse as that ambiguous
form in which it is unclear whether the discourse in question is the character's or the narrator's
text. See Neumann, "Characterization and Comment in *Pride and Prejudice*: Free Indirect
Discourse and 'Double-voiced' Verbs of Speaking, Thinking, and Feeling," *Style* 20 (1986):
376.

31. See Margaret Doody, "George Eliot and the Eighteenth-Century Novel," *Nineteenth
Century Fiction* 35 (1980): 260–91.

32. See, for example, Burney's *Cecilia* (Harmondsworth, England: Penguin/Virago, 1986),
51, in which the narrator can indirectly lament through Cecilia's perceptions the demands
on women's time; and Charlotte Smith's *The Old Manor House*, 336, in which strong positions
against war and slavery are rendered in the narrator's voice through Orlando's perspective.

33. John Bender goes so far as to associate free indirect discourse with "the genius of
modern forms of bureaucratic control," which absorb "heteroglossia" into "a container of
authority" (*Imagining the Penitentiary*, 177, 211–13).

authorial voice and that character. At the same time, generalizations thus temporalized and qualified by their adherence to a character lose, as Roy Pascal argues, their "claim to absolute truth."[34]

All of Austen's novels contain such generalizing comments and judgments rendered indirectly and often indefinitely in a dialogized voice. There are times when the ideological positions seem distinct from the authorial consciousness—as, for example, when Sir John Middleton believes that "to be unaffected was all that a pretty girl could want to make her mind as captivating as her person" (*Sense and Sensibility*, 7.33)—and times when an indirectly rendered judgment seems to belong as much to the narrator as to the character, as when Elinor reads Willoughby's letter of defection and is grateful for Marianne's "escape from the worst and most irremediable of all evils, a connection, for life, with an unprincipled man" (*Sense and Sensibility* 29.184). Some are sharply ambiguous: when the narrator reports Emma Woodhouse's response to Harriet Smith's parentage, is it only Emma who thinks that "the stain of illegitimacy, unbleached by nobility or wealth, would have been a stain indeed" (*Emma*, 55.482)? (After all, no "gentleman" marries Harriet, and the verb tense "would have been" could belong to either the narrator or the character.) And when the narrator of *Pride and Prejudice* says that "without thinking highly either of men or of matrimony," Charlotte Lucas had always had marriage as her goal, to what extent does the narrator concur in the sentence that follows—"it was the only honourable provision for well-educated young women of small fortune, and however uncertain of giving happiness, must be their pleasantest preservative from want" (22.122–23)? Some indirect judgments, indeed, seem even more likely to be the narrator's than the character's, such as this statement about the gothic: "Charming as were all Mrs. Radcliffe's works, and charming even as were the works of all her imitators, it was not in them perhaps that human nature, at least in the midland counties of England, was to be looked for" (*Northanger Abbey*, 25.200): even in *Northanger Abbey*, where an authorial generalization would not have been remarkable, Austen may not have wished to criticize another woman novelist directly, especially one whose works were still popular.

On the other hand, free indirect discourse stands in a position of greater power than characters' discourse, especially when it is "indefinite," not firmly or immediately attached to markers of a char-

34. Pascal, *The Dual Voice*, 49.

acter's perception, speech, or thought. This is perhaps why Austen does not embed her most controversial generalizations even in this hybrid form. While *Northanger Abbey* was outspoken about both women and fiction, in the later works oppositional gender ideology is almost entirely embedded in the direct speech of characters (as will be true also of novels by Eliot and Woolf), often of characters who are foolish, misguided, or morally ambiguous. Consider, for example, the following statements concerning marriage and woman's place: "I see no occasion for entailing estates from the female line"; "Happiness in marriage is entirely a matter of chance"; "There is not one in a hundred of either sex, who is not taken in when they marry. . . . it is, of all transactions, the one in which people expect most from others, and are least honest themselves"; "It is poverty only which makes celibacy contemptible to a generous public! . . . a single woman, of good fortune, is always respectable"; "When one lives in the world, a man's or woman's marrying for money is too common to strike one as it ought." Can the validity of these assertions, uttered respectively by Lady Catherine de Bourgh, Charlotte Lucas, Mary Crawford, Emma Woodhouse, and Anne Elliot's friend Mrs. Smith, be sustained on the merits of the character who utters them?[35] Or is Austen dispersing judgment among a community of individuals—the majority of them women—who, while fallible and far from heroic, may still have wise (and cynical) perceptions about matters that concern their lives? Perhaps the oppositional stances of these women might well, if the *Northanger Abbey* narrative liberties had continued, have been spoken in the authorial voice. Certainly Austen's letters, even in the censored versions left by Cassandra, betray similar sexual attitudes: the lament, when her niece Anna became pregnant for the third time, that she would "be worn out before she is thirty"; the caustic recommendation of separate rooms after one couple's announcement of pregnancy; the quip that "single women have a dreadful propensity for being poor"; the defense of Queen Caroline on grounds of sisterhood— "poor woman, I shall support her as long as I can, because she *is* a woman, and because I hate her husband"; the complaint upon the engagement of her niece Fanny, "What a loss it will be when you are married. You are too agreeable in your single state. . . . I shall hate you when your delicious play of mind is all settled down into conjugal

35. The passages come respectively from *Pride and Prejudice* 29.164; and 6.23; *Mansfield Park* 5.46; *Emma* 10.85; and *Persuasion* 21.201.

and maternal affections."[36] Austen's private discourse suggests, in other words, some of the caustic wisdom of Austen's more spirited female characters.

Persuasion, however, attempts a new practice that I will associate with a reach toward the overt authoriality that disappeared after *Northanger Abbey*'s failure: the gradual authorization through a nonironic, nondistanced free indirect discourse, of Anne Elliot as wholly reliable focalizing consciousness. This position, occupied by no previous Austen heroine, seems to me Austen's preparation for a return to some of the overt content of *Northanger Abbey* without yet attempting its overtly authorial form. After *Northanger Abbey*, allusions to both gender and literature (excepting, say, the ambiguous use of *Lovers' Vows* and the reading of Shakespeare in *Mansfield Park*) have gone largely underground. Having created through a nonironized free indirect discourse a completely authoritative heroine in *Persuasion*, the narrator uses the character's discourse as a surrogate through which to return to questions not only about writers (Scott and Byron) and writing (poetry and prose) but about gender and authority, particularly in the extended discussion near the end of *Persuasion* between Anne Elliot and Captain Harville about men's literary advantages: "Education has been theirs in so much higher a degree; the pen has been in their hands" (23.234). While in *Northanger Abbey* it was the authorial narrator who defended the novels and voices of women while the character's judgments were rendered with distance and often with irony, here the character is authorized to speak virtually in the narrator's stead.

This direct discourse that is the formal opposite of authorial voice may have helped Austen find her way back to it: I am certainly reminded of *Northanger Abbey* in the passage in chapter 8 of *Sanditon* that begins with an unequivocal and unironic "the truth was," and goes on not only to chastize Sir Edward and all those who "derive only false Principles from Lessons of Morality" by misreading "our most approved Writers," but also to criticize Richardson and his successors on feminist grounds: Sir Edward's fancy "had been early caught by all the impassioned, and most exceptionable parts of Richardsons; and such Authors as have since appeared to tread in Richardson's steps, so far as Man's determined pursuit of Woman in

36. Letters of 23 March 1817 (*Letters*, 488); 13 March 1817 (483); and 20 February 1817 (478–79).

defiance of every opposition of feeling and convenience is concerned" (404). It is possible, then, that Austen's narrative practices, perhaps stimulated by the recovery of *Northanger Abbey*, would have changed once more; certainly the draft of *Sanditon*'s first twelve chapters reveals Charlotte Heywood's perspective to be far less central than that of Fanny Price or Emma Woodhouse, let alone Anne Elliot.

As I indicated at the outset, it has been argued that Austen's achievements are greatest in those works where authoriality is most covert. A similar argument has been made for those early works by Burney and Edgeworth that do not adopt an authorial voice: *Evelina* was spared the charges of didacticism laid in increasing measure on Burney's three subsequent books; Edgeworth's first novel, *Castle Rackrent* (1800), written in the voice of a male Irish servant, is likewise proclaimed her "masterpiece," while *Belinda* and *Patronage* are criticized for their "preachiness," just as Charlotte Smith's authorial narratives are considered too "bitter," and Susan Ferrier's "caustic."[37] Certainly Austen's work has for over a century been compared favorably to that of her contemporaries precisely for its absence of erudition, "preaching," and explicit politics.[38] Yet Austen seems to have longed for precisely these possibilities when she writes, in a famous letter of 1813, that *Pride and Prejudice*—a novel with virtually no explicit references to literature, history, or anything beyond its own representational boundaries— is "rather too light, and bright, and sparkling," that it "wants shade; it wants to be stretched out here and there with a long chapter of sense, if it could be had; if not, of solemn, specious nonsense, about something unconnected with the story; an essay on writing, a critique of Sir Walter Scott, or the history of Buonaparte." These are *authorial* acts that Austen is wishing for, the acts of Fielding or Staël or Scott himself, and the hesitation to write them seems more Cassandra's than Jane's: "I doubt your quite agreeing with me here. I know your starched notions."[39] The sense of reticence that trans-

---

37. Of *Patronage*, for example, Elizabeth Harden notes Edgeworth's admission that she sacrificed story "to the good of our moral": "I am well aware by woeful experience (vide Patronage) of the danger of making the morality of a fiction too prominent—I have repented—& hope never to be *found out*, in a moral again whilst I live." Letter to J. L. Foster of 28 October 1816, quoted in Harden, *Maria Edgeworth* (Boston: Twayne, 1984), 198. See also Walter Pollock, *Jane Austen, Her Contemporaries, and Herself* (Brooklyn, N. Y.: Haskell House, 1970), 41, 53, 44; and Elizabeth Harden, *Maria Edgeworth's Art of Prose Fiction* (The Hague: Mouton, 1971), 74, 235, 238.

38. See, for example, Harden, *Maria Edgeworth's Art of Prose Fiction*, 235 and 238, and Harden, *Maria Edgeworth*, 74.

39. Letter of 4 February 1813, in *Letters*, 300.

formed Austen's authorial voices from their early audacity would have been reinforced not only by Cassandra's "starched notions" but by the increase of isolation and dependence effected by the death of Austen's father and the move from Bath, where Austen almost surely wrote *Northanger Abbey* and from where she tried to publish it. Austen's touted reticence about authorship, like her reticent authoriality, seems best explained not as modesty or lack of literary ambition but as a self-protective shield for her desires for recognition and approval both from the public and from friends. Those passages in her letters (and one can only imagine what audacities Cassandra censored out of them) so often used to "prove" Austen's modesty are easily read as barely veiled glee—as, for example, in this passage marked by well-placed Capitals:

> The caution observed at Steventon with regard to the possession of the book is an agreeable surprise to me, & I heartily wish it may be the means of saving you from everything unpleasant—but you must be prepared for the neighbourhood being perhaps already informed of there being such a Work in the World & in the Chawton World![40]

Such uppercase letters show signs of the same delight in authorship that characterizes Austen's juvenilia; consider too this breathless passage in which questions of personal acknowledgment, public fame, literary success, and financial recompense are so delightfully mixed:

> Oh! I have more of such sweet flattery from Miss Sharp!—She is an excellent kind friend. I am read & admired in Ireland too.—There is a Mrs. Fletcher, the wife of a Judge, an old Lady & very good & very clever, who is all curiosity to know about me—what I am like & so forth—. I am not known to her by *name* however. This comes through Mrs. Carrick, not through Mrs. Gore—You are quite out there.—I do not despair of having my picture in the Exhibition at last—all white & red, with my Head on one Side;—or perhaps I may marry young Mr. D'arblay.—I suppose in the meantime I shall owe dear Henry a great deal of Money for Printing &c.—I hope Mrs. Fletcher will indulge herself with S & S.[41]

In today's critical climate, where indirection, irony, ambiguity, and "coherence" are privileged as they were not in Austen's time, it is

40. Ibid.
41. Letter to Cassandra of 3 November 1813, in ibid., 368.

difficult to see the journey from *Northanger Abbey* to the later novels as less than triumphant. Perhaps this is why, in curious double-talk, Park Honan maintains that "what is weak in *Northanger Abbey* is its freshest and most innovative feature—its narrative voice," which he calls "a lithe and slippery eel of great energy which is less than fully controlled," and why Honan is perplexed that, although Austen "had a good deal of time for revising between 1799 and 1803," she never "mended" its "fault[s]."[42] Since by modern norms of textual unity Austen's desire for "shade" and "contrast" would have produced only "flaws," one may have to acknowledge that Austen's values are not necessarily the values of her modern admirers. While twentieth-century readers might be horrified to see the novels "marred" by "digressions" and "intrusions," the realist pretense to the narrator's absence was not Austen's primary value or the primary value of her period, and Austen seems at least momentarily to have wanted a broader range of authorial voice. Austen did, of course, find what is now probably a secure place in literary history, but perhaps not entirely in the way *Northanger Abbey* suggests she originally desired; it is no accident that her reputation ebbed (and Scott's grew) in the Victorian age when, as my next chapter will demonstrate, authorial voice was expected to reach farther than Austen had taken it. As a lover (no lesser word will do) of Austen's writings and a profound admirer of her brilliant narrative techniques, I can hardly wish the published novels to have been different from what they became. At the same time, I can see the cost of *Northanger Abbey*'s failure and the climate that spawned it—the loss of that bold young narrator who openly claimed a place in literature in a voice as daring as Fielding's but written insistently in the "mother tongue." To the extent that Austen came to stand for "woman writer," or even woman writer of her period—the model against whom other women were often pronounced didactic or dull—the practices that have guaranteed her canonicity have also helped to construct female narrative authority *as* indirection and ambiguity. Thus "Austen" stands as an equivocal identity, authorizing female voice as a voice that "tells it slant."

42. Honan, *Jane Austen*, 141, 143.

5

Woman of Maxims: George Eliot and the Realist Imperative

Much quotation of any sort, even in English, is bad.
> —Sir Hugo, in GEORGE ELIOT's *Daniel Deronda*

A quotation often makes a fine summit to a climax, especially when it comes from some elder author... But I hate a style speckled with quotations.
> —GEORGE ELIOT, Letter to Alexander Main

Good phrases are surely, and ever were, very commendable.—Justice Shallow
> —GEORGE ELIOT, *Middlemarch*

Fielding lived when the days were longer (for time, like money, is measured by our needs)... We belated historians must not linger after his example; ... I at least have so much to do in unraveling certain human lots and seeing how they were woven and interwoven that all the light I can command must be concentrated on this particular web, and not dispersed over that tempting range of relevancies called the universe.
> —GEORGE ELIOT, *Middlemarch*

All people of broad, strong sense have an instinctive repugnance to the men of maxims because such people easily discern that the mysterious complexity of our life is not to be embraced by maxims and that to lace ourselves up in formulas of that sort is to repress all the divine promptings and inspirations that spring from growing insight and sympathy.
> —GEORGE ELIOT, *Mill on the Floss*

If we judge from the content of these passages, it would seem that George Eliot considered quotation and generalization at worst odious and irresponsible, at best the product of an age when "unraveling human lots" was easier. Mary Jacobus has argued that not only Maggie Tulliver but her creator professed distrust for maxims and the men who made them. In a similar spirit, Susan Gubar and Sandra Gilbert describe *Middlemarch*'s narrator as "highly provisional and tentative." Carol Gilligan even makes the narrator of *The Mill on the Floss* her paradigm of "feminine" moral consciousness, and the "master-key that will fit all cases" her trope for a disfavored "male" hierarchy of right.[1] And where, indeed, *could* one find a more Gilliganesque position than *The Mill on the Floss*'s assertion that "moral judgments must remain false and hollow unless they are checked and enlightened by a perpetual reference to the special circumstances that mark the individual lot"?[2] Such criticism has constructed a George Eliot who sets herself against the very concept of authoritative voice.

Ironically, however, Eliot's professed distrust of quotation and maxim stands in Archimedean tension with her formal practices: if Eliot is suggesting that the authority of such forms is but a fiction, she does so through fiction's arguably most authoritative, "nonfictional" structures— precisely maxims and quotations, the conventional forms for authorial wisdom, detachable from the story proper and able to engage "that tempting range of relevancies called the universe." Eliot's insistence that imaginative discourse could perform an "office for the mind" that no philosophical pronouncement could achieve, her strenuous objections to "the artistic mind which looks for its subjects into literature instead of life," belie the degree to which her own narrators ground their authority in literature and philosophy and express it in nonrepresentational forms.[3] When Alexander Main sought permission to compile a collection of these copious passages, Eliot protested that her works could not be reduced

---

1. See, respectively, Mary Jacobus, "The Question of Language: Men of Maxims and *The Mill on the Floss*," in *Writing and Sexual Difference*, ed. Elizabeth Abel (Chicago: University of Chicago Press, 1982), 44; Sandra Gilbert and Susan Gubar, *The Madwoman in the Attic: The Woman Writer and the Nineteenth-Century Literary Imagination* (New Haven: Yale University Press, 1979), 523; and Carol Gilligan, *In a Different Voice: Psychological Theory and Women's Development* (Cambridge: Harvard University Press, 1982), 69, 130–31, 143–44, 148–49.

2. George Eliot, *The Mill on the Floss* (New York: New American Library, 1965), book 7, chap. 2, 521. All further references will appear in the text.

3. Letter to Mary Sibree (1843), cited in Jennifer Uglow, *George Eliot* (London: Virago, 1987), 39.

to an "assemblage of extracts": "I have always exercised a severe watch against anything that could be called preaching," and "never allowed myself, in dissertation or in dialogue [anything] which is not part of the *structure* of my books." "Unless I am condemned by my own principles," she concluded, "my books are not properly separable into 'direct' or 'indirect' teaching."[4] Yet she allowed Main to create *The Wise, Witty, and Tender Sayings of George Eliot* (1871) and apparently authorized a *Wit and Wisdom of George Eliot* that was published in 1873 (and updated in 1876) consisting precisely of extracted, nonnarrative elements of text. The contradiction is clear even in the passages with which I opened, since four of them are extractable "direct teaching" from the very novels that supposedly reject such practices.

If Eliot is saying that neither men nor maxims can be trusted, then, she says so in a syntax of authority that appropriates the very forms she is questioning, just as she authorizes and profits from the "assemblages of extracts" that confirm "George Eliot" as major literary capital. Although Eliot may not be "condemned by [her] own principles," her narrators appropriate the structures and strategies of the "men of maxims" as, I believe, a way out of separate but intersecting dilemmas of gender and narrative voice. I will argue that in Eliot's novels the impulse to "maximize," while complicated by a semantics of ambiguity, constitutes both a vexing dilemma and a major factor in narrative design. Postmodern critics who want to emphasize Eliot's deconstruction of authoritative discourse, and feminist critics who value women writers precisely for their rejection of authority as "masculine," seem to me to be overlooking the degree to which the rhetoric of Eliot's fiction arrogates authority in a project designed precisely to construct a narrative hegemony. Such a project is consistent with the historical situation in which Eliot wrote, and in which the place of the novel in public culture was dependent on specific forms of authorial voice.

Narrative authority gets worked out in Eliot's novels in two distinctly different formations that correspond to early and late periods of her career. I will speculate that these shifts in narrative practice, which include changes in the narrators' status, in their modes of contact with narratees, and especially in their strategies for repre-

---

4. George Eliot, 12 November 1873, in *The Letters of George Eliot*, ed. Gordon S. Haight (New Haven: Yale University Press, 1954), vol. 5, 458–59.

senting narrative stance, stem from the convergence around 1860
of three factors: an instability in the project of realist fiction that
Adam Bede had already begun to recognize; the professionalization
of the novel in a way that meant the (re)masculinization of its
authority; and the public revelation that "George Eliot" was not a
"University man" as "all the Oxford and Cambridge gents" may
have imagined, but "only a poor woman" living in sin.[5] These are
the primary factors, I believe, that turn Eliot from "intrusive" narrators who temper the authority they appropriate, to remote narrators who appropriate the authority they seem to be tempering.
While the crisis of *Northanger Abbey* produced in Austen's work a
narrative reticence, Eliot's narrative crisis leads to an extraordinary
appropriation of a cultural intertext.

Speculating about the novels Jane Austen would have written had
she lived beyond 1817, Virginia Woolf suggests that Austen was beginning to discover a "larger" world that explored "not only what
[people] are, but what life is."[6] Woolf's hindsight points less, I think,
to potential changes in Austen than to actual changes in the tradition
that followed her. The kind of novel emerging in Europe during the
1830s and 1840s, epitomized in the ambition of Balzac's *Comédie humaine*, embraces a new representational imperative: not simply to delineate "human nature" in its "varieties," as Austen described the
novel's project, but to produce, in Pierre Macherey's words, a *"book
which shall be like a world."* Such an imperative requires the text to
construct a "dispersion" or "diversity" through a proliferation of detail
and a "broken plot" with "several abruptly discontinuous fore-
grounds," all signified in the trope—adopted by Eliot, Stendhal, and
other nineteenth-century realists—of the novel as a mirror reflecting
whatever passes by.[7]

While such a program would seem to constitute the narrator as
mere transcriber, leaving no place for the pedagogic imperative by
which the previous century had justified literature, in realist narrative

5. Letter from George Henry Lewes to Barbara Bodichon of 5 May 1859, in ibid., vol. 3,
65; Letter from George Eliot to Georgianna Burne-Jones, cited in Deirdre David, *Intellectual
Women and Victorian Patriarchy* (Ithaca: Cornell University Press, 1987), 168.

6. Virginia Woolf, "Jane Austen," in *The Common Reader* (New York: Harcourt Brace,
1925), 148–49.

7. Pierre Macherey, *A Theory of Literary Production*, trans. Geoffrey Wall (London: Routledge, 1978), 268, 271. The notion that the novel produces a "world" has grounded novel
theory at least since Lukács. On the novel as "mirror," see the epigraph to chap. 13 of
Stendhal's *The Red and the Black*, and chap. 17 of *Adam Bede*.

the moral project actually takes on new urgency. Since the novel is to produce a diversity, its coherence must come from the narrator, who mediates this complexity not only aesthetically but ideologically. These demands, however, generate another paradox: as Macherey explains, the novel is expected to show "things as they are," but also to show things as they should and should not be. As Eliot formulates them in chapter 17 of *Adam Bede*, such imperatives compel the narrator on the one hand to "tell you, as precisely as I can, what that reflection is, as if I were in the witness-box narrating my experience on oath," and on the other to partake "in the secret of deep human sympathy" that transforms the "common" and "coarse" to the cherished.[8] Such a contradiction between representation and evaluation creates an acute instability in narrative form: the illusion of what is (mimesis) interferes with the declaration (diegesis) of what ought to be. In this economy an explicit narrative stance provides the readiest mechanism for shaping judgment but also arrests representation and ruptures the mimetic illusion on which the realist novel depends. The representation of "things as they are" implies the narrator's ostensible absence, while the expression of judgment implies the opposite.[9]

One project of the realist novel, therefore, is to accommodate the contradictions between knowing and judging, or representation and ideology, through an unprecedented authorization of the heterodiegetic voice, which must stand against the realist novel's necessary production of "speaking persons" whose discourses threaten to destabilize any ideological hegemony.[10] Hence the abandonment of eighteenth-century homodiegetic and multivocal narrative forms in favor of the pervasive structure of classic realism: the single, extradiegetic and public voice, sole mediator of the fictional world, who occupies a "higher" discursive plane than the characters, entering into a compact with public narratees who, if they read rightly, are privileged to share the narrator's enlightened place.

It is only a slight exaggeration to suggest that upon this narrator rested the demands and powers of divinity itself, trusted at once to know all and to judge aright, the self-authorizing authority "who does

8. George Eliot, *Adam Bede* (Harmondsworth, England: Penguin, 1980), 221, 224. Further references will appear in the text.

9. See Gérard Genette, *Narrative Discourse: An Essay in Method*, trans. Jane Lewin (Ithaca: Cornell University Press, 1980), 166.

10. Mikhail Bakhtin, *The Dialogic Imagination*, trans. Caryl. Emerson and Michael Holquist (Austin: University of Texas Press, 1981), 332.

not require verification" and who "verifies all other statements"[11] so
that "the source and evidence of the truth of the [narrator's] interpretation" is not, as it was a century earlier, (the illusion of) empirical
evidence, but (tautologically) the narrative voice itself.[12] Whether one
imagines such a narrator as Balzac's statesmanlike "tutor of men," as
Robert Scholes's "benevolently despotic" entrepreneur ruling the textual world "as the laissez-faire capitalists ruled their factories," as J.
Hillis Miller's "all-embracing consciousness which surrounds the
minds of the characters," as Lennard Davis's imperious master who
demands the reader's submission, or as what we might today understand as the very spirit of imperialist Europe fulfilling its mission to
colonize subjects with an unshakeable confidence in its moral and
intellectual superiority, narrative voice in the mid-nineteenth-century
realist novel operates on the startling myth that, as Davis bluntly puts
it, a person "who spends a good deal of his or her life making up
stories" is somehow both an "archivist of knowledge" and a philosophical and moral arbiter of "real life."[13] Realist "omniscience," then,
means far more than a narrator's privileged knowledge of fictional
facts.

By the mid-1850s, when Eliot began publishing novels, these conflicting textual imperatives were connected to equally conflicting institutional ones as fiction became increasingly prestigious and lucrative.
Eliot, with her legendary longing at once for literary, popular, and
financial success,[14] tries to set up a positive relationship between com-
mercialism and artistry when she complains that "silly novels" are
written not by the genteel poor but "in elegant boudoirs, with violet-
colored ink and a ruby pen" by women irresponsibly "indifferent to
publishers' accounts, and inexperienced in every form of poverty

11. Stanislaw Eile, "The Novel as an Expression of the Writer's Vision of the World," *New
Literary History* 9 (Autumn 1977): 120.
12. Catherine Belsey, *Critical Practice* (London: Methuen, 1980), 70–72.
13. See, respectively, Balzac, preface to *La Comédie humaine*; Robert Scholes, "The Liberal
Imagination," *New Literary History* 4 (1973): 526; J. Hillis Miller, *The Form of Victorian Fiction*
(Notre Dame: University of Notre Dame Press, 1968), 83; and Lennard Davis, *Resisting Novels:
Ideology and Fiction* (London: Methuen, 1987), 142–43. See also Carl D. Malmgren, "Reading
Authorial Narration: The Example of *The Mill on the Floss*," in *Poetics Today* 7 (1986): 478–
79.
14. On Eliot's intellectual aspirations see especially David, *Intellectual Women*. On Eliot's
desires for commercial success see especially Ruby Redinger, *George Eliot: The Emergent Self*
(New York: Knopf, 1975); and Catherine Gallagher, "George Eliot and *Daniel Deronda*: The
Prostitute and the Jewish Question," in *Sex, Politics, and Science in the Nineteenth-Century Novel*,
ed. Ruth Yeazell (Baltimore: Johns Hopkins University Press, 1986), 39–62.

except poverty of brains."[15] With the superiority of the middle-class "organic intellectual,"[16] Eliot links bad literature with the extremes of both "the old Grub Street coercion of hunger and thirst" and the "gratuitous productions of ladies and gentlemen whose circumstances might be called altogether easy."[17] But the figure of the author as godly father was tarnished by the writer's participation in what was viewed as a prostituting economy. Commercial success also required care in constructing the authorial narrator's relationship to the public narratee, lest the contact between (textual) "author" and (textual) "reader" deter a paying audience.

I want to speculate that one narrative mechanism for "solving" simultaneously both of the contradictions I have been describing—a way, that is, to obscure both the author's economic dependence on her reading public and the formal contradiction between representation and judgment—was to purge from a novel's narrative surface all explicit markers of narrative status, contact, and stance. I refer here, as the "solution" to the problems of both realism and professionalism, to the Flaubertian model of "effacing" overt authoriality and its potential for direct contact between narrator and narratee; this gesture is represented clearly within *Madame Bovary* (1857) when the "we" who is the text's initial narrator dissolves into an unidentified impersonal voice. Eliminating the overt narrator "resolves" realism's conflicts by conflating representation and ideology and subsuming the commercial enterprise beneath the artistic one, modeling a specular technology (the forerunner of cinematic realism) that manipulates the "mirror" without revealing the hand that holds it. Eliot's narrators never go this far, but neither do the later novels follow *Adam Bede* in exposing the "mirror" as "doubtless defective" or in making direct, often ironic jibes at the foibles of various narratees. Opposition to such "authorial intrusion" becomes "firm" in England as early as 1865,[18] and as I will suggest in Chapter 6, by the next century overt authoriality will cede to selectively focalized, "figural" narration in

15. George Eliot, "Silly Novels by Lady Novelists," in *Selected Essays, Poems and Other Writings*, ed. A. S. Byatt and Nicholas Warren (London: Penguin, 1990), 142.

16. The term is Antonio Gramsci's. See *Selections from the Prison Notebooks* (London: Lawrence and Wishart, 1971), 18.

17. George Eliot, "Diseases of Small Authorship" in *Impressions of Theophrastus Such*, vol. 20 of *The Writings of George Eliot* (Boston: Houghton Mifflin, 1908), 205.

18. Kenneth Graham, *English Criticism of the Novel 1865–1900* (Oxford: Clarendon Press, 1965), 123.

which the narrator's text is formally inseparable from the texts of characters.

What I have been describing as a multifaceted rise in the novel's authority in the nineteenth century undermined the authority of women novelists in ways easily obscured by the numbers of women in the literary marketplace. Athough women helped to make the novel a powerful social vehicle in the period from 1847 to 1860 that Nancy Armstrong identifies with the "domestic" authority of such writers as Elizabeth Gaskell, Charlotte Brontë, and Harriet Beecher Stowe, "feminine authority" was becoming a fiction. Gaye Tuchman and Nina Fortin convincingly demonstrate that the professionalization of the novel especially after 1860 tended to squeeze women out of the production of "serious" fiction despite (or because of) their role in making the novel a professional genre.[19] As Mary Poovey comments, "If the feminization of authorship derived its authority from an idealized representation of women and the domestic sphere, then for a woman to depart from that idealization by engaging in the commercial business of writing was to collapse the boundary between the spheres" as well as "the ideal from which her authority was derived."[20]

It seems likely that realism's conventions of powerful, public narrative voices authorized to mediate important contemporary questions at a time of particularly rigid separations between "male" and "female" spheres, supported a masculine authorial identity and legitimated the squeezing out of women from the ranks of "serious" novelists. The contradiction between female status and narrative authority is signaled by the widespread use after 1860 of the male pseudonym by women novelists in nineteenth-century England and France, at just the moment when the novel was becoming a serious literary form; such a practice acknowledges that narrative status is authorized diegetically according to the social identity of the (presumed) author rather than, as in early periods, mimetically according to the truth

19. Gaye Tuchman with Nina Fortin, *Edging Women Out: Victorian Novelists, Publishers, and Social Change* (New Haven: Yale University Press, 1989), 215. See also "Edging Women Out: Some Suggestions about the Structure of Opportunities and the Victorian Novel," *Signs* 6 (1980): 308–25. Tuchman and Fortin show that from 1866 to 1887 the "growing prestige of the novel in England" reduced "the opportunities for women to have their work seriously considered and to achieve fame." Terry Lovell makes a similar argument in *Consuming Fiction* (London: Verso, 1987), 43.

20. Mary Poovey, *Uneven Developments: The Ideological Work of Gender in Mid-Victorian England* (Chicago: University of Chicago Press, 1988), 125.

claims made for the narrative itself. Richard Simpson, in an essay of 1863 that attacks Eliot (along with Behn, Staël, Sand, Charlotte Brontë, and others who "misuse their sex"), articulates the fear of women's power as a sexual fear and urges women to restrict themselves to "indirect" strategies: "Women work more by influence than by force, by example than reasoning, by silence than speech: the authoress [Eliot] grasps at direct power through reasoning and speech. Having thus taken up the male position, the male ideal becomes hers,—the ideal of power,—which, interpreted by her feminine heart and intellect, means the supremacy of passion in the affairs of the world."[21] Such attitudes were likely to constrain the forms through which women might effectively constitute authorial narrative. For example, reviews of *Uncle Tom's Cabin*, unquestionably the most socially influential novel of the century, criticize the authorial voice for attempting "imperiously and violently to dictate" to readers or for allowing "anti-slavery sentiment" to "obtrude by the author in her own person,"[22] but George Sand suggests the sexual double standard at work in these judgments: "For a long time we have striven in France against the prolix explanations of Walter Scott. We have cried out against those of Balzac, but on consideration have perceived that... every stroke of the pencil was needed for the general effect. Let us learn then to appreciate all kinds of treatment, when the effect is good, and when they bear the seal of a master hand.... In matters of art there is but one rule, to paint and to move. And where shall we find creations more complete, types more vivid, situations more touching, more original, than in 'Uncle Tom'?"[23] The dilemma I associated in my first chapter with the use of "women's language" is now enacted on the terrain of authorial voice: restrained "lady novelists" are not taken seriously (this is precisely the period when Austen's reputation drops), but powerful female voices are condemned. Eliot's "Silly Novels by Lady Novelists," with its complaint that women without talent receive "journalistic approbation" at "the boiling-pitch," while for women of genius "critical enthusiasm drops to the freezing

21. Richard Simpson, "George Eliot's Novels," in *George Eliot: The Critical Heritage*, ed. David Carroll (New York: Barnes and Noble, 1971), 241.
22. Anonymous reviews in *London Times*, 3 September 1852, and *Putnam's Monthly*, January 1853.
23. George Sand, review in *La Presse*, 17 December 1852, cited in *Critical Essays on Harriet Beecher Stowe*, ed. Elizabeth Ammons (Boston: G. K. Hall, 1980), 4. Sand does not recognize any racism in Stowe's "vivid" representations.

point,"[24] both criticizes and perpetuates this growing male hegemony and, functioning as it does as a prelude to her first published fictions, seems to be clearing the space for her own authority.

As Simpson's comment implies and "Silly Novels by Lady Novelists" anticipates, Eliot's literary imperatives crystallized the contradictions both between gender and authority in Victorian England and between representation and judgment in realist narrative. A scholar and essayist before she was a novelist, Eliot brought to her fiction an intellectual agenda that, Tuchman and Fortin would suggest, could at that time only have hindered a woman novelist's career. No realist novel had yet turned the genre to imperatives as pedagogic and intellectual as Eliot's, nor was Victorian culture amenable to a woman's bold appropriation of the philosopher-historian's role, which centuries of Western tradition had deemed the right of privileged-class white men. Together, these transgressions produced criticisms of Eliot's work such as the *Westminster Review*'s complaint that her novels are "elaborately tedious" because they fail to subordinate "clevernesses, or eruditions, or sciences" to the all-important "tale"; Eliot is derided as one of those "inferior writers" who have "to prove that they are excellent story-tellers, or that they know all science, or are 'well up' in art" and who have failed "to subordinate [their] personal interests to the larger interests of [their] art."[25]

Eliot's novelistic career also spans the transitional period I have been describing in which the novel is moving from the uneasy early-realist coexistence of representation and overt ideology to the late-realist practice of representation "alone." The disclosure, as she was finishing *Mill on the Floss*, that Eliot was a woman and an unlawful wife converges with the novel's increasing stature and an incipient cultural preference for Flaubertian narrative strategies, to explain the shifts in narrative practice between Eliot's early and late works—shifts marked by the abandonment of an uninvolved eyewitness male narrator, of explicit generalizations, and of direct contact between narrator and narratee in favor of a surprisingly little-noted development of new "extrafictional" structures that constitutes "Eliot" as an ultimate literary authority even as her narrators withdraw from the obviously "intrusive" practices of the early works. In the guise of accommodating

24. Eliot, "Silly Novels by Lady Novelists," 161.
25. *Westminster Review* (July 1878), cited in *George Eliot and Her Readers: A Selection of Contemporary Reviews*, ed. John Holmstrum and Laurence Lerner (New York: Barnes and Noble, 1966), 176–77.

a more restricted narrative authority, in other words, Eliot's later narrators inaugurate even more appropriative practices.

As early as "Mr. Gilfil's Love Story," Eliot's narrators are producing long passages of explicit comment linked to the narrative through various formal strategies: beginning with generalization and then moving to the perspective of a character (chap. 5); narrating an event, pausing to comment on its general significance, and returning to the event (chap. 6); embedding a generalization in the middle of a paragraph (chap. 16).[26] As a compensatory gesture, however, these early texts adopt several strategies that appear to render this authority contingent, personal—and male. I refer to three particular practices: direct contact with the narratee; quasi-dramatized narrators, and the use of qualifying or perspectivizing language for expressing narrative stance. Eliot invented none of these strategies, and each was practiced by at least one contemporary woman novelist whom Eliot admired: Sand, Gaskell, Brontë, Stowe.

Robyn Warhol has already written of the "engaging" narrator who directly addresses a public readership, discusses the characters as if they are historical individuals, and guides the narratee's sympathies.[27] This "earnest" address, practiced by women such as Gaskell and Stowe, with whom Eliot corresponded, was, used, says Warhol, "to bridge the gap between strictly literary utterances and serious statements"[28] by exhorting the narratee to a moral or political stance. Warhol suggests that the "engaging narrator" has a historical specificity, reflecting perhaps "certain nineteenth-century women's impulses to speak—if not from a pulpit then from a text—directly, personally, and influentially in the only public forum open to them."[29] These narrators attempt, in other words, to balance "masculine" assertiveness with "feminine" concern for audience.

---

26. See George Eliot, *Scenes of Clerical Life* (Harmondsworth, England: Penguin, 1973). Citations will appear in the text.

27. Robyn R. Warhol, "Toward a Theory of the Engaging Narrator: Earnest Interventions in Gaskell, Stowe, and Eliot," in *PMLA* 101 (October 1986): 811–18.

28. Warhol, *Gendered Interventions: Narrative Discourse in the Victorian Novel* (New Brunswick: Rutgers University Press, 1989), 169. Warhol believes "engaging address to the reader is a sign of these women's conceptions of the purpose of art; as such, it signifies a gendered gesture" (169–70). I would say that any number of male writers, including Dickens and Balzac, shared this referential purpose although they engage much less frequently in direct address. Frederick Douglass's *Narrative*, for example, does not directly address its narratee while Harriet Jacobs's *Incidents in the Life of a Slave Girl* does, yet both works share an urgent referential earnestness. If "engaging" narration is gendered, it is gendered as a question of authority rather than one of pedagogical intent.

29. Warhol, "Engaging Narrator," 817.

The narrative "engagements" in Eliot's first two novels, which are more elaborate and more frequent than in Gaskell's or even Stowe's, support the novels' generalizing practices by establishing a similar sense of connection with the narratee. Because neither her life nor her philosophy was conventionally Christian, Eliot had even more reason than the clergymen's wives Gaskell and Stowe to seek narrative "engagement": even her publisher worried that she took "the harsher Thackerayan view of human nature," and urged her "to *soften* your picture as much as you can."[30] But Eliot does not construct the domesticated female narrators chosen by Gaskell and Stowe; rather, the model for her early narrators came quite probably from George Sand. Openly committed, like Eliot, to the practice of serious literature and to the intellectual and moral questions of her day, and living and writing outside the bounds of propriety, Sand was like Eliot unable to call upon the "feminine" authority, however limited, that Gaskell and Stowe could exploit. Moreover, Aurore Dupin Dudevant and Marian Evans Lewes created their professional identities upon fictions of biography, exploiting the male pseudonym and creating masculine narrative voices to support this fictive identity. While Sand's novels (over seventy in number) adopt a range of narrative practices, one of her most typical narrators is a male figure whose presence is manifestly gratuitous—a narrator who could easily have been an ordinary heterodiegetic voice of indeterminate sex but who turns up, sometimes at the very end of the novel (in *Indiana*), or sometimes at the beginning (in *Mauprat*), as an explicitly male eyewitness or author-surrogate— the kind of narrator created as female in the novels of Aphra Behn.

Eliot adapts for her earliest fictions this quasi-dramatized narrator modeled by Sand. Because such a narrator is represented as a kind of character—an uninvolved eyewitness recalling his past—there is a mimetic legitimation for his presence in the text and thus a mimetic basis for his status as knower and judge; such a narrator's ideological comments, rather than detracting from the mimesis, might well enhance the illusion of a true history. This use of the male narrator is thus not only an authorizing strategy but a tempering one: Sand and Eliot bring their narrators down to human scale, novel becomes story, the personal context of speaking and listening is implicitly engaged, and narrator and reader are established as a community. At the same

30. Letter from John Blackwood to George Eliot of 8 June 1857, in *George Eliot: The Critical Heritage*, 57.

time, the sex of this mediating narrator allows the text to partake of the professional authority that, in mid-nineteenth-century France even more than in England, was resoundingly masculine.

In the first three novels, Eliot's narrators also contextualize the grounds of their authority by generalizing in a language of perspectival contingency. Many of the "maxims" in these novels carry qualifying tags: "Yet surely, surely" (*Clerical Life*, 322); "if I have read religious history aright" (*Adam Bede*, 81); "I believe" (*Adam Bede*, 198); "I cannot say" (*Adam Bede*, 241); "I have often wondered" (*Mill on the Floss*, 19); "I have understood from persons versed in history" (*Mill on the Floss*, 267); "In natural science, I have understood" (*Mill on the Floss*, 287); "I suppose this is the reason" (*Mill on the Floss*, 306). Through such practices the narrator's totalizing potential is tempered by strategies that Robin Lakoff has associated with "women's language" or "language of the powerless," but which Julia Penelope Stanley identifies more positively as the recognition of contingency and perspectivity.[31] By representing understanding as conditional, such tags qualify not only the generalizations but the authority of the voice that utters them.

All of these early strategies, whether deliberate or not, temper a woman's usurpation of public authority; the strategies of the later novels, in contrast, insist on that same authority without acknowledging or engaging its terms even at the risk of offending audiences to whose opinions Eliot was keenly and often debilitatingly sensitive. For readers of *Clerical Life* and *Adam Bede* were engaging a masculine voice they did not take to be fictional; Eliot's gender had not yet been revealed even to her publisher, and her friends may well have been right to believe that *Adam Bede* "could not have succeeded if it had been known as hers; *every newspaper critic would have written against it.*"[32] Eliot was in fact extremely successful in creating her fiction of authorship; letters to her and to Lewes suggest that many believed the author to be a clergyman—which distanced the narrative voice even further from the freethinker and "adulteress" Marian Evans, who had translated Ludwig Feuerbach and David Friedrich Strauss and written "atheism" in the pages of the *Westminster Review*. The choice of pseudonym had been calculated to serve just this end; as

---

31. Julia Stanley, "The Stylistics of Belief," in *Teaching about Doublespeak*, ed. D. J. Dietrich (Urbana: National Council of Teachers of English, 1976).

32. Letter from Barbara Bodichon to George Eliot of 28 June 1859, in *The Letters of George Eliot*, vol. 3, 103.

Lewes wrote to Barbara Bodichon, "the object of anonymity was to get the book judged on its own merits, and not prejudged as the work of a woman, or of a particular woman. It is quite clear that people would have sniffed at it if they had known the writer to be a woman but they can't now unsay their admiration."[33]

As the remarkable rereviewing of *Adam Bede* by Athenaeum proved,[34] people could in fact "unsay their admiration." But the overtly authorial narrators of the early novels had provoked resistance even before Eliot's identity was revealed. A reviewer of *Clerical Life*, for instance, objected to the number of sentences that "finished in an epigram or aphorism" and commented that "casual phrases like these betray a mind of philosophic culture, but they mar the simplicity of the style."[35] A reviewer of *Adam Bede* found similar fault with the way in which "the author intrudes himself in the book. . . . He makes a great deal too much of a very slight novelty of opinion at which he himself has arrived, and he puts the merit of holding this opinion on much too grand a footing."[36] This may be one reason why, as Warhol notes, Eliot (like Stowe and Gaskell) "eschewed engaging narrative in later works."[37] But in Eliot's case there was almost surely at work the public disclosure that put her in a more vulnerable relationship with the reading public on whom her fame and fortune relied—especially after *The Mill on the Floss*, which generated more negative criticism than the earlier novels for representing a rebellious and passionate heroine who, it was said, carried the reader's sympathies into moral "chaos." This may explain Eliot's turn after *Mill on the Floss* to the pastoral *Silas Marner*, by far the thinnest novel in generalizing comments and one of her most popular works among Victorians, and then to the distanced setting of fifteenth-century Italy for *Romola*, which forced her to abandon her dramatized reminiscing narrator and allowed her to write her most intellectual (and partly for that reason her least popular) book.[38]

33. George Lewes, in ibid., 106 (30 June 1859).
34. See Elaine Showalter, *A Literature of Their Own: British Women Novelists from Brontë to Lessing* (Princeton: Princeton University Press, 1978), 95.
35. Unsigned review in *Saturday Review* (29 May 1858), in *George Eliot: The Critical Heritage*, 69–70.
36. Ibid., 76.
37. Warhol, "Engaging Narrator," 816.
38. One contemporary review, for example, lamented the "tax on our patience" generated by the novel's "long accounts," "translations of sermons," and "extracts from chronicles" (*Saturday Review*, 25 July 1863), in *George Eliot and Her Readers*, 65.

When Eliot returns to nineteenth-century English settings in *Felix Holt, Middlemarch,* and *Daniel Deronda,* she has abandoned the dramatized narrators and most of the narrative engagement of the early novels in favor of more distanced strategies for expressing narrative stance. Perhaps because the disclosure of Eliot's identity ruptured the rapport between narrator and narratee that had been generated through the fiction of maleness, in the later novels Eliot's narrators assert authority without engaging the reader in its construction or acknowledging dependence on an audience. That this new posture came to be lauded as a move toward propriety—a propriety perhaps sexual as well as textual—is suggested in the language, strikingly like that of the Victorian reviewers, with which Walter Allen later describes the change:

> After *The Mill on the Floss* [Eliot's] digressions were much more *curbed,* her asides much less *flagrant* and her comment much more closely woven into the texture of her narrative. After *Adam Bede* there is nothing quite so *obtrusive* as [chap. 17], and when one turns from *The Mill on the Floss* to *Felix Holt,* written several years later, one is conscious immediately of a sharp increase in dramatisation; the action is allowed much more to speak for itself. W. J. Harvey . . . gives the ratio of omniscient intrusions in terms of pages as, in *Adam Bede* 1:10, in *Mill on the Floss* 1:14, in *Middlemarch,* 1:33. Once she has learned how to *control* them they are, of course, much more *acceptable.*[39]

But even the reduction Allen claims for *Middlemarch* is a difference less in the degree of authoriality than in the forms it takes, and Eliot was certainly criticized for didacticism in her last two novels.[40] What

---

39. Walter Allen, *George Eliot* (London: Weidenfeld and Nicolson, 1965), 89 (my italics). Neither Allen nor Harvey explains what counts for an "omniscient intrusion."

40. For example, the *Spectator* of 1 June 1872 grudgingly admitted that "we all grumble . . . that there is too much parade of scientific and especially physiological knowledge in it, that there are turns of phrases which are even pedantic, and that occasionally the bitterness of the commentary on life is almost cynical; but we all read it, and all feel that there is nothing to compare with it appearing at the present moment in the way of English literature." The reviewer attributes most of the "unhappiness" in *Middlemarch* to "the authoress's own comments on the universe and its structure" ("The Melancholy of *Middlemarch,*" in *George Eliot: The Critical Heritage,* 297). *Daniel Deronda* received much more negative press, including Saintsbury's regret that "the characters are incessantly pushed back in order that the author may talk about them and about everything in heaven and earth while the action stands still." In the *Academy* (9 September 1876); reprinted in *George Eliot: The Critical Heritage,* 374. One should not discount the discomfort readers may have experienced over the Jewish—and pro-Jewish—content of *Daniel Deronda;* one review complains that the reader never or rarely "feels at home" in the novel: "the author is ever driving at something foreign to his habits

does disappear is direct engagement, and despite exceptional passages like the beginning of chapter 15 of *Middlemarch,* which I cite in my epigraph to this chapter, the authorial generalizations in the last two novels are usually brief embeddings within seemingly narrative paragraphs.

Yet these narrators have also found new ways to consolidate their authority. Maxims that in earlier novels would surely have been qualified in some way are simply presented as if they were true; now narrative comments are rarely contextualized. Julia Penelope Stanley describes this phenomenon in which the perceiving and evaluating "I" is removed from the discourse and replaced by passive adjectives, the universal "we," or an enunciation whose source is suppressed. Stanley comments: "The deletion of the experiencer imparts to the statement an impersonal tone of authority, giving a personal observation the weight of 'universal consensus.' By deleting the experiencer, the author conveys the impression that the judgment or perception is one that everyone agrees with, thus claiming universal consensus for individual opinions."[41] The erasure of the enunciator's perspectivity, and the consequent absence of any acknowledgment that an utterance is contingent or contextual, is a phenomenon that Stanley associates with "masculine" language and that I would link to the language of any ideologically dominant group. In *Middlemarch* and *Daniel Deronda,* generalizations are either entirely uncontextualized or connected with a totalizing "we," as in "We do not expect people to be deeply moved by what is not unusual,"[42] a subtle structure that appears to involve the narratee in the enunciation but actually speaks on the narratee's behalf.[43] This is not the explicitly male narrator of the early work; it is the unmarked Male of Authority itself, all the more powerful for being invisible and impersonal rather than particularized and sexualized.[44] Eliot's narrators may be more remote in these later novels, then,

of thought." "Home" is Christian England, and a woman's job is to make "home." Unsigned review in *Saturday Review* (16 September 1876); cited in *George Eliot: The Critical Heritage,* 377.

41. Stanley, "The Stylistics of Belief," 182.

42. George Eliot, *Middlemarch* (New York: New American Library, 1964), chap. 20, 191. Further references will appear in the text.

43. Both Barbara Hardy and J. Hillis Miller see the narrator of these later novels as a collective or communal voice because of the "inclusive use of 'we.' " In Barbara Hardy, *The Novels of George Eliot: A Study in Form* (London: Athlone: 1963), 163; and J. Hillis Miller, *The Form of Victorian Fiction.* But if one examines these passages, the "we" is not the subject of enunciation but only the subject of the the *énoncé.* In other words, the implicit, unnamed subject remains "I," and this "I" is telling "us" what "we" think and feel.

44. See Davis, *Resisting Novels,* 138.

but they are not ceding voice; they have become "imperious, if sympathetic" presences.[45]

Indeed, Eliot devises for the late novels beginning with *Felix Holt* whole new maximizing structures that separate authorial comment from the body of the text—the "extrafictional" structures of introductions, epigraphs, and epilogues. These structures formally distinguish mimesis from maxim, so that authoriality cannot be said to "intrude" upon the representation of "real life." *Romola*, for example, opens with a long "Proem," the term itself suggesting the erudition that the novel will carry and distinguishing the introduction from ordinary (women's?) prefaces. *Felix Holt* begins with an "Introduction," and *Middlemarch* with a "Prelude"; three of the last four novels end with a "Finale" or epilogue. Once again, a contrast is valuable: although she wrote novels that engaged political and social themes as important as Eliot's, "Mrs. Gaskell" declared herself much too modest to address her audience publicly in no-longer-requisite prefaces.[46]

The most pervasive and, I believe, ultimately the most audacious of Eliot's narrative strategies is one that seems to have been the least remarked upon, and that may by why it served Eliot so well: every chapter in the last three novels—and, but for her publisher's objections, *Romola* as well—is introduced with an epigraph ("motto," to Eliot), a vehicle for direct generalizing commentary in an authorized voice.[47] In adopting epigraphs Eliot is again appropriating and transforming a practice far more common among nineteenth-century women than men. Although Scott, who used chapter mottos in the *Waverley* novels, is taken to be the inspiration for Eliot's epigraphy,[48] using epigraphs became a prominent and earnest practice primarily among women novelists in England and America; they appear, for instance, in Susanna Rowson's *Charlotte* (1791), Mary Brunton's *Discipline* (1815), Susan Ferrier's *Marriage* (1818), Susan Warner's *The*

45. David, *Intellectual Women*, 165.

46. On Gaskell's pretense of ignorance, see Lovell, *Consuming Fiction*, 87–88. To my knowledge, the only woman of the mid-nineteenth century who routinely wrote prefaces that engaged current literary and social questions was George Sand, whose prefaces were a model for Henry James and probably for Eliot as well.

47. At least one critic did comment specifically on the "mottos": Sidney Colvin, in the *Fortnightly Review* (1 November 1876), complains that "moral and philosophical problems do not clothe themselves" in Eliot's novels "in appropriate artistic forms. We have passages of first-rate art side by side with passages of philosophy; and sometimes the philosophy comes where we want the art" (in *George Eliot and Her Readers*, 172, 176).

48. *Waverley* itself (1814) has no epigraphs, while Mary Brunton's *Discipline*, published in Scotland in the same year as *Guy Mannering* (1815), does.

Wide, Wide World (1851), Elizabeth Gaskell's *North and South* (1855),
Harriet Wilson's *Our Nig* (1859), and sporadically in *Uncle Tom's Cabin*.
Women writers in the nineteenth century might have had a particular
predilection for the epigraph as a means for suggesting the scope of
their knowledge, giving the novel an intellectual and moral weight,
and lending external authority to their textual stance.

Eliot, however, takes epigraphy to new, self-authorizing extremes.
While other women draw their epigraphs almost exclusively from
English and American sources, Eliot quotes Heine, Dante, Montaigne,
Molière, Musset—in the original. While other women use primarily
brief verses, Eliot often chooses substantial prose passages. While
other women frequently quote scripture, of 225 epigraphs in Eliot's
last three novels, only three are biblical. While other women frequently
cite women as well as men, only one of Eliot's mottos can be attributed
to another woman (Elizabeth Browning).[49] Seventy-five of Eliot's
sources are used only once or twice; while Susan Warner reveals her
knowledge of Shakespeare, Milton, Cowper, and Burns by quoting
them frequently, Eliot's epigraphs suggest an inexhaustible and esoteric store of references. In short, while other women create an evoc-
ative, English-language, and sexually mixed intertext through their
epigraphs, Eliot's epigraphy constitutes a pan-European canon of
learned men that, like Sarah Fielding, she appears to master. If epigraphs reinforce the literary project over the commercial one, and if
Catherine Gallagher is right to suggest that the dominant image
against which Victorian women writers struggled was not the father
but the whore, Eliot's epigraphy uses the literary fathers to cover "the
guilt of usurious and whorish commercial appropriation" and helps
create the "artificial construction of a superseding *moral* economy."[50]

But Eliot's epigraphy goes further still: it transforms the narrator
herself into a literary "father" by reauthorizing her voice as if it belonged to someone else. If one were to construct an Eliot who first
"saw herself not as a creator of literature but only as an editor and
translator whose skills in expression were to be subordinate to the
meaning of another's words,"[51] one might be tempted to see the epi-

---

49. I have drawn most of my information about Eliot's epigraphs from J. R. Tye, "George
Eliot's Unascribed Mottoes," in *Nineteenth Century Fiction* 22 (1967): 235–49; and David Leon
Higdon, "George Eliot and the Art of the Epigraph," *Nineteenth Century Fiction* 25 (1970):
127–51. Especially valuable is Higdon's appendix, which charts the sources and distribution
of epigraphs in the three novels.
50. Catherine Gallagher, "George Eliot and *Daniel Deronda*," 47.
51. Gilbert and Gubar, *The Madwoman in the Attic*, 450.

graphs as a continuation of feminine servitude. But in fact the major contributor to Eliot's mottos, the literary voice that dominates the tradition evoked through these collective passages, is Eliot's own. Of the 225 epigraphs, a full ninety-six, three times the number from Shakespeare and 45 percent of the whole, were probably authored by Eliot. These epigraphs employ a variety of genres from poetry to drama to philosophical prose, as if Eliot's writings could alone constitute an entire literature. They appear without attribution as if their source were obvious, and they often masquerade as sections of longer works, excerpts from apparently nonexistent plays or poems. While *Felix Holt* carries the largest proportion of epigraphs authored by Eliot herself, these are generally brief and in verse, while *Daniel Deronda* is given to long prose paragraphs much like the extended generalizations that often begin chapters in "Janet's Repentence" and *The Mill on the Floss* and seem to have caused so much offense.

Together, then, Eliot's epigraphs create a supertext and intertext in which the extrafictional "George Eliot" stands among male voices as the dominant though unidentified voice. It is significant, I think, that while the authorial acts of the early novels call considerable attention to themselves, these appropriative and more distanced actions are undertaken entirely without acknowledgment. In what we might read simultaneously as an elaborate appropriation and secret joke, George Eliot makes herself her own most quoted sage. Here, in the guise of nonfiction, is perhaps the ultimate fiction of authority. To be sure, Eliot often uses these structures—as my own epigraphs to this chapter already suggest—to problematize the kinds of simple and unqualified judgment she associates with the "men of maxims," just as she had used direct engagement in *Adam Bede* to plead for human sympathy. Eliot's epigraphy thus mediates the tension in her work between a semantics of indeterminacy and a syntax of authority. Critical efforts to erase the tension between these, such as Gilbert and Gubar's suggestion that Eliot creates her own mottos in order to "ridicul[e] the convention of citing authorities,"[52] seem to me groundless denials of the extent to which, as seems consistent with her historical moment, Eliot sought that authority herself.

There is in fact a particular sleight of hand in Eliot's epigraphy that is absent from other mechanisms that embed textual stance. As Bakhtin suggests, epigraphy works dialogically: it constructs an abstract

52. Ibid., 531.

discourse in tension with the chapter's dramatized events; it creates a dialogue between two voices—epigrapher's and narrator's—presumably of different agency. In some four-tenths of Eliot's epigraphs, however, these voices are the "same" voice. Lennard Davis reminds us, of course, that all novelistic "dialogue"— the engagement of textual voice with textual voice—is only a fiction of dialogue, for "everything that comes from the author is autocratically determined," and "the fact that the novel substitutes a simulacrum of conversation does not mean that the truly dialogic is being represented."[53] If Davis's assumption of a monologic authorial subjectivity can be mitigated by an understanding of the dialogic as internal, then the impasse of single- authored "dialogue" becomes less formidable. Nonetheless, in placing the discourse of "George Eliot" in the (superior) textual position reserved for other voices, Eliot actually creates the discourse that validates her own.

Eliot's professed dislike of quotations, abstractions, and "maxims" stands, therefore, in unresolved tension with the pervasive system of generalization in her work and especially with her practices of epigraphy. It is possible that the more Eliot's narrators use maxims, quotations, and authoritative structures that appropriate the cultural authority of men, the more these same narrators protest against such maxims, so that the content of the generalizations often recognizes the contingencies of authority and pluralities of meaning that the form seems to deny. This insistence on a syntax of self-authorization is one sign of what Deirdre David suggests is Eliot's necessary collaboration in her own "iconised" status.[54] If Eliot seems to question everything, if her commentaries are rewardingly complex, still her narrators assert their right to do the questioning: questioning does not necessarily challenge the authority of the questioner.

It seems, rather, that this questioning of authority that characterizes Eliot's later novels is critical to that authority's very maintenance, much as Austen's disavowals of omniscience sustain her appropriation of authorial stance. Speaking of *Middlemarch,* D. A. Miller suggests in *The Novel and the Police* that "by now the gesture of disowning power should seem to define the basic move of a familiar power play, in which the name of power is given over to one agency in order that the function of power may be less visibly retained by another. Im-

53. Davis, *Resisting Novels,* 178.
54. David, *Intellectual Women,* 168.

potent to intervene in the 'facts,' the narration nevertheless controls the discursive framework in which they are perceived as such." Such novels, Miller argues, are "monologic" in the Bakhtinian sense: they are only "sham" struggles. But, as Miller continues, "to speak of sham struggles is also to imply the necessity for shamming them. The master-voice . . . continually needs to confirm its authority . . . "[55] Eliot's epigraphs, imperiously heading each chapter as a first Word, relentlessly masculine in the tradition they canonize, crown a career in which the role of women as predecessors and resources, like the gender of Marian Evans, is erased from the surface of the text.

If Austen's authorial narrators are constructed in sexual difference and assert a gynocentric authority, then Eliot's construct themselves in terms of sexual equality. These tendencies toward "difference" and "equality"—those two terms that modern feminists understand as an entrapping false duality—are not merely personal preferences but play themselves out within the gendered dynamics of fiction writing at what I hope I have demonstrated are two very different moments in literary history. If Eliot's authoriality writes the woman as moralist, poet, and intellectual into literary history, only a reader's "extratextual" knowledge of Eliot's gender rather than any explicit textual sign makes this a feminization of authority. If Austen constructs a voice double with demurral, Eliot's authority rests on what may be the most double voice of all—the voice of a woman writing in the name and company of men.[56] Neither writer yet maps the space where equality, whether narrative or political, can rest on the affirmation of difference.[57]

55. D. A. Miller, *The Novel and the Police* (Berkeley: University of California Press, 1988), 25.

56. Like Austen, Eliot used both indefinite free indirect discourse and the direct discourse of characters for some of her boldest generalizing statements. Is it only Gwendolen Harleth, or also the authorial narrator, who thinks that "to become a wife and wear all the domestic fetters of that condition, was on the whole a vexatious necessity" (*Daniel Deronda*, 4.68)? Certainly it is to Gwendolen and to the princess that *Daniel Deronda* gives its most "feminist" thoughts—for example, the princess's insistence that she "had a right to be an artist," "something more than a mere daughter and mother" (53.728).

57. On difference and equality see Joan W. Scott, "Deconstructing Equality-versus-Difference: Or, the Uses of Poststructuralist Theory for Feminism," *Feminist Studies* 14 (1988): 33–50.

6

Fictions of Absence: Feminism, Modernism, Virginia Woolf

I never meant to preach and agree that like God, one shouldn't.

—Virginia Woolf, Letter to Clive Bell

Nothing seemed to have merged. They all sat separate. And the whole of the effort of merging and flowing and creating rested on her.

—Virginia Woolf, *To the Lighthouse*

When Virginia Woolf proclaimed a modernist fictional aesthetic in "Mr. Bennett and Mrs. Brown" by juxtaposing a famous and sophisticated male novelist with an obscure and threadbare elderly lady, she was obliquely suggesting what she would later articulate as the potential of modernism to allow women to "write of women as women have never been written of before."[1] Modernist fiction was indeed associated with women in a way that the classic realist novel was not. Leslie Fiedler is not alone is arguing with sweeping gen(d)erality that "the whole 'stream of consciousness' movement is a return from an exaggeratedly masculine literature to a feminine one. Wherever fiction turns from outdoors to indoors, from field to boudoir, from flight to love, from action to analysis, from reason to sensibility the female *persona* becomes, even for male authors, an inevitable mouthpiece; and the female author assumes—as in the novel's earliest decades—

1. Virginia Woolf, "Women and Fiction" (1929), in *Women and Writing*, ed. Michèle Barrett (New York: Harcourt Brace Jovanovich, 1980), 49.

first importance."[2] Framing their arguments quite differently, many contemporary feminists have also celebrated modernism as a movement open to the "feminine," to the "androgynous" and cross-sexual, to patriarchal deconstruction, to Julia Kristeva's "semiotic chora," indeed to *écriture féminine*.[3] While I agree that modernism offered new antihegemonic possibilities in which women not only participated but took leading roles, Fiedler's comments and Woolf's "Mr. Bennett and Mrs. Brown" also reveal a troubling underside—the potential of the modernist novel to recuperate female voice and "consciousness." If Fiedler rightly sees feminine "sensibility" or the female "mouthpiece" (re)valorized in modernist narrative, why is it that women *writers* were not accorded "first importance" in modernism either in the period of its development or in the retrospective light of conventional literary history? Woolf's own words in "Mr. Bennett and Mrs. Brown" suggest that canonical modernism was a masculine enterprise: although she does allude to the "men and women [who] write novels," the only female names in her essay are the names of characters, while the writers she identifies—"Mr. Forster, Mr. Lawrence, Mr. Strachey, Mr. Joyce, and Mr. Eliot"—are men.[4] Nor was the "dark country" that Woolf saw women's fiction exploring for the first time, which she hoped would make the novel "more critical of society, and less analytical of individual lives,"[5] the fiction that modernism came to canonize. I propose that one reason for this dissonance is a complicated and contradictory politics of narrative voice that Woolf herself managed only with considerable struggle to negotiate.

Modernism challenged both of the narrative imperatives—knowing and judging—that I have associated with classic realism: in a world in which "nothing was just one thing," in which consciousness was understood to implicate *un*consciousness, and in which traditional foundations of fact and value had been severely undermined, the project of realism was drastically compromised. The realist narrator

2. Leslie Fiedler, foreword to Caesar R. Blake, *Dorothy Richardson* (Ann Arbor: University of Michigan Press, 1960), x. In Chapter 7 I will identify similar assumptions about gender and interiority in Romantic narrative.

3. See, for example, Sandra Gilbert and Susan Gubar, *No Man's Land* (New Haven: Yale University Press, 1987); Rachel Blau DuPlessis, "For the Etruscans," in *The New Feminist Criticism*, ed. Elaine Showalter (New York: Pantheon, 1985), 271–91; Marianne DeKoven, *A Different Language: Gertrude Stein's Experimental Writing* (Madison: University of Wisconsin Press, 1983); and Shari Benstock, *Women of the Left Bank: Paris 1900–1940* (Austin: University of Texas Press, 1986).

4. Virginia Woolf, "Mr Bennett and Mrs Brown" (1924), in *The Captain's Death Bed and Other Essays* (New York: Harcourt Brace Jovanovich, 1950), 96.

5. Woolf, "Women and Fiction," 50.

could no longer pretend to infallibility; the novel no longer required or desired overt authoriality. The new "indirect and oblique" method modeled by Flaubert and James and championed by Percy Lubbock submerged the entire question of narrative voice beneath "point of view"—what Genette calls focalization—just as the new practice claimed to submerge the voice of the "author" beneath the perceptions of characters. The ideal narrator, as Joyce's Stephen Dedalus avows *d'après* Flaubert, supposedly "refines itself out of existence": all "angles of vision" are ostensibly those of the characters.[6] In what Franz Stanzel has called the "figural" narrative situation, the narrative act and the rhetorical relationship of the narrator to both story and narratee become unspeakable.[7]

But it is revealing that Stephen's description of the narrator retains the trope of (masculine) divinity that characterized classical realism's conception of textual voice. Instead of the personal god presiding openly over the textual world and pronouncing judgments upon it, the modernist narrator is closer to the god of the deists, bringing other voices into being and letting them operate as if they were autonomous: "The dramatic form is reached when the vitality which has flowed and eddied round each person fills every person with such vital force that he or she assumes a proper and intangible esthetic life.... The artist, like the God of the creation, remains within or behind or beyond or above his handiwork, invisible, refined out of existence, indifferent, paring his fingernails."[8] Just as a god who can be "paring his fingernails" is not quite "refined out of existence," this aesthetic does not so much dispense with the narrator as require a particular kind of covert authoriality: the illusion of "effacement" that is constructed from a suppression of narrative self-consciousness, of contact between narrator and narratee, and of explicit markers of narrative stance.

The convention of "effaced" authoriality seems to me to have carried particular double edges for modernist women novelists. On the one hand, overtly hegemonic forms of narration such as those appropriated by George Eliot and her successors were (in part perhaps for that reason) no longer desirable as literature; women writers would have to choose, as it were, between authoriality, with its fertile ground

---

6. James Joyce, *A Portrait of the Artist as a Young Man* (New York: Viking, 1964), 215.

7. See Franz K. Stanzel, *Narrative Situations in the Novel*, trans. James Pusack (Bloomington: Indiana University Press, 1971).

8. Joyce, *Portrait*, 215.

for figuring woman's relation to public culture, and canonicity. On the other hand, the deconstruction of realist authority—which had never been significantly feminized—opened spaces for antihegemonic re-presentations and alternative constructions of female subjectivity. But so long as female subjectivity remained marginal, so too could the writings that represented it. The first formulation of novelistic "stream of consciousness" was in fact explicitly female and feminist, and the responses to this project reveal one side of the narrative double bind in which, I will argue, women modernists found themselves. Determined "to produce a feminine equivalent of the current masculine realism,"[9] Dorothy Richardson made the (dis)organizing principle of her multivolume novel *Pilgrimage* an adolescent female consciousness represented primarily through free indirect discourse that attempts a written approximation of Miriam's mental life. When *Pointed Roofs*, the first of thirteen volumes, was published in 1915, its originality was unmistakable; in Fiedler's words, the book was "unequivocally experimental" and "*avant-garde*."[10] No one, not even Joyce, had "refined" the narrator more thoroughly "out of existence" than Richardson: the subtle and arguably ironic distance between narrator and character that in Joyce's novel still implicates a superior narrative consciousness is not to be found in *Pilgrimage*.[11]

The dilemma of women and modernism is perhaps nowhere more ironically evident than in critic Robert Humphrey's well-meaning attempt to restore Richardson's place in the history of narrative form. For all his praise of her methods, Humphrey declared himself unable to "grasp" Richardson's feminist "aims" because "the basic problems and situations of life (hence of art) are neither masculine nor feminine, but simply human." When Humphrey challenges Richardson's call for a "feminine realism," however, it becomes clear that "human" means masculine and that female consciousness means aberrant consciousness: "One might as well propose that Faulkner writes in order to produce a psychotic equivalent of the current sane realism! Faulkner has, certainly, advantages ... in presenting life from an abnormal person's point of view—and likewise there are certain values inherent in the presentation of life from a feminine point of view—but these values cannot be realized in a vacuum. An adequate purpose is not

9. Dorothy Richardson, foreword to *Pilgrimage* (New York: Knopf, 1967), vol. 1, 9.
10. Fiedler, foreword, x.
11. One might compare, for example, the passages in which Miriam and Stephen respond to a sermon; see *Pointed Roofs*, 73, and *Portrait of the Artist*, 143.

found in presenting these viewpoints merely for the sake of novelty. It is hardly justified, at least, for important literature."[12] David Hayman perhaps explains these limits on modernism's comfort with the ordinary when he notes modernism's tendency to "give the commonplace, banal, and frequently unacceptable subject matter a pleasing and subtly distanced formulation."[13] Distance is indeed as important, though a less- acknowledged concept in modernist narrative aesthetics, as the representation of "ordinary" consciousness, which is transformed into "art" through irony, stylization, and some mark of separation between author and character. I suggest that the desire for distance may be particularly acute when the "commonplace, banal, or unacceptable subject matter" is feminine and the authorizing voice female or, worse, feminist. After all, Joyce's *Ulysses* also presents "life from a feminine point of view" in Molly Bloom's long soliloquy.

The revolution in the novel that Woolf calls for and Fiedler hails may have been permitted to challenge masculinist values, in other words, only insofar as the *forms* of those challenges "pleasantly" distanced the content of women's daily lives. "Distance," as Mary Gordon was to write later, gave "grandeur" to otherwise "trivial" female subjects; "distance, then, was what I was to strive for. Distance from the body, from the heart, but most of all, distance from the self as writer."[14] *Pilgrimage* offered what Gordon would call "radical closeness" in attending to the small matters of women's lives in a literary environment where "masculine" aesthetic distance alone made the representation of female consciousness respectable. It is worth noting, therefore, that Stephen Dedalus's description of the modernist narrative situation speaks of the character as "he or she" but of the creator as male. And when Woolf calls for changes in the representation of character in "Mr. Bennett and Mrs. Brown," she does not mention Richardson, even though she is writing about the same failure of "masculine realism" that motivated *Pilgrimage*.[15] The absence of narrative distance in Richardson's repre-

12. Robert Humphrey, *Stream of Consciousness in the Modern Novel* (Berkeley and Los Angeles: University of California Press, 1954), 11.

13. David Hayman, *Re-Forming the Narrative: Toward a Mechanics of Modernist Fiction* (Ithaca: Cornell University Press, 1987), 6.

14. Mary Gordon, "The Parable of the Cave or: In Praise of Watercolors," in *The Woman Writer on Her Work*, ed. Janet Sternburg (New York: Norton, 1980), 29.

15. Woolf was ambivalent about Richardson's work and reluctant to review it. She did praise Richardson for creating "a psychological sentence of the feminine gender" through which to "describe a woman's mind" and for being "neither proud nor afraid of anything that she may discover in the psychology of her sex," in review of *Revolving Lights* (1923), reprinted in *Women and Writing*, ed. Barrett, 191. But in an entry in her diary, Woolf reveals herself to be more critical, lauding the content but lamenting the form: "That one should

sentation of female consciousness may help to explain why her achievement was overlooked and the credit for "stream of consciousness"
narration handed over to Joyce and Proust.[16] Richardson's fate perhaps also reinforced Virginia Woolf's vehement adherence to the modernist predilection for distancing strategies.

Fiedler's comparison of modernist fiction to the "novel's earliest
decades" may be apt, then, in unintended ways. Just as female voice
in the eighteenth century came to be preserved and validated primarily through novels by men, so modernist representations of the
"feminine" may have been most valued when a man created them—
Joyce representing Molly Bloom rather than Richardson representing
Miriam or even Woolf representing Clarissa Dalloway. Canonical
modernism repeats eighteenth-century literary history: despite extraordinary, innovative achievements, writers such as Gertrude Stein,
Colette, Djuna Barnes, Zora Neale Hurston, and Richardson were
dismissed for decades as precious, irrelevant, and eccentric—at best
in danger, as Elaine Marks said in her pioneering study of Colette,
of becoming "immortal and unknown."[17] Shari Benstock observes in
Women of the Left Bank that traditional studies of modernism have
either overlooked "the very existence of women in this literary community" or have devalued female modernists "for not meeting the
'standards' of modernism set by and for men."[18] I propose that Woolf's
own reputation, which received its share of disparagement from male
critics,[19] may have survived the general derogation of modernist
women precisely because of her carefully distanced narrative prac-

---

see it as a superb subject is a tribute to her, but of course, not knowing how to write, she's
muffed it. The interest remains, because she has ridden straight at her recollections, never
swerving & getting through honestly, capably, but without the power to still & shape the past
so that one will wish to read it again. Honesty is her quality; & the fact that she made a great
rush at life." There was clearly a certain competitiveness: "The truth is that when I looked
at it, I felt myself looking for faults; hoping for them. . . . There must be an instinct of self-
preservation at work. If she's good then I'm not." In *Diary of Virginia Woolf*, ed. Ann Olivier
Bell, 5 vols. (New York: Harcourt Brace, 1976–1984), 1.315.

16. Richardson was very disturbed that Proust's work was being credited for "an unprec-
edentedly profound and opulent reconstruction of experience focused from within the mind
of a single individual," when her own work, begun two years before the appearance of *Swann's
Way*, was attempting precisely this. She was equally distressed that once the "lonely track"
on which she had begun "turned out to be a populous highway" whose numbers included
Joyce and Woolf, her own "role of pathfinder" was minimized. See the preface to *Pilgrimage*.

17. Elaine Marks, *Colette* (New Brunswick, N.J.: Rutgers University Press, 1960), 5.

18. Benstock, *Women of the Left Bank*, 26, 32.

19. See, for example, Herbert J. Muller, "Virginia Woolf and Feminine Fiction" (1937),
reprinted in *Critical Essays on Virginia Woolf*, ed. Morris Beja (Boston: G. K. Hall, 1985), esp.
35–36.

tices. For the difficulty of negotiating the opposing problems of distance and "effacement" affected Woolf and Richardson quite differently: while Richardson sought authorial effacement without distance, Woolf sought distance without authorial effacement, a posture rooted in a complex of factors possibly intensified by the reactions of her colleagues to *Pilgrimage*.

Unlike Richardson and Joyce (both of whom she called egotistical) Woolf avoided the single "angle of vision" and in the process distanced her novels from associations with autobiography. While she once wrote that "I sometimes think only autobiography is literature—novels are what we peel off, and come at last to the core, which is only you or me"; while she professed to "see the attraction" of the "personal style" and raved about the autobiographical fictions of Proust and Colette, she also claimed to "hate any writer to talk about himself; anonymity I adore. And this may be an obsession."[20] In Woolf's entire fictional corpus there is not one novel or portion of a novel written in the first person or even focalized exclusively through a single point of view. In this respect Woolf follows Jane Austen and George Eliot, neither of whom adopts a female personal voice or a wholly fixed focalization through a female persona anywhere in her fictional work. Certainly *The Voyage Out*, Woolf's first novel and, like *A Portrait* and *Pilgrimage*, the tracing of an adolescent's coming of age, creates far more distance between its narrator and Rachel Vinrace than Richardson, Joyce, and Proust create between their narrators and their more obviously autobiographical characters.

This does not, however, mean that Woolf sought to "efface" subjectivity from her writing but rather that the subjectivity she sought to represent was not personal but authorial. Despite her questioning of absolute and authoritarian points of view and her repeated insistence that novels were not for "preaching," Woolf's novels struggle against and for the "maximizing" authority I have associated with

20. Letters respectively to Hugh Walpole, 28 December 1932 (*The Letters of Virginia Woolf*, ed. Nigel Nicolson and Joanne Trautmann, 6 vols. [New York: Harcourt Brace Jovanovich, 1975–1980], 5.142); to Ethel Smyth, 26 October 1939 (6.367); and to Ethel Smyth, 6 June 1933 (5.191). So horrified was Woolf at autobiographical interpretations of her work that even though she wrote in diary entries that *To the Lighthouse* was autobiographical—for example, she wrote of feeling "rather queer, to think" that "all these people will read it & recognise poor Leslie Stephen & beautiful Mrs Stephen in it" (*Diary*, 24 February 1926, 3.61)—still she felt "exposed as a novelist," simply for being "told my people are my mother and father, when, being in a novel, they're not" (letter to Shena, Lady Simon, of 25 January 1941, in *Letters* 6.464).

Eliot: Woolf too will use a generalization to declare, for example, that "these generalizations are very worthless. The military sound of the word is enough."[21] While Richardson might have agreed with her character Miriam that "views and opinions are masculine things" and women "indifferent to them really" (3.259), Woolf would seem to resemble Eleanor Pargiter who, when asked, "pulled herself together and gave him her opinion. She had an opinion—a very definite opinion. She cleared her throat and began."[22] Woolf's career, like Eliot's, began with the writing of essays, the quintessential genre for "views and opinions," but unlike Eliot, Woolf wrote at a moment when fictional aesthetics and overt authoriality were seriously at odds. The result is an unstable struggle throughout Woolf's career at once to suppress and to express narrative stance, to negotiate a position between the overt authoriality of an Eliot and the figural effacement of a Richardson.

It is not difficult to see why Woolf might have found narrative authority both attractive and troubling. A woman raised by a man of letters who denied her a formal education, a conscious feminist immersed in and dependent on the approval of a predominantly male avant-garde, a woman acutely conscious of the negative power of individualist (male) subjectivity but aware of the need for silenced subjects to assert themselves, Woolf was in a situation that was pivotal and liminal: she wrote from a divided consciousness to a multiple audience; she had the power—and the burden—of bringing feminist questions to a literary community and modernist questions to a feminist one. Her strategies for creating presence through apparent absence and singular voice through apparent multiplicity emerge, I believe, from the pressure of these conflicting imperatives. Many critics have emphasized the "impersonality" of Woolf's method, her "world without a self," her "annihilation" of the narrator, her "abandonment" of omniscience—that is, her narrative absences.[23] I want instead to stress Woolf's narrative "presences," those qualities that support J. Hillis Miller's comparison of Woolf's narrators to those of Thackeray, Eliot and Trollope, and that lead Maria DiBattista to note that unlike

21. Woolf, "The Mark on the Wall," in *The Complete Shorter Fiction of Virginia Woolf*, ed. Susan Dick (New York: Harcourt Brace Jovanovich, 1985), 80. All further references to the short stories will be from this edition.
22. Virginia Woolf, *The Years* (New York: Harcourt Brace, 1937), 96.
23. See, for example, James Naremore, *The World without a Self: Virginia Woolf and the Novel* (New Haven: Yale University Press, 1973).

other modernists Woolf "preserves in her fiction the figure of the author as a permeating and permeable presence."[24] I am therefore questioning such assumptions as Elaine Showalter's that Woolf responded to "the violence of [male] ego" by "renounc[ing] the demands of the individual narrative self,"[25] and reading Woolf's narrative strategies not as an antiauthoritative "communal" consciousness, as Rachel DuPlessis does, but as a strategy for reinstating the authorial voice.[26] The divergences in these critical positions can, however, perhaps be traced to Woolf's own ambiguous practices, for her work reflects a particularly sharp version of the dilemma that Alan Wilde observes in British modernists generally—how to enact "the moral impulse of modernism" and "disguise" it at the same time,[27] a dilemma frequently complicated by Woolf's ambivalence about whether feminism, or any expression she associated with "grievances," belonged in a work of art. One way to erase or at least disclaim such "pleading" was, of course, to rid the novel of overt authoriality.

If one begins not with the finished novels but with first drafts and unpublished manuscripts, it becomes evident that Woolf struggled with and against authoriality with surprising consistency throughout her career. The narrators of her earliest short stories, the first four of which were written before 1910 but not published within her lifetime, play openly with authorial forms. "Phyllis and Rosamond," for example, adopts the kind of narrator that characterizes George Eliot's first work: a musing, on-the-scenes author-historian directly engaged with an audience: "Let each man, I heard it said the other day, write down the details of a day's work; posterity will be as glad of the catalogue as we should be if we had such a record of how the door keeper at the Globe, and the man who kept the Park gates passed Saturday March 18th in the year of our Lord 1568" (17). This narrator may or may not be female, but (s)he is clearly feminist, and her project is to study young women "born of well-to-do, respectable, official parents" who "must all meet much the same problems, and there can be, unfortunately, but little variety in the answers they make." Most

---

24. J. Hillis Miller, *Fiction and Repetition* (Cambridge: Harvard University Press, 1982), 176; Maria DiBattista, "Joyce, Woolf, and the Modern Mind," in *Virginia Woolf: New Critical Essays*, ed. Patricia Clements and Isobel Grundy (New York: Barnes and Noble, 1983), 112.
25. Showalter, *A Literature of Their Own*, 240.
26. DuPlessis, *Writing beyond the Ending*, 162–77.
27. Alan Wilde, *Horizons of Assent: Modernism, Postmodernism, and the Ironic Imagination* (Baltimore: Johns Hopkins University Press, 1981), 51–52.

revealing of the four earliest stories is "The Journal of Mistress Joan Martyn," in which a fifteenth-century fictional diary is introduced by a learned historian bursting with self-importance: "My readers may not know, perhaps, who I am. Therefore, although such a practice is unusual and unnatural—for we know how modest writers are—I will not hesitate to explain that I am Miss Rosamond Merridew, aged forty-five—my frankness is consistent!—and that I have won considerable fame among my profession for the researches I have made into the system of land tenure in medieval England. Berlin has heard my name; Frankfurt would give a soirée in my honour; and I am not absolutely unknown in one or two secluded rooms in Oxford and in Cambridge" (33). This playful self-promotion, only partly undercut by irony, reminds me of the prefaces Jane Austen wrote in her "juvenilia" (and poignantly recalls Woolf's longing for the Oxbridge education Leslie Stephen gave only to his sons). Explicitly female narrators appear also in published stories such as "An Unwritten Novel" and "A Society," the latter a witty feminist piece that closes by generalizing that when a woman "knows how to read there's only one thing you can teach her to believe in—and that is herself" (130). Although Woolf's early novels do not openly dramatize their narrators as these stories do, *The Voyage Out* and especially *Night and Day* incorporate (relatively nonoppositional) narrative comment ranging, for example, from the beauties of London to the effects of privilege in English society to the search for truth.[28]

If these early works reflect an ease with overt authoriality, successive drafts of some late novels suggest far more conflict. Three of Woolf's last four novels were first conceived as overtly authorial.[29] But early versions of *The Waves* (1931) and *The Years* (1937) seem to have been sites of struggle precisely over the suppression of authorial voice. Perhaps most surprising is Woolf's apparent difficulty in "purging" an authorial narrator from *The Waves*, the novel often considered to be her triumph of "self-effacement." J. W. Graham shows that Woolf first conceived for this novel an omniscient and explicitly female narrator, a "She," who ends up in the drafts as a vague meditative figure

28. Virginia Woolf, *Night and Day* (Harmondsworth, England: Penguin, 1969), 338, 32–33, and 291, respectively.

29. *Orlando*, of course, makes authorial voice most easily legitimate by creating the fiction of the biographer, so that playful "intrusions" become part of the narrative game, and the authoring voice can comment not only on Orlando her/himself and on the process of biography (119, 126), but on diverse subjects from time (98) to sex (188–90).

speaking "briefly in the first person."[30] Woolf held onto this authorial voice for almost four years, says Graham, at great cost to the progress of her manuscript; only in August 1930, three months after having begun the second draft, did she give up the authorial form in favor of "a series of dramatic soliloquies."[31] This "struggle with the point of view in the early stage of composition," Graham concludes, "can only mean that, although there were obvious reasons for abandoning the narrator, there were less obvious but potent reasons for trying to keep her."[32] Eileen Sypher further notes that as Woolf worked on the manuscript, the originally female central consciousness became first an androgynous "lonely mind, man or woman, young or aged" and finally the author figure Bernard, formally distanced from Woolf herself by both gender and fictionality.[33]

The most visible and assertive authorial voice in all of Woolf's fiction was likewise a voice she eventually sacrificed, in this case when she revised her unfinished essay-novel "The Pargiters" (1932) into *The Years* (1937). As innovative a formal hybrid as some of the fictions of Fielding or Diderot, "The Pargiters" is subtitled "A Novel-Essay based upon a paper read to the London/National Society for Women's Service." Its narrator proposes to pursue her topic of women and the professions by reading selections from her newest novel, an ambitious epic about the lives of women over several decades in a family's history "based upon some scores—I might boldly say thousands—of old memoirs" that together "represent English life at its most normal, most typical, and most representative."[34] Structurally, "The Pargiters" alternates essays with chapters from the "novel," the essays commenting on the novel and the world it represents. By becoming her own literary critic and interpreter, Woolf's narrator constructs a fiction of authority rather like the one Eliot creates through her epigraphs. If Woolf's abandonment of "The Pargiters" may suggest, as Rachel DuPlessis has argued, a

---

30. J. W. Graham, "Point of View in *The Waves*: Some Services of the Style," in *Virginia Woolf*, ed. Thomas S. W. Lewis (New York: McGraw-Hill, 1975), 100.

31. Woolf, *Diary*, 20 August 1930, vol. 3 (1980), 312.

32. Graham, "Point of View in *The Waves*," 103.

33. Eileen B. Sypher, "*The Waves*: A Utopia of Androgyny?" in *Virginia Woolf: Centennial Essays*, ed. Elaine K. Ginsberg and Laura Moss Gottlieb (Troy, N.Y.: Whitson Publishing Company, 1983), 192.

34. Virginia Woolf, *The Pargiters*, ed. Mitchell A. Leaskea (New York: The New York Public Library, 1977), 9. What Woolf calls "typical" and "representative" is of course typical only of her class.

discomfort with authoritative (and polemicizing) voice,[35] then the fact that Woolf conceived this project at all, wary as she was of the conjunction of "preaching" and fiction, testifies as eloquently to her impulse even late in her life toward such overt authoriality. The authorial voice also remains visible, of course, in the prefaces that head each section of both *The Waves* and *The Years*.

Thus again and again in Woolf's fiction, from early to late in her career, one witnesses an impulse to retain the kind of voice, associated with the realist novel of the nineteenth century, that modernism supposedly eschews. The fact that authoriality is most prominent in Woolf's first drafts and unpublished manuscripts may signify an increasing distrust of hegemonic voice or may simply be a bow to convention; in either case, as I hope to demonstrate, the forms Woolf substituted for authoriality are subtly hegemonic themselves. I want to turn now to those novels to which critics often point as evidence of a progressive narrative "effacement": *Jacob's Room* (1922), *Mrs. Dalloway* (1925), *To the Lighthouse* (1927), and *The Waves* (1931). During the decade when Woolf produced these novels—in what was probably modernist fiction's most experimental period—she was forging new methods of "submerging" authorial voice. As I identify some techniques by which narrative presence in Woolf's novels masks itself as absence, I will be concerned especially with the ways in which these novels render voice contingent and apparently collaborative through strategies that blur differences between the voice of the narrator and the voices of characters.

Jacob's Room (1922) begins this process through its periodic breakdown of formal distinctions between the narrator's discourse and that of the characters. By employing a continually shifting point of view, focalizing her vision through various characters and speaking "for" them in free indirect discourse or in unmarked direct thought, the narrator creates a discursive surface in which the attribution of particular thoughts or perceptions becomes confusing and sometimes indeterminate. This practice goes beyond the ambiguity of indefinite free indirect discourse that I associated with Austen, for Woolf's narrator speaks in what appears to be the authorial voice but then tries belatedly to pass off the discourse as a character's. For example, while Jacob is reading his mother's letter, this passage appears after a break

35. DuPlessis, *Writing beyond the Ending*, 175.

in the text: "Let us consider letters—how they come at breakfast, and at night, with their yellow stamps and their green stamps, immortalized by the postmark—for to see one's own envelope on another's table is to realize how soon deeds sever and become alien."[36] This voice holds forth for four paragraphs, now colloquially, now lyrically, considering different kinds of letters, lamenting their ephemerality, hailing their value, alluding to Byron and Cowper, and finally discussing the letters of Jacob's mother and other characters. At the end of the fourth paragraph we return to Jacob's perspective with a parenthetical "so Jacob thought" (94), as if to suggest against plausibility that the entire meditation has been Jacob's text.

In the next three novels, Woolf adopts a less obvious and more global strategy that makes the characters extensions of the narrative voice. As the narrators of these novels orchestrate complex systems of focalization, they use this orchestrated whole to disperse a generalizing consciousness among the characters. This dispersal of narrative authority is accomplished through characters who, for all their differences of identity, have a semantically common voice. This means that the narration is not genuinely communal; each voice is part of a single if shared subjectivity. Writing specifically about *The Waves*, J. W. Graham describes this sleight of hand by which Woolf creates what appear to be direct representations of individual characters' minds. Graham observes that "Woolf makes no attempt to distinguish the style of one speaker from that of any other," so that one cannot logically read these speeches as interior monologues or representations of a "stream of consciousness," because the very objective of "stream of consciousness" is to represent the particularity of a psyche, to find a verbal equivalent for each character as Joyce does in *Ulysses* or Faulkner does in *The Sound and the Fury*.[37] Graham comments that "because the consciousnesses of all the speakers are rendered in the same style, the cumulative effect is like listening to a running verbatim translation of speeches by six different speakers: the subject matter alters, the attitudes of the speakers vary, they have their characteristic images and expressions, which the translator [sic] faithfully mirrors; but the words we actually *hear* are his [sic], and are strongly colored by the nuances and rhythms of his own vocabulary and voice."[38] It is

---

36. Virginia Woolf, *"Jacob's Room" & "The Waves"* (New York: Harcourt Brace, 1968), 92. Further citations from these novels will appear in the text.
37. Graham, "Point of View in *The Waves*," 95ff.
38. Ibid., 98.

not surprising, then, that Louis's "life passes" (293), Susan's "the seasons pass" (294), Neville's "let us abolish the ticking of time's clock" (301), and Bernard's "time lets fall its drop" (303) voice a common concern. When the narrator claims to be representing a character's speech by using the identifying phrases "said Neville" and "said Susan" we are in fact being offered neither what the character *says* nor what the *character* says. By representing characters who sound alike, the narrator can use them as generalized and generalizing presences.

While this use of characters is perhaps most dissonant in *The Waves* because that novel purports to consist almost wholly of the discourses of characters, the narrator uses her characters in similar ways in *Mrs. Dalloway* and *To the Lighthouse* to create the "maxims" that modernism disallows the authorial voice. Repeating a particular syntactic form for embedding ideological stance in the discourse of various characters gives these generalizations a structural uniformity across different characters' identities. In *Mrs. Dalloway*, for example, the characters repeatedly construct maxims, usually while they are doing something else, so that the maxim is embedded in representation and its external relationship to the fiction is minimized: "Because it is a thousand pities never to say what one feels, he thought, crossing the Green Park";[39] "To love makes one solitary, she thought" (33); "And there is a dignity in people; a solitude; even between husband and wife a gulf; and that one must respect, thought Clarissa, watching him open the door; for one would not part with it oneself, or take it, against his will, from one's husband, without losing one's independence, one's self respect—something, after all, priceless" (181); "For this is the truth about our soul, he thought, our self, who fish-like inhabits deep seas and plies among obscurities threading her way between the boles of giant weeds" (244); "For she had come to feel that it was the only thing worth saying—what one felt. Cleverness was silly. One must say simply what one felt" (292).

Most of these maxims are rendered in present-tense discourse, the "detachable" form I have been identifying as traditionally authorial, and without the subordinating structure of quotation marks that would emphasize the distinction between the narrator's and the character's text. Together, these comments create a textual philosophy that is reinforced as words and images reappear in the voices of

39. Virginia Woolf, *Mrs. Dalloway* (New York: Harcourt Brace, 1925), 175–76. Further references will appear in the text.

different characters. This is why it is plausible in *Mrs. Dalloway* for a
particular phrase—for example, "the leaden circles dissolved in the
air"—to recur as if it were being thought in identical language, implausibly, by several characters.[40] This language is everyone's, in other
words, because it is actually the language of the narrative voice.

Maxims appear as well in *To the Lighthouse*, although this novel offers
no such regular and obvious structure for generalization, and characters' thoughts are more frequently rendered in indirect discourse
and the past tense: James' recognition that "nothing was simply one
thing," or Lily's understanding that "love had a thousand shapes."[41]
The narrator continues, however, to mix direct and indirect thought
and thereby to embed present-tense comments, sometimes (as in *Jacob's Room*) attached to a character only parenthetically:

> Both of them looked at the dunes far away, and instead of merriment
> felt come over them some sadness—because the thing was completed
> partly, and partly because distant views seem to outlast by a million
> years (Lily thought) the gazer and to be communing already with a sky
> which beholds an earth entirely at rest. (34)

> There is a coherence in things, a stability; something, she meant, is
> immune from change, and shines out (she glanced at the window with
> its ripple of reflected lights) in the face of the flowing, the fleeting, the
> spectral, like a ruby ... Of such moments, she thought, the thing is made
> that endures. (158)

In all three of these high-modernist novels, then, the characters'
thoughts are blended with the text's narrative surface, allowing
Woolf's narrators surreptitiously to accomplish the outmoded, the no
longer acceptable: to ponder, preach, and prophesy. For finally, I
think, it is less the individual character than the idea, the image, the
vision, that Woolf's fiction seems to represent. If one could argue that
Woolf's narrators "share" authorial voice by authorizing characters,
they also absorb the thoughts of the characters into their own discourse. I am unwilling to name this narrative practice "communal,"
as Rachel DuPlessis does, because the voices seem to me to be expressing a single narrative consciousness that, by modernist convention, cannot be represented *as* a singular narrative consciousness. This
practice seems an apt choice for the woman who wrote that the six

40. See, for example, Rezia, 142; Clarissa, 5, 283–84; and Peter, 72.
41. Virginia Woolf, *To the Lighthouse* (New York: Harcourt Brace, 1927), 277, 286. Further
references will appear in the text.

characters of *The Waves* "were supposed to be one" and said in the
next sentence, "how difficult it is to collect oneself into one Virginia."[42]
I want to propose as a model for such a narrator Woolf's own
character Mrs. Ramsay engaged in the effort of "merging and flowing,"
which I have evoked in my epigraph to this chapter. Joan Lidoff has
speculated that the narrative form of *To the Lighthouse* might be connected to what Nancy Chodorow claims are the more "fluid" ego boundaries of women, and although I have strong reservations about the
essentialism of this theory, Lidoff's seems to me a compelling description of the "fluid boundaries" among Woolf's textual consciousnesses
in both *To the Lighthouse* and *Mrs. Dalloway*.[43] In other words, a modernist self-effacement is produced on the basis of an allegedly feminine "merging" of consciousness modeled on the mother who yields
autonomous identity to identities-in-relationship. Such a gesture must
remain equivocal. On the one hand, as Alan Wilde suggests in discussing Mrs. Ramsay, it may conceal a veiled self-centered imperative:
" 'Losing personality,' as she sinks down, away from the surface, Mrs.
Ramsay intimates the abandonment of command in an ecstasy of
selflessness; but what is at issue may be a yet more supreme egoism:
'It was odd, she thought, how if one was alone, one leant to things,
inanimate things; trees, streams, flowers; felt they expressed one; felt
they became one; felt they knew one, in a sense were one; felt an
irrational tenderness thus . . . as for oneself.'[44] By a similar process,
what might seem like narrative effacement in these middle novels may
be read as a means to gain voice(s) by apparently ceding voice. At
stake in the creation of a narrative method that Woolf hoped would
"enclose the whole" and forge a "sense of continuity"[45] is the "whole"
of the narrator's authoriality, which requires the appropriation of
characters for acts that were once the narrator's prerogative. Thus
Woolf's narrators manage to be nowhere by being everywhere. Nonetheless, such a practice is not (as motherhood is not) a simple rein-
statement-by-subterfuge of individualist authority, for if several
characters are speaking the narrator's words, then the narrative also
revises classic realism's stake in a superior, unreproducible authority.
    Between the Acts takes the construction of a narrative voice that is

42. Letter to G. L. Dickinson of 27 October 1931, in *Letters*, vol. 4, 397.
43. Joan Lidoff, "Virginia Woolf's Feminine Sentence: The Mother-Daughter World of
To the Lighthouse," *Literature and Psychology* 32 (1984): 43–44.
44. Wilde, *Horizons of Assent*, 128–29. See *To the Lighthouse*, 97–98.
45. Letters to Clive Bell of 19 August 1908, in *Letters*, vol. 1, 356; and to G. L. Dickinson
of 27 October 1931, in ibid., vol. 4, 397.

"nowhere" in order to be everywhere a step further, suggesting the extension of voice beyond any attributable identity. For Woolf develops in this last novel ambiguous voices that are neither explicitly authorial nor logically attachable to particular characters: it is not always clear from where they come. Under the pressures of fascism and world war, Woolf's sense of moral urgency seems stronger in this novel than in her early works, and so, too, seems her sense of impotence. If *Between the Acts* is about anything it is about silence, the loss of words, the desperate need for community, the difficulty of preserving the harmony that *To the Lighthouse* had been able in 1927 to imagine intact, if only for a moment, in Rose Ramsay's bowl of fruit. In sharp contrast to the long paragraphs of *To the Lighthouse*, in which discourse flows almost imperceptibly from one to another point of view, *Between the Acts*, with its short paragraphs and unidentified voices, maps a typography of distance and separateness.

Such a structure, however, allows even more latitude for the aphoristic, the epigrammatic, the exhortational. Woolf sends these messages repetitively, through voice upon voice—the voices of "no one" and everyone, of gramophones and acting villagers and visitors repeating what the actors have said: *"Dispersed are we; who have come together. But . . . let us retain whatever made that harmony"*;[46] "We are members one of another. Each is part of the whole" (133); "We act different parts but are the same" (149, 134). Some voices are identified; others are uncertain, anonymous, or collaborative: "Was that voice ourselves?" (132). From "scraps, orts, and fragments" (132; see also 131, 149) voice continues even when no one (but the reader) is listening. In a world where people "haven't the words—we haven't the words" (43) or "can't put two words together" (47), where voices "died away" (53) or "petered out" (70), where "the wind blew away the connecting words" (60; see also 89), music and aphorism unite the "dispersed," sending repeatedly, in this new age of mechanical reproduction, the most cogent and urgent of messages.

Paradoxically, *Between the Acts* insists that authoriality can and must survive even the "death" of human speaking and listening—"The cars drove off. The gramophone gurgled *Unity—Dispersity*" (140). I can support Makiko Minow-Pinkney's vision of this novel as Woolf's strongest move toward a "post- individualist future on the other side

___
46. Virginia Woolf, *Between the Acts* (Harmondsworth, England: Penguin, 1953), 137. All further references will appear in the text.

of the apocalypse brought about by the rapacious male 'I.' "[47] But for Woolf the death of individualism is emphatically not the loss of voice, least of all the loss of generalizing voice: some kind of over-voice, organizing and "maximizing" the possibilities of language, must continue to exhort the characters and enable them to survive the apocalypse so that they can begin again to speak. While the gramophone's promptings make possible this future, the future itself is "post-individualist" only in that it belongs to human dialogue. The text gives its last words, therefore, not to the gramophone but to the authorial narrator, who prepares the stage for this conversation that is not yet representable: "Then the curtain rose. They spoke." From the death of human voice must emerge nothing more or less than human voice.

For all their innovative practices, then, in terms of narrative voice Woolf's novels do not quite "destroy the whole of the nineteenth century," as Woolf said that T. S. Eliot thought *Ulysses* had done.[48] Woolf collectivizes authoriality without ceding it, giving a different shape to authorial imperatives rather than refusing them, and thereby writing in a line of continuity with Austen and George Eliot. But if Austen's authority was masked by indirection and anonymity and Eliot's shored by a male pseudonym and the cultural discourse of Western "man," Woolf's represents itself as feminist and bears its author's own name. In the history of female voice, I read in this moment a shift in emphasis from "fiction" to "authority" even as I must recognize, in ways that Woolf herself understood only partially, that such female authority is still marked by the privileges of race and class.

47. Makiko Minow-Pinkney, *Virginia Woolf and the Problem of the Subject* (New Brunswick, N.J.: Rutgers University Press, 1987), 193.
48. Woolf, letter of 26 September 1922 (*Letters* 2.203).

7

Unspeakable Voice:
Toni Morrison's
Postmodern Authority

Toni Morrison is far too talented to remain only a marvelous recorder of the black side of provincial American life. If she is to maintain the large and serious audience she deserves, she is going to have to address a riskier contemporary reality.

—SARA BLACKBURN, Review of *Sula*, in the
New York Times

Critics generally don't associate black people with ideas. They see marginal people; they just see another story about black folks. They regard the whole thing as sociologically interesting perhaps but very parochial.

—TONI MORRISON, Interview, in
Black Women Writers at Work

I begin with these passages in order to suggest the struggle for authority faced by black women writing publicly in white/male-supremacist North America. As African-American feminist critics of the past two decades have made amply clear, devaluation, neglect, and misreading of black women's writings are pervasive practices in which white men, white women, and black men have taken part.[1] In

1. See, for example, Barbara Smith, "Toward a Black Feminist Criticism," *Conditions* 2 (1977): 25–44; Deborah E. McDowell, "New Directions for Black Feminist Criticism," *Black American Literature Forum* 14 (1980): 153–59; Alice Walker, *In Search of Our Mothers' Gardens:*

a society where "All the Women are White, [and] All the Blacks are Men,"[2] fiction by and about African-American women has been marginalized not only as insufficiently "universal" but as insufficiently "female" and insufficiently "black": African-American female voice becomes officially "unspeakable."

Yet in this negating environment Toni Morrison has forged what is by any standard a brilliant career as a novelist whose "verbal authority," as Margaret Atwood said, seems widely to "compel belief."[3] Morrison has testified that constructing such authoritative fiction has meant the complicated negotiation of a narrative quandary. On the one hand, she has been "forced to resort" to certain "strategies" in order to "accommodate the mere fact of writing about, for and out of black culture while accommodating and responding to mainstream 'white' culture" so that potentially hostile readers have no time "to wonder 'What do I have to do, to give up, in order to read this? What defense do I need, what distance maintain?' " On the other hand, she must sustain "a deliberate posture of vulnerability to those aspects of Afro-American culture that can inform and position [her] work," a vulnerability that relies "for full comprehension on codes embedded in black culture" and thus "effect[s] immediate co-conspiracy" with black readers.[4] Morrison is describing the construction of a double-voiced text, like the bride's letter of my first chapter, that African-American readers can decode while white readers think they have done the same. If we rewrite Dale Spender's distinction between private and public discourse in racial terms, Morrison's primary narratee is a "private" one—she once described her writing as "village literature"—which must be filtered through a potentially resistant "public" audience. The consequences for such filtering are evident, for example, in the suppression of anger that Mary Helen Washington identifies in *The Bluest Eye* and which she explains "as a complicated

---

Womanist Prose (New York: Harper and Row, 1983); *Conjuring: Black Women, Fiction, and Literary Tradition,* ed. Marjorie Pryse and Hortense J. Spillers (Bloomington: Indiana University Press, 1985); Mary Helen Washington, *Invented Lives: Narratives of Black Women 1860–1960* (New York: Doubleday, 1987); Bell Hooks, *Talking Back: Thinking Feminist, Thinking Black* (Boston: South End Press, 1989); and *Wild Women in the Whirlwind: Afra-American Culture and the Contemporary Literary Renaissance,* ed. Joanne Braxton and Andrée McLaughlin (New Brunswick, N.J.: Rutgers University Press, 1990).

2. *But Some of Us Are Brave: Black Women's Studies,* ed. Gloria Hull, Patricia Bell Scott, and Barbara Smith (Old Westbury, N.Y.: Feminist Press, 1982).

3. Margaret Atwood, "Haunted by Their Nightmares" (review of *Beloved*), *New York Times Book Review* (13 September 1987), 50.

4. Toni Morrison, "Unspeakable Things, Unspoken: The Afro-American Presence in American Literature," *Michigan Quarterly Review* 28 (1989): 26, 33.

response to the dilemma of being a black writer whose audience is primarily white. Is it possible," she asks, "to tell a 'black' story without taking the sensitivities of the white audience into account and somehow trying to assuage their fears and anxieties?"[5] Nor are white people Morrison's only "potentially hostile" audience; few reviews are as unforgiving as Stanley Crouch's castigation of *Beloved* as a novel "designed to placate sentimental feminist ideology" in which the narrative is "perpetually interrupt[ed]" with "maudlin ideological commercials."[6] And the narrative project becomes even more complicated when the work seeks not only to be published and recognized but to challenge the foundations of fictional and social authority.[7]

It is Morrison's engagement within a literary culture that is not only predominantly white and androcentric but philosophically "postmodern" with which this chapter is concerned. A number of African-American critics have explored the oral and communal qualities of Morrison's narrators, their use of a black cultural idiom, and their racial politics.[8] My focus here, in keeping not only with the emphasis of this study but with my limited perspective as a white reader of works coded to speak as much around me as to me, is upon this question: Through what narrative strategies does Morrison authorize, in ways that seem to have been persuasive for most of her "private" and "public" readers, narrators who are not only implicitly black and female but overtly authorial, at a historical moment when narrative authority has been radically compromised? I will suggest that Morrison "accommodat[es] and respond[s] to mainstream 'white' culture" not only politically but formally by constructing a narrative stance that reconfigures authority in "postmodern" terms. In suggesting that Morrison seizes a particular literary-historical moment in which her vision of narrative authority converges with and transforms "mainstream" possibilities, I am also speculating that what I will describe below as a certain kind of postmodern novel—a novel that recognizes the radical contingency of all authority and the limits of a positivist

---

5. Mary Helen Washington, "Toni Morrison," in *Black-Eyed Susans/Midnight Birds* (New York: Doubleday, 1990), 58–59.

6. Stanley Crouch, review of *Beloved*, in *The New Republic* (19 October 1987). On black men's responses to Morrison, see Calvin Hernton, "The Sexual Mountain and Black Women Writers," in *Wild Women in the Whirlwind*, 202–3.

7. Morrison, "Unspeakable Things, Unspoken," 33.

8. See, for example, Joseph T. Skerrett, Jr., "Recitation to the *Griot*: Storytelling and Learning in Toni Morrison's *Song of Solomon*," in *Conjuring*, 192–202; Valerie Smith, *Self-Discovery and Authority in Afro-American Literature* (Cambridge: Harvard University Press, 1987); and Washington, *Black-Eyed Susans/Midnight Birds*, 55–59 and 77–79.

world view—may offer possibilities for authorizing hitherto "unspeakable" voices that realism (and even modernism) did not provide.

Morrison is by no means the first African-American woman to write novels in an authorial voice or to use it for ideological purposes openly concerned with race and sex. The narrative difficulties Morrison describes in directing African-American authorial voice toward "potentially hostile" white readers are already evident in the first known novel published by an African-American woman: Harriet Wilson's *Our Nig: or, Sketches from the Life of a free Black in a Two-story White House, North. Showing that Slavery's Shadows Fall Even There* (1859). At a time when, as I suggested in Chapter 5, other narrators were making wide use of authorial strategies, Wilson's narrator evokes the "gentle reader" only rarely and cautiously, and she reserves her strongest ideological statements for the discourse of characters rather than for the narrator's own voice. Through such strategies the novel is able, for example, to use free indirect discourse to condemn its own implied readers, the "professed abolitionists who did n't want slaves at the South, nor niggers in their own houses, North. Faugh! to lodge [a black]; to eat with one; to admit one through the front door; to sit next to one; awful!"[9] Rather than defending her heroine openly, the narrator usually lets Frado authorize herself; she tells us, for instance, that Frado *"felt* herself capable of elevation" rather saying Frado *was* capable (124, my italics). In short, read alongside other antislavery novels of the period such as Stowe's *Uncle Tom's Cabin* and William Wells Brown's *Clotel, or the President's Daughter* (1853), *Our Nig* is markedly cautious in its use of authorial voice.

In the 1890s the intersection of African-American and feminist movements fostered an extensive social and literary activism among African-American women, some of whom also pioneered in turning American fiction toward openly political and intellectual purposes. Like Wilson directing their works explicitly to an audience that included whites, Frances E. W. Harper hoped in *Iola Leroy, or Shadows Uplifted* (1892) to "awaken in the hearts of our countrymen a strong sense of justice," and Pauline Hopkins sought through *Contending Forces* (1899) to "cement the bonds of brotherhood among all classes and all complexions" by portraying "the inmost thoughts and feelings

9. Harriet Wilson, *Our Nig* (New York: Random House, 1983), 129. I will discuss this novel more fully in Chapter 11.

of the Negro" that were "as yet, unrecognized by writers of the Anglo-Saxon race."[10] Yet both novels carefully contain their representations of female authority. While Iola Leroy is a passionate advocate for her race and sex, she is usually the lone female voice in a dialogue among men, an exceptional figure with a white father, a white education, and the option to "pass." In *Contending Forces* the sexual division is even more conservative: in a chapter called "The Sewing Circle," women discuss "the place which the virtuous woman occupies in upbuilding a race," while such chapters as "The American Colored League," "Will Smith's Defense of His Race," and "The Canterbury Club Dinner" engage men in questions of public politics. Hopkins's unsigned preface to *Contending Forces* similarly qualifies her own narrative as a "humble" effort to create a "simple, homely tale, unassumingly told," and implicitly contrasts its author to "men of brilliant intellects" who serve as "historians, lecturers, ministers, poets, judges and lawyers." Scholar William Still's patronizing introduction to *Iola Leroy*, which "confess[es]" his "doubts" that Harper could write a novel "of merit and lasting worth to the race" (11) and circumscribes the audience for this "interesting, moral story-book" to "the thousands of colored Sunday-schools in the South" (13), similarly undermines Harper's authority.

   Nonetheless, these novels represent the first moment when African American women are engaged in the ambitious intellectual project I described in Chapter 5: the construction of diverse fictional "worlds" whose narrative voices mediate the imperatives of knowing and judging associated with the realist enterprise. They aim, in other words, to re-present African-American people and experiences "as they are"—in their diversity—and at the same time guide the reader's judgment toward what "should be." Insofar as they are addressed to a white readership in a virulently racist Jim Crow society, however, such novels face the narrative dilemma of authorizing a discursive community that is identifiably African-American within the frame of a realist ethic dependent on the construction of a superior narrator for whom the "King's English" is a master sign. It is therefore not surprising that in both *Iola Leroy* and *Contending Forces* the narrator and the most authoritative characters are educated African-Americans

10. Frances Harper, *Iola Leroy* (1892; reprint, Boston: Beacon Press, 1987), 282; and Pauline Hopkins, *Contending Forces: A Romance Illustrative of Negro Life North and South* (Boston: The Colored Co-operative Publishing Company, 1900; reprint, Miami: Mnemosyne, 1969), 14. Further references to both novels will appear in the text.

whose voices are indistinguishable formally from those of educated whites: in this historical moment, the sign of narrative authority is a language without traces of social or culture difference. The equality/difference dilemma of which I spoke in relation to Eliot is enacted here in racial terms.

At the same time, however, *Contending Forces* and (especially) *Iola Leroy* work against this association of authority with privileged-class English culture through techniques of polyphony that mitigate the realist conventions by which the narrator is the highest authority and the characters' positions are contingent upon their relationship to that authority. The novels rely heavily on dialogue, and both extend ideological authority to unlettered former slaves. This polyvocal dialogue among characters and their "contending" ideologies, which can be contrasted to those realist novels like Eliot's in which the narrator occupies a more solitary ideological position, presents textual authority much less as an individual construction than as the collectively created consensus (or nonconsensus) of a community.

Yet within the hierarchical structures of the realist novel, any project to authorize characters outside the social hegemony is already undermined by the conventions of narrative form. As Judy Grahn observes, "an outside and all-knowing narrator...speaks standard English while quoting characters who speak what is called 'dialect' or slang, or people's English.... [as if to say] that the occupation of writer belongs only to the upper class and those who can *pass* by using its standards; no one else need apply—except as a *character*, an object to be quoted and described, and in effect, looked down upon from a class distance."[11] The containment of black vernacular in *Iola Leroy* and *Contending Forces* to orthographically marked and framed "dialect" is an emblem of a larger containment of folk cultures in novelistic worlds where social and textual success is measured by educated white standards. Such a practice leaves formally unchallenged the implied race and class of realism's "generic" voice, the overarching consciousness that adopts an authorized language in order to forge a collusion between narrator and narratee.

When modernism and feminism began in the early twentieth century to deconstruct the divine right of such a narrator, African-American women writers faced challenges more complicated than

11. Judy Grahn, "Murdering the King's English," introduction to *True to Life Adventure Stories* (Oakland: Diana Press, 1978), 10–11.

those facing such novelists as Woolf and Richardson. The call by Harlem Renaissance writers for a specifically African-American literary vernacular allowed a writer like Zora Neale Hurston to transform narration itself into a black medium—to use words and images that would identify her narrative voice as African-American and perhaps also as female. As I shall discuss in chapter 11, however, Hurston's narrators are still distinguished from her characters, whose discourse is rendered in a vernacular that contrasts visibly to the narrator's grammatically and orthographically standard text. And while the Harlem Renaissance did give Hurston and other African-American women writers a validation for new representations of both narrators and characters, the movement remained predominantly masculinist. A writer such as Hurston with a woman-centered vision thus faced reactions both within and outside the Renaissance similar to those Woolf faced inside and outside Bloomsbury, while the novels of Jessie Fauset, which like those of Dorothy Richardson usually represent a single female consciousness, have according to Deborah McDowell been wrongly consigned to a genteel and conservative "narrow groove."[12]

The decades of Morrison's career coincide with another convergence of African-American and feminist movements that intersect with a very different moment in the history of narrative voice: the moment I am calling "postmodern." The postmodern aesthetic, as it is associated with hegemonic literature in the United States especially after 1960, presses modernist skepticism to an extreme: while modernism understood narrative authority as conditional, postmodernism finds it a sham. Meaning is now not merely contingent but indeterminate, and the notion of a narrator as a textual "higher" authority—or of any textual figure as privileged knower—becomes not merely hollow but absurd. Yet the "postmodern" decades have also been a time of new discursive activity by previously suppressed communities who might be less enthusiastic than hegemonic writers about dispensing with narrative authority. Attempting to explain the paucity of experimentalist, antimimetic fiction by contemporary feminists, Bonnie Zimmerman argues persuasively that such groups understandably seek "to create an authoritative voice, not to undermine an already existing one."[13] Clearly, to accept or celebrate the demise of

12. Deborah E. McDowell, "The Neglected Dimension of Jessie Redmon Fauset," in *Conjuring*, 87.
13. Bonnie Zimmerman, "Feminist Fiction and the Postmodern Challenge," in *Postmodern*

all narrative authority is of questionable value for creating "art forms" that, as Morrison hopes, still "have much work to do."[14]

Yet the very shift in discursive relations of power that enables the emergence of hitherto marginalized voices exposes the constructed and conditional status of all authority, just as the "demise" of white male narrative voice stand as a cautionary tale against reproducing realism's fiction of godly authority in the name of a different god. I am speculating that the success of once disauthorized voices engaged in political transformation within a "postmodern" literary environment has depended on their ability to reconstitute the grounds of knowledge and judgment in terms compatible with, if not transformative of, late-twentieth-century Western consciousness. Mark Edmundson calls this a "positive postmodernism" in which the recognition "that we live in a world without stable truths or the possibility of transcendency" becomes an "*opportunity . . .* for people to invent themselves anew."[15] Alan Wilde gives the name "midfiction" to forms that avoid the extremes of "naive" realism and antimimetic experimentalism by attempting to create from "a world that is itself, as 'text,' ontologically contingent and problematic," with provisional "enclaves of value in the face of—but not in place of—a meaningless universe."[16] For Wilde, whereas contemporary realism "illustrates, somewhat meagerly, the arts of coping and survival," a resigned and "resentfully cynical acquiescence to things 'as they are' and, so it is implied, must be," and whereas the "boisterous deconstructions" of "experimentalism" have "left us with emblems of a world hardly less narrow and restricted," midfiction "responds, with a greater sense of risk, by acts of redefinition and creation, by an imaginative reinterpretation of the place human beings hold, or may hold, in the world."[17] Both Edmundson's and Wilde's formulations thus understand "postmodernism" to be capable of generating not only hedonistic reflexivity or unqualified despair but determined reinvention and qualified hope. Challenging the Eurocentrism of conventional constructions of

---

Fiction: A Bio-Bibliographical Guide, ed. Larry McCaffery (Westport, Conn.: Greenwood Press, 1986), 176–77. McCaffery's book is extremely androcentric, listing only ten women in his "guide" to 106 authors and critics. The list does include Morrison and Walker.

14. Morrison, "Unspeakable Things, Unspoken," 33.

15. Mark Edmundson, "Prophet of a New Postmodernism: The Greater Challenge of Salman Rushdie," *Harper's* (December 1989), 62–63.

16. Alan Wilde, *Middle Grounds: Studies in Contemporary American Fiction* (Philadelphia: University of Pennsylvania Press, 1987), 34; Wilde, *Horizons of Assent: Modernism, Postmodernism, and the Ironic Imagination* (Baltimore: Johns Hopkins University Press, 1981), 148.

17. Wilde, *Middle Grounds*, 4, 108.

the postmodern, Cornel West also calls for "possible critical positions" through which African-American culture "can be viewed as sites of a potentially enabling yet resisting postmodernism."[18]

All three of these critics, from different vantage points, lay an implicit theoretical ground for redefining postmodernism—or distinguishing one of its main tributaries—in terms of the politically and culturally oppositional. Although Alan Wilde names Toni Morrison along with Max Apple, Grace Paley, Jerome Charyn, Stanley Elkin, Don DeLillo, Russell Banks, and Robert Coover, he does not suggest that "midfiction" might have a particular relevance or urgency for silenced or dominated communities. Edmundson associates his "positive postmodernism" primarily with "bicultural" writers like Salman Rushdie, Gabriel García Márquez, and Milan Kundera though he does not mention the bicultural position of African-American writers like Morrison. West remains skeptical about whether the "parochially" white term "postmodern" can be usefully reclaimed, and I share his uncertainty even though I will use the term in this chapter to designate a generalized literary vision with permutations that may be rooted in the experiences of specific communities. I want to speculate that certain groups of writers are especially drawn to "midfictional," "enabling yet resisting" forms of the postmodern because several ironies associated with postmodern consciousness—that subjectivity is not coherent and singular, that "freedom" may not always liberate nor "choice" provide alternatives, that not everyone (or anyone) is the "master of [her] fate," that events may not have rational explanations—are also philosophical implications of the historical experience of African-Americans, Holocaust survivors, colonized peoples, and other displaced and dominated groups. This, I believe, is one reason why the philosophical positions of some people of color parallel (and predate) those of some white poststructuralists despite obvious divergences in political commitment and theoretical terminology.

It is the compatibility of "midfictional" postmodern values with a major impulse in contemporary political consciousness that I want to posit as an enabling basis for Toni Morrison's bicultural narrative authority. Just as the realism of Harper and Hopkins suited a moment in which many African-Americans saw education and "uplift" as viable paths to racial equality, so postmodernism may recognize realism's—

18. Cornel West, "Black Culture and Postmodernism," in *Remaking History*, ed. Barbara Kruger and Phil Mariani (Seattle: Bay Press, 1989), 96.

and with it Western humanism's—failed promises for rational reform. Morrison's novels change the terms of narrative authority by deconstructing the rationalist humanism that grounds the realist novel and reconstructing authoriality in ways that seem to me to exploit the space where a hegemonic postmodern sensibility converges with an African-American politics. Through shifts from the double narrative structure of *The Bluest Eye* to the complex "fluidity" of *Beloved*, authoriality remains a powerful practice in Morrison's novels, but the white narratee's position becomes increasingly marginalized and ironized and the use of Western culture as a source of authority virtually disappears.

The narrative choices Morrison has faced as a bicultural United States novelist begin, as my discussion of Hopkins and Harper might suggest, at the level of orthography. Instead of opposing "dialect" and "white English," Morrison's narrators adopt a vernacular that is neither dialect nor white; "black language," Morrison has said, means for her "not so much the use of non-standard grammar" as "the manipulation of metaphor."[19] While some of Morrison's characters do use vernacular grammatical and lexical forms that the narrator herself does not employ, the novels do not translate the inflections of spoken Black English into a deviant typography, eliminating a visual class distinction between narrator and characters. This egalitarian narrative surface is also enabled by the narrator's register: all of Morrison's narrators speak a colloquial, conversational discourse that makes each one a persona(lity) among personalities: "Corinthians was naïve, but she was not a complete fool"; "Women who drink champagne when there is nothing to celebrate can look like that: their straw hats with broken brims are often askew; they nod in public places; their shoes are undone"; "A joke. A nigger joke. That was the way it got started . . . Still, it was lovely up in the Bottom"; "Yet there was this heavy spice-sweet smell that made you think of the East and striped tents and the *sha-sha-sha* of leg bracelets."[20]

This choice of register for her narrators supports Morrison's insistence in several interviews that her own voice is authorized in and

19. "An Interview with Toni Morrison Conducted by Nellie McKay," *Contemporary Literature* 24 (1983): 427.

20. See, respectively, *Song of Solomon* (New York: Knopf, 1977), 191; *Beloved* (New York: Knopf, 1987), 50; *Sula* (New York: Knopf, 1973), 4–5; and *Song of Solomon*, 185. *Tar Baby* is also published by Knopf (1981), and *The Bluest Eye* by Holt, Rinehart, and Winston (1970). All further references to the novels will appear in the body of the text.

through African-American community.[21] I propose that Morrison's
first novel, *The Bluest Eye* (1970), constitutes an authorizing preface
for that voice by acknowledging the necessity, for a readership that
has suffered from centuries of external misrepresentation, of establishing a narrator's social identity. I read this novel, the only one that
will have a place in all three sections of this book, as Morrison's self-
locating entry into literature (as *Northanger Abbey* was for Austen) at
a time when, as Morrison says, no one was authorizing or even authoring African-American female experience. By constructing both
the personal voice of Claudia MacTeer looking back on her childhood
and the omniscient voice of an authorial narrator, Morrison creates
in *The Bluest Eye* a double and alternating structure—two voices, two
sets of titles, even two different typographies (one narrative has right-
justified margins; the other does not). But in the novel's last section
these narrators seem to converge: the typography reserved previously
for the authorial narrator is adopted by a voice that appears to be
Claudia's but speaks as "we." The convergence of the two narrators
at the end of *The Bluest Eye*, which had been suggested all along by
the strong similarities in their diction and imagery, legitimates personal experience as the basis for authorial voice. Such a project deconstructs the conventional opposition between "first" and "third"
person, mimetic and diegetic voice, at once authorializing the personal
and personalizing the authorial. In this humanizing of the authorial
narrator that is reminiscent of Eliot's early novels, the distance of a
century is profoundly measurable: while *Clerical Life*'s witness is an
elderly white gentleman, Morrison's is a young black girl.

None of Morrison's subsequent novels has used a personal narrator;
except for a brief middle section of *Beloved*, Morrison has turned since
The Bluest Eye to the authorial mode favored by Austen, Eliot, and
Woolf. Read as Morrison's prefatory novel, however, *The Bluest Eye*
authorizes subsequent "Morrison" narrators as African-American
women and also undermines the conventions of narrative omniscience
in a manner Eliot's early novels only suggest—for if Claudia is also
the "omniscient" narrator, how can she, a character, know the other
characters' private stories and intimate thoughts? Claudia's knowledge
of the Breedloves and Soaphead Church must rest on a different
foundation: her "omniscience" must come not from superhuman understanding but from social experience. Austen's and Woolf's nar-

21. Morrison, interview by Nellie McKay in *Contemporary Literature*, 425.

rators play from time to time with conventions of omniscience, pretending to lack the knowledge narrators are supposed to possess.[22] While these strategies mock assumptions of narrative godliness, Morrison's more radical gesture undermines conventional narrative possibility: if "omniscience" is redefined as imagination grounded in collective experience, it is also limited by the human inability to make sense of the nonsensical and explain the inexplicable.

For it is not simply narration but Western realist epistemology that Morrison's narrators undermine. Using authorial structures to make clear that certain kinds of authority may be futile or impossible, the narrators of the first two novels deconstruct realism, while the later narrators reconstruct the "real" on different ground. *The Bluest Eye* and *Sula* embody the (postmodern) recognition that realism cannot finally explain human actions or prescribe solutions in the way that postbellum novels like *Iola Leroy* sought to do. At the beginning of *The Bluest Eye* (1970), Claudia questions the very foundation of realist ideology—the presumption that one can know and therefore judge: "There is really nothing more to say—except why. But since *why* is difficult to handle, one must take refuge in *how*" (9). The novel tells the outcome of the story before it begins, leaving a series of questions: why did Cholly rape his daughter Pecola, why did Pecola want blue eyes, why didn't marigolds blossom in the fall of 1941? In "answering" these questions, however, the authorial narrator piles up explanations that replicate the chaos of life rather than the clarity of art. Thus we learn about Pauline's lame foot, her lonely childhood, her need for crayons, her rotten tooth, her fascination with movie stars, her experiences of racism in the North, her marital unhappiness, her longing for the order she finds only in the white house with its pink and yellow child. All of this information overdetermines her role in Pecola's tragedy and makes it impossible to assign causes to effects or to delineate clear boundaries of responsibility. What Valerie Smith calls the "hard questions—why Black Americans aspire to an unattainable standard of beauty; why they displace their self-hatred onto a communal scapegoat; how Pecola's fate might have been averted"—the narrator does

---

22. Austen's narrators claim as early as *Lady Susan* to lack certain kinds of information about their characters, and Woolf's narrators are often so unwilling to own conventional narrative knowledge that Erich Auerbach mock-laments that Woolf "does not seem to bear in mind that she is the author and hence ought to know how matters stand with her characters" but acts "as though the truth about her characters were not better known to her than it is to them or to the reader." In *Mimesis* (Princeton: Princeton University Press, 1953), 469, 472.

not even try to explain.[23] As she describes the impossibility of making order of Cholly's life, Morrison's narrator could be speaking as well of her own refusal of causalities:

> The pieces of Cholly's life could become coherent only in the head of a musician. Only those who talk their talk through the gold of curved metal, or in the touch of black-and-white rectangles and taut skins and strings echoing from wooden corridors, could give true form to his life. Only they would know how to connect the heart of a red watermelon to the asafetida bag to the muscadine to the flashlight on his behind to the fists of money to the lemonade in a Mason jar to a man called Blue and come up with what all of that meant in joy, in pain, in anger, in love, and give it its final and pervading ache of freedom. Only a musician would sense, know, without even knowing that he knew, that Cholly was free. (125)

This acknowledgment is compatible with the creation of a narrative voice like the eyewitness Claudia's, which can imagine but never really know her characters with certainty, but it also suggests the unrepresentability of African-American subjectivity or perhaps any subjectivity in a linear, verbal form.

Sula (1973) takes the opposite strategy: rather than overloading the novel with causes, the narrator underexplains and leaves the most important narrative events to the realm of mystery. The narrator never tells us the truth about Eva's amputated leg; about whether and why Sula "watched her mother burn"; about what Shadrack did and did not understand; just as she tells us that it is "for no earthly reason, at least no reason that anybody could understand," that Helene Wright "smiled dazzlingly and coquettishly at the salmon-colored face of the conductor" (21) in the white railroad car. And even where race, sex, or class can explain characters' reactions (for example, the workers' disillusionment with the tunnel), Sula herself remains the figure of unknowability and the narratee remains dislodged from any comfortable complicity with a "superior" narrative voice. In a delicate balancing of political conviction and postmodern skepticism, the narrator suggests that although racism and sexism are certainties, human behavior remains only partially amenable to explanatory forms. I do not mean to suggest that realist novelists such as Eliot supply causalities, even complex ones, for every narrated act—I think, for example,

23. Valerie Smith, "The Quest for a Discovery of Identity in Toni Morrison's *Song of Solomon*," *Southern Review* 21 (1985): 731–32.

of Gwendolen Harleth's inexplicable terrors—but Morrison uses authorial voice as the explicit mechanism for questioning and rejecting the explanations that authorial voices are supposed to provide. Since it is the narrator whose voice announces these inexplicabilities, however, her own authority is not diminished but merely altered in the shift to assert the unknowable. Like Eliot, Morrison creates a syntax of authority in tension with a semantics of abdication; narrative stance in *Sula* entails knowing—and proclaiming—what it is that cannot be known. If (in keeping with their different moments) the authoritative syntax is more pronounced in Eliot, the refusal of explanation is more pronounced in Morrison.

The over- and underexplanation represented respectively in the narrative practices of *The Bluest Eye* and *Sula* provide the initiating extremes that lead Morrison's next novels from a refusal of rational explanation to the assertion of what realism has designated nonexistent or impossible. The events of *The Bluest Eye* are firmly grounded in empirical verisimilitude; everything that happens in the novel is plausible, and "magic" is only a desperate girl's delusion perpetrated by a misguided and embittered old man. Nothing that breaches realist convention occurs in *Sula* either, but the magical is suggested, for example, in the "plague of robins" that accompanies Sula's return to Medallion and in Shadrack's preternatural consciousness. And although in *The Bluest Eye* tragedies are determined by social circumstance, the inexplicable haunts *Sula* as it haunts Sula herself: Chicken Little's and Hannah's deaths remain pointless postmodern accidents that are horrifying precisely because they frustrate and thus expose conventional novelistic rationality.

But Morrison's next three novels selectively reject empirical or even "psychological" realism in favor of the "magical" modes represented in such works as García Márquez's *One Hundred Years of Solitude*. *Song of Solomon* (1977) creates a "magical" character in Pilate as part of a project to expose the inadequacy of white European ways of knowing and the wisdom available only through folkloric and mystical sources associated especially with women and Africa and never fully articulable: "I don't know who and I don't know why. I just know what I'm telling you: what, when, and where" (42), Pilate says. *Tar Baby* (1981) does not transgress verisimilitude on the level of plot, but its narrator pushes authorial omniscience beyond the divine posture of white realism by representing the thoughts not only of characters but of animals and plants: she insists that "the clouds looked at each other,

then broke apart in confusion" (10), discusses the feelings and behavior of bees and sky (82), and comments archly, after Jadine has
said "horseshit," that "the avocado tree standing by the side of the
road heard her and, having really seen a horse's shit, thought she
had probably misused the word" (127). Such uses of narrative authority either elaborately mock realist omniscience, or they establish
this narrator as even more godlike than the narrators of the white
West. *Beloved* goes further still, incorporating the spirit world as the
cornerstone of its plot and hence as the narrator's most direct responsibility: Beloved's return from the dead must be accepted or the
entire story fails. Since white racism is responsible for this ghost and
perhaps all the ghosts in which white folks are unlikely to believe—
"not a house in the country ain't packed to its rafters with some dead
Negro's grief" (5)—the inadequacy of Western epistemology is here
exposed through the consequences of its cruelest practices of dominance.

These various movements into the rationally unknowable place a
particularly strenuous demand on narrative authority. In realist fiction, characters may imagine the "magical," but the narrator's superiority lies precisely in refraining to corroborate such imaginings as
truth. But in the last three novels and most dramatically in *Beloved*,
Morrison's narrators must authorize the supernatural or "magical" if
the narrative is to exist at all. In *Song of Solomon* the narrator takes
some care not to assert directly what an audience schooled in European empiricism would find incredible. While the narrator uses authorial voice for speculation—for example, telling us that "it must
have been Mr. Smith's leap from the roof over their heads that made
them admit" Ruth to the white hospital (5)—when there is "magic"
to report, she usually takes refuge in free indirect discourse, locating
herself on one side or the other of a fine line of accountability. The
narrative makes sense only if Pilate actually has no navel, but the
narrator represents this information as Macon Dead's indirect perception in which her own participation is indefinite: "After their
mother died, [Pilate] had come struggling out of the womb without
help from throbbing muscles or the pressure of swift womb water.
As a result, for all the years he knew her, her stomach was as smooth
and sturdy as her back, at no place interrupted by a navel. It was the
absence of a navel that convinced people that she had not come into
this world through normal channels..." (27–28). The narrator's
stance toward Pilate's alleged supernatural gifts is even more equiv-

ocal: Pilate, she says, "*was believed* to have the power to step out of her skin, set a bush afire from fifty yards, and turn a man into a ripe rutabaga—all on account of the fact that she had no navel" (94, my italics). In *Beloved* the narrator also hedges: she tells us that "a fully dressed woman walked out of the water," but does not tell us who that woman is; tells us she had "new skin, lineless and smooth," but does not tell us why (50). She does not participate in the characters' attempts to explain Beloved empirically, but neither does she assert in her own voice, as the community does, that "baby ghost came back evil" (267). And after the climactic confrontation at 124, the narrator restricts herself only to other people's perceptions: "Paul D knows Beloved is truly gone. Disappeared, some say, exploded right before their eyes. Ella is not so sure" (263). Yet the very telling of this story requires the narrator's belief, which is finally signified in the novel's last word, "Beloved," uttered unambiguously in the authorial voice. African in its cosmology, the novel's deconstruction of empiricism is also compatible with what Hans Bertens calls a "mystical attunement" in Western postmodern consciousness.[24]

There is a similar convergence of African-American consciousness with European postmodern sensibility in the ways in which Morrison "maximizes" this deconstruction and transformation of realist authority. All of Morrison's narrators generalize at least occasionally in their own voices and more frequently through the indefinite free indirect discourse of characters. But while modernist constraints on Woolf's narrative practices could be circumvented, for example, by dispersing abstract generalizations among her characters, Morrison writes at a moment when the problem is not simply which voice is allowed to generalize, but whether any generalizations can claim validity. Morrison uses two particularly important strategies for instituting the "maxims" that are crucial to her political aims. The first is locating such commentary in a concrete instance, which is narrated in the past tense and rendered it specific to a particular group, rather than resting such comment upon a superior narrator's claim to know the way things universally "are." For example, the openness of the pronoun "they" in this passage in *The Bluest Eye*, purportedly about Aunt Jimmy's friends, evokes the experience of African-American women generally: "Everybody in the world was in a position to give

24. Hans Bertens, "The Postmodern *Weltanschauung* and its Relation with Modernism: An Introductory Survey," in *Approaching Modernism*, ed. Douwe Fokkema and Hans Bertens (Amsterdam: John Benjamins, 1986), 28.

them orders. White women said, 'Do this.' White children said, 'Give me that.' White men said, 'Come here.' Black men said, 'Lay down.' The only people they need not take orders from were black children and each other. But they took all of that and re-created it in their own image...(109). Even brief and aphoristic comments are often historicized—"as always the Black people looked at evil stony-eyed and let it run" (*Sula*, 113)—to give the narrator a didactic latitude that postmodern fiction disavows. At the end of *The Bluest Eye*, for example, the narrator takes several paragraphs to identify the community's complicity in tragedies like Pecola's; the past-tense discourse transforms the general to the apparently specific: "we were not free, merely licensed; we were not compassionate, we were polite; not good, but well behaved" (159). Morrison has insisted, in language reminiscent of Eliot's, that she tries "to avoid editorializing emotional abstractions" in favor of letting her readers "see the person experiencing the thing."[25] These passages do editorialize emotional abstractions, but they operate simultaneously in narrative contexts that let us "see the person experiencing the thing."

Second, Morrison synthesizes postmodern consciousness with African-American politics when she uses a generalizing discourse of negation to "Signify" upon racism in America.[26] While the generalizations of Woolf's and Eliot's narrators are almost always positive assertions, Morrison's narrators exercise a kind of negative omniscience by asserting a knowledge of what is not there and what is not possible. In a discursive gesture something like the young bride's, Morrison uses a double-voiced syntax to juxtapose African-American deprivations to white American opportunities. *The Bluest Eye*, for example, opens with a typographical deconstruction of the Dick-and-Jane myth, moving from "Here is the house. It is green and white. It has a red door" to the irregular but still readable "Here is the house it is green and white it has a red door" to the chaotic and bitterly ironic "Hereisthehouseitisgreenandwhiteithasareddoor." Morrison's narrators thus represent white privilege as the shadowy presence against which their black characters must struggle both materially and psychically. The discourse of negation that *Northanger Abbey*'s narrator

25. Morrison, interview in *Black Women Writers at Work*, ed. Claudia Tate (New York: Continuum, 1983) 127.
26. I am using "Signifying" here to designate a coded, double-voiced verbal act specific to African-American culture, which glosses, challenges, ironizes, dismantles, or otherwise revises another verbal act. See Henry Louis Gates, Jr., *The Signifying Monkey* (New York: Oxford University Press, 1988), 44.

performs as lighthearted literary parody—for example, in distinguishing the ordinary Morelands from the heroic families of fictional fantasy, Morrison's narrator turns to tragedy as she describes the Breedloves' lodgings in terms of the life they cannot sustain:

> There is nothing more to say about the furnishings. They were anything but describable, having been conceived, manufactured, shipped and sold in various states of thoughtlessness, greed, and indifference.... No one had lost a penny or a brooch under the cushions of either sofa and remembered the place and time of the loss or the finding.... No one had given birth in one of the beds ... No thrifty child had tucked a wad of gum under the table....
> There were no memories among those pieces. Certainly no memories to be cherished. (31–32)

Such narrative acts, disrupting the conventions of novelistic description, expose the legacy of material absence that racism has forced on the African-American community so that it becomes visible to the text's readers even when it remains unrecognized by the characters. Thus in *Song of Solomon*, we learn that "Bryn Mawr had done what a four-year dose of liberal education was designed to do: unfit [Corinthians] for eighty percent of the useful work of the world.... After graduation she returned to a work world in which colored girls, regardless of their background, were in demand for one and only one kind of work," and so Corinthians "never let her mistress know she had ever been to college or Europe or could recognize one word of French that Miss Graham had not taught her" (190–91). Similarly, *The Bluest Eye*'s narrator tells us that Pauline "missed—without knowing what she missed—paints and crayons" (89) and that the men who marry girls like Geraldine who aspire to white ideals "do not know ... that this plain brown girl will built her nest stick by stick, make it her own inviolable world, and stand guard over its every plant, weed, and doily, even against him" (69). In this way, the narrator is asking her (white?) readers to know through negativity and gaps the horrors of deprivation and suffering.[27] *Beloved* goes further still, inverting the ideology of slavery so fully that it becomes quite clear who are the "animals" and who are human beings: the "jungle" that became the

----

27. Such a practice is present in at least one novel by a black female predecessor, Jessie Fauset's *Plum Bun: A Novel without a Moral* (1928; reprint, London: Routledge/Pandora, 1985), whose very title announces the ironic definition-by-negation practiced earlier by Austen and later by Morrison. See, for example, the description of Opal Street that opens the book.

racist trope for Africa gets exposed as a construction by which white people have dehumanized themselves: "The screaming baboon lived under their own white skin" (199).

In the movement from *The Bluest Eye* to *Beloved*, which is also a movement away from the fictions of Western epistemology that exposes the racist foundations of the culture in which those fictions have flourished, Morrison makes another critical move: her narrators increasingly refuse to accommodate a white audience. In "Unspeakable Things, Unspoken," Morrison accounts for the differences in attitude that, she says, led her from the carefully explanatory practices that begin *The Bluest Eye* to the refusal of *Beloved*'s opening sentence to explain anything. One sees this refusal as well in a gradual decrease in her novels of the kind of Western intertext I have associated with writers such as Sarah Fielding and George Eliot, as allusions to Roman and Christian characters and rituals give way to African names and cosmologies. In this change Morrison is in effect making her work less bicultural, giving white readers less and less familiar material on which to ground readings that would assimilate her novels to a white tradition and "universalize" what is historically particular. If it is possible to read *Sula* (though not *The Bluest Eye*) as a novel about "evil" in ways that the narrator does not insist are wholly attachable to race,[28] the evils represented in *Beloved* are unquestionably linked to the pan-Evil of slavery. If *Sula* provides the white narratee a space in which race is not central, *Beloved*'s narrator denies its narratee any such racially unmarked space, any location outside the anguished memories of slavery; the multiplicity of perspectives filtered as free indirect discourse through the narrative voice disallows the safety of distance, while narrative comments make clear who is responsible for the horrors the novel represents. Perhaps *Beloved* is finally the novel without those separate private and public narratees, as if the American bride has forced her husband to read the letter in the "right" way without handing him the key. Perhaps this, finally, is what it means to speak the unspeakable: to return narrative to the site of a black woman's silencing by naming at once the crimes and the criminals who have wrought that silencing, and from the fragments of "rememory" to make voice whole, not falsely coherent but free from narrative servitude.

28. Morrison, interview in *Black Women Writers at Work*, 118.

Part II

PERSONAL VOICE

I understand the secret of the third person, who...can bring down more reality upon herself than the first person: I. The difficulty of saying "I."

—CHRISTA WOLF, *The Quest for Christa T.*

What would happen if one woman told the truth about her life?
The world would split open

—MURIEL RUKEYSER, "Käthe Kollwitz"

8

Dying for Publicity:
Mistriss Henley's Self-Silencing

"Oh, none of this really matters," Mr Henley said, smiling.
"But it matters to me!"
—ISABELLE DE CHARRIÈRE, *Lettres de Mistriss Henley*

So it is better to speak
remembering
we were never meant to survive.
—AUDRE LORDE, "A Litany for Survival"

I argued in my discussions of Riccoboni's writings that the epistolary voices produced in the eighteenth-century "heroine's text" offered a very limited fiction of female authority. Nevertheless, women writing from the late seventeenth to the late eighteenth century seem to have avoided the public form of personal voice represented by novels such as *Robinson Crusoe, Tristram Shandy* and *Les Égarements du coeur et de l'esprit*. Fictional memoirs such as Jane Barker's *Love Intrigues* (1713), Mary Hearne's *The Lover's Week* (1718) or Eliza Haywood's "secret histories" were, as Haywood's generic title implies, addressed to private narratees, locating the (unacknowledged) public reader as eavesdropper or voyeur. Ironically, if not surprisingly, the first European novels in which a female narrator addresses a public narratee seem to have been man-made—Defoe's *Moll Flanders* (1722) and *Roxana* (1724)—and the way in which Defoe's "editor" tampers with his heroines' texts (as he does not tamper with Crusoe's) suggests precisely the constraints that may have inhibited women from producing public

voice. While Richardson and Marivaux construct "editors" who claim
to be mere transcribers, Defoe's mock-editor seeks to compensate for
the insufficiency of his narrating characters; he styles himself a "Re-
lator" who will put Moll's and Roxana's stories "into new words" so
they might be properly "prepared for the World"— "dressed up" in
order to "keep clear of Indecencies and immodest Expressions," and
"made to tell [their] own tale in modester words than [they] told it at
first."

In light of these suggestions that a woman's discourse must
be covered up, the virtual absence of public personal voice from
eighteenth-century novels by women suggests that the dichotomy between public/male and private/female discourse holds for personal as
well as authorial voice: a "proper" woman does not narrate her own
story to an audience that includes (strange) men. A male editor is one
obvious device for "clothing" the narrator's nakedness and might have
kept Defoe from being conflated with his heroines, but writers known
to be female have had to contend with readers who identify first-
person narrators with the authors who created them. Such an equation
of author and narrator seems to me more likely to occur when narration is public rather than epistolary, for by repeating the names of
the sender and receiver, the epistolary form makes a visible distinction
between the letter-writer and the novelist. In public narration, in
contrast, the narrator appears primarily as an "I" and speaks to an
unidentified and readerly "you," thus mirroring the narrative situation of nonfictional autobiography and encouraging readers to conflate
writer and character in ways that anonymous publication, and fluid
boundaries between fact and fiction, could only reinforce.[1]

I want to speculate that in the wake of the solidifying sexual spheres
that I described in Chapter 2, constructing the personal narrator as
a married woman might have been a particularly problematic enterprise. As both Ossery's appropriation of Juliette Catesby's pen and
the bride's letter of my first chapter vividly illustrate, the voice of the
married woman has not been unequivocally her own; could such a
voice be trusted if an insistence on happiness were suspect and an
account of unhappiness unseemly or even dangerous? Moreover, notwithstanding the second half of *Pamela*, there was little precedent in

---

1. The dearth of fictional autobiography by eighteenth-century women is at odds, at least
in England, with the emergence of factual autobiographies both spiritual and "scandalous."
See Felicity Nussbaum, *The Autobiographical Subject: Gender and Ideology in Eighteenth-Century
England* (Baltimore: Johns Hopkins University Press, 1989).

eighteenth-century fiction for representations of ordinary married life. The woman writer who would construct an authoritative personal-voiced novel about marriage might face multiple challenges: to find shape for a fiction that by conventional standards would contain either the "trivial" or the unspeakable; to balance the powers of publicity with the protections of privacy by preserving a distinction between author and narrating character; and to sustain narrative reliability in a system where marriage asks a woman to submerge her public identity beneath a man's. These challenges form the implicit agenda of Isabelle de Charrière's *Lettres de Mistriss Henley, publiées par son amie* (1784), possibly the first novel by a European woman to attempt even a quasi-public personal voice, which in its very effort to move outside epistolarity surpasses *Juliette Catesby* in exposing female voice as impotent and marriage as (living) death. While Riccoboni was financially constrained to repeat masterworks that she could undermine only subliminally, the aristocratic Charrière was able to take on a specific novel and through her countertext enter public debate about women's rights.[2] *Mistriss Henley* suggests that the way out of the marriage plot is through public voice, but it represents marriage as the very prohibition of that publicity; paradoxically, then, it is only through an act of self-silencing that Mistriss Henley can "speak."

Lettres de Mistriss Henley begins where the conventional courtship plot ends: with marriage to a storybook husband, a "mari de roman."[3] Charrière wrote this book to disarm one particular and popular "mari de roman": the victim-hero of Samuel Constant de Rebecque's epistolary novel *Le Mari sentimental, ou le mariage comme il y en a quelques-uns* (1783).[4] Constant's narrator, a sensitive and contented middle-aged bachelor named Bompré, marries a wife so domineering and foolish that she destroys his happiness and ultimately his life through increasingly serious misdeeds, from removing his father's portrait to selling his favorite horse, causing the death of his dog, dismissing his most faithful servant, destroying his relations with neighbors and

2. Joan Stewart makes a similar contrast in "Sex, Text, and Economic Exchange: *Lettres neuchâteloises* and *Lettres de Milady Juliette Catesby*," *Eighteenth Century Life* 13 (February 1989): 60–68.

3. Isabelle de Charrière, *Lettres de Mistriss Henley*, in *Oeuvres complètes* (Geneva: Slatkine, 1980), vol. 8, 101. All further references will appear in the text. The English text is sometimes my own, sometimes from an unpublished translation by Jack Undank.

4. Samuel Constant de Rebecque, *Le Mari sentimental ou le mariage comme il y en a quelques-uns* (1783; reprint, Milano: Cesalpino-Galiardica, 1975).

relatives, and finally accusing him publicly of seducing a peasant girl to whom he has in fact extended charity. In a grotesque exaggeration of woman-worship, Bompré continues through all of his wife's treachery to insist that she is "reasonable," merely exercising the "rights of her sex," and that all the "errors" are his own. Abandoned and disgraced, completely "subjugated to a woman's rule [l'empire d'une femme]," Bompré finally sees no choice but suicide.

Charrière's novel disrupts Constant's narrative configuration by giving voice not to the upright husband but to the restless wife, who is represented as the victim of her husband's very righteousness through a dissociation of "right" (*raison*) from "reason" (*raison*) that provides a new interpretation of a woman's "wrongs." Mrs. Henley's proclaimed motive for this anatomy of marriage is her concern for women readers who, "simply because they are women," she says, will blame themselves, while men (simply because they are men?) will all believe they are beleaguered Bomprés. This sense of collective injustice becomes the pretext for publicizing a personal history: although the title announces a private correspondence between confidantes, and although the work is technically a series of letters, this is not a conventional epistolary novel claiming to expose discovered documents never meant for public eyes. Instead, Mrs. Henley conceives her story as a public narrative and her confidante as a channel to that public readership. That is, in order to create a mechanism for making her voice public without speaking publicly, Mrs. Henley sets aside some "light scruples" and asks her narratee to become her translator-editor, to turn English autobiography into French *roman à clef*, and not incidentally to adopt a language that Mrs. Henley has already suggested her husband cannot read:[5] "Shall I tell you what occurs to me? If my letter or letters strike you as authentic, and if they stand a chance of arousing some interest, translate them into French—but change the names, and omit whatever you find boring or irrelevant" (102). In this way the private narratee becomes the editor—implicitly Charrière herself—and the text a collaborative work in which fiction is openly presented as a mask for autobiography. What we are reading as the *Lettres de Mistriss Henley*, then, is presumably that translated and edited version already prepared for private protection and public display.

5. Charrière notes that her novel was widely taken to be either biography or autobiography: "Never did fictional characters seem so real; everyone was asking me for explanations as if I knew more of these characters than what was on paper." In a letter to Gérard Godard Taets van Amerongen van Schalkwijk (January 1804), in *Oeuvres*, vol. 6, 559 (my translation).

The novel underscores its public status by omitting epistolary trap-
pings—datelines, salutations, signatures, small talk, even the addres-
see's name—in favor of simple headings ("TROISIEME LETTRE") that
resemble the chapter divisions of a public text.

Mrs. Henley's history is explicitly designed to break down the gen-
der/genre dichotomies that keep women's voices private and powerless
and shield men from women's criticism of patriarchal practices: "I
believe there are many wives [*femmes*] in my predicament. I would
like, if not to change their husbands, at least to inform and warn
them; I would like to set things straight again and have everyone
submit to what is just. [Je crois que beaucoup de femmes sont dans
le même cas que moi. Je voudrois, sinon corriger, du moins avertir
les maris; je voudrois remettre les choses à leur place, & que chacun
se rendît justice.]" (102). In this way Mrs. Henley becomes one of the
first personal narrators in Western fiction explicitly to bind her life
to the lives of other women, to see hers as a general case, and to seek,
if through elaborate subterfuge, a public audience that includes men.
She harbors as well some ambivalent desire to reach her own husband:
"No one will recognize Mr. Henley; he probably won't ever read what
I have written, and if he did, if he ever recognized himself! . . . " (102).

Mrs. Henley represents herself as an educated but orphaned young
woman in need of a husband (and thus for gender-specific reasons
different from the older M. Bompré, who had no need of a wife).
She has already lost "everything a woman can lose" through the infidelity and death (by syphilis) of her childhood sweetheart, and she
is convinced that the other men around her are her intellectual and
spiritual inferiors. Socially and financially desperate, she foregoes an
ambivalent attraction to a pleasure-loving sophisticate who has made
his fortune by exploitations in the West Indies,[6] for a "fully reasonable
happiness" with the landed and titled country widower Mr. Henley,
whom all her acquaintances ("toutes les voix") proclaim to be the ideal
match: a "witty, elegant, modest, gracious, affectionate" man "of reason, learning, fairness" and "perfect equilibrium" (103–4). This split
between personal desire and public judgment lies at the heart of the
novel's conflict as the very qualities that make Mr. Henley a "mari de
roman" become precisely the source of his wife's misery. While Constant's Madame Bompré represented an inept and dangerous female

6. The colonialist dynamics of the novel are complex: although at first it seems that this
suitor is to be rejected on moral grounds, he later turns up as "Governor Bridgewater" and
a member of Mr. Henley's social set.

rule, it soon becomes apparent that "Mistriss" Henley commands nothing at all. In the aptly named Hollowpark, custom, law, common sense, and his own paternalism all designate Mr. Henley as his wife's superior.

Such a consequence of "storybook" marriage exposes the traditional novel's courtship plot as that "ceaseless repetition of the Preliminaries" that Charlotte Perkins Gilman considered hardly "any sort of picture of a woman's life,"[7] and turns the ground of domestic tragedy away from "important" concerns such as adultery and abuse. Mrs. Henley is continually aware that, as the (surprisingly similar) narrator of Gilman's *The Yellow Wallpaper* would put it, "my case is not serious!"[8] At the start she avows that she has "no serious complaints" to make about her husband; later, reporting that "everyone admires Mr Henley and congratulates me on my good fortune," she acknowledges herself "all the more unhappy for the fact that I have nothing to complain of, no change to request, no one but myself to reproach for my unhappiness" (107). In the fourth letter, despite her discomfort, the narrator recognizes that this piling up of "little things" is the necessary foundation for her narrative: "I carry on, my dear friend, about uninteresting things—and at great length, and in great detail! —But that is the way they come to mind, and I would feel I had told you nothing if I did not tell you everything. Little things are precisely what both irritate me and cause me to do wrong [d'avoir tort]. Here then is a pack of little things" (112). Since this focus on "little things" accompanies an insistence that "beaucoup de femmes sont dans le même cas," the *Lettres de Mistriss Henley* suggests the basis for a new and oppositional narrative form in which domestic "trivia" are exposed as a source of oppression in women's lives. As Virginia Woolf wrote much later, "when a woman comes to write a novel, she will find that she is perpetually wishing to alter the established values—to make serious what appears insignificant to a man, and trivial what is to him important. And for that, of course, she will be criticized." In other words, "This is an important book, the critic assumes, because it deals with war. This is an insignificant book because it deals with the feelings of women in a drawing-room."[9]

7. Charlotte Perkins Gilman, *The Man-Made World: or, Our Androcentric Culture* (New York: Charlton, 1911), 94, 96, 102.
8. Charlotte Perkins Gilman, *The Yellow Wallpaper* (1892; reprint, Old Westbury, N.Y.: Feminist Press, 1972), 14.
9. Virginia Woolf, "Women and Fiction," in *Women and Writing*, ed. Michèle Barrett (New

In rewriting both *Le Mari sentimental* and the conventional courtship novel, Mrs. Henley must rewrite both literary and moral value as she enters the contemporary debate about female rationality and its political implications for women's rights. Mrs. Henley and Constant's Bompré accuse themselves of "wrongs" (*torts*) in ways that are ironically but very differently misplaced. Bompré claims to be "wrong" for disagreeing with his wife; actually he *is* "wrong" to be enslaved against his better judgment by an exaggerated reverence for "the sex." In fact, Constant's novel never presents a real conflict between right and wrong because however "wrong" M. Bompré may be, his wife is never right. Bompré's own language suggests as much, since his acceptance of her "right" is always hypothetical: "ma femme a de l'esprit, *donc* elle a de la raison" or "Mme Bompré a de l'esprit; elle *aura* de la raison" (94, 103; my italics). Such remarks challenge the very existence of female reason, a challenge underscored by Bompré's lengthy excursus on women's inability to master science and philosophy (letter 7). The conflict that besets the "mari sentimental," then, is that of a man of feeling whose reason fails him in the face not of "right" but of a distorted surrender to a capricious woman whose behavior is then used to prove women unfit to rule.

In responding to this representation Charrière does not invert the old opposition of irrational woman to rational man by creating an irrational husband and a rational wife. Her gesture is rather more subtle and more radical: she challenges the linguistic and moral yoking of "right" and "reason" (*raison*) and with it the Enlightenment justification for patriarchal rule. In the first conflict between the Henleys, when the narrator decorates her five-year-old stepdaughter with baubles and Mr. Henley disapproves, this moral structure is made clear: "You are right, Sir; I was wrong [*vous avez raison*, Monsieur; *j'ai eu tort*]" (104). In these early pages of the novel the words "raison" and "tort" become an insistent refrain in which Mistriss Henley deplores her "torts," which are "even worse than I believed" (108), and tells her husband, over and over, "you are right."

This very repetition, however, gives the discourse a double voice: the weight of Mistriss Henley's statements begins to expose the oppositions "right" and "wrong" as a matter less of truth and fault than of power and resistance: "I tell the truth, but I am wrong" (107).

York: Harcourt Brace Jovanovich 1980), 49, and *A Room of One's Own* (New York: Harcourt Brace, 1929), 77.

Eventually Mrs. Henley lets herself question openly so many "wrongs": "Could he be right, my dear friend? Could I be wrong again, wrong forever, wrong in everything? No, I don't believe it" (111). But Mrs. Henley is *not* always reasonable—she is often outspoken, fanciful, impetuous—so that if she is not to be wrong, then reason must be acknowledged not always to be right. Certainly she has begun to find Mr. Henley's very perfection a source of misery: "a punching would be better than all this reason/right [des coups de poing me seroient mois fâcheux que toute cette raison]" (107). "Right" and "wrong" have begun to reverse themselves; to be wrong, if it is not yet to be right, is at least to be human, feeling, interesting.

As this questioning of Mr. Henley's "rights" that begins in the privacy of Mrs. Henley's letters erupts into the plot, it also becomes clear that her critique of pure reason cannot in itself undermine the balance of marital power: the Henleys' differences in personal value and taste assume the force of moral absolutes in the face of the husband's dominance. Thus, as Mistriss Henley struggles to assert herself in small matters of domestic life, she finds that Mr. Henley *is* right after all, because power is his. The novel's challenge to the linguistic coupling of "right" and "reason" becomes, therefore, a challenge as well to the coupling of "woman" and "wife" in *femme*. The first major conflict reveals the futility of the narrator's complex efforts to "right" herself in a system where the different meanings of *femme* also yield different meanings of right. The issue that generates the conflict is a "trivial" matter of dress rooted in the larger question of Mistriss Henley's right to her body; it is therefore also a question of which meaning of *femme* shall prevail. Disapproving her choice of costume for a longawaited ball, Mr. Henley remonstrates that "a woman of twenty-six should not dress like a girl of fifteen, nor a wife like an actress" (112). Yet when her sister-in-law appears at the ball in similar dress, he expresses no disapproval because "she is not my wife" (115). And although he responds to her protests by trying to dismiss the entire issue as trivial (see my epigraph to this chapter), it must be remembered that he is in fact the one who brought it up.

The extremes between which Mistriss Henley fluctuates in her response to this episode suggest the impossibility of negotiating the literally unutterable difference between "woman" (*femme*) and "wife" (*femme*). When her flirtations at the ball fail to distress her husband, she first attacks him for coldness—"the injustices of a jealous man, the excesses of a brute, would be less annoying than the impassivity and sterility of a sage"—and then grovels when she realizes her step-daughter has been listening: "Pardon, Sir! Pardon, dear child!...I set a bad example...I should have taken the place of your mother ...yet I say in your presence things that you are fortunate not to understand!" (116). Here are the extremes of eccentricity and imitation that Claudine Hermann associates with feminine discourse: even as the woman explodes in excess, the wife/mother imposes conformity. Female subjectivity is so visibly split that having finally voiced her anger and misery, Mistriss Henley must punish herself with submissiveness. Whose, then, is the married woman's voice?

This conflict between assertion and self-effacement gets "resolved" by an assertion *of* self-effacement as Mistriss Henley enacts a caricature of wifely submission in a letter she writes to her husband immediately after this episode. The draft, which she sends to her correspondent, is an erasure-filled palimpsest that parades its self-censorship; there are "almost as many words erased as words left in" (117). First, flinging the loaded words "raison" and "tort" at her husband at last, accusing him of the "wrong" of marrying a woman he so clearly disdains, she announces a refusal of "reason" itself: "a reasonable woman could not help but be happy" but "I am not a reasonable woman" (117). To be "unreasonable," however, means admitting to the very arguments by which contemporary philosophy has reasserted the subordination of woman to man—what Kant describes as the "natural superiority of the husband's faculties compared with those of the wife," a superiority that Kant among many other philosophers proclaims as the sole basis for "the right [of a husband] to command."[10] And so it is not entirely a contradiction that in the face of this political double bind Mistriss Henley takes the desperate measure of empowering her own impotence: she "chooses" her husband's "natural superiority" and stages an aggressive erasure of her own will by asking him to become her conscience, to help her "arrange my conduct in a way that will compensate for my greatest wrongs" (117). She, in turn, will work to understand what he wants without his having to tell her so, and if she fails, he is simply to "tell me what you would like me to do in place of what I am doing" (118).

In this way, like Juliette Catesby but with the crucial difference of manifest irony, Mrs. Henley substitutes a man's sense of right and wrong for her own in order to become a proper "femme," enacting

10. Immanuel Kant, *The Philosophy of Law* (Edinburgh, 1887), I: 24–26.

a grotesque exaggeration of wifely submission as if to expose—to her narratee if not to Mr. Henley— the marriage price. For clearly this bitter gesture is a submission in name alone, indeed in *his* name alone, since the narrator signs her letter to her husband only "S. Henley," withholding the proper name. The process here is more insidious than Ossery's appropriation of Juliette's pen: Mistriss Henley does not need a husband to write for her because she will compose his version of her herself. Her voice, and by implication women's writing to men with power over them, is flagrantly compromised. Such self-erasure in the name of marriage means, of course, that *Lettres de Mistriss Henley*, much more openly than *Juliette Catesby*, redefines marriage as death, a death underscored when Mr. Henley responds only obliquely and uncomprehendingly to this carefully crafted letter of surrender from his wife. It is no coincidence that just after this episode Mistriss Henley begins to find writing to her female friend onerous, as if she can no longer operate in the space explicitly designed to separate "woman" from "wife." Such a separation, in other words, is now as impossible psychically as linguistically: the married woman's voice is only a fiction of autonomy.

It is Mistriss Henley's strength and hence also her tragedy, however, that she is unable simply to submit; she must still test her husband's authority at every turn, as if to make clear to herself or her reader how "wrong" he is. Her pregnancy, announced joyfully in the brief fifth letter, provides the occasion for the final erasure of the woman and writer beneath the wife. The sixth letter narrates a series of conversations that reveal the degree to which Mistriss Henley is courting her own psychic death in a display of either a doomed desire for her husband's approval or a perverse desire for his hostility. First she divulges her anxieties about nursing her infant and discovers that "of myself, my health, my wishes" Mr. Henley utters "not a word: it was only a question of this child who did not yet exist" (120). Then she blurts her fantasies of raising a daughter whose "brilliant talents, cultivated by the most striking education, would arouse the admiration of the entire country or even of all Europe" (120) and she is devastated when Henley insists that he wants his daughters trained for domesticity: "modest, gentle, reasonable, compliant women/wives and careful mothers" (121)—*Hen*-ley girls indeed. Since there is no possibility for Mrs. Henley to alter the marital relations of power that govern her opportunities, such moments can only reproduce the same insoluble confrontation between "right" and "wrong."

It is in dashing his wife's fantasies about a daughter who would live the life Mrs. Henley has been denied that Mr. Henley delivers the climactic revelation: he has turned down an appointment at Court and hence shattered her dream to escape the isolation and boredom of Hollowpark. So painful is this news that even in recounting it Mistriss Henley is "forced to put down her pen" (121). Responding with the self-censorship that now marks all her communications with her husband, speaking "slowly with a voice that I forced to be natural" (121), Mrs. Henley is able to find out that his reasons are predictably righteous ones: politics might corrupt him, or make him dissatisfied with provincial life when he has to return to it. He is only telling her about the appointment, in fact, for the sake of marital appearances, the matter having become, "pour ainsi dire, publique" (122). Should she hear the news from others, he fears that she "might be too affected by it, and show too publicly, by an initial reaction of regret, that husband and wife are not one in spirit, do not have a common way of feeling and thinking" (121). It is not her "chagrin" but its public representation that he wants to avoid; if husband and wife are properly one, and that "one" is the man, then insofar as Mrs. Henley fails to speak her husband's discourse she fails as a wife. For Mr. Henley, a woman's voice *is* properly a fiction reflecting a husband's will; a wife cannot *have* a personal voice.

Mrs. Henley's response to her husband's proof of control over her destiny only confirms this lack of authority as the puppet-voice affirms her husband's rectitude: "I revere you, sir, I said, and in effect I had never revered him more; the harder it was for me, the more I revered him; the more I revered him, the more distinctly I saw his superiority" (121). Like M. Bompré, Mrs. Henley pays homage to the spouse who is destroying her, but Mistriss Henley's spouse, unlike Bompré's, still has "toutes les voix" on his side. The price for Mistriss Henley's capitulation to this hegemony is appropriately the loss not only of voice but of consciousness: "I wanted to say something, but I had been so attentive, so torn between esteem for so much moderation, reason, rectitude in my husband and the horror of finding myself so estranged in his sentiments, so fully excluded from his thoughts, so useless, so isolated, that I could not speak. Exhausted by so much effort, I grew faint and passed out" (122).

This self-silencing of the character becomes the grounds for the self-silencing of the narrator as well: the sixth letter begins and ends with announcements that it will be her last. The woman who once wrote freely and urgently is now too "tired" to continue telling her "long and hardly pleasant" (119) tale. At this moment she also recognizes openly that her story can be read in two different ways: "Either everything I feel is absurd, or Mr. Henley is insensitive and unyielding" (120). Yet these different readings yield equally "frustrating" alternatives: she can "blame a fate [le sort] that I cannot change, or blame and despise myself" (119). The two readings are not really opposed because if one interpretation accuses the woman, the other stops short of accusing the man. If "fate" and not Mr. Henley is responsible, then to relive her miseries in discourse—"par mes récits" (119)—can have no personal benefit. Since Mrs. Henley still has no authority, the letters leave her paralyzed by a heightened consciousness that only deepens her despair. Here private personal voice is not just impotent, as in Riccoboni's novels; it is insidious, for it produces knowledge that cannot be translated into material change.

It is appropriate, then, that Mrs. Henley refuses either to continue her narration or to resolve her misery.[11] She will not follow Bompré into suicide because "je ne suis qu'une femme": only a woman? only a wife? the two words have collapsed anyway. But there is no need for outright suicide, since "sorrow also kills"; the last letter ends with the prediction that "in a year or two, you will learn, I hope, either that I am reasonable and happy, or that I no longer exist" (122). Since this is clearly no "reasonable" woman, and since any happiness could be only a masquerade, one way or the other Mistriss Henley "dies." In this sense the ending is not open at all, and it is fitting that the translator-editor provides no concluding epilogue. Marriage kills, and marriage is deadliest with a husband who (unlike Ossery) is by conventional (fictional) measures without fault. What is playful subtext in *Juliette Catesby* is dark and open here: the condition of *femme* is the condition of silence; Mistriss Henley's "choice" to be silent only repeats the conditions of her "choice" to be a wife.

In denying its heroine an official death, *Lettres de Mistriss Henley* refuses to end with one of the large disasters on which the eighteenth-century novel usually relies: adultery, abandonment, abuse, rape, financial ruin, kidnapping, illness, suicide. In substituting for the large gesture the daily "little things that afflict or frustrate me" (112), Charrière engages in an act of fictional revision that parallels her revision

---

11. On this refusal of closure see Susan K. Jackson, "The Novels of Isabelle de Charrière, or, A Woman's Work Is Never Done," *Studies in Eighteenth-Century Culture* 14 (1985): 299–306.

of *Le Mari sentimental* and of the traditional opposition of irrational woman to rational man. It seems no accident that this novel was written in the 1780s, the decade of wide and high revolutionary fervor that was to yield after the French Revolution to the sexual and political conservatism I described in Chapter 4. At least in Charrière's own upper-class and cosmopolitan Swiss community, early reaction to the *Lettres de Mistriss Henley* was divided primarily along lines of sex; it "caused a schism in Genevan society. All the husbands were for Mr. Henley, most of the wives for Madame; and the young ladies didn't dare say what they thought."[12] One male reviewer may have been speaking for many men when he judged the novel an " '*inviting yet cruel little book*' excellent in literary quality but in my opinion morally dangerous in several ways."[13] Predictably, this novel born in rebuttal also spawned a rebuttal of its own: in 1785 there appeared a *Justification de M. Henley*, which continued the debate initiated by *Le Mari sentimental*. Thus a novel such as *Mistriss Henley*, written explicitly against the patriarchal text in order to "put things back in place" could only enter an endless oppositional struggle for which there was as yet no solution either fictional or historical; this is why going "beyond the Preliminaries" to make a truer "picture of a woman's life" was likely to end in narrative death, and it may also be why Charrière turned, as I will suggest in the next chapter, to a safer, Wertherian fiction in her next book.

There is, however, a crucial positivity to Mistriss Henley's self-silencing, for the "death" of Mistriss Henley's private voice is of course the condition for the very life—the publication—of her history. According to the contract established with the narratee in the first letter, the cessation of the letters is the precondition and signal for the narratee to translate and publish them. Just as the bride of Chapter 1 finally had to transfer to her confidante the possibilities for resolving the married woman's plight and plot—"may you be as blest as I am unhappy"—so here the letters, in becoming public, transfer to other women who are "dans le même cas" the tenuous possibility of change. In this case, self-silencing is not simply an end, as it is for the narrator of *L'Abeille*, or even the prelude to an unwritten story, as it is when

---

12. Letter to Gérard Godard Taets van Amerongen van Schalkwijk (January 1804), in *Oeuvres*, vol. 6, 559 (my translation).

13. Cited in Charrière, *Oeuvres*, vol. 2, 420. This comment was passed on to Charrière in a letter from her husband of 15 June 1784. The phrase "aimable et cruel petit livre" is drawn from the first sentence of *Mistriss Henley* and refers there to *Le Mari sentimental*.

Juliette Catesby writes her last words of desire to Henriette; here a private self-silencing is the very condition for public voice. Thus, even as Mistriss Henley moves from speech to silence, marking the death of voice as the correlative to a woman's transformation into a wife, Charrière's novel reverses the process by restoring that voice to its proper—which is to say public—place.

9

Romantic Voice: The Hero's Text

> I did not make myself the heroine of my tales. Life appeared
> to me too common-place an affair as regarded myself. I
> could not figure to myself that romantic woes or wonderful
> events would ever be my lot.
> —MARY SHELLEY, *Frankenstein*

> I am utterly and completely Lélia.
> —GEORGE SAND, Letter to Sainte-Beuve

> Genius has no sex.
> —GERMAINE DE STAËL, Letter to Benjamin
> Constant

When Isabelle de Charrière wrote the *Lettres de Mistriss Henley* as an
immediate response to *Le Mari sentimental*, she was interrupting the
longer novel that would become her best-known work—the *Lettres
écrites de Lausanne* (1785) and its sequel, *Caliste, ou suite des lettres écrites
de Lausanne* (1787). The double title of this novel is no casual choice:
it figures deep dualities that critics and readers have usually "resolved"
by renaming the entire novel *Caliste*. The work begins as a series of
letters by an anonymous Mme de *** about her daughter Cécile's
(economically necessary) foray into the marriage market, but just
when a serious and troubling match seems to be developing between
Cécile and the Englishman Edouard, this plot is abandoned for a long
narrative about the ill-fated love of Edouard's cousin William for a
woman he calls Caliste. In this way, a courtship story narrated by a
woman turns into a Romantic tragedy narrated by a man.

This split in both story and discourse, underscored by the abandonment of Cécile's history at its moment of greatest intensity, marks a larger turning point in the history of narrative: a displacement of female personal voice that will characterize European fiction for half a century. If the eighteenth-century novel is the "heroine's text," the Romantic novel is even more fully the hero's,[1] for Romanticism gives new primacy to the singular voice representing the singular (if non-coherent) subject who "holds the center of works whose primary purpose is the presentation of his character."[2] To the list of novels I named in Chapter 2—*Pamela, Clarissa, Moll Flanders, La vie de Marianne, La Religieuse, Julie ou la nouvelle Héloïse, Fanny Hill*—European Romanticism counterposes titles like *René, Adolphe, Obermann, Die Leiden des jungen Werthers, Hyperion, Heinrich von Ofterdingen, Alastor, La confession d'un enfant du siècle*. This narrative masculinization is far more complete than any feminization that preceded it, for while eighteenth-century fiction gave place and voice to male figures from Crusoe, Des Grieux, and Grandison to Tristram Shandy, Humphry Clinker and Valmont, Romanticism's "great myths"—Prometheus, Satan, Faust, Don Juan, Napoleon—are ineluctably male,[3] and women figure in high Romantic fiction almost entirely as repressed "others" virtually without voice. Femininity is of course routinely bound to the male subject in the Romantic images of the twin and the androgyne, but the central figure in this union remains male; woman is muse, object or servant of the male quest, source of sorrow or ecstasy, at best the man's double, a "narcissistic projection" of himself.[4] Goethe's Werther, Chauteaubriand's René, Byron's Childe Harold, Musset's Octave, Constant's Adolphe all absorb "feminine" affectivity into "masculine" genius, unconventionality, physical and sexual freedom,

1. I intend here a traditional understanding of "Romanticism" rather than a redefinition that might account for writers and texts of the period from 1780 to the 1830s who are usually excluded from Romantic canonicity. I retain the traditional conception because I see Romanticism as a male-centered movement in which women struggled against severely masculinist biases. See, for example, Margaret Homans, *Women Writers and Poetic Identity: Dorothy Wordsworth, Emily Brontë, and Emily Dickinson* (Princeton: Princeton University Press, 1981); and Marlon B. Ross, "Romantic Quest and Conquest: Troping Masculine Power in the Crisis of Poetic Identity," in *Romanticism and Feminism*, ed. Anne K. Mellor (Bloomington: Indiana University Press, 1988), 26–51. On redefining Romanticism, see Stuart Curran, "Romantic Poetry: The I Altered," in *Romanticism and Feminism*, 185–207, and Marlon Ross, *Contours of Masculine Desire: Romanticism and the Rise of Women's Poetry* (New York: Oxford University Press, 1989).

2. Lilian Furst, *The Contours of European Romanticism* (London: Macmillan, 1979), 43.

3. Lloyd Bishop, *The Romantic Hero and His Heirs in French Literature* (New York: Peter Lang, 1984), 19.

4. James D. Wilson, *The Romantic Heroic Ideal* (Baton Rouge: Louisiana State University Press, 1982), 96. See also Leslie Rabine, *Reading the Romantic Heroine: Text, History, Ideology* (Ann Arbor: The University of Michigan Press, 1985).

intellectual and spiritual quest,[5] splitting sensibility from domesticity and thus from the heroine's "sphere."

It does not seem impossible that this subsumption of the "feminine" was in some part a reaction to the increasing presence of female voice in fiction, just as male modernism has been considered in part a reaction to women writers at the end of the next century. But whatever the causes of this shift to a male-centered narrative economy, the result is a virtual disappearance from the novel of female personal voice: just when the single narrating subject becomes most insistently the center of narrative, in other words, that subject becomes masculine.[6] The narrative divide in Charrière's novel tells us that well before *René* and *Adolphe*, and before the post-Revolutionary backlash against women writers and intellectuals that I described in Chapter 4, at least one woman was actively repeating the male-centered personal voice that *Werther* had employed with such electrifying results. Startlingly, not one of the women (or men) associated with high Romanticism seems ever to have published a novel written exclusively in the female personal voice. While it is crucial to examine this absence novel by novel, the larger pattern is an important sign of the complicated relationship of women to Romantic ideology and especially to Romantic subjectivity. The evidence of narrative voice suggests that Romanticism offered women the lure of the universal, the escape from gender and thus from the always-problematic female body by which a woman's genius, spirituality, and freedom were denied. Yet the strategies for this escape from gender ("genius has no sex") end up signifying its impossibility. I do not see the nonachievement of female autodiegetic voice as a refusal of hegemonic authority or subjectivity, as some postmodernist feminists have argued, but rather as a historically situated struggle with contemporary social values and literary forms. Before I turn to the problematic status of female voice in fiction by the three women novelists most closely identified with European high Romanticism—Germaine de Staël, Mary Shelley, and George Sand—I will look briefly at the *Lettres écrites de Lausanne*, with the *Lettres de Mistriss Henley* as a hinge for the novel's two sections, in order to

5. For a recent discussion of this phenomenon, see Margaret Waller, "*Cherchez la Femme*: Male Malady and Narrative Politics in the French Romantic Novel," *PMLA* 104 (1989), 141–51.

6. One could argue that formally speaking the heroine's text made the hero's possible, that the interiority Romanticism celebrates is already configured in female voices such as Clarissa's and Julie's. See Alan Richardson, "Romanticism and the Colonization of the Feminine," in *Romanticism and Feminism*, 13–25.

suggest why some women might have had a stake in a Romantic flight from female voice.

Recognizably the prototype of Staël's Corinne, Charrière's Caliste is a brilliant and talented artist-performer with a "compromised" past, who has become passionately involved with the Englishman William, for whom duty is stronger—or courage weaker—than love. The opposing force is William's father, who disapproves of his liaison with Caliste; all the more because the father has already suffered deeply from the death of William's twin brother, both Caliste and William resign themselves to loveless marriages. But William's father has a belated change of heart, and ironies pile up until at last the unhappy Caliste succumbs to a consumptive death and William himself falls dangerously ill from grief.

Sold by her own mother first to the London stage and then to the keeping of a "gentleman," Caliste is clearly a victim of a particular sexual and political economy; indeed, the consequences of Mme de ***'s warnings to her daughter Cécile are evident everywhere in Caliste's story, and since Caliste too is well born, one could surmise that but for circumstance and mother-love Cécile could be in Caliste's place. But the novel never acknowledges these similarities. The title notwithstanding, William, and not Caliste, is the center of the narrative: it is occasioned by Mme de ***'s concern for his welfare, it begins with his family history, and except for a final letter from Caliste's husband, it proceeds entirely from his point of view. William's version emphasizes not sexual politics but sensibility in an insensible society; his anguished despair overshadows his responsibility for Caliste's misfortunes, and he comes to seem equally with Caliste a victim of circumstance. His final litany of self-accusation ("I ought to have . . . I ought to have . . .") identifies him in Romantically self-aggrandizing language as "the *most worthy* of his unhappiness,"[7] and ultimately it is less Caliste's tragedy than his own that he grieves: "Here I am, then, alone on earth. She who loved me is no more. I hadn't the courage to avert this loss; now I haven't the strength to endure it" (231). Even the final letter from Caliste's husband absolves William, and although there is no further response from Mme de *** in the published volume, in a "suite" found among Charrière's papers the

---

7. Isabelle de Charrière, *Lettres écrites de Lausanne*, in *Oeuvres complètes* (Geneva: Slatkine, 1980), vol. 8, 230. All further references will appear in the text. English translations are my own.

mother who had been so critical of patriarchy's double standards goes to some length to exonerate William: "If you neglected her you neglected yourself as well" (240).

It is through William's narrative dominance, then, that Caliste's plight, manifestly a function of the gender and class politics that Mme de *** exposes, gets re-presented as personal fatality, the suffering of the exceptional soul. The longing for death, which in *Mistriss Henley* was grounded in feminist despair, gets mystified in *Caliste*, and the gender-specific causes of her tragedy disappear, along with William's own culpability, beneath the twinning of William and Caliste as Romantic suicides. Critics have perpetuated this mystification by treating *Caliste* as if it were the entire novel rather than a dependent part and by emphasizing in Charrière's fictional philosophy not a feminist protest, but a Wertherian death wish.[8]

Read against *Mistriss Henley*, however, the unarticulated shift in *Lettres écrites de Lausanne* from a female voice preoccupied with the material plight of women to a male voice preoccupied with the spiritual plight of "men" becomes less curious. The impasse generated by the courtship plot, vividly dramatized in *Mistriss Henley*, makes it virtually impossible for Charrière to bring Cécile's story to a happy end: sexual and economic double standards have already structured her relationships as they structure the Henleys' and, as Jean Starobinski points out, Cécile's suitor Edouard resembles his cousin William in loving less completely than the woman who loves him.[9] The "Romantic death-wish" that Janine Rossard identifies in *Caliste* and associates with "the emptiness of the philosophy of happiness at the end of the eighteenth century; the futility of heroic struggle in this same society; and the impotence of reason"[10] might stem in *Caliste*, as it clearly does both in *Mistriss Henley* and in Charrière's own history, from the particular emptiness of an educated woman's restricted life. Nor was Charrière insensitive to the somewhat different futilities of a poor woman's situation: both *Lettres neuchâteloises* (1784) and *Mistriss Henley* represent working-class women as victims of double standards and indeed of sexual abuse.

But since neither the conventions of the novel nor the society on which Charrière depended were amenable to these feminist questions,

8. See especially Janine Rossard, "Le Désir de mort romantique dans *Caliste*," *PMLA* 87 (1972), 492–98.
9. Jean Starobinski, cited in Charrière, *Oeuvres complètes*, vol. 8, 129.
10. Rossard, "Le Désir de mort," 492. Translation mine.

it is plausible that she might turn to a Wertherian *mal du siècle* in which gender is recuperated into a "universal" (upper-class) malaise. An unpublished epistolary novel that Charrière began in 1796 makes explicit the attractiveness of a Wertherian ethos as an antidote to feminist anxiety: to Emily's reproaches for her romanticism, Harriet retorts, "is it not much safer to love an imaginary object than an unworthy one? I had in mind to say a *real* one.... There, there, is *danger*, true *danger*—As long as I love no body but Werther no dangerous command shall be exerted over me." Although Emily argues, in turn, that "those heroines whose virtues are but paper and ink may be what they please.... Let them have fifty children about them they will not suffer of the head ach [*sic*]," and although Charrière's writings of the 1790s will suggest a return to a materialist ideology, becoming "Werthered" and 'Romanticated" in the mid-1780s allowed Charrière to avoid confronting men as oppressors and to join with them in their quest for the Ideal.[11]

A crucially placed passage in the *Lettres écrites de Lausanne* demonstrates dramatically this slide from the specific and material to the generic and spiritual. Having nursed a black man dying in the neighborhood, Cécile acknowledges, if with some equivocation, the tragic dimensions of colonialism and slavery: "So this is how one ends, Mama...?What a strange lot! to be born in Guinea, to be sold by one's parents, to plant sugar in Jamaica, to serve the English in London, to die near Lausanne!...This poor Negro!" [Quel étrange sort! naître en Guinée, être vendu par ses parens, cultiver du sucre à la Jamaïque, servir des Anglois à Londres, mourir près de Lausanne! ...Ce pauvre nègre!] (187). But she immediately "corrects" herself: "But why say this poor Negro? To die in one's own country or elsewhere, to have lived a long time or a little, to have had more or less trouble or pleasure—there comes a moment when none of this matters: the King of France will be like this Negro one day." [Mais pourquoi dire ce pauvre nègre? mourir dans son pays ou auilleurs, avoir vécu long-temps ou peu de temps, avoir eu un peu plus ou un peu-moins de peine ou de plaisir, il vient un moment où cela est bien égal: le Roi de France sera un jour comme ce nègre.] (187). If the king will be like the slave, then no revolution, no material change, no protest, is needed: in death, social imbalance will equalize itself. Here is the legitimation for Charrière's reconciliation with the status quo, her

11. Isabelle de Charrière, "A Correspondance," in *Oeuvres complètes*, vol. 8, 491, 495, 497.

choice of Enlightenment idealism over the incipient materialism of Revolutionary ideology. If idealism could have served social interests by arguing that the slave and the king must have nothing more or less than equal rights, here a Romantic fatalism turns away from such an opportunity.

It seems therefore extremely significant that this isolated and apparently gratuitous episode of the dying man appears at just the moment when the novel will abandon Cécile's history for the fatal story of Caliste. For the entire *Lettres écrites de Lausanne* repeats the gesture of this episode: while it begins with the specific and political, it ends with the generic and metaphysical, "Romanticating" a woman's material life. What enables this transformation, I believe, is the shift to male voice, the voice of "universal" suffering, which offers Charrière a distance from the feminist impasse her works repeatedly inscribe. At the very least, *Caliste* was able to escape the controversies generated by all three of Charrière's earlier published fictions and to place her in a less embattled avant-garde: it is no accident that her best-known and most-loved work is the *Caliste* section of the *Lettres écrites de Lausanne*.

Yet I will argue that this refuge that generic Romanticism seemed to offer women was also illusory: women could never fully exploit the radical potential of Romantic ideology because the "human" was not the "female." The Romantic woman's "splendid" escape from the body and the body politic into transcendence was, as Margaret Homans also argues, repeatedly undermined or thwarted by Romanticism's double messages.[12] By the turn of the nineteenth century, the association of Romantic subjectivity with male voice had solidified so that constructing a female "Romantic hero" demanded a double overturning of Romantic norms: the displacement of male subjectivity from center to periphery, and the transformation of plot to allow the tropes of Romantic questing a plausible female form. It is these historically situated literary conditions, rather than any antiauthoritarian "feminine" or even feminist refusal of voice, that I believe are responsible for the forms of women's Romantic narratives.

One result is that most women writing from 1790 to 1830 simply did not participate actively in the creation of (what has passed for) Romantic fiction. Jane Austen might be said to have created a Romantic subject in Anne Elliot, who is *Persuasion*'s superior and sen-

12. Homans, *Women Writers and Poetic Identity*, 4.

sitive, lonely and misunderstood outsider-protagonist, but Anne's
longings are always tempered by social morality and are ultimately circumscribed by the marriage quest, and she is not given the utter cen-
trality of personal voice. Other women writers simply repeated the
male Romantic text. Beneath its deceptive title, for example, Barbara
de Krüdener's *Valérie* (1803) is little more than a reproduction of
Werther: Gustave, hopelessly in love with the married Valérie, is at once
the heroic character and the narrating voice, while the loved object who
gives her name to the novel is a nearly silent figurehead. Charlotte
Smith's authorial novel *The Old Manor House* (1793) also creates a Romantic protagonist in the adventurer and sometime poet Orlando,
whose cherished Monimia is little more than his passive double.

I want to turn, however, to the three novelists who do seem to have
attempted, at separate moments across three decades, to create female
counterparts to the Romantic hero's text. Staël, Shelley, and Sand
were all deeply involved both with Romantic thought and with men
who were constructing the kind of subject-centered narratives that I
have been describing. Each of these women wrote a novel in which a
woman is a Romantic hero, but none of them—nor, to my knowledge,
any woman writing Romantically before the 1840s—ever published a
novel written exclusively in the female hero's voice. *Corinne*, *Lélia*, and
Mathilda offer different, autobiographically resonant configurations
for female subjectivity that together sketch in the particular resistances
of high Romanticism to female voice.

It is difficult to overestimate the historical impact of Staël's *Corinne,
ou l'Italie* (1807) in figuring the woman of genius. Undoubtedly and
indeed disturbingly indebted to *Caliste*,[13] the novel constructs its female hero's inner life in ways that Charrière's novel does not ap-
proach. From her first "Improvisation at the Capitol" to her "Last
Song," Corinne's public speeches and private writings are represented
by the authorial narrator (as William almost never represents Caliste's)
and at midtext Corinne and Oswald narrate their personal histories.
Yet from the beginning the novel's dominant focalizing consciousness
is Oswald's; Corinne is seen first and last through his perspective, and
although her thoughts are also represented, Oswald's constitute the

---

13. On the "disturbingly strong resemblances" between *Corinne* and *Caliste* see Madelyn
Gutwirth, *Madame de Staël, Novelist: The Emergence of the Artist as Woman* (Urbana: University
of Illinois Press, 1978), 165–66. Gutwirth considers it "lucky" that Charrière died the year
before *Corinne* appeared, "or else she might have felt that not only her lover [Benjamin
Constant], but her novel as well had been appropriated by her rival."

framing subjectivity. These narrative practices not only distance the female Romantic hero from her creator but authorize Corinne through the perspectives of men. Indeed, the text uses an entire community of voices to prepare for the introduction of Corinne as "a goddess amid the clouds,"[14] and the narrator underscores Corinne's superiority as a "refined sensitive woman . . . with no one to turn to but herself" (338). When the narrator explains that "it is impossible for a woman living independently to be pleased with herself" (129), she may be hinting that the extraordinary woman is never in a position to authorize her own exceptionality. Corinne is thus given the status of Romantic hero but not fully of Romantic subject: hers is the prophetic voice and vision *in* the text without being the prophetic voice and vision *of* the text.

I am not suggesting that Corinne "ought" to have been the novel's narrator or even its dominant focalizing consciousness, or that the work was ever intended to be written otherwise, but I do want to point to the difference between the narrative representation of first-generation Romanticism's most heralded female figure and the figures of such male counterparts as Werther, René, and Adolphe. It is understandable that Staël would adopt an authorial voice for this novel, for as its double title suggests, *Corinne, ou l'Italie* is almost as much the study of a culture as of a character: the work is replete with extensive discussions of literature, history, and art. Yet it is also possible that this broader design was imposed precisely to keep Corinne from "hold[ing] the center" of the text: according to Avriel Goldberger, Simone Balayé's research reveals three complete revisions of *Corinne* that suggest Staël "worked to put a distance between her own life and the world of her novel" (for example, by giving Oswald some of her own history).[15] Marie-Claire Vallois hails *Corinne*'s narrative structure as a fortunate "escape" from "the trap of autobiography, the ritual of confidence and penitence performed by an 'I,' which imprisons once and for all—the trap of the 'I' that could only repeat, as Napoleon would have it, that anatomy is destiny."[16] If Staël did find autobiography a "trap," might this have been because her society would indeed have used the novel to entrap her? As my discussion

---

14. Germaine de Staël, *Corinne, or Italy*, trans. Avriel Goldberger (New Brunswick, N.J.: Rutgers University Press, 1987), 21. All further references will appear in the text.

15. Avriel Goldberger, introduction to *Corinne, or Italy*, lii.

16. Marie-Claire Vallois, "Voice as Fossil: Madame de Staël's *Corinne or Italy*: An Archaeology of Feminine Discourse," *Tulsa Studies in Women's Literature* 6 (Spring 1987): 50.

of Shelley's and Sand's Romantic fictions will make clearer, I find it significant that Vallois sees the female body as the obstacle to personal voice.

Corinne stands, then, as both a sign and a legacy. As a sign, it suggests that the female heroic subject is more easily a thematic than a formal center of narrative; as the most famous "first-generation" construction of female Romantic identity read avidly by both Mary Shelley and George Sand and influential on women writers for decades to come, *Corinne* patterns a formal separation of the female hero from the text's narrative voice and sustains the distinction between female and male Romantic fictions that I have been describing. Shelley's unpublished novel *Mathilda* (1819–20), on the other hand, does reproduce the Romantic pattern of a single personal voice. I will propose that *Mathilda* was made possible for Shelley by the writing of *Frankenstein*, and that the failure of *Mathilda* to be published is not unrelated to the problems of constructing Romantic heroism in female terms.

In its surface manifestations, of course, *Frankenstein* (1818) shares none of the gynocentric impulses of *Corinne* or even *Caliste*: it is virtually a caricature of Romantic male-centeredness. Mrs. Saville, the empty signifier toward which the narrative supposedly directs itself,[17] well represents the place of female subjectivity in this novel: women are peripheral and almost interchangeable figures readily sacrificed to male pursuits, offering tenuous links to a domestic community that most of the male characters claim to honor but repeatedly reject. Except for two letters written by Elizabeth, women's voices figure significantly only on the occasion of Justine's trial, and the result simply underscores their impotence: Elizabeth's words further condemn the woman she is trying to save, and Justine's false confession seals her doom. Despite its array of female characters, then, Rosemary Graham is right to call *Frankenstein* a novel "about a world without women"; it is no wonder that readers were shocked that a woman had authored it.[18] Indeed, the novel is so blatantly male-Romantic

17. For a more positive reading of Mrs. Saville's "emptiness," see Gayatri Chakravorty Spivak, "Three Women's Texts and a Critique of Imperialism," in *"Race," Writing, and Difference*, ed. Henry Louis Gates, Jr. (Chicago: University of Chicago Press, 1986), 278.

18. Rosemary Graham, "For Want of a Wife: The Influence of Mary Wollstonecraft's *Vindication of the Rights of Woman* on Mary Shelley's *Frankenstein*," unpublished paper written at the University of Virginia. Graham notes that Frankenstein does not even protect Elizabeth's life because he is so certain that the Creature's warning is a threat against his life and not hers.

that it provides a grudging Harold Bloom with "one of the most vivid versions we have of the Romantic mythology of the self" despite or because of its "flaws."[19] *Frankenstein* has now become one of the novels most fully subjected to feminist scrutiny, and I do not wish here to enter the debates about the ways in which it is or is not a "woman's book."[20] I can see the possibility of a subversive reading of *Frankenstein* as antiheroic and even antimasculine, but I agree with Mary Poovey and Robert Kiely that the novel ultimately valorizes Frankenstein more than it undermines him and that the self-ironizing of its voices serves conventional, self-authorizing purposes. Read against other Romantic narratives, in other words, *Frankenstein* does not stand out as a critique of the tradition in which it takes part.[21]

Rather than argue for the female in *Frankenstein*, I prefer to suggest that the very "maleness" of the novel allowed Shelley to move toward female voice by working out in "universal" or "generic" space gender-specific anxieties about authorship and autobiography, imitation and originality. *Frankenstein* assumes, as this chapter's epigraph from its preface suggests, that Romantic heroism and Romantic writing are male projects, and inscribes a woman's desire for authority in a re-peating structure of male voice that may have been superimposed upon the novel's original design. Precisely because it represents the exaggerated inefficacy of female voice and the exaggerated potency of male voice, I believe *Frankenstein* permitted Shelley to write out male Romanticism and to move on in her next novel to a female-centered narrative about a different kind of parentally created "mon-strosity." In other words and to exaggerate somewhat, *Frankenstein* is

19. Bloom's *ad feminam* afterword to the Signet edition claims that precisely "because it lacks the sophistication and imaginative complexity" of *Manfred* and *Prometheus Unbound*, *Frankenstein* "affords a unique introduction to the archetypal world of the Romantics" (New York: New American Library, 1965), 215.

20. See especially Sandra Gilbert and Susan Gubar, *The Madwoman in the Attic* (New Haven: Yale University Press, 1979), 213–47; Barbara Johnson, "My Monster/My Self," *Diacritics* 12 (1982): 2–10; Mary Jacobus, "Is There a Woman in This Text?" *New Literary History* 14 (1982): 117–41; and Devon Hodges, "*Frankenstein* and the Fem-inine Subversion of the Novel," *Tulsa Studies in Women's Literature* 2 (Fall 1983): 155–64.

21. I am disagreeing here with Devon Hodges' claim that Shelley's use of multiple narrators "undermines the stability of the male voice" through its aberrant narrative practices ("*Fran-kenstein* and Feminine Subversion," 157). I agree rather with Robert Kiely that *Frankenstein* uses relatively conventional Romantic narrative strategies; see *The Romantic Novel in England* (Cambridge: Harvard University Press, 1972). However, *Frankenstein* might lend itself to an *esoteric* feminist rereading if one reads as gendered rather than generic its many negative uses of the word "man" (see xi, 88, 114, 137).

not only, as Barbara Johnson says, a novel about the writing of *Frankenstein*,[22] it is a novel about the writing of *Mathilda*, the then-unwritten story of a woman's "romantic woes."

Shelley's nervously self-centered 1831 preface provides a link with each of *Frankenstein*'s narrators and narratees. Beginning with Mrs. Saville, whose "feminine" position is mirrored in Shelley's description of herself as a "devout and nearly silent listener" to the conversations of men,[23] the narrative agents of *Frankenstein* become vehicles for exploring Shelley's isolation in a male literary world, her fears of both eccentricity and conformity, of creating but also of failing to create the "unbidden"—*for*bidden?—tale. To paraphrase Gilbert and Gubar speaking of Eve,[24] the part of Shelley is all the parts: Walton is the author reduced to copyist, Frankenstein the author whose creative dreams have gone awry, and the Creature a text whose voice, if not yet female, is also not humanly male.

As critics note repeatedly, by naming her novel a "hideous progeny" Shelley has begged readers to see her alliance with Victor Frankenstein, who is also terrified by his "odious handiwork" (54). Frankenstein is indeed the ultimate innovator, creating what was supposed to be a copy (of a man) but what turns out to be an aesthetically unacceptable product, entirely without precedent (if, arguably, but the incarnation of Frankenstein's own grotesque soul). Shelley, the devotee striving for acceptability, likewise ends up with a wholly original novel that does not "owe the suggestion of one incident, nor scarcely of one train of feeling" (xi) to Percy Shelley or to anyone—not even, as Anne Mellor perceptively notices, to the conventional sources in folklore and legend from which other Romantic mythmakers drew their ideas.[25] It is precisely this originality that I believe is mitigated by the framing device of epistolarity. If we take the preface to be accurate on this score, the first words Shelley thought of were Frankenstein's—that sentence about the "dreary night in November" that now constitutes the beginning of Chapter 5. On Percy's "incitement," says Shelley, she turned a short tale into a novel and created "the

22. Johnson, "My Monster/My Self," 7.
23. Mary Shelley, *Frankenstein* (New York: Signet, 1965), x. All further references will appear in the text.
24. Gilbert and Gubar, *The Madwoman in the Attic*, 230.
25. Anne K. Mellor, *Mary Shelley: Her Life, Her Fictions, Her Monsters* (New York: Methuen, 1988), 38. Mellor shows, however, that Percy Shelley undertook considerable stylistic editing, including Frankenstein's much-discussed references to himself as "author" and numerous changes that make Frankenstein appear more sympathetic and the Creature more monstrous.

form in which it was presented to the world" (xi), possibly at that point buffering Frankenstein's horror story with Walton's relative normalcy.

As an "author," indeed, Walton is to imitation what Frankenstein is to originality. Much as the author of *Frankenstein* sought to "prove herself" by inscription on "the page of fame" (viii), Walton had hoped to "obtain a niche in the temple where the names of Homer and Shakespeare are consecrated" (16). But he enters this text as a disappointed poet reduced to the (feminine) act of private letters, bearing "heavily" his "failure" to achieve the poetic "paradise" he had sought from childhood (16). It is also as a literary failure that Shelley first represents herself in the preface to *Frankenstein*: the stories she "scribbled" as a child manifest a "most commonplace style" and imitative content, "rather doing as others had done than putting down the suggestions of my own mind" (vii–viii). When Percy Shelley began urging his wife to write, he did not, she reports, expect her to "produce anything worthy of notice," and when the group made a pact to write ghost stories, Mary Shelley felt only "that blank incapability of invention which is the greatest misery of authorship." Even success would be failure, since the "illustrious poets" Shelley and Byron, "annoyed by the platitude of prose," had already given up the "uncongenial task" of inventing a story's "machinery" (ix). For both Shelley and Walton the solution is Frankenstein, appearing Romantically as the figment of dream. Beholden like Walton to the "unbidden," the daughter of one of the eighteenth-century's most openly autobiographical writers can only claim to record someone else's "infinitely more interesting" tale.

In giving the Creature a voice, however, Shelley undertakes a different kind of authorial project that extricates her from both the unbidden and the imitative: the struggle for an authoritative basis— a language, a literary tradition, a credible voice—through which to represent an unauthorized search for subjectivity. Other feminist critics have argued persuasively that this Creature—denied full humanity, lacking history and language, possessed of an "eloquent and persuasive" voice that men are warned not to "trust" (198), naturally gentle but made "monstrous" from misunderstanding and loneliness—is a figure for Woman, hence for Shelley herself.[26] Although I appreciate

26. See, for example, Ellen Moers, *Literary Women* (New York: Doubleday, 1976); Gilbert and Gubar, *Madwoman in the Attic*; and Johnson, "My Monster/My Self."

the suggestiveness of such readings, it seems to me equally important that materially Shelley's Creature is male, and though it may have been a powerful autobiographical act for her to give him a "feminine" condition and sensibility, female voice and experience (and their particular ways of complicating Romantic "woes" and "wonderful events") are withheld here just as Shelley withheld the "true compositions" of her childhood. Multiply voices as it might, *Frankenstein* is a story not of female subjectivity but of the impossibility of its transcription: like Frankenstein, Shelley "could not compose a female" (143). In its narrative layering, however, one can see in *Frankenstein* a progressive movement from passive reception toward unauthorized autonomy, from Mrs. Saville's silence through Walton's imitation, from Frankenstein's brilliant but frighteningly unconventional creation to the self-construction of a subject who cannot be named woman but who also cannot be named man.

Ironically, although this novel may be grappling with autobiographical and authorial dilemmas that surely stem from the difficulties of writing Romanticism as female, in an important sense Shelley's use of male voices serves the cause of women's authority well. Because convention bids her to tell her Romantic story as a male "generic" text, it is through male voices that Shelley writes out her "anxieties of authorship." Had Shelley created women as unsuccessful poets, physical "monsters," or progenitors of the grotesque, her work could not have failed to support the ethos by which female creation is already seen as imitative, distorted, or misguidedly Promethean. Shelley had wanted in her preface to speak about "authorship alone," and to speak of "authorship alone" was to speak of male authorship. Given the conservatism of Romanticism's literary gender roles, it seems to me that to struggle with questions of authority through female voice would call into question not authority but female voice. Thus the Creature's male gender allows it to be a metaphor for, rather than a representation of, a woman: the monster may figure a woman's anguish, but a woman is not a monster.

Read from the evidence of Shelley's next novel, *Frankenstein* takes on further significance as an elaborate strategy not only for working out authorial anxiety but for working toward female voice. In 1819 the writer who could not "think of a story" created another, more directly autobiographical fiction, which I read as a link between the "feminized" Creature of *Frankenstein* and Shelley's own history. If *Frankenstein* uses male voices to write out a gendered anxiety, *Mathilda* uses female voice to write in a gendered history. Whereas Shelley may have created the structure of *Frankenstein* by adding on layers of male voice, there is clear textual evidence that she created *Mathilda* by stripping away layers of voice until what remained was the single personal voice I have associated with male Romantic literature. Here, as nowhere else in Romantic fiction, is the female voice that "holds the center" of her text in a plot in which the female body becomes the site of conflict.

Mathilda (like Shelley herself) has lost her mother ten days after birth. Left to the care of a cold and stern Scottish aunt, she grows up desperately lonely, her "warm affections finding no return from any other human heart." Books—mostly the same books (Shelley and) the Creature loved—supply "the place of human intercourse."[27] Like the Creature, Mathilda longs for fathering; she imagines running away, "disguised like a boy" to "seek my father through the world" (11). Mathilda's father does return when she is sixteen, but the relationship, like that between Frankenstein and the Creature, goes grotesquely awry, for reasons equally corporeal but sexually differentiated. When the father begins to shun his daughter, she presses from him a confession that his love for her is incestuous; he is convinced that her mother's spirit has been "transferred into [Mathilda's] frame, and she ought to be as Diana to me" (40). Mathilda sends him away with "a daughter's curse" and a double message: to "return pure to thy child, who will never love aught but thee" (34). The father commits suicide; Mathilda blames herself; like both Frankenstein and the Creature, for whom "sorrow only increased with knowledge" (*Frankenstein* 115), Mathilda is destroyed by her (Romantic) need to know. The despairing daughter then arranges her own "death" so that she can escape into solitude and await the "eternal mental union" with her father that death alone will provide. After two years of hermitage, as she begins to long for "the love that is the soul of friendship" (53), she meets the poet Woodville, whose history resembles Percy Shelley's and whose poetry holds Mathilda "enchained to his discourses" (61), although until she is dying she cannot bring herself to "give words" to her own "dark tale."

The language of *Mathilda* is a language of isolation, horror, and anguish whose phraseology strikingly repeats *Frankenstein*'s. In both novels, the monstrosity of a parent begets a "monstrous" child. Like

---

27. Mary Wollstonecraft Shelley, *Mathilda*, ed., Elizabeth Nitchie (Chapel Hill: University of North Carolina Press, 1959), 10. All further references will appear in the text.

Victor Frankenstein, Mathilda's father calls himself a "monster" and
a "fallen archangel" (31); like the Creature, Mathilda laments an "eternal barrier between me and my fellow creatures"; she is "struck off
from humanity; bearing no affinity to man or woman; a wretch on
whom Nature had set her ban" (62), an "outcast from human feeling,
this monster with whom none might mingle in conversation and love";
she wonders why fate had not "from that fatal and most accursed
moment, shrouded me in thick mists and placed real darkness between
me and my fellows so that I might never more be seen" (71), so that
"I should have lived upon this dreary heath unvisited, and blasting
none by my unhallowed gaze" (72). "I was in truth," she says, "a
marked creature, a pariah, only fit for death" (72). The Romantic
conflict of the novel is thus the conflict between gendered and generic
versions of identity that I have already described in Charrière; Mathilda struggles to be a "transcendent" self, while her father reconstructs
her as the object of (his) desire.

The form Shelley ends up creating for this female-centered version
of monstrous alienation and failed fathering is a memoir presented,
like *Frankenstein*, as unbidden: Mathilda composes it only when she is
"too weak both in body and mind to resist the impulse" to tell. Technically the story is private, directed only to Woodville, but Mathilda,
like Mistriss Henley, narrates "as if I wrote for strangers," stretching
private voice toward public ends (and thus implausibly telling Woodville his own history). But Shelley did not come immediately to this
form: *Mathilda* began with the framed structure in which *Frankenstein*
ends up. The original version, entitled "The Fields of Fancy" and
modeled on Wollstonecraft's unfinished "The Caves of Fancy," creates
three narrators who frame one another's texts. Walton's counterpart
is a person of unspecified sex who has "suffered a misfortune" that
"reduced me to misery & despair," and who is conducted by a spirit
to the Elysian Fields to listen to "the Prophetess Diotima the instruc-
tress of Socrates" (94). Among Diotima's disciples is Mathilda, whom
Diotima urges to narrate "her earthly history" (102). The unnamed
extradiegetic narrator thus becomes the scribe of both Diotima's wisdom and Mathilda's tale, so that structurally as well as psychically,
Mathilda occupies the Creature's place in a narrative whose three
voices may well be female.

In revising *Mathilda*, however, Shelley removed the buffers of setting and form that distance Mathilda's narrative, leaving a novel written wholly in a single, female voice. Devon Hodges had suggested on

the basis of *Frankenstein* that for Shelley the singular "I" is a "unifying device that needs transformation if women are to speak";[28] *Mathilda* suggests that it is not singular voice but male voice that Shelley needed to transform. When, in *Mathilda*, Shelley does "compose a female," she strips away the layers of narration built around the equivalent voice in *Frankenstein*.

It is impossible to know whether the fate of this novel might have been different had Shelley kept the original, buffered structure of "The Fields of Fancy." Contrary to Shelley's proclaimed intentions, *Mathilda*, arguably the creature-text "ten thousand times more malignant than her mate" (*Frankenstein*, 158), was never published during her lifetime. It is a powerful and disturbing irony that Shelley put the fate of this manuscript in her own father's hands. As she would later do with *Valperga*, which she also wrote in Italy, Shelley gave her fair copy of *Mathilda* in May 1820 to her friends the Gisbornes, who were returning to England, asking them to deliver it to Godwin so that he could find it a publisher. As Elizabeth Nitchie reports, there is "no record of his having made any attempt to get it into print," and Shelley apparently tried repeatedly through Maria Gisborne to get the manuscript returned to her; the completed novel turned up only after Shelley's death. While the Gisbornes strongly admired *Mathilda*, Godwin apparently considered it uneven in quality and "disgusting and detestable" in subject.[29] Surely a complex psychic history is buried in the saga of this novel's composition, Shelley's decision to send it to Godwin, and Godwin's (non)response.

I would like to read the fate of *Mathilda*, however, as more than an accident of biography. In an important sense, it is fitting that Shelley sent *Mathilda* to Godwin rather than directly to a publisher, for this gesture repeats Mathilda's own self-destructively tenacious subordination to a man who cannot allow his daughter her individuality. In this sense, Mathilda is as much Romantic heroine as Romantic hero; she embodies the spirit of superior sensitivity and genius, alienation, and longings for transcendence, but she cannot untangle these longings from her desire for the father who torments her. While the Creature blamed its father, Mathilda blames herself, and because she

28. Hodges, "*Frankenstein* and Feminine Subversion," 157.
29. See Nitchie, introduction to *Mathilda*, xi; and Mary Shelley's letters of 9 February 1822, 7 March 1822, 10 April 1822, and 2 June 1822, in *The Letters of Mary Wollstonecraft Shelley*, ed. Betty T. Bennett, vol. 1 (Baltimore: Johns Hopkins University Press, 1980). See my Chapter 12 for the similarly negative language Godwin will use to describe the unfinished section of Wollstonecraft's *The Wrongs of Woman*.

continues to hold herself responsible for his death and to desire no other love, she remains not only the victim of the patriarch but his loyal subject as well. It seems likely that Godwin's censorship would have been re-enacted by a publisher; even *Frankenstein* was rejected by several presses before Lackington accepted it in 1817. Godwin's refusal to return *Mathilda* suggests the dangers female voice poses when it turns the tables on male Romantic subjectivity. Shelley apparently never confronted her father directly about this manuscript, and she did not write another novel in a female personal voice.

George Sand's *Lélia* (1833) reveals the dissonance between Romantic representation and Romantic subjectivity from virtually the opposite stance; its project is precisely the refusal to reduce desire to the gendered shape that even *Corinne* and *Mathilda* give it. Ellen Moers exults that Lélia "claim[s] all of Romanticism for women," "tak[ing] her place beside Werther, René, Obermann, Childe Harold, Adolphe, Alastor, Raphaël de Valentin and the rest of the swollen masculine egos of the age. Lélia feels the guilts, the aspirations, the alienation, the boredom, the sterility, the pride, the rebelliousness of the Romantic hero; she plays the cold dandy, the demon lover, the inspired prophet, the doomed soul—and remains all Woman."[30] Although Sand is able to make Lélia the center of the plot, however, she does not make her the novel's single voice. Instead, if one agenda of *Lélia* is to fulfill Staël's proclamation that genius has no sex, the novel's form dramatizes as an impossible fiction that a woman is as free as a man to express this genius.

Lélia's central conflict concerns the challenge to Lélia's reserve by Sténio, a young poet who loves her passionately at a time when a tormenting and oppressive affair has left her sexually impotent and when she has wearied of ever reaching the transcendent understandings to which she aspires. On guard against the reduction of woman to Romantic object yet on the verge of yielding to Sténio, Lélia fears that "it's scarcely a soul you want: it's a woman, isn't it?" (142), and sends her courtesan sister Pulchérie in her place. The "Lélia" to whom Sténio makes love—vowing that he has never loved more deeply—is thus actually Pulchérie (a hoax the text also perpetrates upon the reader). When the truth is revealed, Sténio turns in despair to de-

---

30. Moers, *Literary Women*, 201; Moers, foreword to *Lélia*, trans. Maria Espinosa (Bloomington: Indiana University Press, 1978), vii. Citations of *Lélia* are from this edition and will appear in the text.

bauchery, and even the efforts of their aging and ascetic friend, the reformed gambler Trenmor, do not save Sténio from suicide. Lélia herself dies a violent death that, once again, is inseparable from her sex: she is strangled with a rosary by Magnus, the Irish priest whose tormented passion for her has finally driven him insane.

In form *Lélia* is a pastiche of letters, authorial narration, interior monologues, and dialogues among all the major characters. Often the identities of a narrator and narratee must be inferred; it is not always certain whether a narrator is writing or speaking; and nearly all markers of time and place have disappeared. *Lélia*'s "shapelessness" has led many critics to consider it an aesthetic failure; even its English translator says that perhaps it "should not be judged as a 'novel' in modern terms" (xx). Eileen Boyd Sivert has argued that, on the contrary, the formal eclecticism of *Lélia* functions subversively as a refusal of patriarchal constraints: "Sand's discourse, which offers so many ways of approaching woman's story, does not enclose or smother, it is strikingly open, loose, plural." For Sivert the text's narrative openness gives Lélia "a freedom of movement in narration which contrasts sharply with her position in society." In the novel's multiplicity of narrators, Sivert sees a challenge to "exclusive, appropriating narrative authority" and a willingness on Lélia's part to "admit the 'other' into a kind of shared writing without losing control over the recounting of herself. Having no voice in society, Lélia can be heard in narration, in what slips out of the norm, out of the dominant (masculine) discourse, in what can only be 'got at' sideways, in the margins, the gaps or breaks, and silences in the text."[31]

But this valorization of pluralism denies the struggle for subjectivity that constitutes Lélia's central quest. I see the form of *Lélia* not as a flight from social constraints but as their necessary inscription. The novel's complicated, unpredictable narrative structure replicates the unpredictable and complicated contestations over Lélia's identity, which can never settle into that of "generic" poet because she is never free from the projections and the desires of men. As she says to Pulchérie, "To be lover, courtesan, and mother . . . These are the three conditions of a woman's fate which no woman escapes" (100). If Lélia's is the text's dominant personal voice, it is the voice almost always

---

31. Eileen Boyd Sivert, "*Lélia* and Feminism," *Yale French Studies* 62 (1981): 47, 48, 64. I do not understand the suggestion that Lélia is "sharing" narrative voice, since the text is not structured as "hers." Such a decision would have to be Sand's, or Sand's authorial narrator's, not Lélia's.

responding to other voices; we first see her through male eyes just as we see nearly all Romantic women from Werther's Charlotte to Oswald's Corinne to Victor's Elizabeth. The novel opens precisely with Sténio's question to Lélia, "Qui t'es- tu?"—"Who are you?"—and with his refusal to accept Lélia's insistence that they are "brothers" (7), that "my soul is the sister of yours" (8). Even the wise Trenmor, who counters Sténio's insistence that "where there is no love, there is no woman" by asking him whether he believed "that where there is no love, there is no man" (30), and who places Lélia in a noble bisexual tradition that includes Galatea, Tasso, Dante, Romeo, Hamlet, Juliet, Lara, and Corinne, imposes gender when he accuses Lélia of having "a woman's ferocious ingratitude and vanity" (32) and appeals to her to "mother" Sténio (33). And Magnus's projection upon her of the "double" (52) who is both angel and demon, spirit and flesh, will literally be the death of her. Lélia's silencing by strangulation occurs precisely because she refuses Magnus's demands to "console me. Love me" (227), and provides fitting closure for a text in which a female voice that "holds the center" would have produced a false representation of Lélia's autonomy.

For all her greatness, Lélia cannot escape being defined from the outside, and it is the struggle within and against such definitions that I believe the narrative form of *Lélia* represents. The men's constructions of Lélia, juxtaposed to Lélia's version of herself, suggest that to allow the female Romantic figure a central or exclusive voice is to perpetuate the illusion that woman can simply constitute her self as generically human and have that construction accepted alongside Goethe's construction of Werther or (Sand's lover) Musset's of Octave. Instead, *Lélia*'s form juxtaposes Lélia's complex subjectivity to the versions of the men who project upon her the shapes of their desires. It is significant that Lélia's deepest secrets are told only to Pulchérie: at the heart of the novel, where Corinne tells her story to Oswald, Lélia tells hers to her sister.

Given the equation between women writers and their first-person subjects that I have suggested in Chapter 8, it is also likely that Sand's reputation could not have sustained the autobiographical implications that a wholly autodiogetic version of *Lélia* would have produced. As it was, *Lélia*'s feminization of Romantic codes turned against Sand; she suffered "emotional agony and personal humiliation" for publishing this book, which was easily the most controversial novel of its day,[32] and she even attempted to replace the original with a toned-down version in 1839—the only substantial revision of a novel that she ever undertook. Although the revised version never caught on, and *Lélia* remained both controversial and widely admired, it is ironically appropriate that the novel that now represents a woman's Romantic "masterpiece" (after its own long-standing trivialization and neglect) is the male-dominated *Frankenstein*.

I stated earlier that women faced two challenges if they were to write Romantic fiction: to displace the male subject and hence male voice as textual center, and to re-present Romantic tropes in female terms. Novels such as *Caliste, Corinne, Mathilda,* and especially *Lélia* suggest that it was possible to construct a female character with Romantic desires and conflicts while also showing the tension between "femininity" and humanity. The second challenge, displacing the male subject as the *narrative* center, clearly proved more difficult. I see no evidence that Romantic women refused personal voice in virtuous avoidance or deconstruction of hegemonic subjectivity. Rather, I see in the complexity of women's Romantic fictions the sign that if Romantic genius was generically "human," its narrative expression was still a matter of sex.

32. Joseph Barry, "George Sand: Our Existential Contemporary," in *The George Sand Papers* (New York: AMS Press, 1980), 19.

10

Jane Eyre's Legacy: The Powers and Dangers of Singularity

It is the fact of your telling, whether they believe you or
not... It will help other women to speak out what they
think, unashamed.

—MARY AUSTIN, *A Woman of Genius*

Discourse conceals its incompleteness.

—LAWRENCE HOGUE, *Discourse and the Other*

Sometimes there appears a work of literature so seemingly singular
that it obscures Virginia Woolf's reminder that "masterpieces" are not
"solitary births."[1] *Jane Eyre* is such a book; when it appeared in 1847
under the sexually ambiguous pseudonym Currer Bell, whether its
originality pleased or scandalized, "for everyone *Jane Eyre* was 'new.' "[2]
No aspect of this novel is more sharply singular in every sense than
its narrative voice, which has been perceived as almost tyrannical in
its power to impose a stance. In the grudging words of Frederic
Harrison, "the plain little governess dominates the whole book and
fills every page. Everything and every one appear, not as we see them
and know them in the world, but as they look to a keen-eyed girl who
had hardly ever left her native village." Yet Harrison believes the
novel "would have been a failure" if "cast into the form of impersonal
narration," while "as the autobiography of Jane Eyre" it is "consum-

1. Virginia Woolf, *A Room of One's Own* (New York: Harcourt Brace, 1929), 68–69.
2. Miriam Allott, ed., *"Jane Eyre" and "Villette": A Casebook* (London: Macmillan, 1973), 20.

176

mate art."[3] One of the earliest fictional autobiographies directed to a public narratee, *Jane Eyre* has no precedent in the authority it claims for a female personal voice. Yet *Jane Eyre*'s voice is not quite a "single and solitary birth"; it is a transformation of possibilities already present in fiction but segregated along gender lines. I will suggest that the form of *Jane Eyre* involves the imposition of the self-authorizing and totalizing voice I have associated with the Romantic hero upon a very different and particularly female genre.

Fictional autobiography was still young in 1847, and not surprisingly nineteenth-century women published fewer fiction or "nonfictional" autobiographies than men. While Jerome Beaty may be right to claim that by 1847 "a novel in the autobiographical mode appearing in England" might be "an apologia or an exemplum, egoistic and Byronic, or humbly Providential,"[4] "egoistic and Byronic" fictions in the female voice seem not to have existed, as Beaty's own examples suggest. Instead, female personal voice took form at least in early nineteenth-century England by synthesizing two fictions of dependency—the courtship novel and the spiritual autobiography—into the "governess tale," the story of a dependent woman's progress to spiritual and material happiness. At least three such novels precede *Jane Eyre* in creating a public voice: Mary Brunton's *Discipline* (1815); Mary Martha Sherwood's *Caroline Mordaunt* (1835); and Anne Brontë's *Agnes Grey*, published in 1847 but written before Charlotte Brontë wrote *Jane Eyre*.[5] While each of these novels adopts a voice grammatically female, however, each also limits the narrator's personal authority by appealing to (masculine) authorities outside the self. The governess tales that make *Jane Eyre* possible, therefore, also make it unique, for Jane will challenge these limits on female authority in her attempt to create an "egoistic" if not "Byronic" narrative subject engaging with uncommon insistence a public narratee. At the same time,

3. Frederic Harrison, cited in Kenneth Graham, *English Criticism of the Novel 1865–1900* (Oxford: Clarendon Press, 1964), 129. Note Harrison's typical conflation of author and character: "as the autobiography of Jane Eyre—let us say at once of Charlotte Brontë..."
    4. Jerome Beaty, "Jane Eyre at Gateshead: Mixed Signals in the Text and Context," in *Victorian Literature and Society: Essays Presented to Richard D. Altick*, ed. James R. Kincaid and Albert J. Kuhn (Columbus: Ohio State University Press, 1983), 186.
    5. The relationship between Jane Eyre and other governess novels is discussed, though not in terms of voice, by both Jerome Beaty in "Jane Eyre at Gateshead" and Inga-Stina Ewbank in *Their Proper Sphere* (Cambridge: Harvard University Press, 1966). On the material situation of the governess and its representation in *Jane Eyre*, see Mary Poovey, *Uneven Developments: The Ideological Work of Gender in Mid-Victorian England* (Chicago: University of Chicago Press, 1988), chap. 5.

as I will argue at the end of this chapter, Jane's voice has a dangerously unacknowledged dependence of its own.

The governess narrative that I believe *Jane Eyre* is rewriting traces the fortunes of an intelligent gentlewoman in reduced circumstances. Although Ellen Percy, the clever, beautiful, and spoiled heroine of *Discipline*, begins life in the bosom of luxury, she eventually finds herself orphaned, penniless, and ill; her deprivations foster a conversion to virtue that is ultimately rewarded by marriage to the excellent man she once proudly spurned. Sherwood's spoiled, outspoken, and arrogant Caroline Mordaunt chafes at her subordination as governess and ends up leaving or being dismissed from post after post until she is inspired to holiness by her pupil Emily Selburn, probably a prototype for Helen Burns, who dies at fourteen after "a rapid ripening for a higher state of being."[6] Although no love plot runs through this book, Caroline is rewarded on the final page when the "humble rector of the parish" seeks her hand. Agnes Grey, virtuous from the start, is sorely tested by humiliations and deprivations that, all three novels stress, are the particular lot of the governess, but in the end it is the plain Agnes, not her beautiful and wealthy charge, who gets the handsome clergyman.

It is not surprising, since public personal voice is still so unconventional in fiction by women, that each of these narrators takes some trouble both to bolster her authority and to mitigate the self-centeredness of her narrative act. *Discipline*, which may well be the first novel written by a woman anywhere in Europe that uses a public female personal voice exclusively, places itself in the tradition of spiritual autobiography by titling itself after an abstract, virile ideal and by beginning the character's story with so much focus on patrilineage that only midway into the first chapter does a coy reference reveal that the protagonist is of "feminine character."[7] The narrators of all three novels construct their narratees as judges to be pleased, appeased, or instructed, and they address these "readers" only in distanced, often anxious, third-person forms. Caroline Mordaunt will ask regularly whether her reader is "weary" (232), or "tired of me"

6. Mary Martha Sherwood, *Caroline Mordaunt, or, The Governess*, in *The Works of Mrs. Sherwood* (New York: Harper and Brothers, 1835), vol. 13, 281. Further references will appear in the body of the text.

7. Mary Brunton, *Discipline* (London: Routledge and Kegan Paul, 1986), 4. Further references will appear in the body of the text.

(252) and will report eagerly something she thinks "my pious reader will be pleased to hear" (263). Ellen Percy, though much less servile, uses anticipated judgments as occasions to sermonize: "Before my reader comment on the wisdom of this reply, let him examine, whether there be any more weight in the reasons which delay his own endeavours after Christian perfection" (28), or, "Others may smile at this and many other instances of my folly. I look back upon them as on the illusions of delirium, and shudder whilst I smile" (83). In *Agnes Grey*, which seems to take self-judgment so seriously that one may suspect some irony to be at work, the reader is evoked to forgive behaviors that are hardly culpable, as with Agnes's "confession" that she paid "more attention to dress than I had ever done before," or her fear that "the reader is well-nigh disgusted with the folly and weakness" of feeling worthy of Mr. Weston's love.[8]

As such addresses suggest, it is not only the reader but the older "I" who is constructed as authoritative judge. All three novels are explicitly retrospective, narrated by women who have been "many years a wife" (*Discipline*, 375), and all three profess "instruction" as their goal. In the first two novels, narrative authority demands this temporal gap: the narrator looks back with sharp moral distance at the younger character and can tell her story only because she has changed. This confessional strategy is most obvious in *Caroline Mordaunt*, the most evangelical of the three novels, whose narrator says she does not "have any good to say of myself," but "much, very much to say of the various providences by which I was gradually brought to know myself, to esteem myself as the chiefest of sinners, and to comprehend in some degree what the Almighty has done and is still doing for me" (252). Ellen Percy, having "escaped from eminent peril," hopes "to warn others of the danger of their way" (1–2). These texts must distinguish sharply between the protagonist and the mature, detached narrator who can look back critically upon her former self. Indeed, the narrator is authorized to the extent that she has accepted a truth that is both Christian and male: in all three novels there are wise God-fearing men (Ellen's uncle and later her benefactor-husband, Agnes's clergyman spouse) who "know better" than the heroine. In this respect the novels recall Hannah More's very popular

8. Anne Brontë, *Agnes Grey* (London: J. M. Dent, 1985), chap. 17, 114, 121. Further references are to this edition and will appear in the body of the text.

Coelebs in Search of a Wife (1808), in which a male narrator so self-authorizing that he is his own introducer and editor is presented, as I said in Chapter 4, as the ultimate expert on Christian womanhood.

The governess tales that precede *Jane Eyre* stop short of full self-authorization, then, by making the narrator's authority contingent on submission to an implicit over-voice, the joint construction of the older self and the Christian God who has transformed the protagonist to a worthy autobiographer. In this way, the right to narrate becomes virtue's mandate and reward. In two of the novels the character's (speaking) voice must explicitly be tamed so that the narrator's (writing) voice may serve higher purposes: Ellen Percy's outspokenness lands her in a hospital for the insane and Caroline Mordaunt's costs her several positions. All three novels make clear that silence is the condition of governess, which is in turn but an extreme of the dependent condition of womanhood: "it was my business to hear, and not to speak" (*Agnes Grey*, 18.127). Agnes survives because "I was used to wearing a placid smiling countenance when my heart was bitter within me" (17.120), and she is rewarded because she passively lets "time and patience" improve her situation "slowly, it is true, and almost imperceptibly" (7.59). Despite their suffering, beyond a passing recognition of the limited "market for the fruits of feminine ingenuity" (*Discipline*, 244) none of these narrators explicitly questions traditional gender roles. The counterpart, for example, to Jane Eyre's passionate defense (in chapter 12) of women's need for liberty that begins with "Anybody may blame me who likes" is Agnes's long "confession" defending her preoccupation with physical appearance after she has fallen in love (17.114–15).

At the same time, these novels do bear signs of restlessness with their own submissive and pious femininity. *Caroline Mordaunt* apologizes for recounting a time when "religion had no influence whatever upon my conduct" (212) but takes four-fifths of its pages to present the outspoken, brash, and self-centered behavior of the younger "infidel." Brunton's narrator parades her moral superiority: "there are few who, like me, unfold their temptations, or record their repentance" (243). And each text arguably writes "beyond the ending" by inscribing some ambivalence toward the marriage that ends the tale. Caroline Mordaunt barely mentions her husband, focuses on her children and her "King"; her final word is a reminder that "God is love" (303). Ellen Percy speaks with praise of her unmarried sister-in-law, whom "some misses lately arrived from a boarding school have begun to call... an old maid" and insists that the single state has not "produced any ill effect on Charlotte's temper, or on her happiness." She also refuses to compare her own present happiness to her past pleasures, claiming that "the Lowland tongue wants energy for the contrast" (375). And what are we to make of the ending of *Agnes Grey*, which is surely undercut by this language of negativity surprisingly close to that of the coded letter from the American bride: "I became the wife of Edward Weston; and never have found cause to repent it, and am certain that I never shall.... for whatever his faults may be as a man (and no one is entirely without), I defy anybody to blame him as a pastor, a husband, or a father"? From where would such blame come, when Edward has been presented to us as goodness itself, or are we also to take as literal Agnes's earlier statement that "it is not the man, it is his goodness that I love" (16.111)?

Despite these small signs of resistance, the governess narrators are very distant in spirit from the Romantic voices I described in Chapter 9. In turning the governess tale toward the conventions of Romantic subjectivity, *Jane Eyre* will expose the authority of these earlier governess narrators as only fictively female and singular—as occupying the ideological positions of men. In *Agnes Grey*, of course, both the possibilities and the limits of the governess narrative are literally brought home to the author of *Jane Eyre*: Anne wrote *Agnes Grey* while Charlotte was completing *The Professor*, her novel in a male voice that could not find a publisher; Rebecca Rodolff argues persuasively that *Agnes Grey* probably inspired Charlotte Brontë to begin a new novel in a female voice.[9] *Agnes Grey* also attempts, if obliquely, to transform the indirect narrator-narratee relationship of the earlier governess tales to the direct contact represented in *Jane Eyre*. In its promise "candidly [to] lay before the public" the substance of Agnes's diaries, which "I would not disclose to the most intimate friend" (1.1), *Agnes Grey* constructs a bridge between the private forms of eighteenth-century fiction and the public autobiography of *Jane Eyre*. Yet Anne Brontë's narrator also models a feminine submissiveness that Charlotte's will openly reject.

If *Jane Eyre* has a dominant agenda, I believe it is to crowd out

9. Rebecca Rodolff, "From the Ending of *The Professor* to the Conception of *Jane Eyre*," *Philological Quarterly* 61 (Winter 1982): 71–89.

competition in order to authorize as original and self-sufficient the
voices of both "Charlotte Brontë" and "Jane Eyre." As Brontë writes
in a letter to W. S. Williams in 1848,

> The standard heroes and heroines of novels are personages in whom
> I could never from childhood upwards take an interest, believe to be
> natural, or wish to imitate. Were I obliged to copy these characters I
> would simply not write at all. Were I obliged to copy any former novelist,
> even the greatest, even Scott, in anything, I would not write. Unless I
> have something of my own to say, and a way of my own to say it in, I
> have no business to publish. Unless I can look beyond the great Masters,
> and study Nature herself, I have no right to paint. Unless I can have
> the courage to use the language of Truth in preference to the jargon
> of Conventionality, I ought to be silent.[10]

Not only does this letter insist upon an ethos of originality that women
like Mary Shelley were shy to claim, it also rejects an explicitly male
literary tradition in preference for a (female) "Nature" that gives
Brontë not just "something of my own to say," but "a way of my own
to say it in." A close look at the narrative practices that create Jane
Eyre's singular voice suggests that virtually trait for trait Brontë is
rejecting the fictions of authority that fashion the governess tales.

While the governess novels rely on temporal and spiritual differences between narrator and protagonist, *Jane Eyre* relies on their identity. The absence of any attention to the act of narration in the chapters
preceding Jane's arrival at Thornfield reinforces a more general masking of the distinction in *Jane Eyre* between the experiencing child and
the narrating adult. Although the young Jane does learn from her
mistakes, the narrator never seriously criticizes her, and the narrator's
values are more- or-less continuous with those of the younger character. In the famous passage in chapter 12 about a woman's need for
liberty, for example, Jane's discourse mingles past and present tense,
as if evoking the experiencing and the narrating selves at once: "Who
blames me? Many, no doubt; and I shall be called discontented. I
could not help it: the restlessness was in my nature; it agitated me to
pain sometimes . . . It is in vain to say human beings ought to be satisfied with tranquillity: they must have action . . . women feel just as
men feel" (95–96). Brontë's generalizing "I" emphasizes syntactically

---

10. Charlotte Brontë, letter to W. S. Williams of September 1848, cited in *Jane Eyre*, ed.
Richard Dunn (New York: Norton, 1971), 424. References to *Jane Eyre* are from this edition
and will appear in the text with chapter numbers given first.

the harmony between the younger protagonist and the older voice: what the one did the other still supports. The young Jane, in sharp contrast to the earlier characters, is already her own moral authority even when her understanding is admitted to be limited. While containment or diminution of voice was necessary for the progress of Ellen Percy, Caroline Mordaunt, and Agnes Grey, nothing is more crucial to the development of Jane's character than the preservation of her right to speak. For voice is the trope par excellence of power in *Jane Eyre*.[11]

It is difficult in retrospect to grasp the radical departure represented by the first scene of the novel, as the orphan girl refuses the silent dependence that the governess novel established as necessity. As Ellen Moers says, "Before she gives Jane Eyre a name, or a class, or an age, Brontë makes her speaker both a person and a female in the quickest shorthand available to women writers: she has her say no."[12] This refusal, which in contrast to similar rebellions in the governess novels has implicit narrative sanction, becomes translated in chapter 4 into the trope that will structure virtually every narrative turn: Jane's rejection of other people's representations of herself in favor of a "new way of talking" based on the authority of her own perceptions, feelings, and experience—that is, on an essentially Romantic authority. While the adult Mistriss Henley could question only in an ironic double voice her right to speak the truth against her husband, the child Jane can insist that she is "quite right" to speak ill of Mrs. Reed: "How dare you affirm that, Jane Eyre?" "How dare I, Mrs Reed? How dare I? Because it is the *truth*." Such "truth" telling gives Jane "the strangest sense of freedom, of triumph, I ever felt" (4.31). When telling her story to Miss Temple earns Jane public absolution from the accusations of Mr. Brocklehurst, the child has learned most of what she needs to know about voice: to refuse silence (and hence the values of the governess tale) as one refuses death: "I was no Helen Burns" (7.57).

Jane's struggle, then, is not to gain a voice but to sustain it in the face of increasingly seductive pressures to yield. Although she is submissive to Rochester in ways I find disturbing, she always bristles when

11. Several feminist critics have explored the importance of voice in *Jane Eyre*. See especially Janet H. Freeman, "Speech and Silence in *Jane Eyre*," *SEL* 24 (1984): 683–700; and Rosemary Bodenheimer, "Jane Eyre in Search of Her Story," *Papers on Language and Literature* 16 (1980): 387–402.

12. Ellen Moers, *Literary Women* (New York: Doubleday, 1976), 24.

he attempts to harness her voice or to disallow her point of view. She will not flatter him, will not be commanded to speak "for the mere sake of talking and showing off" (14.117), and when she refuses to become his mistress, it is the exercise of voice that licenses her as a "free human being with an independent will": "I have spoken my mind, and can go anywhere now" (23.223). Likewise, Jane is able to resist St. John Rivers's demands in a discourse in which, even though "he had not imagined that a woman would dare to speak so to a man," she herself "felt at home" (32.330), nor is she daunted when he tells her that "your words are such as ought not to be used: violent, unfeminine, and untrue" (35.363).

In order to have the authority to redefine both the "feminine" and the "true," Jane proceeds as if she must not only have *a* voice but must have—and be—*the* voice. To achieve this hegemony, she must first of all vanquish the verbal authority of men, beginning with "Master Reed"—the master-reader?—whose rights Jane usurps when she throws his book at him.[13] Mr. Brocklehurst, the clergyman who in a traditional governess tale would be a voice of truth, is entirely discredited. Rochester the "Master" tells outright lies about matters of which Jane has a crucial right to know. And holy as St. John Rivers may be, his coldness renders his voice mechanical, "his tongue a speaking instrument—nothing more." In refusing these male authorities, *Jane Eyre* severs the identification assumed in the governess novels between God's authority and man's. Jane's spiritual development is predicated on becoming her own religious authority, rejecting both Rochester's relativism and St. John's absolutes in order to fashion a morality and even a scripture of her own.[14] Thus when Helen Burns tells her, for example, to "read the New Testament, and observe what Christ says, and . . . make his word your rule," she flatly states that loving an enemy like John Reed is "impossible" (6.50), nor does the older narrator correct her as the narrator of the governess novel would be compelled to do. This moral self-centeredness is what allows Jane finally to leave first Rochester and then St. John despite each man's persuasive rhetoric; when she returns to Rochester, it is through neither God's power nor man's will: it was "*my* time to assume ascendancy.

13. On reading in this novel see Mark M. Hennelly, Jr., "*Jane Eyre*'s Reading Lesson," *ELH* 51 (1984): 693–717; and Carla L. Peterson, *The Determined Reader: Gender and Culture in the Novel from Napoleon to Victoria* (New Brunswick, N.J.: Rutgers University Press, 1986), 82–131.

14. For a fuller discussion of this point see Linda Peterson, *Victorian Autobiography: The Tradition of Self-Interpretation* (New Haven: Yale University Press, 1986), 132–35.

My powers were in play and in force" (35.370). Given the audacity of this position, the curious last paragraph of *Jane Eyre*, with its emphasis on St. John Rivers and its concession to the voices of man and God, might be read as a reversion to the safe conventionality of the governess tale: "No fear of death will darken St. John's last hour: his mind will be unclouded; his heart will be undaunted, his hope will be sure, his faith steadfast. His own words are a pledge of this:—'My Master,' he says, 'has forewarned me. Daily He announces more distinctly,—"Surely I come quickly!" and hourly I more eagerly respond,—"Amen; even so, come, Lord Jesus!" ' " (398). The dissonance of this bow to Christian rhetoric only underscores the degree to which *Jane Eyre* has been written against the authorities that license the governess tale.[15] As character Jane has squelched every attempt to take over her story; as narrator she has been equally aggressive in suppressing points of view that differ from her own. For its historical moment, Jane's voice is an extraordinarily defiant fiction of authority. This is also, I think, why as both narrator and character Jane risks no humor, conscious ambiguity, or verbal play: her energies are necessarily bent upon keeping others—perhaps especially her "dear Reader"—from creating versions of her that might entrap her or threaten her representation of herself.

One cannot, of course, know the degree to which Charlotte Brontë was conscious of the unconventional narrative act that *Jane Eyre* constitutes, but this unconventionality might account for the narrator's self-conscious relationship with her narratee. One of the novel's oft-remarked features is the frequency of its direct address: some thirty instances clustered toward the latter third of the narrative. I have already indicated that such consciousness also characterizes the governess novels but that contact in those novels takes the form of indirect acts of deference or defense; even *Agnes Grey*, which claims to be an intimate self-revelation, addresses the reader only in third-person forms. Nowhere in previous literature have I found a female *personal* voice so insistently, even compulsively, in contact with a public narratee in the manner of the "engaging" authorial narrators I described in Chapter 5.

Some critics have noticed—or deplored—the seemingly gratuitous

---

15. The ending is also, as Gayatri Chakravorty Spivak argues and as my discussion below will reinforce, a re-turn toward imperialist evangelism as the pre-text for this text. See "Three Women's Texts and a Critique of Imperialism," in *"Race," Writing, and Difference*, ed. Henry Louis Gates, Jr. (Chicago: University of Chicago Press, 1986), 267–68.

nature of these addresses. Sylvère Monod finds them defensive and intrusive; Karl Kroeber notes they are rarely "required by the immediate situation," and thus seem arbitrary like the comments of Eliot's narrators in *Clerical Life* and *Adam Bede*.[16] This "arbitrariness" suggests that the desire to evoke the reader is motivated less by the daring nature of the story than by the daring nature of its voice, or rather by the narrator's wish to be accepted despite her unconventional assertiveness. Just as the novel's suppression of retrospectivity re-creates the immediacy of epistolary fiction, I believe the name "Reader" functions as a substitute for the epistolary proper name, recapturing in a public fiction the intimacy of epistolarity in a way much more immediate than *Agnes Grey*'s effort to capture the intimacy of the diary. The fact that "Reader" is always named in the singular— a distinct contrast to the "engaging" practices of Stowe and Eliot, who construct various narratees of both sexes—reinforces the use of the public narratee as confidant in evocations that resemble acts of epistolary address: "True, reader, and I knew and felt this . . . "(Chap. 9); "I have told you, reader, that I had learnt to love Mr Rochester" (Chap. 18); "Gentle reader, may you never feel what I then felt!" (Chap. 27); "Reader, it was on a Monday night . . . " (Chap. 37). The search for contact implied in these addresses certainly corresponds to the behavior of Jane as character, for voice is to her as much the trope of intimacy as of power. Jane "could never rest in communication with strong, discreet and refined minds, whether male or female, till I had passed the outworks of conventional reserve, and crossed the threshold of confidence, and won a place by their heart's very hearthstone" (32.330). It is of course through voice—the mysterious voice Jane hears from "somewhere" that cries "Jane! Jane! Jane!" (35.369)—that she is called back to Rochester, and marital happiness is the pleasure of talking "all day long" (38.397). The goal for Jane as both narrator and character is to achieve this intimacy without trading voice for love.

A kind of public epistolarity becomes the narrative sign, then, of Jane's quest for such a blend of intimacy and autonomy. Who can blame her (to paraphrase Jane) if, abandoned by family and publicly shamed, Jane might anxiously seek the approval of a larger audience? At Lowood, when Jane is afraid that "everybody" will think her a liar,

16. Sylvère Monod, "Charlotte Brontë and the Thirty 'Readers' of *Jane Eyre*," in *Jane Eyre* (New York: Norton, 1971), 496–507; and Karl Kroeber, *Style in Fictional Structure* (Princeton: Princeton University Press, 1971), 46.

Helen Burns answers whimsically, "Everybody, Jane? Why, there are only eighty people who have heard you called so, and the world contains hundreds of millions" (8). Jane can address these "hundreds of millions" by writing her story as a kind of public letter to the world. It is no accident, I think, that in this same chapter she tells us she has been learning to conjugate the French verb *être*, or that, as Mark Hennelly observes, Jane's initials, which identify her paintings and which remain unaltered even when she takes on a pseudonym at Marsh End, spell the French *je*.[17] For Jane, the orphan-woman asserting personal identity against the powers of silencing, to tell is to exist. And although the novel ends in marriage, so that at the time of writing Jane Eyre is in fact Jane Rochester, the narrator never yields her "J-E," her proper name, and her autobiography appropriately remains *Jane Eyre*. One could argue that this retention of her name, along with Jane's "Reader, I married him" (38.395), in contrast to Juliette Catesby's passive "they married me" and Ossery's appropriative "there is no more Juliette Catesby," takes control of the conventional marriage plot so that, as Rachel Brownstein says, her marriage "defiantly affirms not the heroine's transformation but her remaining herself."[18] In this respect *Jane Eyre* also rewrites the tradition in which marriage effects the heroine's silence, though the fact that the story ceases with marriage perpetuates what I suggested in Chapter 8 (and will suggest again below) to be a continuing problem in the history of female voice.

Because its singular and insistent voice does not falter before a public audience, *Jane Eyre* dramatically widens the space for female personal voice in fiction: it extends to privileged-class women the fiction of individual authority that Romanticism had consolidated for privileged-class men. If "books continue each other,"[19] *Jane Eyre* surely helped to foster the tradition of the Bildungsroman that burgeons after 1847. It is conventional in literary criticism to assume a one-way influence of men's work upon women's; I suspect that the influence of *Jane Eyre* upon fictional autobiography by men has not been told, and that the similarities Carla Peterson has noted between *Jane Eyre* and *David Copperfield* may be more than shared signs of the literary times.[20]

17. Hennelly, "*Jane Eyre*'s Reading Lesson," 703.
18. Rachel Brownstein, *Becoming a Heroine* (New York: Viking, 1982), 156.
19. Woolf, *A Room of One's Own*, 84.
20. Carla L. Peterson, *The Determined Reader: Gender and Culture in the Novel from Napoleon to Victoria* (New Brunswick, N.J.: Rutgers University Press, 1986), 84–85. See also F. R. Leavis and Q. D. Leavis, *Dickens the Novelist* (London: Chatto and Windus, 1970), 108–10.

Ellen Moers suggests as much when she notes that the first three chapters of *Jane Eyre*, "including the crisis of pre-pubic sexuality that is their climax, is the female equivalent to chapters 2, 3, and 4 in *David Copperfield*, the classic Victorian dramatization of the Oedipal crisis in a boy's life, which Dickens wrote after he read *Jane Eyre*." Moers also reminds us how daring Jane's voice is when she notes that David would never use the "hostile negatives" that Jane spits at John Reed.[21]

If the influence of *Jane Eyre* on male novelists remains unacknowledged, women writers from Elizabeth Barrett Browning and Harriet Martineau to Doris Lessing and Adrienne Rich have named the novel as a primary authorizing source. Even Virginia Woolf, in the guise of criticizing Brontë in *A Room of One's Own*, uses Jane's outspoken voice when she cites at length the "who shall blame me?" passage that she is ostensibly condemning for "sex-consciousness."[22] *Jane Eyre* seems to have been the acknowledged starting point for a tradition of fictional autobiography by women in a way that, as Elaine Showalter says, was "felt to have been revolutionary."[23] One early successor, perhaps the first female autobiography in American fiction and written by a proclaimed admirer of the Brontës, is Elizabeth Stoddard's *The Morgesons* (1862), which (using the first name of another Jane's sister) creates in Cassandra Morgeson a strong-willed figure whose fictional story begins like Jane's when she is ten and avidly reading ("unprofitable stories" rather than religious tracts), and ends like Jane's with an epilogue announcing her marriage and describing her happiness. In later decades other women in Europe, the United States, and the British Commonwealth constituted outspoken narrators who claim and defend forms of independence more radical than Jane's, often eschewing marriage for sexual freedom and professional life: Miles Franklin's *My Brilliant Career* (1901), Mary Hunter Austin's *A Woman of Genius* (1912), Colette's *La Vagabonde* (1911).

Still, "the difficulty of saying 'I' " in public voice is by no means ended with *Jane Eyre*. Brontë herself, perhaps responding, as Nina Auerbach suggests, to her own overconsolidation of subjectivity in *Jane Eyre*, creates in *Villette* a far more elusive and complex narrator

---

21. Moers, *Literary Women*, 24.
22. Woolf, *A Room of One's Own*, 71–73.
23. Elaine Showalter, *A Literature of Their Own: British Women Novelists from Brontë to Lessing* (Princeton: Princeton University Press, 1977), 122.

who withholds her story as compulsively as Jane tells hers.[24] *Jane Eyre's*
(and for that matter *Villette's*) fidelity to marital teleology may only
have reinforced the conventions that, I argue, restrain personal voice
for married women, for the ambiguous voice of the censored woman
continues most visibly in fictions that represent their narrators as wives
or fiancées. In both Dinah Craik's *A Life for a Life* (1859) and Charlotte
Perkins Gilman's *The Yellow Wallpaper* (1892), for example, the narrators speak a complex language of indirection even though their
writing is ostensibly directed only to the "dead paper" of a diary. And
until the 1970s personal voice has remained unquestionably a practice
chosen less frequently by women than by men. For Marguerite Yourcenar, writing in the 1920s, for example, the representation of female
voice was simply unthinkable: "Another thing virtually impossible, to
take a feminine character as a central figure, to make Plotina, for
example, rather than Hadrian, the axis of my narrative. Women's
lives are much too limited, or else too secret. If a woman does recount
her own life she is promptly reproached for being no longer truly
feminine. It is already hard enough to give some element of truth to
the utterances of a man."[25] This may be why Proust's *A la recherche
du temps perdu* is a personal narrative while Dorothy Richardson's
Pilgrimage is not—a difference of major significance, I argue, insofar
as the "I"-protagonist can represent the act of narration as well as the
narrated event. There is clearly some relationship between political
progress and personal voice: when Sylvia Plath's *The Bell Jar* appeared
in 1963, it ruptured an American literary scene shaped by the conservative gender ideology of the 1950s and dominated by the male
narrators of J. D. Salinger, Norman Mailer, and Philip Roth, while
the feminist movement of the early 1970s soon produced female autobiographical fictions like Rita Mae Brown's lesbian picaresque *Rubyfruit Jungle* and Erica Jong's heterosexual adventure *Fear of Flying*
(both 1973). Yet even in the 1970s, Mary Gordon admits to writing
the first draft of *Final Payments* (1978) "in the third person" because
"I wanted to sound serious. I didn't want to be embarrassing."[26]

24. Nina Auerbach, "Victorian Players and Sages," paper delivered at Georgetown University Literary Criticism Conference, June 1988.
25. Marguerite Yourcenar, "Reflections on the Composition of Memoirs of Hadrian," in
Memoirs of Hadrian and Reflections on the Composition of Memoirs of Hadrian, trans. Grace Frick
(New York: Farrar, Straus, and Giroux, 1963), 327–28.
26. Mary Gordon, "The Parable of the Cave or: In Praise of Watercolors," in *The Writer
on Her Work*, ed. Janet Sternburg (New York: Norton, 1980), 30.

By the mid-1980s, however, public female personal voice in fiction had become for white Western women as conventional as private female voice was two hundred years ago.[27] One sign of this conventionality also repeats eighteenth-century literary history: today men are once again writing fiction in the female voice. Such novels, which include (to name a random few) Wright Morris's *Plains Song* (1980), Reynolds Price's *Kate Vaiden* (1986), J. M. Coetzee's *Foe* (1986), Richard Babcock's *Martha Calhoun* (1987), Michael Dorris's *A Yellow Raft in Blue Water* (1987), John Updike's *S.* (1988), and Allan Gurganus's *Oldest Living Confederate Widow Tells All* (1989), offer perhaps as varied a spectrum of representations of female voice as did men's fictions two hundred years earlier: primarily sympathetic, sometimes feminist, occasionally misogynist. Like the eighteenth-century parallel, this resurgence in men's writings suggests to me both a new empathy and an old opportunity to recuperate female authority.

If *Jane Eyre* helped to inaugurate the tradition that has led to this new resurgence of female voice, however, Brontë's novel and the tradition it launched have also created a dangerous legacy signified by the gaps in my own examples—a legacy I suspect is a logical rather than accidental result of the terms of Jane Eyre's authority. I have already stated that Jane the character must silence all voices; I want to argue now that Jane's authority is also predicated upon the novel's production—precisely in order to dehumanize and disempower it— of a voice far bolder and more singular than hers: the voice of the Creole woman Bertha Mason Rochester. Brontë's use of a Caribbean woman as Jane's "mad" and silenced double is of course the very sign of the subjugation that Victorian Empire demands.[28] *Jane Eyre*'s project to construct the outspoken and insubordinate Jane as legitimately feminine succeeds by denying Bertha's femininity: she is large and "virile," "athletic" and "corpulent" (25.250), her face is "discoloured"—not white?—and "savage," (25.249); she has a "pigmy intel-

---

27. William H. Gass claimed in 1987 that of 195 recent novels he had examined, "eighty-one were in the first person"; he (unhappily) proclaimed the three most visible trends in fiction to be "an increase in women, first persons and present tenses" in numbers that go "through the roof." In "A Failing Grade for the Present Tense," *New York Times Book Review* (11 October 1987), 32.

28. This recognition is, of course, what impelled Jean Rhys to give Bertha a narrative voice and a West Indian name in *Wide Sargasso Sea* (1966). The best-known critical reading of the relationship between Jane and Bertha reproduces the text's own relations of power by making Bertha Jane's mirror. See Sandra Gilbert and Susan Gubar, *The Madwoman in The Attic* (New Haven: Yale University Press, 1979), 336–71.

lect," is but a "demon," a "harlot," a "thing" (27.271). Here blatantly dramatized is the "splitting of the female image" for purposes of domination,"[29] in which the black woman is first exoticized and then bestialized into a "masculinized, domineering, amazonic creature" of "animalistic, subhuman strength" who gives the white "lady" her identity.[30] In a fictional world whose pervasive imperialism is also reflected in the missionary activities of St. John Rivers, and whose Anglocentrism discredits even the "foreign" European women with whom Rochester associates, the most foreign woman of all must be "killed off," as Gayatri Spivak says, so that "Jane Eyre can become the feminist individualist heroine of British fiction."[31]

While this novel clearly reveals imperialism to be the unacknowledged foundation for its narrator's hegemonic authority, what is especially significant for the purposes of my discussion is the representation of Bertha as a woman with a voice gone wrong. None of Bertha's qualities receives more attention than her voice: the "mirthless" laugh (11.93), as "tragic" and "preternatural a laugh as any I ever heard" (11.94), which gives Jane the first clues to Bertha's existence; "her eccentric murmurs; stranger than her laugh," the "oral oddities" and frightening "sounds" for which Jane cannot "account" (12.96), the doglike snarls, "savage, sharp, [and] shrilly," that "ran from end to end of Thornfield Hall" (2.181). As Jane's voice signifies her fitness for Rochester, Bertha's crystallizes her failures as wife: conversation with her is impossible "because whatever topic I started immediately received from her a turn at once coarse and trite, perverse and imbecile"; servants refused to live with "the continued outbreaks of her violent and unreasonable temper" (27.269); "no professed harlot ever had a fouler vocabulary than she" (27.271); and it is her "yells" that finally lead Rochester to leave the "hell" of the Indies for England's "whispering" wind (27.271).

But what is Bertha's voice if not the voice of the woman who refuses entirely both "women's language" and woman's place—in-

---

29. Adrienne Rich, "Disloyal to Civilization: Feminism, Racism, Gynephobia" (1978), in *On Lies, Secrets, and Silence*, 291. Rich, too, slides past the question of race when writing in 1973 about Bertha as Jane's double. See "*Jane Eyre*: The Temptations of a Motherless Woman," in *Lies, Secrets, and Silence*, 98–100.

30. Bell Hooks, *Ain't I a Woman? Black Women and Feminism* (Boston: South End Press, 1981), 81–82.

31. Spivak, "Three Women's Texts and a Critique of Imperialism," 265.

deed, the entire symbolic order—the voice (of the semiotic chora?) against which Jane's verbal audacity gets contained and normalized?[32] The fact that Jane is not a "blonde, blue-eyed doll" but is herself dark and as a child was "savage" suggests that she is already dangerously like Bertha; that Jane is not the submissive traditional governess suggests that her voice must be shown to have limits of its own. Bertha's uncontrollable voice, which insists on being heard even when her body is shackled, is the frame that makes safe Jane's outspokenness and reveals it as ultimately unthreatening to the social order: precisely because Jane's voice must vanquish the voices of men, it must also be distinguished from the violent, angry mockery of the woman whom white patriarchy cannot restrain, the dark woman brought in chains to foreign shores. Thus just as Romantic narrative constructed authority as essentially masculine, so *Jane Eyre* legitimates female authority as essentially white. Indeed, authoritative voice in *Jane Eyre* is even more parochial, for it belongs finally only to white educated Christian Englishwomen of the middle class; Mrs. Fairfax, the housekeeper, has "no notion of sketching a character, or observing and describing salient points" (11.92), the housemaid Sophie is "not of a descriptive or narrative turn" (12.96), and the wealthy Blanche Ingram "was not original; she used to repeat sounding phrases from books" (18.163).

In this light, Jane's extraordinary narrative authority becomes insidious. At Lowood, Jane must learn to temper her voice for reasons of strategy; under Helen's advice she is able to "arrange" her story "coherently," so that "thus restrained and simplified," it "sounded more credible" (8.62). If *Jane Eyre* repeats for a more public audience precisely this gesture, then the text has revealed in spite of itself the concealed incompleteness that its own singular authority demands. If the powerful voice achieved by Jane Eyre helped to foster a tradition of outspoken white female narrators in novels since the mid-nineteenth century, the very hegemony of that tradition, brought into being by the dramatized silencing of Bertha Mason, must also have helped to foreclose narrative possibilities for women novelists of color writing in the West. I make this claim as more than hypothesis, for the evidence at least of the African-American women's writings discussed in the next chapter over-

---

32. Such a notion is supported by Gilbert and Gubar's observation that Bertha's entrances in the text are typically "associated with an experience (or repression) of anger on Jane's part." In *The Madwoman in the Attic*, 360.

whelmingly supports just this racial split in women's narrative possibilities. If Jane's voice can be empowered only through the silencing
of other women's voices, then *Jane Eyre* unwittingly exposes the
dangers of its own authority and makes clear that the difference of
gender is not difference enough.

11

African-American Personal Voice: "Her Hungriest Lack"

She could neither resolve nor dismiss. There were these scraps of baffled hate in her, hate with no eyes, no smile and—this she especially regretted, called her hungriest lack—not much voice.
—GWENDOLYN BROOKS, *Maud Martha*

What I see is the millions of people, of whom I am just one, made orphans: No motherland, no fatherland, no gods, . . . and worst and most painful of all, no tongue. (For isn't it odd that the only language I have in which to speak of the crime is the language of the criminal who committed the crime? And what can that really mean? For the language of the criminal . . . can explain and express the deed only from the criminal's point of view.)
—JAMAICA KINCAID, *A Small Place*

In 1859, twelve years after the publication of *Jane Eyre*, Harriet Wilson wrote the first African-American novel published in the United States.[1] Like Brontë's novel, *Our Nig* by "Our Nig" represents itself as autobiography. Its external signs point to first-person narrative: the preface connects the story to its author's "own life" and the first three chapter titles are constructed from the position of a narrating protagonist: "Mag Smith, My Mother," "My Father's Death," "A New Home for Me." Although the protagonist is not named as "I" in these

1. The first known African-American novels, William Wells Brown's *Clotel* (1853) and Frank J. Webb's *The Garies and Their Friends* (1857), were published in London.

194

chapters, no dissonance is immediately evident because most of the narrated events antedate the heroine's conscious life. However, by the fourth chapter, "A Friend for Nig," the discrepancy between these early chapter titles and the body of the text is evident: *Our Nig* is not a fictional autobiography but, as my discussion in Chapter 7 has already indicated, a heterodiegetic text.

There are persuasive explanations for Wilson's choice to write a book that would be taken for a novel rather than an autobiography: the profitability of the novel for a destitute mother whom poverty had "forced to some experiment"; the literary aspirations manifested in Wilson's verse epigraphs from Shelley and Byron and in her apologies for the book's "defects"; the utility of fully authoritative heterodiegetic voice for authenticating Frado's narrative to skeptical northerners; the value of novelization as a pretext for omitting material that "would most provoke shame in our good anti-slavery friends at home"; and the formal differentiation of this book from slave narrative so that *Our Nig* would in no way "palliate slavery at the South."[2] It seems to me significant, however, that in choosing heterodiegetic voice, Wilson nonetheless retained the signs of autodiegesis in her preface, in her pseudonym (which is also the epithet given to Frado), and in the titles for the first three chapters of the book.

I would like to place *Our Nig* as an inaugurating emblem of both the absence and the traces of presence of personal voice in African-American women's novels.[3] Although black women in the Americas have been writing novels about black women for over a century, I have not located a single novel before 1970 that adopts a public personal voice, and only one that uses a private personal voice. This "difficulty of saying 'I' " is all the more striking in contrast not only to the history of personal narration by white women that I have been describing and to a similar though later development in the writings of black men that begins with James Weldon Johnson's *The Autobiography of an Ex-Coloured Man* (published virtually "in secret" in 1912),[4] but also to the strong tradition of African-American autobiography that begins with slave narrative. Certainly Henry Louis Gates, Jr., is right to see *Our Nig* as "a missing link" between "the sustained and

2. "Our Nig" [Harriet Wilson], preface to *Our Nig; or, Sketches from the Life of a Free Black, in a Two-story White House, North. Showing that Slavery's Shadows Fall Even There* (Boston: Rand and Avery, 1859; reprint, New York: Random House, 1983), 3.

3. I am not suggesting a direct influence of *Our Nig* on subsequent narratives. Virtually lost until the 1980s, Wilson's novel could not be more unlike *Jane Eyre* in manifest influence.

4. See Arna Bontemps's introduction (New York: Hill and Wang, 1960), v.

well-developed tradition of Black autobiography and the slow emergence of a distinctive Black voice in fiction."[5] Yet in light of the particularly "slow emergence" of personal female voice in black fiction, Gates's comment has an ironic underside: although *Our Nig* charts the emergence of its protagonist Frado's ability to speak, it does not allow her a narrating voice. *Our Nig* thus initiates what I see as the first of three overlapping moments in the history of African-American female voice, a period of almost a century in which autodiegetic voice is present only through traces within heterodiegetic narratives. It is not until the mid-twentieth century that first private and then public female voice appears in black women's novels, circling back with a critical difference to the form of narration with which an African-American prose tradition began.

Before exploring the ways in which individual novels have negotiated the question of personal voice, I wish to speculate about possible causes for this difference between African-American women's novels and the novelistic practices of European and Euro-American men and women and African-American men. Although a large tradition of slave narratives, written from the eighteenth century until well after Emancipation, establishes an African-American voice in American literature, the great proportion of slave narratives were written by men.[6] Because enslaved women had less access than enslaved men to both the means of writing and the means of escape, because the "universal" slave experience tended to be figured in the masculine, and because the histories of female slaves so frequently involved rape by white masters and therefore "compromised" the teller's virtue according to white patriarchy's double standards, the voice of the slave narrative was predominantly male, and those few slave narratives written by women were until very recently overlooked by critics and historians.[7]

5. Henry Louis Gates, Jr., introduction to *Our Nig*, lii.

6. Estelle Jelinek figured the proportion of women's to men's slave narratives at about 12 percent, but additional works may have been uncovered since she made that judgment in *The Tradition of Women's Autobiography* (Boston: Twayne, 1986). Antebellum slave narratives written by black women include *The History of Mary Prince, a West Indian Slave* (1831), *The Life and Religious Experiences of Jarena Lee, a Coloured Lady* (1836), Zilpha Elaw's *Memoirs* (1846), *A Narrative of the Life and Travels of Mrs. Nancy Prince* (1853), *The Autobiography of a Female Slave* (1857), Harriet Jacobs's *Incidents in the Life of a Slave Girl* (1861); and *Memoirs of Old Elizabeth* (1863). The Schomburg Library of Nineteenth-Century Black Women Writers includes a volume entitled *Six Women's Slave Narratives*, ed. William Andrews (New York: Oxford, 1988), including works written from 1831 to 1909.

7. There is evidence of bias, for example, in the Federal Writers Project Collection, which during the 1930s gathered over six thousand oral narratives from former slaves. In his book

I also want to distinguish the kind of voice required of slave narrative from the voice of European autobiography. In a sense, because of its public mission the slave narrator's voice is only technically personal, for it is bound by rhetorical imperatives so urgent as to require a very careful fiction of autobiography. Since the writer's freedom (whether bought, bestowed, or "illegally" taken) was virtually the condition for telling the story of slavery, the narrator was almost never writing to plead his or her own case. In ways that had probably never before been true of an entire literature, the "I" of slave narrative was responsible to and for a community of other *I*'s whose lives might literally depend upon the construction of the narrator's history as both credible and representative. This burdened voice had to direct itself to a readership primarily of northern whites who, even though they might abhor slavery, were likely (as Harriet Wilson makes clear in *Our Nig*) to share the racism that sustained it. This meant that the voice of the slave narrative had to negotiate the fine line between the writer's truths and the fictions of the audience. I have already suggested that to the extent that any group controls the means by which books are published and read, the discourse of another group will have some orientation toward this hegemony; in slavery, however, these power structures controlled not only the literary means of production but the very lives of the producing community. As William Andrews says, the dilemma of these and later black writers was that "to *sound* authentic to whites required them to adopt a mask, to play a role, to feign authenticity in and through a carefully cultivated voice."[8]

Such conditions expose graphically the dissonance between the "I" who writes and the "I" that is written and may suggest that a community forced to begin its literary life by producing careful, public first-person narratives might have welcomed the freedom and flexibility of fiction's alternative techniques. It is also possible that generic differences are significant, that despite the crucial continuities between African-American fiction and African-American autobiography, there are also crucial differences in the conventions available within

---

of selections from this material Norman Yetman notes that males are "disproportionately represented" in the collection: "Whereas the Black population eighty-five and over was characterized by an extremely low ratio of males to females (.74), the ratio in the Collection is unaccountably high (1.43)." See *Voices from Slavery*, ed. Norman R. Yetman (New York: Holt, Rinehart, and Winston, 1970), 3.

8. William Andrews, "The Novelization of Voice in Early African-American Narrative," *PMLA* 105 (January 1990): 24.

the two genres for representing black subjectivity. To the extent that the novel has been a European genre, imperalist virtually from its origins, it has constructed black identity and especially black female identity as negativity and absence, as Bertha Mason inhabits *Jane Eyre*, as Topsy inhabits *Uncle Tom's Cabin*, as the unnamed servants inhabit Kate Chopin's *The Awakening*, as "blackness" inhabits Western discourse generally.[9] The titles of the two earliest autodiegetic novels by African-American men expose and disrupt precisely this semiotic negativity: in Johnson's *The Autobiography of an Ex-Coloured Man* (1912) the unnamed narrator's identity is constituted by passing for what he is not; in Ralph Ellison's *The Invisible Man* (1947) the visibly black male is, ironically, the unseen, "without substance, a disembodied voice."[10] It would not be surprising for the pervasive erasure of black women's subjectivity to mark itself in the narrative forms of black women's novels as well.

The historical constraints upon African-American female voice are the explicit focus of Sherley Anne Williams's 1986 novel *Dessa Rose*.[11] Through its own complex narrative structure, *Dessa Rose* illustrates the misuses of a black woman's voice and makes clear why private rather than public voice seems to be for black narrators a necessary first location of power. The first two sections of *Dessa Rose* are focalized through the perspectives of whites who need Dessa Rose's story for their own purposes: an ambitious southern schoolteacher making his reputation by writing manuals for slaveowners, and an abandoned wife who harbors runaway slaves on her rundown plantation in exchange for their labor power. In constructing her novel through shifting narrative practices, Williams represents the appropriations of voice that a black woman must evade in order to "write herself into the dominant discourse and, in the process, transform it":[12] when Dessa Rose is forced to speak, she either tells fictions or exposes truths her white listeners do not want to hear. The transformation of this pseudopersonal voice must therefore entail the right not simply to

9. On this question see Henry Louis Gates, Jr., "Criticism in the Jungle," in *Black Literature and Literary Theory* (New York: Methuen, 1984), 7.

10. Ralph Ellison, *Invisible Man* (New York: Signet, 1947), 503.

11. I am indebted for my inclusion of this novel to Deborah E. McDowell. For a fuller reading, see "Negotiating Between Tenses: Witnessing Slavery after Freedom—*Dessa Rose*," in *Slavery and the Literary Imagination*, ed. Deborah E. McDowell and Arnold Rampersad (Baltimore: Johns Hopkins University Press, 1989), 144–63.

12. Mae Gwendolen Henderson, "Speaking in Tongues: Dialogics, Dialectics, and the Black Woman Writer's Literary Tradition," in *Changing Our Own Words*, ed. Cheryl Wall (New Brunswick, N.J.: Rutgers University Press, 1990), 35.

speak but to speak freely, to choose a narrative situation and an audience that can be trusted not to appropriate her discourse for its own objectifying and annihilating purposes. This voice is represented in the novel's final section in the memoir Dessa Rose dictates to her grandchild, which is addressed to the private audience of her own "people."

Dessa Rose suggests that the absence of public personal voice in black women's novels from *Our Nig* to the 1970s may be an act of resistance, an important gesture of self-silencing. If so, the traces of personal voice in novels like *Our Nig* stand as visible signs of refusal or impossibility. Since little is known about Harriet Wilson or the composition of *Our Nig*, there is at this moment no recourse to historical documents that might explain why Wilson kept the pseudonym ("Our Nig"), chapter titles, and preface that prepare the reader for autobiography. If one looks at the chapter titles in relation to the novel's development, however, it becomes clear that the "I" is suppressed just at the point when Frado is taken into servitude—and almost immediately beaten for speaking an unwelcome truth. It is also in this chapter that she begins to be called "Nig." Except for one other chapter, "Spiritual Condition of Nig." (Chap. 7), even the name "Nig" disappears from the chapter titles, which come to reflect the events in the white family's history that determine Frado's fate but are beyond her control: "Departures." (Chap 5), "Visitor and Departure." (Chap. 8), "Death." (Chap. 9), "Perplexities.—Another Death." (Chap. 10), "Marriage Again." (Chap. 11), and finally "The Winding Up of The Matter." (Chap. 12), in which in the space of a few pages Frado herself marries, is abandoned by her husband, gives birth, falls ill, and is left struggling to survive in a racist "free" North.

One could argue on structural grounds, then, that the section of *Our Nig* in which the "I" is represented in chapter titles is that section in which personal voice is still possible, and that the enslavement of Frado as "Nig" is inscribed in the suppression of her narrative voice. Certainly the novel is filled with perils to the character Frado's voice: Mrs. Bellomont threatens to "cut her tongue out" (72) if she tells the sympathetic son James that she is beating her, and several times when Frado is beaten, a towel or a wedge of wood is stuffed in her mouth (35, 82, 93). All this because she is insistently a teller of her story, and without any comforting fictions, from the moment when she rightly accuses the daughter Mary of lying (34) to the moment when she tells in a religious meeting about Mrs. Bellomont's abuse (103), to the

200

successful utterance of a fierce "Stop!" (105) that succeeds in staying Mrs. Bellomont's blows.

The "emergence" of Frado's voice as a character, then, is structurally contradicted by her narrative "disappearance" from the text. It is as a mark precisely of this dissonance that I want to read the traces of autodiegesis in *Our Nig*: as an act of overt self-silencing like those eighteenth-century gestures I have already described. Gates speaks of these traces as "lapses," but Wilson, clearly a careful craftswoman, could easily have corrected such obvious "mistakes."[13] I see in *Our Nig* the attempt to find some hybrid form for representing the particularly complicated dynamics of African-American female voice through textually marked, hence reluctant or ambivalent, absences. While in the century after *Our Nig* black women created many novels that, as Barbara Omolade says, seem to "take us straight into the insides of Black women"[14]—novels such as Nella Larsen's *Quicksand* (1928) and *Passing* (1929), Jessie Fauset's *Plum Bun* (1929), Zora Neale Hurston's *Their Eyes Were Watching God* (1937), Ann Petry's *The Street* (1946), Dorothy West's *The Living Is Easy* (1948), Gwendolyn Brooks's *Maud Martha* (1953), Paule Marshall's *Brown Girl, Brownstones* (1959), Kristin Hunter's *God Bless the Child* (1964), Ellease Sotherland's *Let the Lion Eat Straw* (1979); and Ntozake Shange's *Betsy Brown* (1985)—not one of these is a first-person narrative, although most make extensive use of free indirect discourse and "figural" narration to represent a female character's consciousness. In a repetition of the eighteenth-century phenomenon I mentioned in Chapter 8 and perhaps for similar reasons, two of the earliest novels narrated in black female voices were written by men: Ernest Gaines's *Autobiography of Miss Jane Pittman* (1971) and James Baldwin's *If Beale Street Could Talk* (1974).

It is possible that these women use heterodiegetic narrators to guarantee the authority of their characters or to "protect" them from direct

13. Gates speculates that these early moments "reveal the author's anxiety about identifying with events" that "she cannot claim to recollect clearly," while "in later chapters Mrs. Wilson had no need to demonstrate or claim the direct relation between author and protagonist" because of the coincidence between the fictional and the biographical facts (Gates, introduction to *Our Nig*, xxxvii). Even if one assumes that Wilson's major structural imperatives were autobiographical rather than fictional, the beginning of the novel is apparently not autobiographically accurate.

14. Barbara Omolade, "The Silence and the Song: Toward a Black Woman's History through a Language of Her Own," in *Wild Women in the Whirlwind: Afra-American Culture and the Contemporary Literary Renaissance*, ed. Joanne M. Braxton and Andrée Nicola McLaughlin (New Brunswick, N.J.: Rutgers University Press, 1990), 290.

contact with an unfriendly or uncomprehending readership. It is also possible that the writers wished to keep a clear formal distance between author and character. I would like to extend here my discussion in Chapter 8 of the hazards of public voice for women writers by theorizing that the more a group has been subject to class stereotyping, the more likely an "I" will be seen as a figure at once (and paradoxically) of the author and of the entire group or class. In the words of Gayl Jones, author of two novels in the personal voice: "There are some critics who feel the character's preoccupations are those of the author's. I don't think this would be as true if the stories were written in the third person, and if there were some sense of the author's responding to experiences, directing how they're to be taken, or if the author wasn't also female and Black."[15] While readers might of course make autobiographical connections between a heterosexual, white, privileged-class male narrator and the heterosexual, white, privileged-class author who created him, they would probably not see this figure as representative of all white privileged-class heterosexual men; the voice that stands as universal reaps the luxury of being seen as particular.

Although no black woman in the United States seems to have published a complete novel in the public personal voice for almost a century after *Our Nig*, Zora Neale Hurston's long-neglected but now canonized *Their Eyes Were Watching God* (1937) and Gwendolyn Brooks's lyrical and still seriously neglected short novel *Maud Martha* (1953) straddle a double structure that suggests the desire to balance "distance" with "radical closeness" (to repeat Mary Gordon's terms) by representing the possibility, if not the achievement, of personal voice. Although these two novels construct different narrative dynamics, placing them within a history of personal voice suggests an axis of commonality.

The dissonance between personal and authorial narration that Wilson creates in *Our Nig* is reenacted even more dramatically in *Their Eyes Were Watching God*, a novel that is often praised by feminist critics for representing the emergence of a black woman's voice. Hurston's novel is indeed a record of Janie Crawford's struggle to find voice and through voice an identity that is ultimately both enabled and signified by her success in defending herself publicly

15. Gayl Jones, interview in *Black Women Writers at Work*, ed. Claudia Tate (New York: Continuum, 1983), 96–97.

in a court of law. To trace this development would be to traverse what is now extremely well traveled terrain.[16] Let me say here only that the text makes clear both Janie's verbal power—she is by the community's testimony "uh born orator" who "put jus' de right words tuh our thoughts"[17]—and its suppression especially by her second husband, Jody Starks, who "aim[s] to be uh big voice" himself.

Only after the character Janie has "found" her voice and spoken publicly in her own defense does the retrospective narration begin. The novel constructs itself as a frame story for this personal voice, creating an oral context in which Janie (a namesake of Jane Eyre?) can tell her history, and the narrative purports to be the history that Janie tells her friend Pheoby as they sit on the porch at sundown after Janie has returned to Eatonville. Yet *Their Eyes Were Watching God* does not give narrative voice to the character it claims is narrating it: after Janie has recounted only the earliest years of her childhood (roughly the same period encompassed by the first-person chapter titles of *Our Nig*), the text slips smoothly back into the authorial narration of the frame:

> "Nanny didn't love tuh see me wid mah head hung down, so she figgered it would be mo' better fuh me if us had uh house. She got de land and everything and then Mis' Washburn helped out uh whole heap wid things."
>
> Pheoby's hungry listening helped Janie to tell her story. So she went on thinking back to her young years and explaining them to her friend in soft, easy phrases while all around the house, the night time put on flesh and blackness.
>
> She thought awhile and decided that her conscious life had commenced at Nanny's gate. On a late afternoon Nanny had called her to come inside the house because she had spied Janie letting Johnny Taylor kiss her over the gatepost.

16. Studies that focus centrally on the development of Janie's voice include Wendy J. McCredie, "Authority and Authorization in *Their Eyes Were Watching God*," *Black American Literature Forum* 16 (Spring 1982): 25–28; Maria Tai Wolff, "Listening and Living: Reading and Experience in *Their Eyes Were Watching God*," *Black American Literature Forum* 16 (Spring 1982): 29–36; Barbara Johnson, "Metaphor, Metonymy, and Voice in *Their Eyes Were Watching God*," in *Black Literature and Literary Theory*, ed. Henry Louis Gates, Jr., 205–19; Elizabeth A. Meese, *Crossing the Double-Cross: The Practice of Feminist Criticism* (Chapel Hill: University of North Carolina Press, 1986), 41–53; Henry Louis Gates, Jr., *The Signifying Monkey*, 170–216; Mary Helen Washington, *Invented Lives: Narratives of Black Women 1860–1960* (New York: Doubleday, 1987), 237–54; Henderson, "Speaking in Tongues"; and Molly Hite, "Romance, Marginality, and Matrilineage: *The Color Purple* and *Their Eyes Were Watching God*," in *Reading Black, Reading Feminist*, ed. Henry Louis Gates, Jr. (New York: Meridian, 1990), 431–53.

17. Zora Neale Hurston, *Their Eyes Were Watching God* (Urbana: University of Illinois Press, 1978), 92. Further references will appear in the body of the text.

It was a spring afternoon in West Florida. Janie had spent most of
the day under a blossoming pear tree in the back-yard. (22–23)

With this sleight of hand, the text expropriates voice from Janie and
gives to the heterodiegetic narrator virtually the whole of Janie's history—and hence the whole novel—except for a portion of the last
chapter, which reinstates Janie's voice. Hurston does make copious
use of free indirect discourse to represent Janie's consciousness, but
Janie is no longer the narrator of her history. I want to suggest that
in this act the narrator comes close to doing to Janie the narrator
what Joe Starks did to Janie the character: keeping her from having
a public voice.

The important question for my purposes is not why Hurston uses
the frame device, which clearly creates important continuities between oral and written culture, black and white forms, writing and
telling, reading and listening. My question is why, having set up far
more explicitly and extensively than *Our Nig* the conditions for
personal voice, Hurston does not give Janie the *narrative* voice the
story claims she has gained. I am surprised that with the almost
singular exceptions of Mary Helen Washington and Robert Stepto,
critics who write about this novel's narrative strategies describe the
text as Janie's "narration of her own story," stressing the triumph
of storytelling made possible through Janie's voice even when they
acknowledge the narrative indirection at work in this text.[18] Formally,
however, the novel inscribes not Janie's verbal achievement but her
silencing.[19]

The dissonance between form and content in the novel's representation of Janie's voice seems to me most striking when she is called
upon to defend herself for shooting Tea Cake. Her courtroom speech
is meant to give the climactic proof of her narrative authority; it is
the discourse on which her very life depends; yet not one word of
what Mae G. Henderson calls her triumphant "testimonial" is directly

18. Missy Dehn Kubitschek, " 'Tuh de Horizon and Back': The Female Quest in *Their Eyes Were Watching God,*" *Black American Literature Forum* 17 (Fall 1983): 114. I cite Kubitschek here, but similar statements are made by Barbara Christian in *Black Women Novelists* (Westport, Conn.: Greenwood Press, 1980), 57; and by McCredie in "Authority and Authorization," 25. Even critics who acknowledge the heterodiegetic narrative structure go on to talk about Janie as if she is narrating the text: Elizabeth Meese in *Crossing the Double-Cross* contemplates Janie as "speaking subject" (51); even Henry Louis Gates says that Janie is able "to recapitulate, control, and narrate her own story of becoming" (see *The Signifying Monkey*, 185).

19. For a similar reading on somewhat different textual grounds, see Washington, *Invented Lives*, 243–45.

represented in the text.[20] While the scene in the courtroom is described at some length and other characters speak directly, Janie's
speech is only summarized: "She tried to make them see how terrible
it was that things were fixed so that Tea Cake couldn't come back to
himself until he had got rid of that mad dog that was in him and he
couldn't get rid of the dog and live. He had to die to get rid of the
dog. But she hadn't wanted to kill him. A man is up against a hard
game when he must die to beat it. She made them see how she couldn't
ever want to be rid of him. She didn't plead to anybody. She just sat
there and told and when she was through she hushed" (278). One
could plausibly argue, of course, that for Hurston to have Janie tell
the entire story would be redundant, or that there is more artistry in
the mere suggestion of the narrative than any direct rendering would
allow. But the choice is also, I believe, ideological; Wollstonecraft's
The Wrongs of Woman, as I will note in the next chapter, chooses just
this "redundancy" that allows Maria to model public female voice.
This absence of Janie's speech is indeed not an isolated phenomenon.
Although the text *says* that Janie tells stories or delivers speeches to
the community, these are not usually reproduced in the text although
other characters' speeches are represented, and so the textual silence
in the more public arena of the courtroom is in fact consistent with
the narrator's practice throughout, ironically reinforcing Joe Starks's
insistence that "mah wife don't know nothin' 'bout no speech-makin'"
(69).

   I propose as a lens for exploring this dissonance between story and
discourse the particularly complicated narrative situation that Janie
faces in the court. Everyone present is potentially a hostile or uncomprehending misreader: the judge and jurors and attorneys, "strange
[white] men who didn't know a thing about people like Tea Cake and
her" (274); "all of the colored people"—implicitly men—"standing up
in the back of the courtroom . . . with their tongues cocked and
loaded," (275) who are eager to testify that "Tea Cake was a good
boy" and "no nigger woman ain't never been treated no better" (276);
and "eight or ten white women" who are "nobody's poor white folks"
(276). It is these white women on whom Janie's hopes rest: she must
"make *them* know how it was instead of those menfolks" (276). Race
and gender collide uneasily: when the blacks in the courtroom are

---

20. Henderson, "Speaking in Tongues," 21. Echoing the pervasive practice I described
above, Henderson discusses Janie's "speaking" in the courtroom scene without mentioning
that her speech is not represented textually.

reprimanded for speaking out, the white women applaud. Near the close of this novel in which there has been almost no white presence at all, Hurston constructs a scene in which a black woman's voice faces an audience in which white men make the formal judgments, white women carry emotional authority, and black women like Pheoby, to whom Janie "tells" her story, seem to be absent entirely. Janie's speech, then, must satisfy three potentially unreceptive audiences, none of which is black and female.

Perhaps this audience parallels the complex and divided readership that Hurston herself faced writing a feminist novel in a male-dominated Renaissance within a white literary establishment. Hurston's narrative choices, when considered in relation to the complexity of her own audience, lead me to wonder whether one crucial issue at stake in the narrative structure of *Their Eyes Were Watching* is the question of black vernacular or "dialect" that I raised in Chapter 7. By maintaining the authorial frame, Hurston produces a voice rich in vernacular imagery as Frances Harper's and Pauline Hopkins's narrative voices were not, but the narrator's orthographically "standard" language still contrasts with that of the characters. Giving voice to Janie in the courtroom or on the porch means giving voice to a language with an ambivalent status in white literary (and social) America. The narrative form Hurston adopts allows her to have it both ways, creating a private structure in which one black woman is alleged to tell her story to another, but using a heterodiegetic voice to authorize Janie's story for a public readership presumed to be racially and sexually mixed. In a rich and provocative essay, Barbara Johnson suggests that the form of *Their Eyes Were Watching God*, which she describes rather too loosely as constructed of "shifts between first and third person, standard English and dialect," expresses a "self-division" healthy for black women who, in the face of racism and sexism, must maintain precisely the distinction between "inside" and "outside" that Janie learns when she realizes she no longer loves Jody Starks. For Johnson this "self-difference" that African-American literature "always has to assume" is "the sign of an authentic voice." Thus she regrets that "the search for wholeness, oneness, universality and totalization can...never be put to rest" no matter how "rich, healthy or lucid fragmentation and division may be."[21] In conflating the divid-

---

21. Johnson, "Metaphor, Metonymy, and Voice in *Their Eyes Were Watching God*," 212–13. It seems to me significant that Johnson laments that "*narrative* seems to have trouble resting content" rather than saying *individuals* might have such difficulties (213, my italics).

edness of all subjectivity with the self-division that emerges from oppression, Johnson ends up citing W.E.B. DuBois and James Weldon Johnson without commenting on the obviously painful language through which these men speak of "double consciousness": an identity of "warring ideals" and "unreconciled strivings" (DuBois) that has a "dwarfing, warping, and distorting influence" (J. W. Johnson).[22] If there is "health" in Hurston's narrative choice, I believe it is the health of recognizing institutional narrative pressures not unlike those Jane Austen "healthily" recognized after the failure of *Northanger Abbey* to see print. I find it surprising, therefore, that Henry Louis Gates goes to significant lengths to read the free indirect discourse Hurston sometimes adopts in this novel as a way of representing "an oral literary tradition," and I suggest that there is a recognition of Hurston's literary dilemma in Gates's comment that free indirect discourse "aspires to resolve the tension between standard English and black vernacular."[23]

While its strategies are different from Hurston's and less obviously at cross purposes, Gwendolyn Brooks's *Maud Martha*, written in the early 1950s during what was surely one low point of possibility for African-Americans (and for all women), also shows traces of the difficulty of personal voice for black women even after Ellison's *Invisible Man* had brought black male voice into the literary consciousness of postwar America. Using a lyrical, modernist form that replaces traditional narrative continuity with a series of vignettes, Brooks renders Maud Martha's life as a Chicago housewife primarily through free indirect discourse. But what makes *Maud Martha* seem "hungry" for voice, to use the text's own image, is its frequent representation of Maud Martha's thoughts as if they were direct speech. Modernist literature usually represents direct thought in the form of interior monologue, but this novel gives its character whole passages of quoted thought that approximate what Maud Martha might speak aloud if she had someone to speak it to:

> "He'll have to take me," thought Maud Martha. "For the envelope is addressed to 'Mr. and Mrs.,' and I opened it. I guess he'd like to leave me home. At the Ball, there will be only beautiful girls, or real stylish ones. . . .
> "I'll settle," decided Maud Martha, "on a plain white princess-style

22. Ibid., 214–15.
23. Gates, *The Signifying Monkey*, 181, 215.

thing and some blue and black satin ribbon. I'll go to my mother's. I'll work miracles at the sewing machine.

"On that night, I'll wave my hair. I'll smell faintly of lily of the valley."[24]

In contrast to the conventional strategy of free indirect discourse, which Brooks does employ elsewhere in this novel, this quoted direct thought seems awkward and archaic, recalling techniques virtually unused since the seventeenth and eighteenth centuries. Transposed in this manner—He'd have to take her, thought Maud Martha. For the envelope was addressed to 'Mr. and Mrs.,' and she'd opened it. She guessed he'd like to leave her home. At the Ball, there would be only beautiful girls, or real stylish ones. . . . —such a passage would blend into the structure of indirection that is in fact the novel's primary mode. Instead, *Maud Martha*'s "unnecessary" use of quoted direct thought constitutes a formal sign of its protagonist's longing for personal voice that also seems to me a longing for audience—in this Chicago of the 1950s there seems to be no Pheoby and no porch—at a moment when personal voice in Black American women's fiction still has no formal precedent.

The first example I have found of such a voice in an entire novel follows soon upon *Maud Martha*, inaugurating a second stage in the history of black female personal voice: the adoption throughout a novel of the private narrative form that Janie is supposed to be using in *Their Eyes Were Watching God*. The first novel of playwright, actor, director, and political activist Alice Childress, *Like One of the Family: Conversations from a Domestic's Life* (1956) creates a virtual foil to Maud Martha in its narrator Mildred, who is probably the most outspoken black woman then to have appeared in American fiction. In a series of some sixty individually titled monologues on subjects from the mistreatment of domestic workers to Hollywood misrepresentations of blacks, from drug addiction to religion, from slavery to northern racism to the budding civil rights movement in the South, Mildred reports, ponders, and holds forth to her friend Marge—an entirely silent presence like Juliette Catesby's correspondent Henriette—about black life in white America, often recounting her own successes at turning the tables on the white families for whom she works. Mildred's discourse does make use of a black vernacular, but without the sharp differences in orthography used to represent characters in *Their Eyes*

24. Gwendolyn Brooks, *Maud Martha*, in *The World of Gwendolyn Brooks* (New York: Harper and Row, 1971), 207.

Were Watching God: "How 'bout them pictures where people are always passin' for white? You know, they are always about some colored person bringin' misery down on themselves by passin' for white. Only the person actin' out the part *is* always white!"[25] Because this vernacular is the primary narrator's voice, it does not occupy the subordinate position Judy Grahn associates with the incorporation of "dialect" in a "standard" frame.

I find it striking that this first personal-voice novel adopts a form closer to the eighteenth-century epistolary method than to any contemporary mode—each monologue the oral equivalent of a letter (one chapter actually is a letter) complete with copious direct address. Like Riccoboni's letter-novels, *Like One in the Family* counters its character's ideological boldness with a privatization of narrative voice that contains the outspokenness. In this way, for example, Mildred's retorts to her white employers are buffered by narrative strategy: they become reports that Mildred repeats to Marge and that "we" merely overhear. But the use of private voice also stems from an important reversal of the condition Mistress Henley dramatized: while the public voices of white women have been mostly discouraged, the public voices of black men and women have been forced into servitude. There is thus a particular power in a narrative structure that eliminates the public, white narratee and requires the reader to "overhear" the private monologues of a black woman. At the same time, that the text represents the private narratee Marge's shock at Mildred's outspokenness may be a strategy for comforting the nervous reader that Mildred's behavior is not necessarily normative. In this way, *Like One in the Family* dramatizes the racial split between public and private voice that I suggested in describing the novels of Toni Morrison.

How this novel might have been received by a racially diverse audience, however, is impossible to assess. According to Trudier Harris, some of the monologues were originally published in Paul Robeson's newspaper *Freedom* and in the *Baltimore Afro-American*, but the book itself, brought out by a small Brooklyn-based press, was apparently reviewed in only one journal during the four years after it was published. Probably no buffering strategies could have saved a novel with

25. Alice Childress, *Like One of the Family: Conversations from a Domestic's Life* (1956; reprint Boston: Beacon Press, 1986), 123. Introduction by Trudier Harris.

such a radical agenda, written by a woman known to be associated with leftist politics in the reactionary mid-1950s, and the novel quickly disappeared from view. As far as I can tell, it took another fourteen years, and the convergence of feminist and African-American liberation movements, to produce further instances of first-person voice in African-American women's novels.

I have already mentioned Toni Morrison's *The Bluest Eye* (1970) in order to explain the way in which Claudia legitimates Morrison's authorial voice, but Claudia must also be recognized as one of the first public female voices in black women's fiction along with Francie Coffin, the narrator of Louise Meriwether's *Daddy Was a Number Runner* (1970). These novels inaugurate through similar narrative situations a third moment in the history of African-American personal voice: each is told by an adolescent girl living in the North in the 1930s and 1940s and coping with racism, poverty, and the threat of sexual abuse. The degree to which a simple "I"-narrative of growing up constitutes within African-American women's writing a revolution in form more than a century after *Jane Eyre* is suggested in James Baldwin's foreword to Meriwether's book: "we have seen ... life from the point of view of a black boy growing into a menaced and probably brief manhood; I don't know that we have ever seen it from the point of view of a black girl on the edge of a terrifying womanhood."[26] Annis Pratt has commented that women protagonists of the bildungsroman grow up and then grow down;[27] for Francie Coffin and Claudia MacTeer, growing up means watching everyone around them grow down. *Daddy Was a Number Runner* begins by portraying a poor but relatively happy and united black family doing its best to survive Depression-era Harlem; by the novel's end, Daddy has gone off to another woman, one of Francie's brothers has been in jail and both boys seem doomed, her mother is condemned to a future of housework in white homes, and various neighbors have met bad ends. Francie's own future seems hardly less bleak; her modest aspiration to become a secretary instead of a seamstress has already been greeted by one teacher's muttering that "I don't know why they

26. Baldwin, foreword to Louise Meriwether, *Daddy Was a Number Runner* (Englewood Cliffs, N.J.: Prentice Hall, 1970), 5. Further references to Meriwether's novel will appear in the text.

27. Annis Pratt, et al., *Archetypal Patterns in Women's Fiction* (Bloomington: Indiana University Press, 1981), 14.

teach courses like that to frustrate you people" (144). In the novel's final scene, Francie, her brother Sterling, and her friend Sukie are sitting on the apartment stoop:

> The sun was sinking fast and soon a dusty blanket of darkness would settle over the avenue, hiding some of its filth, but not all. The street was filled with colored people scurrying in and out of doorways, coming and going, crowding each other off the sidewalk. It was all too depressing. James Junior hadn't come to see Mother like he promised and I guess he didn't have a job after all, at least not an honest one. Vallie and them were going to get the electric chair and if they did get an appeal they'd be behind bars the rest of their life, so what was the difference? And Daddy didn't come home anymore.
>
> I tried to get again that nice feeling I had for all of Harlem a few weeks ago, but I couldn't. We was all poor and black and apt to stay that way, and that was that. (207–8)

In this atmosphere of death and despair echoed in Francie Coffin's family name, the narrator closes her story by repeating, after her brother, "Shit."

Francie's narrative voice is held to an adolescent's perspective and focuses primarily on external events, as if, desperate to remain intact against the destructive forces of white racism and male predation, she is unable to look too deeply within. Yet clearly narration is serving a critical function in this text: it is both a means and a sign of survival. The fact that Francie is able to tell her story, all the way through to the discouraged but rebellious final epithet, testifies to a positive textual movement that is contradicted by the narrated events. Narration serves a similar purpose for the more self-reflective Claudia MacTeer who, faced with similar happenings less in her own home than in Pecola's, is hardly more optimistic than Francie; her last textual words, "it's much, much, much too late," are no more hopeful than Francie's "Shit." In both novels, as in *Jane Eyre*, a female voice takes on narrative authority, but the difference of vision makes the narrative act the antithesis of Jane Eyre's triumph; both novels focus less on the narrator's development than on the decline of those around her, and the very fact of narration replaces a "happy ending" as the locus of possibility.

In the 1970s and early 1980s, personal voice is most often represented in black women's novels, when at all, as a thematic problem with ramifications for narrative. Gayl Jones's brilliant, disturbing, and

underread novels, *Corregidora* (1975) and *Eva's Man* (1976), are interior monologues, structurally excluding any textual audience, that
explore complex notions of both narration and self.[28] Both novels use
associative rather than linear structures through which the narrator
recalls (and the reader reconstructs) the sources of her anger and
pain. Ursa Corregidora, the protagonist of the first novel, has grown
up with the legacy of the Portuguese slaveowner and pimp whose last
name she bears—a man who raped and prostituted both her great-
grandmother and her grandmother, his own daughter. The repeated
telling of this story by Ursa's female ancestors becomes the barrier to
Ursa's construction of her self, to knowing "how much was me ... and
how much was Great Gram" (184). Imprisoned in (horror) stories,
Ursa's struggle is to separate "the lived life" from "the spoken one"
(108) and finally to tell—and live—her own story rather than
"bear[ing] witness," as her mother had done "to what she'd never
lived, and refus[ing] me what she had lived" (103). The narrator of
Eva's Man, on the other hand, must overcome the silence her mother
taught her; as the novel opens (she is in a psychiatric prison for the
murder and castration of the man who oppressed her) she must piece
together confusing memories and images and at the same time ward
off the officials and "helpers" who insist that she speak.

In both of these interior monologues the speaker works through
the fictions that have constructed her. Through narrative methods
that frustrate the traditional conventions of fictional reliability, Jones's
novels blur distinctions both among voices and between imagined and
lived event; all voices and memories are "real" in that they coexist in
the narrator's consciousness. For Corregidora though not yet for Eva,
the narrative itself enacts the journey Bakhtin speaks of as the novel's
central quest: "the process of coming to know one's own language,"
learning to distinguish one's voice from a myriad of voices.[29] In this
way, these novels repeat the very process of creating a "personal"
voice and make clear as well the constituents of silence: racism, sexism,
poverty, abuse.

It is precisely from this position of silencing that Alice Walker's

28. Gayl Jones, *Corregidora* (1975; reprint, Boston: Beacon Press, 1986); and *Eva's Man*
(1976; reprint, Boston: Beacon Press, 1987). Further references to both novels will appear
in the text.

29. M. Bakhtin, *The Dialogic Imagination*, ed. Michael Holquist; trans. Caryl Emerson and
Michael Holquist (Austin: University of Texas Press, 1981), 365.

Celie moves to voice as both narrator and character. Like *Their Eyes Were Watching God*, *The Color Purple* (1982) engages the search for voice on the level of content, but Walker's novel also succeeds in creating personal voice in its narrative form. Indeed, Walker recuperates and transforms the entire epistolary tradition by rewriting an eighteenth-century European form in twentieth-century African-American terms and ultimately by moving private voice into a quasi-public mode. Like many epistolary narrators, moreover, Celie and her sister Nettie are recorders not only of their own histories but of others' lives; each is what Gates calls "a mimetic voice masking as a diegetic voice, but also a diegetic voice masking as a mimetic one."[30]

Celie's search for voice, like Janie Crawford's, is visibly marked as a textual theme. Celie's text, a series of letters at first entirely private, exists only because she has been forbidden to speak: "You better not never tell nobody but God."[31] Writing is thus represented in *The Color Purple* not as a form superior to speech but as its substitute. Celie's letters trace the struggle to speak out that is made possible by the support of her sister Nettie and her lover Shug, so that finally she can walk out on her abusive husband: when he tells her she can leave only "over [his] dead body," she simply retorts, while "folkses mouths be dropping open": "You a lowdown dog is what's wrong.... It's time to leave you and enter into the Creation. And your dead body just the welcome mat I need" (181).

While Janie Crawford's coming to voice is denied a commensurate representation in narrative form, Celie comes to voice through her own narrative acts as she writes first to God and then to her sister Nettie and finally to "everyone." This makes *The Color Purple* probably the first and only epistolary novel written by a black woman in America; as such, it claims for a poor and poorly lettered black woman of the American South a tradition that has been European, white, and privileged. (Celie's references to her husband as Mr. —— remind me of Pamela's references to Mr. B——.) However, by eliminating most of the markers that distinguish written letters from oral discourse, including place names and dates, and by eliminating quotation marks for characters' speech, the text "oralizes" the written word. What Walker gives her character, then, is not only the textual voice Hurston

---

30. Gates, *The Signifying Monkey*, 243. Gates reads *The Color Purple* as a novel that Signifies upon *Their Eyes Were Watching God*.

31. Alice Walker, *The Color Purple* (New York: Simon and Schuster, 1982), 11. Further references will appear in the text.

did not give Janie, but a place in a specifically female-voiced tradition, the tradition of private writing I associated with the "heroine's text."

If, as I have indicated, African-American literature was born in the slave narrative and hence in the public voice, then in adopting the epistolary form Walker not only gives Celie a necessary outlet but reclaims for African-American women the right to privacy and reveals that the private voice of epistolarity may have a more positive value for African-American narrators than the restrictive place I have said it occupied for white narrators in the eighteenth century. As Celie's inscribed reader changes from God to her sister Nettie (I think here of Lélia telling her story to Pulchérie), Walker is also restoring to the black female narrator a black female audience, fulfilling the narrative situation that Hurston generates but does not accomplish when she puts Janie and Pheoby on the porch. And when, in the end, Celie can write to everyone—"Dear God. Dear stars, dear trees, dear sky, dear peoples. Dear Everything. Dear God" (249)—she has effected yet another transformation: her voice becomes public, but on her own terms. Because there are no dates on any of the letters, and because the letters are not even a realized, intersecting correspondence but a set of parallel epistolary histories,[32] the entire text presses toward this public voice. At the same time, the fact that Celie's and Nettie's letters do not always reach one another also keeps visible the material difficulties across which black women have had to maintain communication and community.

Black, poor, lesbian, Celie also writes in the only language she knows, and this is another reversal that *The Color Purple* undertakes. Because the dominant first voice of the novel is Celie's, Black English becomes the standard as it does in Alice Childress's *Like One of the Family*, reversing the tradition of framed "dialect" represented, for example, in *Contending Forces* and *Iola Leroy* and even in *Their Eyes Were Watching God*. For many readers, this inversion of convention seems to be so effective that when they come upon Nettie's letters midway through the novel, it is Nettie's proper and formal (acquired) white English that may get marked as "other" and seem stilted and foreign; certainly most of my students have been impatient to return to Celie's rich and lively voice. This strategy makes it, as Eliza-

---

32. Although Nettie's letters eventually reach Celie, they are intercepted by Albert and therefore do not reach her when they are intended to. There is no sign that any of Celie's letters reach Nettie. On the epistolarity of *The Color Purple*, see also Valerie Babb, "*The Color Purple*: Writing to Undo What Writing Has Done," *Phylon* 47 (1986): 107–16.

beth Fifer put it, "the educated language of the outside world that must be translated, not the other way around."[33] Given the self-perpetuation of white racism, of course, Celie's discourse, transcribed as "dialect," may still carry for some readers a diminished authority. To the extent that Celie's voice is read as authoritative, *The Color Purple* marks a turning point in the history of narrative voice: it creates a positive space in literature for a black female narrator who "murders the King's English."[34]

Like *Their Eyes Were Watching God*, *Corregidora*, and *Eva's Man*, however, and like such works as Maxine Hong Kingston's *The Woman Warrior* (1976) to which it is often compared,[35] *The Color Purple* represents voice as a luxury of birth and circumstance, tracing a character's escape from silencing. I shall turn now to a novel that does not represent this movement from silence to voice but assumes from the beginning the right to narrate, and which seems to me in this and other ways both to resemble and to revise *Jane Eyre*: the bildungsroman of an Antiguan writer whose narrator is able to live without the daily oppression experienced or witnessed by Celie and Francie Coffin and Claudia MacTeer and the narrators that Gayl Jones creates. Jamaica Kincaid's *Annie John* (1985) may be the first novel published by a black woman in the United States in which a black girl is allowed not only to grow up without growing down but to say so in her own sure voice, a voice so solid that its sound is "a calming potion" to her.[36] Since the only textual voice Annie John acknowledges wanting to vanquish is her mother's, and since that battle is as much internal as exterior, the novel eschews *Jane Eyre*'s predilection for direct discourse that engages the narrator in struggles with other voices. Instead, *Annie John* is marked by a striking absence of dialogue, so that the prevailing voice is even more prominent than Jane's without Jane's combativeness: it is *a* voice, not *the* voice. There is, however, a muted narrative struggle in this novel, a struggle with and against *Jane Eyre* and its confusing mix of female autonomy and British imperialism. In *A Small Place*, Kincaid proclaims that "I met the world through England, and

---

33. Elizabeth Fifer, "The Dialect and Letters of *The Color Purple*," in *Contemporary American Women Writers: Narrative Strategies*, ed. Catherine Rainwater and William J. Schick (Lexington: University Press of Kentucky, 1985), 158.

34. Judy Grahn, "Murdering the King's English," in *True to Life Adventure Stories* (Oakland: Diana Press, 1978), 14.

35. See, for example, King-Kok Cheung, "'Don't Tell': Imposed Silences in *The Color Purple* and *The Woman Warrior*," *PMLA* 103 (1988): 162–74.

36. Jamaica Kincaid, *Annie John* (New York: Farrar, Straus, and Giroux, 1985), 41. Further references will appear in the text.

if the world wanted to meet me it would have to do so through England."[37] Annie John meets narrative authority through England in the form, among other cultural artifacts, of *Jane Eyre*.

Although Kincaid's novel is clearly no direct revision like Jean Rhys's *Wide Sargasso Sea*, Annie's revelation that *Jane Eyre* is her "favorite novel" (92) more than invites comparisons. There are a few superficial similarities between the novels: both are named for their narrator-heroines; both characters are ten when their stories begin; Annie's friend the Red Girl might recall the Red Room in *Jane Eyre*; each girl attends a girls' school where she forms a close romantic attachment, the explicitness with which Annie describes her passion for Gweneth Joseph teasing out what is more covert in Jane's relationship to Helen Burns. The chapter titled "Somewhere, Belgium" describes a fifteen-year-old's fantasy world chosen explicitly because Charlotte Brontë "had spent a year or so there" (92), and in this chapter we also learn that Annie's middle name, which the novel's title pointedly elides, is Victoria. When Annie wins a school award, the prize is *Roman Britain* (the young Jane reads the *History of Rome*), and like Jane, Annie takes books that do not belong to her.

As Annie's middle name and the book she is awarded suggest, the novel engages simultaneously in evoking and revoking *Jane Eyre* as it reinstates the voice of the West Indian woman as English and marginalizes the English woman's voice.[38] Annie's education and citizenship are British, so that when she speaks of "our country, by which was meant England" (115), she is rewriting the national identities so crucial to *Jane Eyre*, and her childhood incorrigibility, in spirit like Jane's, is devoted not only to "boyish" behaviors like collecting marbles, but to politically charged acts such as defacing with "old English lettering" (78) the picture of Columbus in her schoolbook.

Even as the narrator seems to honor the paradigmatic female voice of white nineteenth-century British fiction, then, a major project of *Annie John* is to reverse the racism of Brontë's novel by re-presenting British characters and values through Antiguan eyes. Of the headmistress Miss Moore (a name evoking Brontë country?), Annie says:

> I knew right away that she had come to Antigua from England, for she
> looked like a prune left out of its jar a long time and she sounded as

37. Jamaica Kincaid, *A Small Place* (New York: Farrar, Straus, and Giroux, 1988), 33.
38. Actually, Rhys's novel is told only partly in the voice of Bertha ("Antoinette"), for Rochester narrates the middle section. *Annie John* is thus formally closer to *Jane Eyre* than is *Wide Sargasso Sea*.

if she had borrowed her voice from an owl. . . . [H]er throat would beat
up and down as if a fish fresh out of water were caught inside. I
wondered if she even smelled like a fish. Once when I didn't wash, my
mother had given me a long scolding about it, and she ended by saying
that it was the only thing she didn't like about English people: they
didn't wash often enough, or wash properly when they finally did. My
mother had said, "Have you ever noticed how they smell as if they had
been bottled up in a fish?" (36)

Such a passage turns on a white British woman the dehumanizing
animal imagery through which *Jane Eyre* describes Bertha and the
equally dehumanizing imagery attached to Caliban in *The Tempest*—
precisely the book Annie's teacher is reading on the first day of the
new term (39). Similarly, Ruth, the blonde-haired daughter of the
English minister, turns out to be the class dunce. But Annie John
feels sorry for Ruth because she is sure that Ruth, living in Antigua,
must realize "the terrible things her ancestors had done; perhaps she
had felt even worse when her father was a missionary in Africa"—as
St. John Rivers was. The Christian imperialism that enables *Jane Eyre*
is thus exposed in *Annie John* as a source of shame: "I could see how
Ruth felt from looking at her face. Her ancestors had been the masters, while ours had been the slaves. She had such a lot to be ashamed
of, and by being with us every day she was always being reminded.
We could look everybody in the eye, for our ancestors had done
nothing wrong except just sit somewhere, defenseless" (76). Just as
Annie John is not interested in overturning *Jane Eyre*, neither is she
intersted in a reversal of political dominance: "I was sure that if the
tables had been turned we would have acted differently; I was sure
that if our ancestors had gone from Africa to Europe and come upon
the people living there, they would have taken a proper interest in
the Europeans on first seeing them, and said, 'How nice,' and then
gone home to tell their friends about it" (76). But the novel engages
in a powerful if subtle exposition of *Jane Eyre*'s insidious representational authority, for the single moment when Annie becomes a racial
Other to herself occurs precisely in the chapter titled "Somewhere,
Belgium," just after she has revealed that her favorite novel is *Jane
Eyre*. First her beloved friend Gwen suddenly looks foreign, and then
Annie contemplates her own reflection in a store window and sees
herself become grotesque:

My whole head was so big, and my eyes, which were big, too, sat in my
big head wide open, as if I had just had a sudden fright. My skin was

black in a way I had not noticed before, as if someone had thrown a lot of soot out of a window just when I was passing by and it had all fallen on me. On my forehead, on my cheeks were little bumps, each with a perfect, round white point. My plaits stuck out in every direction from under my hat; my long, thin neck stuck out from the blouse of my uniform. Altogether, I looked old and miserable. (94)

What is of course on one level simply an adolescent's horror at the ravages of puberty is rendered ideological not only by the framing through *Jane Eyre* and the fantasy of Belgium, but by the passage that follows:

> Not long before, I had seen a picture of a painting entitled *The Young Lucifer*. It showed Satan just recently cast out of heaven for all his bad deeds, and he was standing on a black rock all alone and naked. Everything around him was charred and black, as if a great fire had just roared through. His skin was coarse, and so were all his features. His hair was made up of live snakes, and they were in a position to strike. . . . At heart, you could see, he was really lonely and miserable at the way things had turned out. . . and suddenly I felt so sorry for myself that I was about to sit down on the sidewalk and weep. (94–95)

While the racism of such representations is obvious, this passage also carries veiled allusions to *Jane Eyre*, from St. John Rivers's harsh proclamations about damnation (chap. 35) to Bertha's fiery destruction of Thornfield into a "blackened ruin," a "lonesome wild" of deathlike silence where the signs of "conflagration" are obvious in the "grim blackness" of the stones (chap. 36).

Annie John thus rewrites Charlotte Brontë's novel in a very different and more indirect way from that of *Wide Sargasso Sea*: it creates the voice of a West Indian girl mothered as Jane might have longed to be, a cherished daughter encouraged to read and to learn. When Annie John goes off to study nursing in England at the novel's end, England is neither a motherland of freedom and opportunity nor a place of colonialist captivity; it is an equivocal site of passage to a struggle of another kind: "I did not want to go to England, I did not want to be a nurse, but I would have chosen going off to live in a cavern and keeping house for seven unruly men rather than go on with my life as it stood" (130). Annie John takes to England only her name, which is "written in big, black letters all over my trunk, sometimes followed by my address in Antigua, sometimes followed by my address as it would be in England" (130): she is and will remain a subject with a dual (hence an uncertain) address.

This uncertainty of address operates not only in theme but in narrative voice. Just as the Antiguans are represented as uninterested in reversing British white supremacy with Antiguan dominance, so in rewriting *Jane Eyre* Kincaid seems uninterested in replicating Jane Eyre's totalizing and vanquishing voice. One moment in the novel is particularly illustrative if we recall that at a similar age Jane Eyre, when accused of lying, learns to tell her story more convincingly not by changing the facts but by controlling the rhetoric. While Jane insists that her story is the absolute truth, Annie John proves her storytelling authority by writing lies or fictions about her life. When she is assigned an autobiographical essay at school (which she must read aloud much as Jane must tell her story) Annie's piece turns out to be the best one. This triumphant occasion, which also marks the first time her name appears in the narrative, "cheats" the class assignment by being (like *Annie John*) a fictive autobiography: Annie does not "exactly tell a lie," but she tells "what would have happened in the old days" (45). While Jane Eyre must insist on absolute truth as a way to construct an impenetrable and falsely coherent identity, Annie John can acknowledge the fictions of—and fissures in—her subjectivity.

Nor, of course, can the public personal voice of an Annie John simply occupy the space of Jane Eyre, because to (be able to) occupy that space is also to have to articulate what centuries of silencing have cost. This may be why Kincaid followed *Annie John* with *A Small Place*, in which the racial anger muted in the novel erupts into a scathing narrative essay on postcolonialism whose initial subject of discourse is not the narrator but the narratee: "If you go to Antigua as a tourist, this is what you will see . . ."[39] The "you" of this essay—the narratee that is not addressed explicitly in *Annie John* and with whom the "I" seeks not to bond, as Jane Eyre did, but to generate a rift—is the "you" of the white West—the "you" responsible for Bertha Mason, the "you" descended from the likes of Rochester, who "should never have left their home, their precious England, a place they loved so much, a place they had to leave but could never forget. And so everywhere they went they turned it into England; and everybody they met they turned English. But no place could ever really be England, and nobody who did not look exactly like them would ever be English, so

---

39. Kincaid, *A Small Place*, 3.

you can imagine the destruction of people and land that came from that" (24). It does not seem to me too fanciful to name this voice as the voice *Jane Eyre* refuses Bertha Mason, the furious and cursing voice that mocks the brutalizers, appropriates their terminology, relocates the blame: "Even if I really came from people who were living like monkeys in trees, it was better to be that than what happened to me, what I became after I met you" (37). The language of *A Small Place*, which, as one reviewer says, "screams with hate," is a language that slave narrative could not have risked.[40] In refusing to speak of the crime from "the criminal's point of view" (32), the black female "I" of *A Small Place* insists on an authority that is not fictional. That no similarly outspoken voice has yet found its place in Kincaid's own novels suggests that the authority of fiction may still exercise its quieting influence on personal voice.

40. Review in *Richmond Times-Dispatch*, cited as front matter to the paperback edition of *A Small Place*.

Part III

COMMUNAL VOICE

Until we find each other we are alone.
—ADRIENNE RICH, "Hunger"

12

Solidarity and Silence: *Millenium Hall* and *The Wrongs of Woman*

Proletarians say "We"; Negroes also. Regarding themselves
as subjects, they transform the bourgeois, the whites, into
"others." But women do not say "We."

—SIMONE DE BEAUVOIR, *The Second Sex*

In a now famous passage in *The Second Sex*, Simone de Beauvoir
distinguishes the condition that, she believes, prevented women from
creating the collective consciousness that has characterized other oppressed groups. Women have been unable to say "We" and transform
men into "others" because they "lack concrete means for organizing
themselves into a unity which can stand face to face with the correlative
unity ... They live dispersed among the males, attached through residence, housework, economic condition and social standing to certain
men—fathers or husbands—more firmly than they are to other
women. If they belong to the bourgeoisie, they feel solidarity with
men of that class, not with proletarian women."[1] When Beauvoir wrote
her monumental study she did not have the benefit of feminist scholarship that has uncovered resisting female communities across the
world and the centuries. But if Beauvoir had been writing about the
Western novel, there could be little challenge to her claim: its con-

---

1. Simone de Beauvoir, *The Second Sex*, trans. H. M. Parshley (New York: Knopf, 1952),
xviii–xix.

ventions of plot have worked to rupture female relationships and attach individual women to individual men,[2] while its conventions of narration have kept women's voices separate and individualized. If Juliette Catesby's last word of desire is for Henriette, the narrative struggle has been precisely to undermine her alliance with women, and while Mrs. Henley hopes her story will help wives in her situation, and shows an unusual concern for women servants, Hollowpark offers no space for constructing female community; both novels expose women's wrongs but neither establishes women's rights. The one canonical novel of the period that represents women in community, Diderot's *La Religieuse* (ca. 1770), presents that community as a prison house of perversity, pathological not only because it is clerical but also, I believe, because it is female.[3]

At first glance, the technical conventions of eighteenth-century narrative would seem especially amenable to some form of communal narrative voice. As I mentioned earlier, one important difference between eighteenth-century and classic realist practice is the frequency with which eighteenth-century novels incorporate multiple voices and stories, whether through the polyphony of epistolary writing (*Clarissa, Les Liaisons dangereuses, Lady Susan*, Hannah Foster's *The Coquette*) or through the insertion of autodiegetic narratives into the main narrator's text (*Amelia, David Simple*, Claudine de Tencin's *Les Malheurs de l'amour*). Such narrative forms could readily be used to constitute novels in which different narrative voices collaborate to create a collectively authorized discursive solidarity. But as the examples I have given would testify, the spirit of eighteenth-century fiction is the spirit of "difference"; the novel is virtually born in the recognition of perspectivity, and the multiplicity of narrative voices functions precisely to represent these individual differences. In the process, and consistent with the project of "humanist" capitalism, the larger Differences that structure individual relations—that is, the power relations of race, class, sex, nationality, sexuality—become far less perceptible.

These narrative conventions that deter the construction of both female communities and communal voice are negotiated very differently, and with commensurately different public reactions, in Sarah

2. On this dynamic see, for example, Joseph Allen Boone, *Tradition Counter Tradition: Love and the Form of Fiction* (Chicago: University of Chicago Press, 1987).

3. On "pathology as femininity" in *La Religieuse*, see Rita Goldberg, *Sex and Enlightenment: Women in Richardson and Diderot* (Cambridge: Cambridge University Press, 1984), 169–204.

Scott's popular *Millenium Hall* (1762) and Mary Wollstonecraft's controversial *The Wrongs of Woman or, Maria* (1798). As different in mood and setting as Enlightment from Revolution, *Millenium Hall* creates a utopia of rich single and widowed women who have turned a large country estate into a class-stratified, female, charitable society, while *The Wrongs of Woman* creates a dystopia of women wrongly accused, abused, and abandoned, set in an asylum that is also a metaphor, for "was not the world a vast prison, and women born slaves?"[4] Both novels create the conditions for "saying 'We' " by bringing together those who have been "dispersed among the males" and by representing women to be disadvantaged (in Scott's case) or oppressed (in Wollstonecraft's). Neither novel is able to sustain what I am calling a communal voice, but both novels bear the formal marks of their own self-silencing: *Millenium Hall* succeeds by evading communal narration but subtly undermines the narrative authority on which the public text depends, while *The Wrongs of Woman* fails precisely because it remains in paralyzed suspension between individual and communal narrative. I will suggest as well that the differences in these two novels and their narrative strategies are remarkably homologous to the differences in ideology and social position of the respective novelists.

For the women of accomplishment and sensibility who constitute Millenium Hall's society, theirs is a community of choice, indeed an "earthly paradise" explicitly preferred over marriage, which most of the women have come to Millenium Hall to avoid, escape, or recover from.[5] For a patriarchal readership, such a community is surely, to cite Nina Auerbach, "a rebuke to the conventional ideal of a solitary woman living for and through men, attaining citizenship in the community of adulthood through masculine approval alone."[6] The narrative is therefore under significant pressure to provide some sign of this "masculine approval" in order to defuse the gynocentricity that Millenium Hall's existence signifies. For the clear message of *Millenium Hall* is not only that there are virtuous, intelligent women who would rather be with one another than with men, but that some of them

4. Mary Wollstonecraft, *The Wrongs of Woman: or Maria. A Fragment*, in *"Mary, A Fiction" and "The Wrongs of Woman"* (London: Oxford University Press, 1976), chapter 1, 79. All further references will appear in the text, with chapter number given first.

5. Sarah Scott, *Millenium Hall* (1762; reprint, Harmondsworth, England: Penguin/Virago, 1986), 6. Further references to this novel will appear in the body of the text.

6. Nina Auerbach, *Communities of Women: An Idea in Fiction* (Cambridge: Harvard University Press, 1978), 5.

have managed, in spite or because of men's absence, to form what is presented as a virtually perfect society. Precisely because the novel not only describes this society but accounts in detail for the circumstances that led five of the principal members to live together, *Millenium Hall* also subverts the mid-century "heroine's text" by presenting the company of women as the highest reward for the ideal heroine.

The novel legitimates its own project by providing on the level of discourse precisely the "masculine approval" that a female community would seem by definition to flaunt. As in a typical utopian narrative, the representation is textually mediated by an outsider who stumbles upon the community and becomes its ethnographer and advocate. In this case, however, narrative strategy places story and discourse sharply at odds, for the voice that authorizes this female community is male. One of two travelers forced to take shelter when their carriage breaks down, the narrating "gentleman" can neither enter the community nor represent it *as* a women's community; it is always filtered through a voyeuristic paternalism apparently designed to guarantee the women's virtue to the male narratee, an unnamed "Sir" to whom the narrator sends his "volume" and whom (after the fashion of Mrs. Henley) he authorizes to publish it. Like the narrator's omnipresence, the novel's elaborate title, *A Description of Millenium Hall and the Country Adjacent Together with the Characters of the Inhabitants And such Historical Anecdotes and Reflections as May excite in the Reader proper Sentiments of Humanity, and lead the Mind to the Love of Virtue. By 'A Gentleman on His Travels'*, conceals the community's most significant and threatening quality: its exclusion of men. Supporting this structure of legitimation is a pervasive Christian discourse like the authority that sustained the governess tales I described in Chapter 10: what the narrator emphasizes in his account is the elaborate social system through which the women sustain the disabled and the poor; support a community for middle-class women who have been sexual victims; and engage in myriad acts of charity. This is not, however, a classless utopia in which all women are equal: the "ladies" live together in the main house and each of their dependent communities is structured separately according to upper-class assumptions about different social groups.

The novel's male narrator and narratee, its coded title, its Christian ideology, and perhaps also its class stratification conspire to reassure readers that women without men need not threaten the patriarchal status quo. At the same time, this safe narrative surface is always tenuous because the "gentleman" clearly cannot narrate without intelligence from the women themselves. I propose that although the novel legitimates itself through its single male narrator, its avoidance of communal voice is also a subtle rejection of the traveling gentleman's entire narrative enterprise just as the histories of the individual women, which the gentleman does not narrate and which he therefore cannot turn to his purposes, emphasize the affectional preferences that lead these women to one another's company.

The double gesture by which the narrator is both authorized and disqualified is most obvious in the text's treatment of the women's individual histories, which are marked off within the narrative as long, separately titled inserted texts. Given the emphasis in mid-eighteenth-century fiction on the authority of personal experience and the importance of personal voice, the obvious narrative choice would have been to allow each woman to tell her own history; such a project would have constituted, on the intradiegetic level framed by the gentleman's public text, a series of mutually reinforcing narrators or what I am calling sequential communal voice. Instead, the individual histories are narrated by one member of the group, Mrs. Maynard, who turns out to be a cousin of the narrator and who, I argue, is repeatedly "pumped" by the narrator for information that is not quite yielded willingly. For instead of authorizing Mrs. Maynard as a communal voice, the novel exposes her position as compromised and the gentleman's demand for the women's stories as a voyeuristic invasion that comes to resemble just the kind of behavior the women have come to Millenium Hall to evade.

Mrs. Maynard speaks on the other women's behalf allegedly for reasons of propriety: she insists that the women are "never the subject of their own conversation" although they "are above wishing to conceal any part of their lives" (24). Since these women clearly have told their stories to one another or Mrs. Maynard could not be repeating them, the "never" must refer to public conversation, discourse directed toward outsiders or perhaps toward men. Since according to Mrs. Maynard the women also do not wish "to be present while their actions were the subjects of discourse" (70), they are textually distanced from their own stories, which Mrs. Maynard relates heterodiegetically, as if she were an authorial voice, but to a private audience. It seems significant that before any of their stories of female affiliation are narrated, the women's charitable way of life has been explicated and praised.

But the propriety in question seems to be required less by the fictional circumstances than by the culture in which this novel would be published and read. Heterodiegetic voice even in a private mode is surely the most authoritative choice for narratives in which women collectively reinforce the superiority of female community over heterosexual relationships. At the same time, the distancing of these stories of heterosexual unhappiness and female friendship from the voices of their protagonists, the physical separation of these acts of storytelling from the community, and the women's apparent unwillingness to speak for and of themselves, all suggest that the women are not authorizing this recounting of their histories—that while they understand that Mrs. Maynard must oblige her cousin, the gentleman, they do not endorse her narrative acts. Mrs. Maynard herself appears to be a reluctant reporter; the narrator must repeatedly maneuver "to be alone with my cousin, in hopes I might from her receive some account" of the women (24); must "call upon" his cousin "to perform her promise" (123) and "to continue her task" (152, 179). Her own justification for telling is as lame as it is arch: " 'It would be unnatural,' said she, 'for a woman to quarrel with curiosity; so far from complaining of yours, I am come merely with a design to gratify it, and only expect you will judge of my desire to oblige you by my readiness in obeying your commands' " (72). And she never tells her own story, claiming that to speak about herself would be "equivocal" (72), as if dividing her voice.

This tension between the women and the male narrator is mirrored by a broader tension between the histories told by Mrs. Maynard, which emphasize the women's ill fortunes with men, their intellectual interests, and their enduring female friendships, and the version constructed by the gentleman, which stresses the women's Christian virtues, social vision, and good deeds. The reconciliation of these differences is sometimes visibly disingenuous, as when a member of the community justifies the women's aversion to the "general duty" of marriage by comparing them to knights who send "deputies" in their stead or to devout persons who pay others to pray for them (115).

Moreover, the narrator is visibly motivated by a curiosity, indeed a voyeurism, that is precisely what the women have sought to escape in creating their private community. His earliest acts are descriptions of the estate and of the physical appearance of each woman, and although he himself deplores "curiosity" as "one of those insatiable passions that grow by gratification" (5), he intrudes himself into a woman's cottage and insists on being admitted within the enclosed space where physically "deformed" women are allowed to live free from just this kind of prurience. The ground for the women's resistence to male "curiosity" is also suggested in a discussion the narrator reports. Early in the novel Miss Mancel attempts to explain to the narrator's insensitive companion Lamont a Rousseauesque distinction among kinds of societies and their attendant possibilities for freedom of speech:

> "What I understand by society is [not large numbers assembled but] a state of mutual confidence, reciprocal services, and correspondent affections; where numbers are thus united, there will be a free communication of sentiments, and we shall then find speech, that peculiar blessing given to man, a valuable gift indeed; but when we see it restrained by suspicion, or contaminated by detraction, we rather wonder that so dangerous a power was trusted with a race of beings who seldom make a proper use of it. (61)

Among themselves, the women "can with safety speak our own thoughts": they "are not afraid of shewing our hearts," and have, therefore, "no occasion to conceal our persons, in order to obtain either liberty of speech or action." They engage in a "reciprocal communication" that is only possible among "friends" who "serve and oblige each other" (62). If this position can be taken as a communal philosophy, then the women's resistance of the intruding men may be a pointed refusal to give over their stories to outsiders—the same refusal of men that led them to Millenium Hall, and a refusal that makes one wonder whether the "race of beings" who so poorly use the gift of speech is the generic or the specifically masculine "man." At the same time, the very legitimation of the novel depends on minimizing this resistance to the narrator lest the community seem to be dangerously hostile to men in general.

If the women are engaging in acts of fiction rather than conviction in allowing the narrator to study them, they are subverting the very strategies through which the narrator establishes his authority. The fact that the name "Millenium Hall" is the narrator's invention, a pseudonym designed to protect the women's privacy, also suggests that he is creating his own fiction of female community. And most tellingly, there is no evidence that the community has authorized— or even knows about—the narrator's written account, which he sends to his narratee with the express hope that the recipient will see fit to publish it. While Mistriss Henley also asks her confidante to undertake this kind of publication of her text, the history she authorized her to publish was in fact her own. Given the appropriative nature of the gentleman's relationship to this female utopia, the inserted histories told by Mrs. Maynard stand as resistant, autonomous, and, by virtue of the structural superiority of heterodiegesis, perhaps most authoritative, against the narrator's otherwise dominant voice: had he told these stories himself rather than only recorded them, they would surely have been told differently.

Millenium Hall's narrative situation is thus at odds with itself. In order to reach a public for whom the idea of female community as an alternative to marriage might be unacceptable, Scott uses the voice of a respectable and conventional Christian "gentleman." At the same time, the women in the community withhold from this narrator the open discourse that characterizes their own society, and he is not permitted control over their personal histories. The tensions in the novel between Christian (and class) convention and what I consider to be lesbian sensibilities are replicated in the tensions between the "gentleman" narrator's ideology and the women's subversion of his authority. A novel *about* a (privileged-class) female community, *Millenium Hall* is not yet a novel *of* the community. Its narrative compromises, by which signs of resistance remain subtle and signs of lesbian eroticism are indirect, and its voyeuristic structure by which men "penetrate" women's secrets, are surely connected to the novel's successful reception, measured by its run of four editions in sixteen years.

Wollstonecraft's *The Wrongs of Woman*, unfinished at her death and published posthumously by her husband William Godwin in 1798, is less obviously a novel about female community and by no means a novel about lesbian community though it is more explicit in its communal politics. Yet it attempts more directly to authorize the "we" of which Beauvoir speaks, a "we" that tries to bridge, if only through two voices, the class boundaries marked geographically at Millenium Hall. Without yet shedding its own class biases or its investment in heterosexual narrative conventions, Wollstonecraft's project is much more openly critical of patriarchy rather than only of individual men, aiming "to show the wrongs of different classes of women, equally [*sic*] oppressive though, from the differences of education, necessarily various" (74). In *The Wrongs of Woman* "wrongs" articulated only tentatively as common in *Mistriss Henley*, and common but not communal in *Millenium Hall*, are argued not in a drawing room but in a court of law. Wollstonecraft's novel sets out explicitly to compose a history that "ought rather to be considered, as of woman, than of an individual" (73). It is a sign of the degree to which the novel is (read as) an individualist enterprise, however, that although Wollstonecraft's book was originally titled *The Wrongs of Woman, or Maria*, it has been reissued at least twice with title and subtitle reversed, and *Maria* is the name by which it is best known. While this reversal obscures the novel's explicit agenda, the easy slippage suggests that, as Mary Poovey has persuasively argued, Wollstonecraft could not save her own project from making its middle-class character an individualist heroine.[7] On the other hand, the various and conflicting conclusions Wollstonecraft attempted before her death signify her struggle to construct a narrative of female community and to authorize a female voice that would speak not simply for herself but, she imagined, for all women.

In contrast to the static structure of *Millenium Hall*, in which past problems have already been resolved by the creation of a (privileged) community, *The Wrongs of Woman* struggles to deconstruct the ideology that attaches women more firmly to men of their class than to one another across class boundaries. In this process, female voice must be transformed from the asylum's impotent verbal extremes—"groans and shrieks" that alternate with a "suffocation of voice"—to private personal narration, and then to public speech. The surreptitious discursive acts in which Maria, Jemima, and Maria's lover, Darnford, engage as they construct and interpret their histories become the means for solidifying community and escaping the patriarchal prison house. The novel attempts this transformation by shifting its narrative authority from authorial to personal voice and from separate but corroborating private voices to a voice both public and communal. Because the public voice it can construct is in important ways only a fiction, however, the project of constructing a "we" leads the novel into a narrative impasse that amounts to self-silencing.

The novel's first business is to authorize its own characters, who, especially by the standards of the late 1790s, are hardly fit for narrative authority: a disheveled, seemingly mad woman straining at her manacles, and a gruff servant whose "honor" has long ago been compro-

---

7. Mary Poovey, *The Proper Lady and the Woman Writer* (Chicago: University of Chicago Press, 1984), 94–113.

mised. Wollstonecraft uses an authorial voice rather than the voice of a "gentleman," but this narrator must establish the credibility of women who stand visibly outside the bounds of propriety and law. Like Burney, Edgeworth, and Austen, Wollstonecraft uses free indirect discourse to validate the feelings, thoughts, and perspectives of her characters and hence to establish their authority. Through a strategy of shifting perspective, in which the narrator focuses alternately upon Jemima and Maria, the text establishes the reliability at once of the characters and of their points of view, constituting the two women as a microcosmic cross-class community by recording the process through which they learn to accept one another as reliable. Thus Maria comes to recognize that Jemima "had an understanding above the common standard" (178), and Jemima develops an "involuntary respect for [Maria's] abilities" (1.80). Class distinctions, never erased but at least confounded by Jemima's role as Maria's guard, weaken beneath a common sympathy and shared oppression, and at times the textual boundaries between the two characters' perspectives become indistinguishable.

Having legitimated these characters, the narrator can yield them personal voice in an authorizing chain that also incorporates a man's discourse without giving it privilege. Darnford is the first of the three to tell his story, but his is markedly the shortest narrative (just three pages); he begins it with a fear that he will "weary" his listeners by his "egotism" (3.94), and after he speaks, his role as textual voice virtually disappears, so that Maria will even represent him in a court of law.[8] Jemima's story is six times the length of Darnford's, and she tells it because she "felt herself for once in her life, treated like a fellow-creature" (4.101). Significantly, Jemima's narrative leads Maria away from her preoccupation with Darnford and the novel away from the romantic plot and toward communal concerns: "Active as love was in the heart of Maria, the story she had just heard made her thoughts take a wider range.... Thinking of Jemima's peculiar fate and her own, she was led to consider the oppressed state of women" (6.120). Inspired explicitly by "the compassion I feel for many amiable women, the *outlaws* of the world" (10.156), Maria adds her own story

---

8. We can see how far Wollstonecraft has come in this novel in minimizing male authority by comparing *The Wrongs of Woman* to her first novel, *Mary, a Fiction* (1788). Although *Mary* sets out to create a book in which "the mind of a woman, who has thinking power, is displayed," Mary almost never speaks in her own voice, and Henry is represented as the source of her intellectual birth.

to Jemima's, writing it down for her infant daughter but giving it to Darnford and Jemima to read.

These histories, offered as representative, reveal both similarities and differences of class and argue that female community and even seemingly natural "femininity" depend on material circumstance. In Jemima's world, women routinely abandon and betray one another out of fear or need: her stepmother and half-sister have treated her "like a creature of another species" (5.104); she is abused by the wife of a master who seduced her; rescued by a "gentleman" for a sexual price, she loses everything once more when this man dies and his heir's wife—"why must I call her woman?" (5.112–113)—leaves her destitute and demoralized; she herself turns her anger on a pregnant servant and drives her to suicide. In Jemima's story, women fail each other again and again, beginning with that first failure of female community, the loss of a "bosom to nestle in" and "the grand support of life—a mother's affection" (5.103; 5.106). Maria, far more privileged materially, is able to support her sisters and to provide for her husband's illegitimate child, but she becomes a victim of patriarchal power when her husband, after she refuses to be prostituted in the settlement of an unpaid debt, uses his legal prerogatives to take away her infant daughter, confine her to an asylum, and appropriate her funds. Capitalist patriarchy is here exposed as a system that conquers women by dividing them; ironically the asylum, by throwing these different women together, offers a way out.

Since Jemima and Maria also tell other women's stories in the process of telling their own, the text becomes a narrative by, for, and about (wronged) women that generates a movement from experience to theory to political acts. Communal understanding, emerging from the recognition of mutual oppression as a basis for analysis and change, reveals the insufficiency of individual solutions; Maria and Jemima must escape the asylum and its private discursive space and take their story into a forum so "public" that it does not even allow women to speak. Maria prepares openly to defend herself "from a charge [of adultery with Darnford] which she was determined to plead guilty" by refusing publicly (as Mistriss Henley refused privately) the very grounds on which "right" and "wrong" have been constructed, transforming an analysis of individual wrongs into a proclamation of collective rights. Since by law and custom the woman cannot address the court on her own behalf, Maria provides a written analysis that she bases on the personal histories exchanged in the asylum. The private texts now become transformed into a purportedly public discourse speaking a collective vision that faces the Law (of the Father) and refuses it.

Maria's address to the court, which constitutes most of the last completed chapter of the book, thus authorizes her voice in a new way, but for that very reason creates a collision with institutionalized authority from which the novel never recovers. Since her statement more or less repeats the memoirs that the novel's audience has already read, Wollstonecraft would not have needed to include the courtroom speech in its entirely (recall Hurston's contrary practice in *Their Eyes Were Watching God*). That she does so, providing in substance no new "information," suggests a textual desire to model a public, communal discourse in which the individual story, linked to the stories of other women, can yield a new set of philosophical and hence legal principles:

> Various are the cases, in which a woman ought to separate herself from her husband; and mine, I may be allowed emphatically to insist, comes under the description of the most aggravated. (17.195)

> While no command of a husband can prevent a woman from suffering for certain crimes, she must be allowed to consult her conscience, and regulate her conduct, in some degree, by her own sense of right. The respect I owe myself, demanded my strict adherence to my determination of never viewing Mr. Venables in the light of a husband, nor could it forbid me from encouraging another. (17.197)

That Maria is not able to appear in her own person to speak these words directly—that they must be read out by a man—is, however, a reminder of the equivocal position of female voice. When Maria's "paper" is finished it is the Judge who has the last word, not only in the courtroom but in the chapter and indeed the completed portion of the book. Immediately expressing his concern that "letting women plead their feelings"—he uses the phrase twice—will open "a floodgate for immorality" (149), the judge denies Maria effective voice just as the law has denied her the right to appear in court: he undermines the public (philosophical and legal) nature of her speech by relegating it to the discourse of "feelings," the stereotypical quintessence of private female voice. Such a gesture recalls Ossery's reduction of Juliette Catesby's rights to the display of her "charms."

It is no wonder that at this point the novel reaches an impasse of both voice and plot; having "gone public" with Woman's wrongs, neither Maria nor Wollstonecraft can recover Maria's, let alone Woman's, rights. Maria is unfit after all to speak for her sex, not simply because she has committed adultery and refuses to be ashamed, but because the sex is unfit to speak. It is thus appropriate that although as character Maria speaks to a public audience, as narrator Maria's discourse remains private (intradiegetic), addressed only to the courtroom audience inscribed in the text itself. The only *public* voice in the novel is the authorial narrator's voice, and, as in Riccoboni's *L'Abeille*, this novel's most radical statements are the statements not of the public, authorial narrator but of fictional characters speaking only to other characters.

Perhaps it is not surprising, then, that while *The Wrongs of Woman* does not bear an explicit proclamation of self-silencing as do *L'Abeille* and *Mistriss Henley*, Wollstonecraft experienced uncharacteristically severe difficulties in completing it. What Godwin describes in his "Advertisement" preceding chapter 15 as "broken paragraphs and half-finished sentences" (186) already mark the drafts of the courtroom scene; much more fragmented still are Wollstonecraft's multiple and sometimes contradictory attempts to resolve the plot. Scholars have understandably wondered why, since these signs of self-censorship and paralysis are not evident in her earlier works (some of which she completed in a matter of weeks), it took Wollstonecraft a full year to draft the first volume of *The Wrongs of Woman*; why she "began in several forms, which she successively rejected, after they were considerably advanced," "wrote many parts of the work again and again," and could not settle upon a direction for the plot. Godwin attributes the difficulties to a heightened awareness of her own capabilities and the attendant difficulty of writing the "truly excellent novel" to which she now aspired.[9] Wollstonecraft's correspondence suggests that this unconventional novel may have disconcerted even her closest male supporters. On 4 September 1796 she wrote to Godwin that she was "labouring . . . in vain to overcome a depression of spirits, which some things you uttered yesterday, produced. . . . I allude to what you remarked, relative to my manner of writing—that there was a radical defect in it—a worm in the bud—&c. What is to be done, I must either disregard your opinion, think it unjust, or throw down my pen in

---

9. William Godwin, *Memoirs of the Author of "A Vindication of the Rights of Woman"* (London, 1798), 171.

despair.... I have scarcely written a line to please myself (and very little with respect to quantity) since you saw my M.S."[10] Godwin's own language in the Advertisement preceding the final chapters, with his anxiety that readers will be put off by the sketchiness of her notes for ending the novel (but which may be anticipating the public outcry against this book not for its form but for its politics) suggests a personal distaste; he calls it "repell[ent]", "incoherent," "imperfect," and "mutilated" (186). And Wollstonecraft writes to their friend George Dyson on 15 May 1797 that "I am vexed and surprised at your not thinking the situation of Maria sufficiently important, and can only account for this . . . by recollecting that you are a man."[11]

This lack of support from Wollstonecraft's immediate literary community would only have reinforced the fictional and political conventions internalized, as Mary Poovey argues, in Wollstonecraft's own literary consciousness.[12] Mitzi Myers has observed that it was nearly impossible for anyone to "weave radical ideology into the fictionalized texture" of female experience as the novel imagined it.[13] Although the essay form in which Wollstonecraft published her *Vindication of the Rights of Woman* required no major transformation to suit Wollstonecraft's feminist ideas, the novel did not yield easily in either plot or voice to a discourse "rather . . . as of woman than of an individual." There is thus a sad and unintended irony in Wollstonecraft's claim in her preface that her desire to portray "the misery and oppression peculiar to women" had "restrain[ed] her fancy."

The Wrongs of Woman does stand as a challenge, then, but if its lack of closure is a refusal of "mastery" as Mary Jacobus argues,[14] the refusal is hardly a triumphant one. In contrast to Riccoboni and Charrière, who deliberately truncated their works in displays of self-silencing, Wollstonecraft apparently generated ending after ending without being satisfied. Most of these endings, whether they resolve in marriage or death, whether they bring Maria and Darnford together or separate them disastrously, suggest individual rather than

10. Mary Wollstonecraft, *Collected Letters*, ed. Ralph M. Wardle (Ithaca: Cornell University Press, 1979), 344–45.

11. Wollstonecraft, *Letters*, 391.

12. Poovey, *The Proper Lady and the Woman Writer*, 94–112.

13. Mitzi Myers, "Unfinished Business: Wollstonecraft's *Maria*," *Wordsworth Circle* 11 (1980): 110.

14. Mary Jacobus, "The Difference of View," in *Women Writing and Writing about Women* (London: Croom Helm, 1979), 15–16.

communal resolutions. The one conclusion Wollstonecraft did write out in more than a few words and phrases, however, appears as Godwin noticed "to deviate from the preceding hints": Jemima rescues Maria from death and restores her lost daughter, and Maria exclaims, "The conflict is over!—I will live for my child!" (153). This resolution does keep Jemima, Maria, and her daughter together, evading the heterosexual-individualist plot that returns women to live "dispersed among the males."

Although differences between Scott and Wollstonecraft have not been the focus of my argument, the vastly different public responses to these novels, as well as their different ideological positions, seem to me inseparable from biographical and historical differences: Scott was a woman of considerable intellectual and class privilege, the sister of Elizabeth Montagu, a "Bluestocking" and a Christian who lived entirely with public approval although her desires were perhaps lesbian;[15] Wollstonecraft was largely self-educated, forced early to earn her living, associated herself with radical causes, and lived her (hetero)sexual life in ways that were publicly unconventional. The narrative forms of the two novels are manifestly homologous to these differences in self-presentation, and I imagine that not only the differences between their novels but the differences in the writers' reputations generated such different public reactions to their work. Told differently, and by a woman of different status, the story of "Millenium Hall" could have seemed as dangerously gynocentric as Wollstonecraft's widely condemned, unfinished narrative.

On the other hand, while Wollstonecraft might eventually have finished her novel, *The Wrongs of Woman* would probably not have resolved its contradictory imperatives toward conventional novelization and communal form. Against the successful patriarchal cover Scott constructed for her novel, Wollstonecraft's exposure of patriarchy stands as proclamation of narrative and social impossibility. Both works suggest that whatever formal conventions for communal voice were available to the eighteenth-century novel, eighteenth-century (English) discourse lacked the valorization of female community— especially lesbian community or community across class lines—that

15. Scott was married briefly and unhappily in 1751, and lived during and after her marriage with her close friend Lady Barbara Montagu until the latter's death in 1765. Scott curtailed public knowledge of her private life by directing that all her papers be destroyed after her death.

could have transformed these technical possibilities into authoritative text. Ironically, this impasse will be reversed in the next century as a form of female community becomes ideologically feasible in the novel at the same time that the narrative techniques for representing it disappear from currency.

13

Single Resistances: The Communal "I" in Gaskell, Jewett, and Audoux

Here then was I (call me Mary Beton, Mary Seton, Mary Carmichael or by any name you please—it is not a matter of any importance).
                        —VIRGINIA WOOLF, *A Room of One's Own*

By the mid-nineteenth century, as I discussed earlier, some women especially in the United States and England were using the novel to construct a "separate," morally if not always canonically authoritative domestic "sphere." As the histories of nineteenth-century feminism, abolition, unionization, temperance, and other more-and-less radical reform movements have underscored, the alleged moral superiority of women became a basis from which to intervene in the public domain with the discourses of home and church. Such a movement opened space for—and was itself opened by—novels in which formal and informal female communities, explicitly or implicitly utopian, offered "feminine" solutions for a transformed world.

It is ironic and symptomatic that this potential for a communal female authority was emerging at the same time that fictional narration was becoming overwhelmingly singular, a choice between the hierarchically superior authoriality of a "Balzac" or "Eliot" and the totalizing autobiography of a David Copperfield, Huck Finn, or Jane Eyre. The dual narrative structure of Dickens's *Bleak House* is a fascinating exception that proves the gender-genre rule: replicating the ideology of separate spheres, it sets the omniscient and implicitly male voice of the authorial narrator next to the personal voice of the female character Esther Summerson without acknowledging this duality: the alternating narratives proceed as if they were independent texts. The visible move from communality to singularity in *Madame Bovary*, which could hardly be accidental coming from the champion of "le mot juste," is another marker of the narrative times: although the novel's first word is *nous* and its initial eyewitness narrator the spokesman for a group of schoolboys, the discourse quickly becomes authorial and the "we" is not heard from again.

At the moment when female community becomes politically feasible, then, narrative convention resists the construction of communal voice. The dissonance is vividly dramatized in Charlotte Perkins Gilman's *Herland* (1915), which imagines a long-standing all-female (but by no means lesbian) child-centered utopian society, reproducing itself through parthenogenesis, which refuses distinctions between "public" and "private" domains by building its communal life on values of cooperation, nurturance, and scientific achievement. As with *Millenium Hall*, however, this all-female world is never presented as such; *Herland*'s story is mediated and legitimated by the voice of the sociologist Van, who becomes much more than an eyewitness when he falls in love with one of *Herland*'s inhabitants. *Herland* is investigated from the outside, as an empirical phenomenon: we enter it with the men who penetrate its borders and we are presented with the men's rather than the women's fears, reactions, and desires. Although the narrative does incorporate dialogue between the Herlandian women and the American men, no woman has a sustained narrative role like Mrs. Maynard's in *Millenium Hall*. And although Van is by no means the novel's dominant ideological authority, the women of *Herland* remain objects in the narrative scheme—a status that, along with their newfound (hetero)sexuality, subtly reinforces the androcentrism and individualism that the story is supposed to be challenging. Angelika Bammer identifies at least two earlier utopias that similarly use a male voice to represent a female society: Mary Griffin's *Three Hundred Years Hence* (1836) and Ella Marchant's *Unveiling a Parallel* (1893).[1]

The three novels I will discuss in this chapter quietly oppose these conventions of utopian fiction and narrative form. Elizabeth Gaskell's

---

1. On these novels and other nineteenth-century female utopias, see Bammer, *Partial Visions: Feminism and Utopianism in the 1970s* (London: Routledge, 1991), chap. 2

Cranford (1853), Sarah Orne Jewett's *The Country of the Pointed Firs* (1896), and Marguerite Audoux's *L'Atelier de Marie-Claire* (1920) all create communities of women, but perhaps because they are not radical utopias like *Herland*, they do construct female narrators who can at least provisionally situate themselves inside the respective communities they seek to represent and authorize. These "singular" communal narrators are constructed through subtle but important departures from autodiegetic practices, for while the narrators retain the syntax of "first-person" narrative, their texts avoid the markers of individuality that characterize personal voice and thereby resist the equation of narrator and protagonist. Rather, the narrator's identity becomes communal: not only is she an authoritative mediator of the community, but the community is represented as the very source of her (textual) identity. Such a departure from conventional autodiegesis, however, implicates not only narration but plot: because the novel traditionally binds the female character in (heterosexual) conflict, novelistic teleology is challenged by articulations of communal voice.

Like *Millenium Hall* if without the wealth of its "society," both *Cranford* and *The Country of the Pointed Firs* represent communities of women set apart from patriarchal-capitalist economies. While *Millenium Hall* actually engages the tropes of conventional fiction by detailing the heterosexual misadventures that have brought its members to the community, Gaskell's and especially Jewett's novels relegate heterosexual intrigue to minor subplots. These novels thus operate on what has been viewed as stasis—the position of utopian fiction—rather than on conventional novelistic movement, and are therefore often claimed not be to be novels at all. *L'Atelier de Marie-Claire*, on the other hand, locates its community of working women, as Wollstonecraft locates Maria and Jemima, in a dystopic social order, and engages a dynamic plot in which the refusal of heterosexual teleology must take a more active form. For this reason, however, Audoux's novel resists autodiegesis with considerably more difficulty, in a "resolution" that stops short of conventional closure, if less dramatically than Wollstonecraft's.

Long (de)valued as a nostalgic idyll of village life, *Cranford* has in recent years been considered a feminine if not a feminist utopia. That the genteel ladies who "possess" Cranford are named in the first sentence as "Amazons," that we are told that "if a married couple comes to settle in the town, somehow the gentleman disappears,"[2] suggests some effort to construct these women as a powerful community. Unlike the autonomous Herland, however, Cranford is a tiny enclave within a capitalist society, and although some of the gentlemen do indeed "disappear," even *Cranford*'s chapter titles confirm that this is not literally a world without men.[3] But the visibility of men is used repeatedly to stage a gynocentric stance. Thus Miss Pole laments that "men will be men. Every mother's son of them wishes to be considered Samson and Solomon rolled into one" (10.145), and Miss Deborah Jenkyns "would have despised the modern idea of women being equal to men. Equal, indeed! she knew they were superior" (2.18).

Cranford's object, it seems, is to absorb men without absorbing what are perceived to be at once male, capitalist, and urban ways. The "I"-narrator that Gaskell constructs to mediate this project is a figure whose liminal position is built into her identity as character: she is a father's daughter—there is no mention of a mother—who has "vibrated all my life between Drumble and Cranford" (16.235). Her narrative purpose seems to be to articulate Cranford to "Drumble" (London?), to explain its "rules and regulations" (1.3), its values, its eccentricities. But unlike the male narrators of female utopias, this narrator comes to speak not only for the community but *as* the community, and in the process she herself becomes the ground on which the clash of cultures gets worked out.

This project of mediation demands of the narrator an implicitly contradictory authority: at once to know Cranford well enough to represent it faithfully, and to be outside it enough for her judgment of Cranford to seem reliable for her Drumble narratees. At the outset, therefore, the narrator's representation of her relationship to the community is ambiguous. On the one hand, her syntax is that of an outsider, fond of and somewhat bemused by "the ladies of Cranford" but ideologically allied with her narratees: "one of them observed to me once"; "I will answer for it" (1.2); "I can testify to" (1.2); "I imagine" (1.3); "I never shall forget" (1.5). But almost as immediately, the narrator claims a place inside the Cranford community, and her pro-

---

2. Elizabeth Gaskell, *Cranford* (London: J. M. Dent, 1977), 1. All further references will appear in the text, with chapter numbers given first.
3. It is probably not in political innocence that when Gaskell prepared *Cranford* for book publication she added androcentric chapter titles ("The Captain," "A Visit to an Old Bachelor," "Poor Peter," "Signor Brunoni," "Samuel Brown") very different from the generic titles Dickens affixed to the serialized version in *Household Words* ("Memory at Cranford," "Visiting at Cranford," "The Great Cranford Panic").

nouns shift from "they" to "we": "we had a tradition" (1.2), "we kept ourselves to short sentences of small talk" (1.3); "we none of us spoke of money" (1.4). In constructing herself as a mediator, the narrator avoids the markers of autobiography; she says almost nothing of her life outside Cranford except for marking events like her father's illnesses that call her back to Drumble, and even when she is away from Cranford the facts of her individual life are suppressed in favor of the communal life that reaches her in letters and reports. In other words, as textual figure the narrator exists only in and through Cranford.

For the narrator to speak for Cranford, as its interpreter and when necessary its advocate, is essentially a matter of "content," but to speak *as* Cranford means representing the community's discursive practices. Thus the narrator creates her text from Cranford women's private forms: their letters, stories, conversations, and gossip. In a text highly conscious of discursive possibilities, the narrator would seem to have rejected two extremes: Miss Jenkyns's imitations of Johnson, which make the narrator long for "facts instead of reflections" (5.70), and the entirely factual letters of her father—"just a man's letter; I mean it was very dull, and gave no information beyond that he was well, that they had had a good deal of rain, that trade was very stagnant, and there were many disagreeable rumors afloat" (13.182). Her own ideal is an "elegant economy" (1.5): she "had often occasion to notice the use that was made of fragments and small opportunities in Cranford" (2.23), and it is from such "fragments" that her own narrative has been composed.

Cranford is so discursively self-enclosed a community that although the narrator tells us "how naturally one falls back into [its] phraseology," (1.5), she must translate rather than simply reproduce its forms. In what seems to signify an unconscious resistance to "male" discursive practices (one thinks of the legendary Amazon language that the Greeks could not decode), the women of Cranford are unable to speak effectively to those outside. When Miss Matty writes to the narrator's father, for example, "words that she would spell quite correctly in her letters to me became perfect enigmas" (14.200–201). When she is upset, even her letters to the narrator in Drumble become "mysterious": "she began many sentences without ending them, running them one into another, in much the same confused sort of way in which written words run together on blotting-paper" (9.122). When Miss Pole attempts to send a coded and anonymous letter to the narrator, she garbles the message and inadvertently discloses her identity. And when the narrator wants information about Miss Matty's brother Peter, she encounters a most uninformative chorus in which "every lady took the subject uppermost in her mind, and talked about it to her own great contentment, but not much to the advancement of the subject they had met to discuss" (12.169). In reporting these incidents, the narrator suggests not simply that the discourse of Cranford is useless outside it, but that Cranford itself is not representable; only a liminal or bicultural consciousness like the narrator's can shape the structures of Cranford's "phraseology" into a form comprehensible beyond Cranford itself. In this sense, the narrator cannot be a fully communal voice and no such voice could be understood.

There is, however, a way for the narrator to become an unequivocal member of the community, maintaining the authority of her representation without relinquishing the authority of her judgment: she must be persuaded and persuade her narratee to accept Cranford's values and shed "Drumble" loyalties. The episode of Miss Matty's financial ruin, which is the major teleological segment of the novel, enacts the conflict of cultures through which the narrator will move from mediator to a leading participant in the community. The battle between what Nina Auerbach calls a "cooperative female community" and a commercial "warrior world that proclaims itself the real one,"[4] is thus a battle not only for Miss Matty's survival but for the narrator's consciousness, and recalls *Mistriss Henley*'s conflicts over right, reason, and wrong. The narrator begins by sounding like her own father, whose logic is "as clear as daylight" (14.214), for example imploring Miss Matty's servant Martha to "listen to reason" when Martha plans to stay on without wages. But Martha dismisses reason as merely "what someone else has got to say. Now I think what I've got to say is good enough reason; but reason or not, I'll say it, and I'll stick to it" (14.197). Sure enough, the Cranfordians end up saving Miss Matty by what the narrator's father will call "great nonsense" (15.220): they transgress good business sense, class hierarchies, and the rules of free enterprise. But even the patriarch himself—"clear-headed and decisive, and a capital man of business" (14.214)—cannot remain untouched when he learns that Cranford's communal strategies have worked: he is reduced to "feminine" muteness and tears, "brushing his hand before

4. Nina Auerbach, *Communities of Women in Fiction* (Cambridge: Harvard University Press, 1978), 87.

his eyes as I spoke" (14.214), and like Matty at her most confused, unable to "get a tail to [his] sentences" (14.215).[5] In the end, then, he too is momentarily Cranfordized, and the narrator is reduced to defending him simply for having "come over from Drumble to help Miss Matty when he could ill spare the time" (14.214).

The narrator's ideological shift is represented by a new textual identity: it is at precisely the moment when she becomes a major force in the community that the text names her for the first time. The name is uttered in full and by a leading Cranfordian, and the identity it suggests could not be less individualized: it is the name of Every[British]woman, Miss Mary Smith. (Lest we think this a name of significance, we have learned otherwise much earlier: when there is some talk about the recent marriage of the butcher's wife, Miss Pole says, "Good gracious me! as if we cared about a Mrs. Smith" [8.108].) And "prim little Mary" the narrator will remain, as Gaskell confirms in a short sequel written ten years after *Cranford* that describes the narrator as "past thirty" and still Miss Smith.[6]

In distinguishing *Cranford* as a communal rather than personal narrative, the text must deny its narrator not only a life apart from Cranford but the conventional resolution of marriage; it must write an alternative story that operates, as Coral Lansbury remarks, "by another order altogether."[7] That this is primarily a discursive order dependent on ways of telling is suggested by a pivotal moment in *Cranford* itself. Matty confides to the narrator that long ago her father had made his daughters "keep a diary, in two columns; on one side we were to put down in the morning what we thought would be the course and events of the coming day, and at night we were to put down on the other side what really had happened" (11.162). Matty's and Deborah's "second column" lives have been very different from the lives they imagined for themselves, and Matty (still grieving an old, lost love) comments in a brave, tremulous gesture of denial that this two-columned system " 'would be to some people rather a sad way of telling their lives' (a tear dropped upon my hand at these

---

5. The women of Cranford take care of Miss Matty with a utopian "simplicity" that the narrator's father says "might be very well in Cranford, but would never do in the world" (15.221): Miss Matty's servant Martha stays on without pay and the ladies concoct a scheme in which each contributes to Miss Matty a monthly sum administered through Drumble to save Matty's pride. The narrator sets Matty up in business selling tea, and the grocer of Cranford, although he sells tea himself, refers customers to her.

6. Elizabeth Gaskell, "The Cage at Cranford," in *Cranford* (London: Oxford University Press, 1947), 248.

7. Coral Lansbury, *Elizabeth Gaskell* (Boston: Twayne, 1984), 72.

words)—'I don't mean that mine has been sad, only so very different to what I expected.' " (11.162). Rowena Fowler suggests that when Miss Matty ends up living in the same household with Martha and Jem's child, who is Matty's namesake, the novel creates a kind of "third column which will retrieve some of the optimism and buoyancy of the first."[8] It is also possible to see *Cranford* as the second column told without being set against the first. The problem is a formal one: it is the "way of telling" that makes "what really had happened" seem sadder than "what we thought would be" (11.162). To give Mary Smith a romantic plot would be to reinstate the first column next to which the second diminishes.

But the narrator's "Mary Smithness" also testifies to the limits beyond which Gaskell could not push her communal world or its communal voice. While *Cranford* honors a "female sphere," it also exposes the limitations of any notion of "spheres": it re-creates only a local and genteel community whose mediation by a single rather than a collective voice underscores its dependence and its insularity. Cranford is not Herland: as Patsy Stoneman argues, "all it can do is make the best of the little space allowed it."[9] And Mary Smith must presumably continue to "vibrate" between Cranford and Drumble, between worlds that remain separate and almost mutually incomprehensible. That Mary Smith apparently does not take up permanent residence in Cranford reminds us that she is still her father's daughter and that Cranford is no permanent motherland.

For the narrator of Sarah Orne Jewett's *Country of the Pointed Firs* the community is likewise a temporary refuge, a world of Maine coastal villages and islands, populated like Cranford primarily by widows and spinsters and a few old men but constructed unlike Cranford without reference to a larger political economy. Its title suggests this contrast with tiny landlocked Cranford: Jewett's "country" extends without definite boundaries into islands and villages, upward toward the heavens, and outward toward the sea. This geographical license is matched by the physical freedom of the inhabitants and by the blurring of traditional gender identities: Mrs. Todd's brother William "looked just like his mother" (42) and is "son an' daughter both" (42); Joanna the hermit can live on an island all alone; and old Elijah the

8. Rowena Fowler, "*Cranford*: Cow in Grey Flannel or Lion *Couchant?*" *SEL* 24 (1984): 717–29.

9. Patsy Stoneman, *Elizabeth Gaskell* (Sussex, England: Harvester Press, 1987), 91.

fisherman spends the winter knitting as his mother taught him long ago (109).[10]

Jewett's novel resembles *Cranford* not only in its absorption of men into a primarily female society but in its absence of conventional narrative linearity and its construction of a singular communal voice. Like Mary Smith, Jewett's unnamed summer visitor mediates the community's life for an audience of outsiders, presenting its folkways, its values, its tales. While *Cranford* finally builds to the crisis of Miss Matty's insolvency, the events narrated in *The Country of the Pointed Firs* exist almost wholly as representations or continuations of the past. This has led some critics to suggest that its form is "nuclear" rather than linear, that the "separate narrative units do not lead inexorably one to the next."[11] But the book does enact a linear process: precisely that of the narrator's integration into and departure from the community. Such a reading, which justifies the order of certain episodes that have otherwise seemed arbitrarily placed, suggests that a critic such as Richard Cary has missed an entire drama when he comments that "the narrator makes no pretense of becoming part and parcel of the community" but rather "raises the curtain on the scene, lets the characters enact their roles, then lowers the curtain and silently steals away."[12] The drama of which I am speaking is staged not so much representationally as syntactically—literally through the grammar that constructs the narrating voice.

The first sign that the narrator is a communal rather than a personal voice is that before she has settled into Dunnet Landing she is not even represented as "I." Until midway into the second chapter, *The Country of the Pointed Firs* appears to be a heterodiegetic text. The character who will become the narrator is mentioned in the third person as "a lover of Dunnet Landing," "a single passenger," "the lodger" (her name is not given), and we observe her from a vantage point outside herself. The text goes in fact to some length to avoid the first person by using impersonal and passive phraseology: "when *one* really knows a village like this"; "*there was* only one fault to find"; "*you* could always tell"; the discovery *was* soon *made*"; "which *made it seem* more attractive" (my italics).[13]

10. Sarah Orne Jewett, *The Country of the Pointed Firs* (New York: Doubleday, 1956), 42, 109. All further references will appear in the text.
11. Elizabeth Ammons, "Going in Circles: The Female Geography of Jewett's *Country of the Pointed Firs*," *Studies in the Literary Imagination* 16 (1983): 85, 87.
12. Richard Cary, *Sarah Orne Jewett* (Boston: Twayne, 1962), 145.
13. To my knowledge, Sivagami Subbaraman is the only other scholar to have noticed this

This heterodiegetically presented character emerges as the narrator only when she has begun to take her place in Dunnet Landing. The transition begins in an awkward passive construction and concludes with a sudden presentation of the narrative subject that is as abrupt as the arrangement with the innkeeper that it describes: "For various reasons, the seclusion and uninterrupted days which *had been looked forward to* proved to be very rare in this otherwise delightful corner of the world. *My* hostess and *I* had made our shrewd business agreement on the basis of a simple cold luncheon at noon" (15, my italics). But this "I" has not yet engaged with the community. If the early references to the unnamed "she" were references to a "stranger," virtually all the early references to the narrating "I" are to a persona seeking not community but writerly solitude. Writing means leaving the community; it forces her to say "unkind words of withdrawal to Mrs. Todd" (16). When the narrator rents the schoolhouse in order to write, however, her first story comes in the person of Captain Littlepage, who sits down at a student's desk and provides the narrator with a "little page" of her own.

This episode suggests not only the imperative for ceding personal for communal voice but the rationale for doing so as well: only by turning the personal project to communal ends, by yielding her own story for the story of Dunnet Landing, can the narrator avoid choosing between love and work, human connection and writerly accomplishment. The narrator can achieve community by writing it, extending into the timelessness of text what would otherwise be only a brief personal experience. It is striking that once the narrator gives over her text to the stories of Dunnet Landing she ceases to present herself as a writer—as if to do so would be to mark her difference from the community in which she implicitly claims membership.

The synthesizing moment in the subtly enacted struggle between writing and community occurs when Mrs. Todd invites the narrator to her mother's home at Green Island, the setting for one of the most intense moments in the narrative. The choice is made explicit when Mrs. Todd says "despairingly" one early morning, "I expect you're goin' up to your schoolhouse to pass all this pleasant day; yes, I expect you're goin' to be dreadful busy" (35). Instead, the narrator decides to accompany Mrs. Todd, and the episodes that follow lead her more

---

characteristic of the early chapters, which she applies to a rather different understanding of narrative communality. See "Rites of Passage: Narrational Plurality as Structure in Jewett's *The Country of the Pointed Firs*," *Centennial Review* 33 (Winter 1989): 61, 70.

and more deeply into intimacy with Mrs. Todd, her family and friends. In a neat reversal, for example, when Mrs. Todd's old friend Mrs. Fosdick pointedly suggests that old friends are best, Mrs. Todd "gave a funny little laugh. 'Yes'm, old friends is always best, 'less you can catch a new one that's fit to make an old one out of,' she said, and we gave an affectionate glance at each other which Mrs. Fosdick could not have understood, being the latest comer to the house" (58). Similarly, the narrator will speak of "the Green Island family" as if it were her own, will know "poor Joanna's" spiritual loneliness "as if she had told me" (75), and will laugh with the solitary old Elijah "like the best of friends" (111).

This movement of the narrator into the community is marked by another subtle shift in narrative strategy. Although the narrative *voice* remains singular, the narrator begins to adopt a collective *vision*, a focalizing consciousness that represents itself in a plural "we" that embraces first only Mrs. Todd and eventually an entire clan. In other words, the narrator reports perceptions and feelings as if she were authorized to represent the thoughts of other characters. The first such instance occurs fairly early in the novel as Mrs. Todd is pointing out the island where she was born:

> We were standing where there was a fine view of the harbor and its long stretches of shore all covered by the great army of the pointed firs, darkly cloaked and standing as if they waited to embark. *As we looked* far seaward among the outer islands, *the trees seemed* to march seaward still, going steadily over the heights and down to the water's edge.
>
> It had been growing gray and cloudy, like the first evening of autumn, and a shadow had fallen on the darkening shore. Suddenly, *as we looked*, a gleam of golden sunshine struck the outer islands, and *revealed itself in a compelling way to our eyes*. (33, my italics)

These plural pronouns that may seem innocuous actually breach the conventions of narrative verisimilitude by constituting a plural perceptual consciousness. I mean that conventionally, in homodiegetic narrative situations, voice and focalization are presumed to be the same: the character who "speaks" is also, to use Genette's formulation, the character who "sees." First-person narrators are expected to report only what other characters say and do, not to have access to what others feel and think. The narrator of *Pointed Firs* should not be able to tell us how something "seemed" to Mrs. Todd or that something was revealed "in a compelling way" to eyes other than her own; she appropriates Mrs. Todd's vision either by eliding the narrative moment in which Mrs. Todd would have told the narrator her thoughts, or by attributing her own thoughts to Mrs. Todd. Such an appropriation of authority breaches narrative decorum in a way similar to if less drastic than that Genette describes in *A la recherche du temps perdu,* when Proust's "I"-narrator Marcel tells us Swann's thoughts as if Marcel were an omniscient heterodiegetic voice.[14]

This communal focalization intensifies and expands when, near the end of summer, the narrator accompanies Mrs. Todd and her mother Mrs. Blackett to the Bowden family reunion. The description of this event is communally focalized: "we began to feel a new sense of gayety" (86); "we watched the boats drop their sails one by one" (88); "we could see now that there were different footpaths" (88); "we hurried on our way, beginning to feel as if we were very late" (88); "we could see the green sunlit field we had just crossed as if we looked out at it from a dark room" (90). Not only does the narrator describe herself as one of this "family," but the three women of three different generations become part of a larger unity: "we were no more a New England family celebrating its own existence and simple progress; we carried the tokens and inheritance of all such households from which this had descended, and were only the latest of our line. We possessed the instincts of a far, forgotten childhood" (90).

This perceptual communality contrasts strikingly with its aftermath: as the narrator and her friends leave the reunion, the plural focalization begins to dissolve and the narrator returns to singularity: "*I* came near to feeling like a true Bowden, and parted from certain new friends as if *they* were old friends" (98); "I hoped in my heart that *I* might be like *them* as I lived on into age, and then smiled to think that I too was no longer very young" (100). The reminder that there is an "I" who is not one of "them" begins the movement out of communal voice that will retrace the process with which the novel began. The penultimate chapter of the book, which is given primarily to the stories of a solitary seagoing man, parallels the early interview with Captain Littlepage and moves the textual focus away from female community. Then, as the narrator prepares to leave her lodgings, she sees her own room in Mrs. Todd's house looking "empty as it had

14. See Gérard Genette, *Narrative Discourse: An Essay in Method* (Ithaca: Cornell University Press, 1980), 241.

the day I came," and narrates the scene of her own absence much as she had narrated herself in the third person before: "I knew how it would seem when Mrs. Todd came back and found her lodger gone. So we die before our own eyes" (159). Finally the narrator can represent herself only "looking back" (160) to catch "a last glimpse" as Mrs. Todd disappears behind "the pointed firs" (159) and Dunnet Landing is "lost to sight" (160). The departure must end the book, for the narrator has no life outside this community: we never know where she is going, just as we never learn her name, her history, or her origins. Textually speaking, in other words, this narrating "I" is an entirely communal entity.

Because it suppresses its narrator's autobiography, because it does not identify contrasting or competing communities or mention any alternative claims upon her sympathies, *The Country of the Pointed Firs* allows its narrator to enter in a much deeper fiction of community than Mary Smith suggests in *Cranford*. Yet in order to achieve this intimacy, the text enacts a dramatic erasure of realist time and space: the narrator has no history and Dunnet Landing no connections to the world "outside." If Mary Smith must "vibrate" between two worlds, reenacting the gendered separation of social spheres, *The Country of the Pointed Firs* attempts to erase the "male" or "public" sphere entirely. The utopia remains localized; there is no mediation that could translate it to a physical space beyond itself.

Marguerite Audoux's *L'Atelier de Marie-Claire* (1920), on the other hand, attempts to represent a female community situated squarely within capitalist patriarchy and encounters in the process the same tension between individual and communal narrative that I described in my discussion of Wollstonecraft. Its narrator, already introduced as a personal voice in *Marie-Claire* (1910), enacts a struggle in this sequel between personal and communal narrative that parallels the character's struggle between heterosexual self-interest and the needs of the women with whom she works. In contrast to Jewett's world-unto-itself or Gaskell's brave village holdout, Marie-Claire's *atelier* is far from idyllic: it is the workroom for a Parisian sewing establishment in which poor women labor desperately to survive conditions so miserable that even the oppressive *patron*, M. Dalignac, barely makes ends meet. Like the narrators of *Cranford* and *Pointed Firs*, this narrator resists autodiegetic voice, but whereas the other narrators can be "everywomen," individuality is a crucial signifier in this world of class struggle in which the loss of identity signifies the loss of control: when the *patron* insists on calling the narrator "Marie" instead of "Marie-Claire," she "responded so poorly" that he is forced to call her by her proper name.[15]

The narrator's struggle at once as voice and as character engages her in telling two intersecting stories that are ultimately at odds. The novel opens with a happy sense of community among the women as the young workers return from the summer layoff, but the "joyful chatter" on the street gives way to the hard work before them as the women begin the long climb to the hot and stuffy *atelier*. The conflict between the competing claims of individual and community is developed most specifically through the courtship plot: Clément, the nephew of Madame Dalignac to whom Marie-Claire reluctantly becomes engaged, is a bourgeois individualist and would-be patriarch dedicated to making money and cavalierly indifferent to the plight of Marie-Claire's friends, unmoved even by the death of Sandrine which is linked unequivocally to the oppressive conditions of her work. Clément's crass self-interest, which becomes still more evident after Dalignac's death as Dalignac's widow faces financial ruin, makes Marie-Claire dread the approaching marriage even though it will, of course, save her from material misery.

The narrator's personal dilemma is also a dilemma of narrative—of what story will dominate and how it will be told. The climax comes three days before Marie-Claire's wedding is to take place, when the ill and exhausted Madame Dalignac collapses on her husband's grave and dies holding Marie-Claire's hand and murmuring "L'atelier." As Jemima's story had turned Wollstonecraft's Maria from her preoccupation with Darnford, so Madame Dalignac's death turns the narrative focus of *L'Atelier de Marie-Claire* away from its progress toward marital closure and toward the needs of the women that the novel cannot, however, resolve. In a dramatic refusal of closure, the narrator totally abandons the personal story of her relationship to Clément, which had become the central issue of the narrative. Instead, there is a brief closing scene that affirms with heavy irony the painful plight of Paris's working women:

> Noontime was ringing from the churches and whistling from the factories as I returned to the *atelier*. All the workers were standing, ready

15. Marguerite Audoux, *L'Atelier de Marie-Claire* (Paris: Charpentier, 1920), 7. All further references will appear in the text. English translations are my own.

to leave. Bergeounette, leaning at the window, was making sure the coast was clear while Duretour sang in her cheerful falsetto:

> Paris, Paris
> Woman's paradise.
>
> [Paris, Paris
> Paradis de la femme.] (259)

When Marie-Claire returns to the "atelier" she enters "de nouveau," as if with new consciousness. At the last moment, the novel has truncated its individual(ist) plot and returned its narrative attention toward the community, reconstituting its narrator as a communal presence. At the end there are only the women; the traditional economic and fictional resolution has been exposed as a "false paradise" and erased along with male and female bosses whether harsh or benevolent. The refusal of personal narration enacts formally and thematically Marie-Claire's commitment to collective politics.

It is notable that in *L'Atelier de Marie-Claire* the struggle against individual voice and story continues almost literally to the novel's end. The evidence of these three texts suggests that the appropriation of singular voice for communal purposes is achieved more readily in the representation of economically and socially separate, relatively autonomous communities than in the novel that represents poor women directly oppressed by capitalist patriarchy. Ironically, the demands of "realist" political struggle seem to leave the narrative more vulnerable to "realist" heterosexual and individualist plot.

This impasse in the novel also exposes the contradictions in what I have been calling, perhaps oxymoronically, singular communal voice or the "communal 'I.'" For all its effort to represent a community with which the narrator is both separate and identified, this discursive singularity means that the narrative "I" is still formally distinct from the community and in control of its representation, just as the most seemingly "communal" of authorial voices remains separate from and in control of a represented world. The narrative singularity that I have suggested as the dominant mechanism for constructing communal voice in the classic realist period inevitably contains and in some sense objectifies female community, recalling the male narrators of *Herland* and *Millenium Hall*. In none of these novels, in other words, does a community "speak" for itself. That each of these narrators has the possibility to leave the community means that their communal identity must remain partial, a kind of fiction; there is still a separate "I" who speaks for "them."

One could argue, however, that within a culture of individual(ist) authorship, in an important way the "communal 'I'" constitutes the most appropriate and honest representation of communal voice. In my next two chapters, I will be looking at some more inclusive forms of communal voice that the narrative technology of modern and postmodern fiction makes possible. These new forms—some of which are reenactments of far older forms—have the capacity to create not only structural equality among voices but contexts in which difference is not subordinated to similarity, where voices may be communal and still diverse. Yet within an individually authored novel, such a communal voice is actually the most fictional of all fictions of authority: the single author "pretends" to speak both for and as an entire community. Communal voice thus exposes the limits of individual authorship however enlightened, complex, and plural the single author's consciousness might be.

14

(Dif)fusions: Modern Fiction and Communal Form

We are
of one mind, tuning
our instruments to ourselves, by our triple light.
                    —OLGA BROUMAS, "Triple Muse"

Where no community exists, "we" may seem to presume
too much.
                    —MARIE PONSOT AND ROSEMARY DEEN,
                    Beat Not the Poor Desk

By recognizing multiple perspectives both formally and philosophically, modernism (re)turns narrative voice from the hegemonic individualism that I have been associating with the nineteenth century
to narrative structures in which two or more characters may constitute
a narrating community without suppressing their personal identities.
This formal possibility coincides with a period in women's writing in
which, according to Rachel Blau DuPlessis, "individual heroes" and
"sealed couples" are often replaced by "collective" protagonists and
"groups which have a sense of purpose and identity, and whose growth
occurs in mutual collaboration."[1] The fictions I will be discussing in
this chapter reflect the intersection of this new communality of representation with conventions that also allow communality of narrative
voice.

1. Rachel DuPlessis, *Writing beyond the Ending: Narrative Strategies of Twentieth-Century Women Writers* (Bloomington: Indiana University Press, 1985), 179.

As I noted in my discussion of *Herland,* representations of female community or what DuPlessis calls "collective" protagonists do not necessarily entail communal voice. *Little Women* (1868–69) constructs a domestic, female community of four sisters, but Meg, Jo, Beth, and Amy are not narrators of their own histories. Bound to the authorial conventions of realist fiction, *Little Women* can create the sisters as a verbal community only through copious direct speech, as black community is constituted in *Contending Forces* and *Iola Leroy.* Conversely, as I have also noted, many novels use multiple voices (and protagonists) without constructing the kind of community DuPlessis describes; the narrating characters do not share "a sense of purpose and identity" and their growth does not occur "in mutual collaboration"; on the contrary, in a novel such as *Les Liaisons dangereuses,* it is disruption and destruction that multiplicity represents.

From among various forms of novelistic multiplicity, then, I am distinguishing the convergence of representation and narration that occurs when a collective or group protagonist is represented through formal strategies that allow the plurality itself to speak. I want to explore in this chapter two different techniques, with different ideological implications, for giving collective protagonists a communal voice: *simultaneous,* first-person-plural narration in a literal "we" that allows voices to speak in unison, and *sequential* narration in which each voice speaks in turn so that the "we" is produced from a series of collaborating "I's." Apart from the not-insignificant challenge that both forms pose to individualist narrative authority, both also entail deviations from narrative conventions: simultaneous communal voice challenges the convention that feelings, perceptions, and thoughts are necessarily individual, while sequential voice threatens conventions of novelistic "coherence" and continuity. In turn, both forms of communal voice are contained and constrained by conventions of representation, not least by the institutionalized heterosexuality that I have been suggesting is at the heart of Western fictional teleology.

I have explained that in *The Country of the Pointed Firs* a plural voice that narrates collective perceptions transgresses Western fiction's conventionally singular notions of consciousness. While this singularity may seem to be a natural extension of the properties of spoken discourse, I want to locate it at least provisionally as the product of individualist cultures which presume consciousness to be unique and literature the "original" product of single authorship. If Western literary cultures do not readily allow for "I's" who speak or perceive as "we," other Western discourses from science to bureaucracy to mass media certainly practice plural narration, and oral traditions in most cultures of the world acknowledge the ways in which an "I" may speak as "we" and collective consciousness be the very foundation of cultural identity.

By *simultaneous voice* I refer to a narrative situation in which both voice and focalization are represented as communal, so that the "we" who perceives is also the "we" who speaks. I am not aware of novels in a white male tradition written in such a voice, but I will examine some of the possibilities and limits of this form through three novels by women in the United States. The first two construct the "we" from an "I" and thus do not entirely reduce the hierarchical distinction between self and other: Sarah Orne Jewett's *Deephaven* (1877) creates a "we" of two women in love; Toni Morrison's *The Bluest Eye* (1970), a "we" of two sisters that comes to include other black adolescents and ultimately a larger community. Joan Chase's *During the Reign of the Queen of Persia* (1983) dispenses with the "I" entirely, constructing (as its predecessor *Little Women* could not) an entirely plural narrative voice that represents four female cousins, two pairs of sisters, whose growing-up years are told as if experienced through a single mind. I shall argue, however, that these exceptional novelistic constructions prove Beauvoir's rule that "women do not say 'we,' " for in all three, communal voice is restricted to the representation of childhood or young adulthood in ways that fail to challenge the novel's adherence to institutional heterosexuality.

While *Deephaven*'s narrator is nominally individual, she narrates almost entirely from the kind of plural consciousness that occurs only momentarily in *The Country of the Pointed Firs*. Although once again this "we" comes formally into being during an idyllic vacation, the voice constructed in *Deephaven* is not produced through a geographic community; it is the voice of two women, Helen and Kate, who spend a long summer together in the house of Kate's late aunt. Helen, technically the narrator, explicitly and emphatically seeks to construct herself as a plurality: "I am not writing Kate's biography and my own, only telling you of one summer which we spent together."[2] The narrator speaks much more about the couple than about either individual,

2. Sarah Orne Jewett, *Deephaven* (1877; reprint, Boston: Houghton Mifflin, 1895), 25. All further references will appear in the text.

recording their thoughts, feelings, fears, desires, as those of a single consciousness: "we are neither of us nervous" (16); "a friendship which we both still treasure" (11); "the west parlor was our favorite room downstairs" (19); "It was very sad work to us—saying goodbye to our friends, and we tried to make believe" (241). The text even sets up a scene of collaborative writing in which on two "old secretaries" that were "facing each other" Helen and Kate "wrote, between us, a tragic 'journal' " and "put it in the most hidden drawer by itself, and flatter ourselves that it will be regarded with great interest some time or other" (16).

Although stories about the villagers are integrated into the novel, Kate and Helen do not require Deephaven, as the narrator of *Pointed Firs* requires Dunnet Landing, to establish a communal voice. This voice, like their relationship, is predicated on their *not* really belonging to Deephaven so that they can deepen an already-established relationship; unlike *Pointed Firs*, this novel begins and ends in Boston. The novel's title, then, becomes not simply the signifier of geographic community, as it does in *Pointed Firs* and *Cranford*, but in a more coded way the deep haven of an essentially lesbian *société à deux*. If anything, the "we" is emphasized rather than diminished in the last chapter; in long passages of dialogue, Kate and Helen reflect together upon their happiness at Deephaven, and the final pages of the book recall not the people of Deephaven but the ways in which two of them spent their time, so that what is emphasized is the "we" that is separate from the larger community and will continue apart from it.

Indeed, the book's innocuous title obscures the central drama of romantic union being inscribed in both story and voice. Just two pages into the book the narrator reports that the two women "kissed each other solemnly" (2) and defends this act with a pert injunction to the narratee: "You need not smile; we are not sentimental girls, and are both much averse to indiscriminate kissing" (2). The narrator freely admits that the pair is an object of village curiosity, and tells us how they would "lie on [the sofa] together" (21); Kate even "laughingly proposed" one evening that they "copy the Ladies of Llangollen, and remove ourselves from society and its distractions" (242). Yet these lesbian suggestions are mitigated by a discourse that renders the characters childlike. Although they are twenty-four-year-old women, "you would have thought we were two children" (3); Deephaven "might be dull...for two young ladies" but not "for two little girls who were fond of each other" (4); "Sometimes in Deephaven we were between six and seven years old" (35); they looked forward to the circus "with as much eagerness as if we had been little school-boys" (120); and each has a favorite children's book that she carries about with her (248–49). This emphasis on childhood desexualizes the relationship and attempts to render it ideologically innocent.

The other two simultaneous communal narratives I want to discuss create their voice literally through children—or rather through adults looking back upon a shared childhood. In Toni Morrison's first novel, Claudia's personal voice frequently becomes the "we" of "my sister [Frieda] and I,"[3] constructing not only shared experience but a shared point of view that presumes Claudia's ability to know Frieda's mind as one would know one's own: "There was no bitterness in our memory of him" (17); "we were full of awe and respect for Pecola" (28); "we looked hard for flaws to restore our equilibrium" (55); "we were sinking under the wisdom, accuracy, and relevance of Maureen's last words" (61); "we were embarrassed for Pecola" (147); "we thought only of this overwhelming hatred for the unborn baby" (148). This repeated "we" suggests— despite explicit differences, for example, in Claudia's and Frieda's reactions to white baby dolls—a commonality of thought and even of memory, a sisterhood that experiences and perceives the world in unison.

This "we" also expands beyond the biological sisterhood to embrace a wider community. In this passage, the narrator is speaking not only for herself and Frieda, but for all black girls oppressed by white standards of beauty: "We were lesser. Nicer, brighter, but still lesser. Dolls we could destroy, but we could not destroy the honey voices of parents and aunts, the obedience in the eyes of our peers, the slippery light in the eyes of our teachers when they encountered the Maureen Peals of the world. What was the secret? What did we lack? . . . We felt comfortable in our skins . . . and could not comprehend this unworthiness" (61–62). Sometimes the "we" includes adults as well: "Black people were not allowed in the park, and so it filled our dreams" (84). And as I proposed in Chapter 7, at the end of the novel the "we" becomes by implication an entire generation of northern African-Americans who "were not strong, merely aggressive," "not free, merely licensed," "not good, but well behaved" (159). Obviously Morrison's message in using the communal "we" is to make clear the

3. Toni Morrison, *The Bluest Eye* (New York: Pocket Books, 1970), 9. All further references will appear in the text.

degree to which the experience of an individual black female "I" is
collective experience; the text sets this "we" of typical black girls
against the overprivilege of Maureen Peal and the underprivilege of
Pecola. Indeed, Pecola is part of the "we" only when she is living with
Claudia's family; it is the absence of the sense and the reality of the
"we" that finally leads after her rape to the madness born of her
longing for blue eyes. Claudia and Frieda, on the other hand, survive
in part because they are allowed to grow up both together and as
individuals, the "I" and the "we" making each other possible.

Joan Chase's *During the Reign of the Queen of Persia* (1983) goes
further still: it has no "I" narrator at all, but only a "we" that becomes
the sole constituent of narrating—though not narrated—identity.
Chase's narrator comprises four girls, "two [Uncle Dan's] own daughters, two his nieces, all of us born within two years of each other,"
who during the 1950s live more-or-less together, with their grandmother and various parents, uncles, and aunts, on the family farm.
The narrative reflects a single group consciousness because people
"treated the four of us the very same and sometimes we thought we
were the same."[4] Thus not only feelings and perceptions but direct
thoughts and direct speech are attributed to this "we": "We accused
her. 'How do you know a thing about it?' " (22); "Didn't she save you,
we thought" (25); " 'He loved her a lot,' we said, recalling his masking
indolence" (44); "We are humiliated. He has shown again that we are
his stupid, flighty, undisciplined daughters" (140); "We were aghast"
(188); "We didn't know what to think" (272); "We had bad dreams,
cried out at night" (196). This "we" survives even the temporary absence of any one or two of its constituents. Any of the four girls—
Anne, Katie, Celia, or Jenny—might be temporarily a "third person,"
a character set apart from the collective voice and thereby individualized, marked in difference. Thus at one moment "Aunt Libby was
still sewing and instructing us . . . while Celia stayed shut away in her
room" (30), or " 'You didn't call me. You left me.' Anne was screaming
at us" (222). The novel is able, in other words, to take advantage of
the semantic fluidity of the "we" to maintain the communal voice despite
the momentary difference or even defection of an individual "I." The
very continuity of the "we" allows each "she" to rejoin it for occasions
of shared narrative identity, as in the powerful moment when all four

4. Joan Chase, *During the Reign of the Queen of Persia* (New York: Harper and Row, 1983),
5. All further references will appear in the text.

are hoping for a miracle to save Aunt Grace, one of the mothers, from cancer: in their "yearning to believe" (194), it seems "as though her presence and our devotion to her had united us at last in a perfect oneness, we four girls thinking, feeling and moving in a dimension that felt like the exact representation of a greater mind" (196). This "exact representation of a greater mind" is indeed what this novel achieves through its unconventional and entirely communal voice.

However, Chase's "we" seems to me viable not only as technique but as representation because the four girls are a "natural" community; they share family and history and live together in a single place. I am theorizing that the "we" is predicated on a kind of unity that the heterosexual conventions of the novel permit far more readily to young girls than to grown women, whose lives are assumed to diverge and become, to recall Beauvoir, "dispersed among the males." The "we" of childhood becomes both nostalgic and utopian, as if community cannot survive as girls grow to womanhood. Even in *Deephaven* the women are still young, their romantic relationship represented as but an episode before the shared life splits into separate, presumably heterosexual histories; it is only "laughingly," after all, that they propose to run off together like the Ladies of Llangolen. It seems significant, therefore, that contemporary novels representing communities of adult sisters or friends do not seem to use such simultaneous communal forms. Maria Katzenbach's *The Grab* (1977), a novel about three sisters whose mother has just died, intersperses direct monologue with authorial narration to render some sense of each sister's feelings about her mother; authorial voice with shifting focalization is likewise the mode of Candyce Flint's novel of three sisters, *Mother Love* (1987). Ntozake Shange's *Sassafrass, Cypress & Indigo* (1982) creates three sisters as a collective protagonist, but each is given her own point of view and her own portions of text, which are organized and orchestrated by an authorial voice who uses free indirect discourse, letters, recipes, journal entries, and other private forms to render each sister's individuality.

Narrative convention may not, however, be the only reason for the paucity of simultaneous voice in the novel; there are good grounds for caution about a narrative method that cannot distinguish among the individual members of a collectivity. If the "we" is at its best the expression of a harmonious unity-in-multiplicity, of what my epigraph from Olga Broumas describes as "one mind, tuning / our instruments to ourselves," it also always risks erasing difference beneath pre-

sumptions of similarity.[5] In the warnings of Marie Ponsot and Rosemary Deen (themselves a "we"), "where no community exists, 'we' may
seem to presume too much."[6] If "we" dissolves the Other/Self dichotomy, its danger lies in its power to reduce each Other to an explicit
or—perhaps more troublingly—implicit norm. The utopian value of
the "we" is counterbalanced, then, by the equally strong dystopian
danger of speaking for women, or a particular group of women, "in
general."

The impulse to balance these tensions of unity and diversity, commonality and difference, surely explains why feminism particularly
in the 1980s produced an entire genre of anthologies based on personal (primarily but not exclusively nonfictional) narratives organized
to show difference within a particular, shared aspect of identity.
Women who identify themselves as members of marginalized ethnic
or political communities have been especially active in writing books
that represent their particular groups through the individual voices
of separate but resonant experiences. These books—I have in mind
such collections as *The Coming Out Stories, This Bridge Called My Back:
Writings by Radical Women of Color, Nice Jewish Girls: A Lesbian Anthology,
With the Power of Each Breath: A Disabled Women's Anthology, You Can't
Drown the Fire: Latin American Women Writing in Exile, Lionheart Gal:
Life Stories of Jamaican Women, Making Waves: An Anthology of Writings
by and about Asian American Women,* and *Charting the Journey: Writings
by Black and Third World Women*—carry the double imperative of constituting an unheard "we" and literally articulating that "we" into its
diverse constitutive elements. Both imperatives are recognized as crucial gestures for inscribing minority identities in a dominant culture
that both disperses and falsely unifies.

Some feminist novelists, especially those who are identified with a
marginalized community, have likewise attempted to represent both
similarity and difference by constituting a multiplicity of individual
female voices that echo one another through experiences and perceptions that are also distinct. These voices are not competing for
authentic versions of a narrative or offering multiple perspectives on
a single story, but are offering multiple stories, each one contributing

5. I have written further about the implications of the pronoun "we" in "Who *Are* the
'We'? The Shifting Term of Feminist Discourse," *Women's Studies Quarterly* 14 (Fall–Winter
1986): 18–20.
6. Marie Ponsot and Rosemary Deen, *Beat Not the Poor Desk: Writing: What to Teach, How
to Teach It, and Why* (Montclair, N.J.: Boynton-Cook, 1982), 137.

to a fuller portrait of a specific community. Ntozake Shange's "choreopoem" *for colored girls who have considered suicide/when the rainbow is enuf* (1975) is perhaps one of the prototypes for such works: seven "ladies," distinguished only by the color of their dress, enact representations of African-American women. Many of the narratives in Shange's text evoke figures of history or myth, but the emphasis is on contemporary black women's experiences, thoughts, and feelings told in their own words. Male voices, when they speak at all, are usually unreliable voices present, as they were in Riccoboni's novels, to be criticized and ironized. Shange sees the separate poems as "a single statement"[7] intended to "sing a black girl's song" and "let her be born."

The sequential communal narratives I wish now to examine function like Shange's "choreopoem," giving voice to a diversity of women of some shared identity without making any single experience or consciousness normative. Such communal narratives are perhaps less common in the novel than in other artistic forms because they necessarily threaten novelistic conventions of representational coherence and structural unity. As I mentioned in Chapter 5, when novels produce what Macherey calls a "dispersal," narrative voice becomes one of the major mechanisms for containing the narrative as a unity. This may be why many novels use communal strategies only momentarily, incorporating women's voices but maintaining authorial narration as their dominant mode. For example, Mary Gordon's *The Company of Women* (1980) represents first the indirectly rendered thoughts and finally the direct voices of a group of women struggling to create their individual and collective identities in a community dominated by a Catholic priest, though the center of the novel is a figural narrative focused on a single character. And Morrison's *Beloved* yields its authorial voice at a particularly intense moment in the relationship of Sethe and her two daughters in order to create interior monologues and finally a communal blend of the three voices. Louise Erdrich's three novels, *Love Medicine* (1984), *The Beet Queen* (1986), and *Tracks* (1988), go further, creating (Balzacian) recurring characters who are represented through a spectrum of voices, both authorial and personal, that together might be said to constitute the voice(s) of a particular, predominantly Native American community.

The retention of authoriality characterizes some recent novels that

---

7. Ntozake Shange, *for colored girls who have considered suicide/when the rainbow is enuf* (New York: Macmillan, 1975), xx. Shange locates the inspiration for her work in Judy Grahn's "Common Woman" poems.

are explicitly structured to represent the intersecting but by no means unified history of a female community. Gloria Naylor's *The Women of Brewster Place* (1982) and Pat Barker's *Union Street* (1983) use place rather than plot as a unifying principle for exploring the lives of poor urban women, respectively African-American and white British, as female communities. Perhaps because they transgress conventional expectations of plot, these books retain authorial voice and rely on free indirect discourse to represent each character's consciousness, constructing formal coherence by narrating diverse stories and characters in a single authorial voice.

On the other hand, the narrative structure of Amy Tan's *The Joy Luck Club* (1989), which Tan claims to have been inspired by *Love Medicine*, does construct through a series of homodiegetic narratives a sequential communal voice. A mah-jongg group becomes the device through which seven women, three Chinese immigrant mothers and four Chinese-American daughters, narrate interlaced segments of their own histories. Here too, of course, family and longtime friendship constitute unifying principles, and even then, the alternation of voices means that most of the stories are not fully developed. The fact that none of the narrator's stories is wholly constituted suggests, indeed, that the book's emphasis is the representation of a spectrum of mothers and daughters, and mother-daughter relationships, within an ethnically and geographically defined community. The orchestration of voices—each character speaks more than once, and in unsystematic order—provides precisely the design that makes the book novelistic rather than a set of stories, and the novel's final image—in which daughters of the same mother finally meet and, in their recognition of one another, recognize their dead mother—constitutes a moving representation of the text's own imperative to balance the samenesses and differences within a community: "I look at their faces and I see no trace of my mother in them. Yet they still look familiar. ...And although we don't speak, I know we all see it: Together we look like our mother. Her same eyes, her same mouth, open in surprise to see, at last, her long cherished wish."[8] Sequential narration, then, allows each narrator a separateness and indeed a separate authority, yet each also helps to create the portrait of an identifiable group.

All these works that I am associating with sequential narration, like

---

8. Amy Tan, *The Joy Luck Club* (New York: Putnam's, 1989), 287–88.

the nineteenth-century novels of "singular" communal voice before them, necessarily deviate from classical fictional form. The need for more open structures than the realist novel to accommodate the narrative effects of sequential communal voice may explain why the contemporary work I have encountered that succeeds most fully in fusing a diffuse group of female voices into a self-conscious, egalitarian narrating community returns to an older form more atomized than the novel even in its modern(ist) modes. The book I have in mind is Julia Voznesenskaya's *The Women's Decameron: A Novel* (1985), which uses the Boccaccian framework to build a female community in which each voice is fully authorized. Ten Russian women who have just given birth, quarantined to the maternity ward with skin infections, decide to pass their ten days of confinement by telling stories; each day has a topic, and the stories usually concern private and unspeakable aspects of women's lives: sexual initiation, rape, infidelity. In contrast to the original *Decameron*, these women tell personal stories as well as stories about others, so that they are homodiegetic and heterodiegetic narrators in turn. Each has her own narrative style and preferences, and through the metanarrative act of creating its characters not simply as voices but as storytellers, the novel legitimates every woman's diegetic and mimetic authority.

Indeed, *The Women's Decameron* creates community precisely through its own narrative acts, as the ten women are transformed through their storytelling from a collection of diverse individuals to a group of narrators and finally to a loving community of considerable shared consciousness. The women start out as a quarrelsome and disparate group who have in common only gender, babies, and boredom: there are party members and political dissidents, proper wives and unmarried mothers, educated women and women of the working class. But as one of the bolder women says, "What's there to be shy about? . . . We're all women, aren't we? We all love with the same part of the body, don't we?"[9] From this rudimentary commonality the women begin to know one another through their stories and to learn that they have much more in common than biological "parts." Brief transitional sections between the stories chart the development of community as the women come to know one another through the intimacy of their narratives. By the seventh day, for instance, the "ice

9. Julia Voznesenskaya, *The Women's Decameron: A Novel*, trans. W. B. Linton (New York: Henry Holt, 1985), 3. All further references will appear in the text.

finally seemed to have melted" (182), even between Valentina the "party bigwig" (3) and Galina the "dissident wife" (22). As the women tell stories that reveal themselves ever more deeply and sometimes more painfully, they also become a caring community: "the women comforted Galya herself as best they could, for she had concluded her story in tears" (188). Two women even become "characters" in another woman's history when they find a way to contact the father of her child.

This movement toward community is not only psychological but ideological, and it is the recognition of shared experience that forges the unity. While the early part of the book featured stories about "mothers-in-law" as "bitches" and nostalgic recollections of heterosexual first love, on the eighth day Galina tells about the "wisdom and goodness" of her mother-in-law (224), and the women joke that "you do occasionally get men who are genuine people" (224). They also begin to identify issues of mutual concern such as physical safety and child care, developing across other ideological differences a shared stance and even rudimentary plans for action. It is significant, however, that the text ends quite abruptly after the tenth story on the tenth day; it inscribes neither the inevitable dispersion of the community nor any continuance beyond the hospital walls.

In *The Women's Decameron*, a group of Soviet women, simply because they are Soviet women and allowed to tell stories of their own choosing entirely among themselves, construct by their own narrative acts a communal voice and a communal history for a communal audience of themselves. By U.S. feminist standards, the ideology of this book is less oppositional than its form might in theory permit: all the women are mothers; the stories still center primarily on heterosexual plots; lesbians get stereotyped with phrases like "butch dyke." Perhaps the very communality of such a narrative project means that certain values and norms may end up constituting their own hegemony. That is, while all narration is of course limited to and by the voices who tell it, this limitation may be obscured in communal narrative situations precisely by narrative plurality; whatever similarities emerge across differences, whatever spaces are not opened to dialogue, are bound to be reinforced. Here, indeed, is the insidious underside of the single author's power to masquerade as a self-reinforcing community. Even the most "open" form for the inscription of communal voice, then, ought not be idealized; form is only possibility, the necessary but never sufficient means for transforming both fiction and consciousness.

15

Full Circle: *Les Guérillères*

we bend
At different temperatures...
Yes, fusion is possible
but only if things get hot enough—
—CHERRÍE MORAGA, "The Welder"

I have been saying that communal narrative voices are produced from intersections of social and formal possibilities. I also proposed that although contemporary feminists have created a political context that makes female community more viable, novelistic conventions of coherence and continuity inhibit the construction of communal narrative forms. My final chapter takes license to return to a somewhat earlier moment when the convergence of two differently radical movements—respectively for an international feminist revolution and a revolution in narrative—creates what may still be the most inclusive, uncompromisingly feminist communal voice in Western literature in a work that also sounds a death knell for that literature. Monique Wittig's *Les Guérillères* (1969), a work in the countertradition of the French *nouveau roman* or *antiroman*, was inspired by the May 1968 political actions in Paris, when women participants recognized that "the vast majority of their male comrades were as deeply phallocratic as the bourgeois enemy."[1] From the vantage point of two decades and an increasingly global consciousness, however, *Les Guérillères* also signifies, in ways it clearly did not "intend," the limits even of feminist

---

1. Elaine Marks and Isabelle de Courtivron, *New French Feminisms: An Anthology* (Amherst: University of Massachusetts Press, 1980), 30.

Western discourse, which unwittingly reproduces its own cultural and linguistic dominance.

Both formally and representationally, *Les Guérillères* constitutes an infinitely expandable community of women at once united and diverse, a community at once mythic and panhistoric, existing in no time and all time, described primarily in a nonspecific continuous present tense. But although *Les Guérillères* begins with female community (or communities), it does not begin with communal voice; rather, it represents the process by which female community develops such a voice. When at the very end of the book the authorial narrator explicitly joins this "we," the narrative also moves from a utopic nowhere/everywhere to contemporary (realist) time and space, in a gesture that is at once a sign of political urgency and an ideological trap.

Les Guérillères goes far beyond any work I have described in this section in rejecting the demands of realist plot and the entire apparatus of what Roland Barthes called "readerly" narrative—identifiable settings, narrative linearity, individualized characters. Physically, the text appears as discontinuous paragraph-long sections whose positioning reflects no absolute continuity in time or theme. The "characters" are a collectivity of "guérillères"—a neologism that evokes not only warfare but healing (*guérir*). What exists of plot is a loose, dialectical division. First the text represents one or many autonomous female communities, describing the myths, rituals, symbols, beliefs, and practices of the self-renewing culture that helps them "beware of dispersal" and "remain united like the characters in a book."[2] In midtext there begins a series of violent struggles against male dominance from which the women, in unity with those "young men" who are willing to understand their struggle, finally emerge victorious. These large developments are impossible to pin to a single textual moment, for the novel's resistance of realism allows the sexual struggles to be occurring at different moments, in different places, on different fronts. What unites the discourse is the fact of community—which, however diverse, is always "elles." The antiphallic signifier of this unity is the "O": an "infinite sphere whose centre is everywhere, circumference nowhere" (69/97), whose movements are revolutions, "the sign of the goddess, symbol of the vulval ring" (27/35) which represents the mirror, the ego, the sun, fullness and emptiness, completion and

2. Monique Wittig, *Les Guérillères* (Paris: Les Editions de Minuit, 1969), 82; English translation by David Levay (New York: Avon, 1971; reprint, Boston: Beacon, 1985), 58. Further references to both editions will appear in the text, with the English cited first.

renewal, perfect equality and equilibrium, union without hierarchy, closure "without limit" (69/97).

The absence of hierarchy and limit also constitutes the ground on which *Les Guérillères* overturns conventional notions of narrator and character. The text's "collective protagonist" and ultimately its narrative authority is the inclusive, infinitely expandable pronoun "elles." The very use of this pronoun is a radical insertion, a form made rare by androcentric language rules that use the feminine plural only for a wholly female community; that the "elles" ultimately embraces not only all women but ultimately also certain men constitutes a pointed reversal of French practice. Wittig chooses "elles" rather than "femmes" because, as *Mistriss Henley* has made painfully clear, the double meaning of "femme" makes the sign of woman's identity always already the sign of her subjection—and her silence—as wife.

This "elles" is not, however, present simply as an anonymous, idealist abstraction that could be (mis)taken for a homogeneous community; it materializes in the blocks of female names printed in large capital letters on every few pages of the book. These "single fore-name[s]" (13), which link the women horizontally in relation to one another rather than vertically in relation to men, posit what Winifred Woodhull calls an antigenealogy, a radical alternative to bourgeois culture and also, I would add, a radical challenge to the bourgeois novel, because "identity can only be thought in terms of the collectivity."[3] The names stand alone in the center of the page like small communities, each uniting women of present and past, "East" and "West," fiction and history—literary and historical names like CLARISSA, CHRYSEIS, ISOLDE, LAMIA; ordinary names like LOUISE, DORIS, ANIKO; and invented names that feminize the masculine, underscore the revolutionary imperative, or signify woman's "place" (HEGEMONIE, ALIENOR, NAUNAME, HEMANE, OSEE, CALAMITA, VILAINE, ANGE), yielding this kind of typical block:

```
METTE   KHADIOTA  MICHAELA
PHANO   HUGUETTE  LELIA
SIDONIA  OMAYA  MERNEITH
INIBRINA  WUANG-QIANG
ASPASIA  HANNAH  LETITIA
NORA  BENOITE  RADEGONDE
```

3. Winifred Woodhull, "Politics, the Feminine, and Writing: A Study of Monique Wittig's *Les Guérillères* and *Brouillon pour une dictionnaire*" (Ph.D. diss., University of Wisconsin, 1979).

The gynomythography that *Les Guérillères* constructs mirrors this project of cultural diversity: the women honor the goddesses Amaterasu and Cihuacoatl (27/34–35), re-create Prometheus and the Round Table as female legends (45/61– 62), remember the warrior Nü Wa's victories (80/112–14), Lei Zu's discovery of silk (81/115), the victories of Vlasta and "the young women of Bohemia" (114/165). Freed from conventional realist continuities of plot, character, and history, *Les Guérillères* can insist on a community that crosses spatial, temporal, and imaginative boundaries. However, in spite of its evident intentions, the text remains European in its cultural base: French names and Western myths dominate, so that the *Les Guérillères* cannot be said to authorize a global community. This problem is most apparent when the text moves into a (rare) moment of quasi-conventional narrativity by naming one of the "elles" with an individual identity: Lucie Maure, Marthe Vivonne, Valerie Céru, Marthe Ephore, Fabienne Jouy, Marie Viarme. I will suggest below that such slips into realist narrativity— into the individuation of realist character, time, and space— inevitably construct some kind of cultural hegemony.

Open and expansive at least in theory, however, the "elles" is not merely the collective "protagonist" of *Les Guérillères* but ultimately its collective authority and its collective voice. Until its last paragraph the narrative voice of *Les Guérillères* is technically heterodiegetic: a "third person" recounts what the women say and do. But this is not the conventional authorial voice that looks down upon and interprets a community. The text avoids the markers that suggest hierarchies of voice; there are no quotation marks, indentations, or shifts between the past tense of a narrator and the present tense of characters. Unlike the authorial narrators I discussed in Part I, the narrator of *Les Guérillères* restricts herself entirely to acts of representation: she is an anonymous and undramatized presence that records what "elles" do and say. Although such a narrator resembles formally the "voiceless" camera eye constituted by *nouveaux romanciers* like Alain Robbe-Grillet and Marguerite Duras, she serves here as a kind of scribe, recording a culture's deeds and words. "Elles" are the source of legends and stories, decisions, warnings and reminders, aphorisms and judgments, political analyses and rituals, all of which the narrator simply passes on.

In substituting this communal source for the individualist "author" of traditional fiction, the text also substitutes oral discourse and provisional textuality for the reified corpus (corpse) of Western patriarchy's written texts. What the "elles" say is contingent not because there is any higher authority but because the community's own truths must continually change. Thus the women decide at one point that their own discourse "denote[s] an outworn language" and that "everything must begin over again [il faut tout recommencer]" (66/93–94). This provisional nature even of communal authority is evident not only in what the women say but in what they write in the "grand registre" and the little "féminaires" that are the community's sacred texts (14/17). Unlike the sacred texts of the fathers, the feminaries are not authorized from outside or above the community. It seems not to matter whether there are "multiple copies of the same original" or "several kinds" (14/17) because all textual authority is limited despite the obvious importance of (provisional) texts. Texts must remain continually (re)inscribable, and by those very persons for whom they hold authority: "when it is leafed through the feminary presents numerous blank pages in which they write from time to time" (15/17–18). No text is the definitive text; there must be no definitive text.

It is clear that the "feminary" and the "great register," with their rejection of conventional linearity, describe Wittig's own book. Like the feminary, *Les Guérillères* "consists of pages with words printed in a varying number of capital letters. There may be only one or the pages may be full of them. Usually they are isolated at the centre of the page, well spaced black on a white background or else white on a black background" (15/18). And like the "great register," which lies always open like a family Bible, it is "useless to open" *Les Guérillères* "at the first page and search for any sequence. One may take it at random and find something one is interested in." Yet, "diverse as the writings are they all have a common feature" (53/74–75). A living and changing record of community, the "great register" continues to be written even as it is being read: "Not a moment passes without one of the women approaching to write something therein. Or else a reading aloud of some passage takes place" (53–54/75). This suggests that the narrative voice of *Les Guérillères* may itself not be singular; that any number of "elles" are its scribes, again dissolving the conventional hierarchy between narrator and characters. And if readers are writers, and all "elles" are authorized to write, then *Les Guérillères* also turns all willing (female and male) readers into writers of "féminaires," scribes of a living and ever-changing collective discourse that is set against the patriarchal text that derives its authority from its implicitly fixed, transcendent voice. Here textuality exists only to serve the women; what is important is the authority over discourse, which includes the right not only to constitute but to discard texts. When the feminaries "have fulfilled their function [rempli leur office]," when the "ancient texts" seem "outdated" (49/67–68), they must be let go. Hence too the emphasis on the temporary, on spoken discourse—the ubiquitous "elles disent"—rather than on writing ("elles écrivent").

But while the "elles" exists from the beginning of the text as the collective protagonist, the women are not from the outset a collective voice. Rather, *Les Guérillères* traces through its own syntax and semantics the very conditions for the emergence of communal voice. At first the women are "huddled [pressées] against each other" and have no voice at all: they "open their mouths to bleat or to say something but no sound emerges" (30/38). The early sections of the book do not employ the "elles disent" at all; the narrator records the women's actions but not their words. We are told that the women shout, laugh, cry, and repeat stories and legends, but these verbal acts are *de*scribed rather than *tran*scribed. Several of these early legends themselves concern voice; the stories of the siren and the echo and the first introduction of the feminaries appear very early in the text (14/16–17).

Significantly, the textual moment in which the women are first said to speak coincides precisely with their recognition and celebration of their sexuality as they name and (re)claim the female body and rewrite a culture in which woman's body is the (unspeakable) source of her silencing: "The women say [elles disent] that they expose their genitals [leurs sexes] so that the sun may be reflected therein as in a mirror. They say that they retain its brilliance. They say that the pubic hair is like a spider's web that captures the rays" (19/24). It is in naming the body that the women begin both to speak and to write (22/29). Implicitly such a conjunction of voice and sexuality refuses both the heroine's text, in which the woman who gives her body gives up her voice, and the representations of female community—in *Cranford, Herland, The Country of the Pointed Firs*, and even *Deephaven*—in which female sexuality is denied. In this way *Les Guérillères* also makes clear why female voice is a crucial signifier for female authority and autonomy, why Hélène Cixous insists that when you "censor the body," you "censor breath and speech at the same time."[4]

---

4. Hélène Cixous, "The Laugh of the Medusa," trans. Keith Cohen and Paula Cohen, in Marks and Courtivron, *New French Feminisms*, 250.

Although *Les Guérillères* has at this point established a collective female cultural authority, the narrator still represents the discourse of the "elles" in indirect forms. Until more than halfway through the text, nearly all of the collective knowledge and wisdom of the "elles" is narrated through tagged indirect discourse, a form that does not, like free indirect discourse, rely on even the flavor of the speaker's own words: "the women say that [elles disent que] they expose their genitals" (19/24); "the women say that [elles disent que] any one of them might equally well invoke another sun goddess" (27/35); "the women say that [elles disent que] references to Ama-terasu or Cihuacoatl are no longer in order" (30/38); "they say that [elles disent que] as possessors [porteuses] of vulvas they are familiar with their characteristics" (31/41); "they say that [elles disent que] the clitoris has been compared to a cherrystone, a bud, a young shoot, a shelled sesame" (32/42); "the women say that [elles disent que] the feminaries give pride of place to the symbols of the circle, the circumference, the ring, the O, the zero, the sphere" (45/61); "the women say that [elles disent que] they perceive their bodies in their entirety," that "they do not want to become prisoners of their own ideology" (57/80).

This indirect discourse creates a slight distance between the words of "elles" and the narrative voice that at the very least denies the women the fullness of textual voice and, it seems to me, renders their authority subtly contingent. But ultimately the narrative shifts defin-itively into a direct discourse that signals the full authorization of the women to speak for themselves. It is ironic and significant that this textual voice is born in revolutionary politics: under the pressure of domination, the women construct a generalizing didactic authority directed at a collective female narratee and designed to empower the women against male dominance. At the same time, the pronominal referents for "elles" become intermingled and interchangeable: they are at once "we," "I," and "you": "The women say [elles disent], the men have kept you at a distance, ... put you on a pedestal, constructed with an essential difference ... described you as they described the races they called inferior" (100–102/146); "the women say [elles di-sent], you are really a slave if there ever was one" (106/153); "the women say [elles disent], I refuse henceforward to speak this lan-guage" (107/153); "the women say [elles disent], unhappy one, men have expelled you from the world of symbols [signes]" (112/162); "they say [elles disent], the language you speak is made up of words that are killing you" (114/162); "the women say [elles disent], whether men [ils] live or die, they no longer have power" (115/165); "they say [disent-elles], we must disregard all the stories" (134/192); "they say [elles disent], if I relax after these great achievements I shall reel drunk with sleep and fatigue" (136/197).

Finally entire passages come to be narrated directly, without even "the women say" to introduce them, as all textual authority combines into a single collectivity that embraces the personal and the authorial, the "I" and "we" as well as the "you" and "they," all pronouns collapsing into communality. The direct discourse becomes, in aggregate, the ultimate "maximizing" text in which generalization does not simply underscore representation but becomes that which must be represented. In other words, *Les Guérillères* remaximizes narrative by writing the ideology of feminist revolution: the rewriting of maxims is part of the revolutionary project and hence of narrative. By the time the women triumph, their authority has become entirely communal and it has become clear that voice is resistance, and discourse one ground on which the "battle of the sexes" must be engaged.

This newly forged community is thus not the "elles" of an old and peaceful order, the "elles" who do not have even to imagine themselves as a "we" against a "they"; it is a revolutionary or postrevolutionary "we" in which "she" also includes "he." That is, the ultimate communal voice, forged when the women embrace the young men and invite them to become part of the collectivity, includes everyone who is willing to "begin again." "Women and the people march hand in hand" (131/189):

> You understand that we have been fighting as much for you as for ourselves.... Today, together, let us repeat as our slogan that all trace of violence must disappear from this earth... The young men [eux] applaud and shout [crient] with all their might. They have brought their arms. The women [elles] bury them at the same time as their own saying, let there be erased from human memory the longest most murderous war it has ever known, the last possible war in history. They wish the survivors, both male and female [aux survivantes et aux survivants], love strength youth, so that they [ils] may form a lasting alliance that no future dispute can compromise. One of the women begins to sing, Like unto ourselves / men who open their mouths to speak / a thousand thanks to those who have understood our language / and not having found it excessive / have joined with us to transform the world. (127–28/184)

It is on this basis that the authorial narrator can also enter the *narrative* "we" to participate in a new order that is grammatically and philosophically feminine. In the final paragraph the narrative shifts simultaneously to a first-person plural voice and to the past tense that is the standard tense of realist narrative. Because of the linguistic transformations it evokes by feminizing all nouns and adjectives, I shall represent this passage in its entirety:

> Mues par une impulsion commune, nous étions toutes debout pour retrouver comme à tatons le cours égal, l'unisson exaltant de l'Internationale. Une vieille soldate grisonnante sanglotait comme une enfant. Alexandra Ollontaï retenait à peine ses larmes. L'immense chant envahit la salle, creva portes et fenêtres, monta vers le ciel calme. La guerre est terminée, la guerre est terminée, dit à mes côtés une jeune ouvrière. Son visage rayonnait. Et lorsque ce fut fini et que nous restions là dans une sorte de silence embarrassé, quelqu'une au fond de la salle cria, camarades, souvenons-nous de celles qui sont mortes pour la liberté. Et nous entonnâmes alors la Marche funèbre, un air lent, mélancolique et pourtant triomphant. (207–8)

> [Moved by a common impulse, we all stood to seek gropingly the even flow, the exultant unity, of the Internationale. An aged grizzled woman soldier sobbed like a child. Alexandra Ollontaï could hardly restrain her tears. The great song filled the hall, burst through doors and windows and rose to the calm sky. The war is over, the war is over, said a young working woman next to me. Her face shone. And when it was finished and we remained there in a kind of embarrassed silence, a woman at the end of the hall cried, Comrades, let us remember [those] who died for liberty. And then we intoned the Funeral March, a slow, melancholy and yet triumphant air.] (144)

This is the utopian "we" that "by a common impulse" "moves" the women and their male comrades to solidarity—to a "we" that has become possible, to quote Cherríe Moraga, only because "things [got] hot enough." It is a "we" open to all women and men who are able to refuse male hegemony. It is fitting that in signifying this "we" the text moves into the time and space of realist narrative: after the reclamation of language, the renaming of the world, representation can begin.

Yet the danger of traditional (Western) narrative is also exposed in this final, communal section of *Les Guérillères* because the passage recircumscribes the community as specifically Western, Marxist, and industrial. Avoiding the greatest danger of utopian literature, the production of stasis, *Les Guérillères* has been careful to show communities always in process, but since narrative closure is itself a kind of stasis, the shift to plural-voice past-tense narration that concludes *Les Guérillères* may be reinforcing a closure that is all too complete. That this passage is only a single moment after an entire book of present-tense, technically heterodiegetic narration is therefore also significant: if *Les Guérillères* transforms fantasy to history, no-time to our time, it must also stop with the single solemn moment when the "new" order begins. That the final singing of the Internationale takes place in a "hall" suggests a Western location, as the reference to Russian revolutionary Alexandra (K)Ollontaï suggests that it is Europe that is to lead the way out of injustice. Thus Europe becomes again the savior in a gesture that, however different its mission, can only reproduce the European colonialist project, and *Les Guérillères*, like any fiction, is revealed as the product of its own cultural positioning.

The limits implicit in the closing paragraph also suggest that the quasi-global communal authority of the rest of the text has depended on the novel's radical antinarrative form. As I pointed out earlier in my discussion, *Les Guérillères* succeeds in representing an inclusive feminist community precisely to the extent that it rejects not only traditional characters but the selectivity and hierarchies imposed by the choosing of protagonists, the constitution of a setting, and the traditional continuities of plot. By postulating a provisional textual authority against an order in which women are imprisoned in reified texts, *Les Guérillères* ultimately constitutes a radical critique not only of phallocentric discourse, and of a literature built on the silencing of female voice, but of those voices that women have inscribed in and as conventional literature. I argued earlier that the eighteenth-century heroine's voice, for all its outspokenness, was a silenced voice, allowed to speak only because of the sharp splits between the private and public, the novelistic and the political. *Les Guérillères* refuses this split between fictions of authority and the authority of the body politic and insists on the necessity to "WRITE VIOLENCE / OUTSIDE THE TEXT / IN ANOTHER WRITING [ECRIRE VIOLENCE / HORS TEXTE / DANS UNE AUTRE ECRITURE]" (143/205). In this sense *Les Guérillères* supports the implications of "self-silencing" eighteenth-century novels such as *Mistriss Henley* and *The Wrongs of Woman* that that there is no viable fiction of authority unless it is also an authority "HORS TEXTE." It is appropriate, therefore, that *Les Guérillères* displaces the conventionally feminine alternatives of death and marriage with the alternatives death and liberty that have long been the male revolutionary imperative.

The "melancholy and yet triumphant" funeral song with which *Les Guérillères* concludes might then be an ode as well to the entire tradition of individual(ist) female voice: necessary but also necessarily sacrificed as "everything must begin over again" and a new "sun is about to rise" (66/131). It is fitting that since its publication in 1969 *Les Guérillères* has fostered not only a generation of utopian fiction but a generation of feminist theory as well, mapping a process of coming-to-community in language, a struggle for authority not only as "content" but as form, modeling the communal writing that is essential if this movement is to exist "hors texte," or in the world-as-text. Wittig's book is a call not to deny the authority of fictions but, on the contrary, to recognize their power as representations by which women live and by which we may therefore reinvent our lives. *Les Guérillères* stands in this sense as a sign of feminist future, pointing to forms of narration that have perhaps not even been imagined, let alone expressed—forms that may give voice to women still not authorized. It is appropriate that Wittig's book invites its own readers to write the texts to come, for *Les Guérillères* is both the culmination of a Western novelistic tradition and the departure point for narrative possibilities as yet unknown.

> We have so many voices to invent in order to express all of us, everywhere, even in our gaps, that all the time there is will not be enough.
> —Luce Irigaray, *This Sex Which Is Not One*

It may seem that this book has given narrative voice an inordinate importance when, as Peter Brooks argues, most of us are "reading for the plot."[5] I have tried to show that voice not only constructs and controls narrative but also enacts more-or-less visibly a "plot" of its own. Perhaps this "plot" has a particular importance for those

---

5. See Peter Brooks, *Reading for the Plot: Design and Intention in Narrative* (New York: Random House, 1984).

whose voices have not been able simply to take for granted their discursive rights. I have emphasized public and private narrative voice, extrarepresentational acts, and self-conscious narrative strategies because I believe that for those without full discursive authority— those who are not, to quote Dale Spender, able to "view *all* audiences and *all* forms of writing as open to them"[6]—novels are able to constrain or to expand the possibilities for voice not only in other novels but in human history. As Chapter 1 suggested, narrative poetics has not, on the whole, concerned itself with these questions that are deeply intertwined with social authority; rather, in opting for a precise and esoteric terminology, it has ruptured the links between narrative and social practices. Likewise, feminist criticism has not, on the whole, attended to the complex interrelationship between representation and voice that, as my discussions of novels like *Millenium Hall* and *Their Eyes Were Watching God* have suggested, are sometimes ideologically at odds.

I said in Chapter 1 that each of the three modes allowed certain meanings and not others to be made visible and that all three forms seemed to me to have been necessary for women to make a place in Western literature. Although the emphasis of this book has been on women's achievement of forms that have been in some way prohibited, I hope I have pointed out the problems attendant on each of these narrative modes. Authorial voice, with its structurally superior position and its superhuman privilege, seems to me always in danger of constructing its own hegemony, yet it can be a powerful tool for dislodging an existing authority. The transformative power of Toni Morrison's *Beloved*, for example, seems to be the effect both of its overturning of white-realist authority and of its rich narrative polyphony, in which the "rememory" of slavery is created through a multiplicity of authoritative characters whose voices often merge in free indirect discourse with the authorial voice.

The differences I have tried to sketch between Jane Eyre's totalizing authority and Annie John's recognition of duplicity suggest the different textual effects that can be created through personal voice. Because its authority is more qualified, personal voice establishes a less certain hegemony, yet it has also the power to engulf the reader

6. Dale Spender, *Man Made Language* (London: Routledge, 1980), 193.

in the vision of a single consciousness. If, on the other hand, the personal voice can represent itself as "interrogative," if it can, as Catherine Belsey puts it, "unfix" itself as subject,[7] then "I" becomes a multiplicity of voices in dialogue. I think of Colette's *La Vagabonde* (1911), for example, as creating such a voice.

Although authorial and personal voice are unquestionably individual(ist) fictions, it seems to me that the construction of such individualist voices has been a necessary if insufficient revolutionary strategy in societies where the alternative to individualism has been oppression in the anonymity of caste. As my discussion of communal voice has indicated, however, there is perhaps a further political potential in forms that constitute the shared and at best also diverse vision of a community. But I have also argued that unlike authorial and personal voice, whose singularity corresponds to that of conventional authorship, communal voice arrogates to an individual author the self-reinforcing pretense of multiplicity.

Each of these three forms of voice—as well as other, hybrid narrative modes that I have not been able to study here—is thus at once determined and open, restrictive and flexible, powerful and dangerous. Every narrative form is already a "content" in that the fact of its existence sends messages, but every narrative form is dependent for its value—hence in a crucial way for its meaning—on the contexts of representation and reception in which it is realized. It is my hope that as new and challenging forms of narrative voice come to be invented, new and supple forms of narrative theory will be able to account for them, so that the political project of finding voices and the theoretical project of naming them can join in the task of repairing the world.

7. Catherine Belsey, *Critical Practice* (London: Methuen, 1980), chap. 4.

Index

Addison, Joseph, 54–56
African-American fiction: and audience, 120–24, 129–30, 138, 197, 204–5, 208; and autobiography, 192–93, 194–98, 200–201, 218; and postmodernism, 122–23, 127, 135–37; and realism, 124–25, 128–29, 131–34
Alcott, Louisa May: *Little Women*, 256
Allen, Walter, 95
Allott, Miriam, 176
Altman, Janet, 45n
Ammons, Elizabeth, 247
Andrews, William, 197
Armstrong, Nancy, 26, 38, 40, 88
Atkinson's Casket. See "Female Ingenuity"
Atwood, Margaret, 121
Audience, women and, 45–46, 87, 142; African-American women, 120–24, 129–30, 138, 197, 205, 208; individual writers: Charrière, 153; Hurston, 205; Morrison, 121–22; Riccoboni and Fielding, 57–58; Sand, 174–75; Shelley, 171–72; Woolf, 109. *See also* Narratee
Audoux, Marguerite: *L'Atelier de Marie-Claire*, 241, 251–53, 254
Auerbach, Erich, 131n
Auerbach, Nina, 189, 225, 244
Austen, Jane, 18, 37, 59–63, 67–80, 100–101, 119, 130; Juvenilia, 68, 79; *Lady*

Susan, 67–68; *Mansfield Park*, 71; *Northanger Abbey*, 61–63, 67–72, 77–80, 84, 136–37; *Persuasion*, 74, 77, 161; *Pride and Prejudice*, 78; *Sanditon*, 77–78; *Sense and Sensibility*, 62–63, 72
Austin, Mary: *A Woman of Genius*, 176, 188
Authoriality, 17; in Austen, 62, 63, 67–69, 72, 79, 80; and charge of didacticism against women, 78, 89, 95, 136, 273; in Morrison, 131–35; in Sarah Fielding, 49, 50, 57; in 1790s, 63, 67–69, 72, 79–80; in Stael, 162; and women writers, 18, 58–59, 65–67, 89; in Woolf, 110–17, 119
Authorial voice, 15–18, 20, 22, 278; in modernism, 103–5, 108, 109; strategies for "humanizing," 92, 129–30; women's use of, 18, 47–49, 89, 93, 123. *See also* Authoriality; Heterodiegesis; Narration, figural
Authority, 6–8; as collective, in *Les Guérillères*, 270, 271; culturally constructed as masculine, 6, 10, 17, 18, 26, 46, 47, 86, 90; material representation of, 35–38; Western, deconstructed in Morrison, 131–35; women's resistance to masculinity of, 69–71, 184; women's strategies for mitigating, 91, 178–80; women's uses of

281

Authority (*cont.*)
    masculine a., 48–49, 52, 83–84, 90, 96–99, 101
Authorship, 6–7, 93; Austen and, 79–80; Hurston and, 205; limits of individual(ist), 254, 266; in novels of 1790s, 63–65; redefined in *Les Guérillères*, 270, 271; Riccoboni and, 52; Shelley and, 166–68; Victorian constraints on women's, 88–90
Autobiography: fictional, 177, 188; and novel, 196–97, 218; and personal voice, 20, 142, 144, 177, 201; and Sand's *Lélia*, 174–75; Stael's avoidance of, 163; Woolf's ambivalence about, 108
Autodiegesis, 19. *See also* Personal voice

Babb, Valerie, 213n
Bakhtin, Mikhail, 5, 8, 16, 46, 73, 85, 99–101, 211
Baldwin, James, 209
Balzac, Honoré de, 86, 89
Bammer, Angelika, 240
Banfield, Ann, 73n
Barbauld, Anna, 36, 47–48
Barker, Pat: *Union Street*, 264
Barry, Joseph, 175
Bauer, Dale, 5n
Beasley, Jerry, 37
Beaty, Jerome, 177
Beauvoir, Simone de, 223
Behn, Aphra, 20, 33, 36–37, 47–48, 89, 91
Belsey, Catherine, 86, 279
Bender, John, 37n, 64n, 74n
Benstock, Shari, 103n, 107
Bertens, Hans, 135
Bishop, Lloyd, 156
Black, Frank, 45n
Blackburn, Sara, 120
Black English, 124, 126, 129, 205–6, 213–14
Bloom, Harold, 38n, 165
Bodenheimer, Rosemary, 183n
Bontemps, Arna, 195
Boone, Joseph Allen, 224n
Booth, Wayne, 18, 61
Bourdieu, Pierre, 63
Braxton, Joanne, and Andrée McLaughlin, 121n
Brontë, Anne: *Agnes Grey*, 177–81, 185
Brontë, Charlotte, 91, 177, 182–83, 185; *Jane Eyre*, 176–78, 181–93, 278; *Jane Eyre* and Kincaid's *Annie John*, 214–19; *The Professor*, 181; *Villette*, 188–89
Brooks, Gwendolyn: *Maud Martha*, 194, 201, 206–7
Brooks, Peter, 277
Broumas, Olga, 255, 261

Brown, Rita Mae: *Rubyfruit Jungle*, 189
Browning, Elizabeth Barrett, 188
Brownstein, Rachel, 27, 30, 187
Brunton, Mary: *Discipline*, 97, 177–81
Burney, Frances (Fanny), 64, 66, 74n, 78

Carrell, Susan Lee, 45n, 47
Carter, Elizabeth, 57
Cary, Richard, 247
Charrière, Isabelle de, 141, 143–44, 153, 155, 157–60; *Lettres de Mistriss Henley*, 143–55, 159, 224; *Lettres écrites de Lausanne (Caliste)*, 155, 158–62, 175
Chase, Joan: *During the Reign of the Queen of Persia*, 257, 260–61
Cheung, King-Kok, 214n
Childhood, as focus for communal plot, 257–61
Childress, Alice, 207; *Like One of the Family*, 207–9
Chodorow, Nancy, 117
Cixous, Hélène, 3, 272
Class: and authority, 49, 56–57, 251–52; in Charrière, 159; in *Les Guérillères*, 274; and individuality, 251, 252; in *Millenium Hall*, 226, 230; and narrative voice, 56–58, 214; and realist narration, 124–25; in *The Wrongs of Woman*, 230–33
Cleland, John: *Memoirs of a Woman of Pleasure (Fanny Hill)*, 35
Coding, 10–14, 59, 121–22
Colette, 107; *La Vagabonde*, 188, 279
Communal voice, 15, 21–22, 90n, 116, 224; implications for plot, 241, 265; movement toward, in *Les Guérillères*, 267–68, 273; problems of, 254, 262, 266, 279; sequential, 21, 256, 263–66; simultaneous, 21, 256–60, 275; singular, 21, 241–49, 253; techniques for representing, 224, 227, 238
Community, female: problems of representing, 224–25, 229, 240–41, 256, 261; relationship to communal voice, 224, 256; in specific novels: *L'Atelier de Marie-Claire*, 251–53; *The Bluest Eye*, 259–60; *Cranford*, 241–46; *The Country of the Pointed Firs*, 246–51; *Deephaven*, 257–59; *During the Reign of the Queen of Persia*, 260–61; *Les Guérillères*, 268–77; *Herland*, 240; *Millenium Hall*, 225, 228–30; *The Women's Decameron*, 265–66; *The Wrongs of Woman*, 230–34
Constant de Rebecque, Samuel: *Le Mari sentimental*, 143–45, 147, 151
Craik, Dinah: *A Life for a Life*, 189
Crebillon *fils*, 36; *Les Égarements*, 141
Crosby, Emily, 58
Crouch, Stanley, 122

Culler, Jonathan, 4n, 18n
Curran, Stuart, 156n

D'Aulnoy, Marie, 36
David, Deirdre, 86n, 97, 100
Davis, Lennard, 37n, 86, 100
Day, Robert Adams, 36n, 45n
Death. *See* Marriage; Plot
Deen, Rosemary. *See* Ponsot, Marie
Defoe, Daniel, 35–36, 141–42
DeKoven, Marianne, 103n
Demay, Andrée, 58
DiBattista, Maria, 109–10
Dickens, Charles: *Bleak House*, 239–40; *David Copperfield*, 187–88
Diderot, Denis, 35, 45; *La Religieuse*, 224
Diengott, Nilli, 4n
Direct discourse (of characters), 75–77, 101n, 113, 115, 206–7, 256, 274
Doody, Margaret, 48, 74
"Double-voiced" discourse, 8n, 12–13, 121, 136, 147. *See also* Coding; Free indirect discourse
Douglass, Frederick: *Narrative*, 91
DuPlessis, Rachel, 39, 103n, 110, 112-13, 116, 255–56
Duras, Claire, 46n

Edgeworth, Maria, 64, 66, 78
Edmundson, Mark, 127–28
Eile, Stanislaw, 86
Eliot, George, 18, 21, 59–60, 81–87, 89–101, 119, 133; *Adam Bede*, 85, 87; *Daniel Deronda*, 96, 101n; early novels, 84, 92, 93; later novels, 84, 87, 97–99; *Middlemarch*, 82, 96, 100; *Mill on the Floss*, 82, 90; *Scenes of Clerical Life*, 20
Ellison, Ralph: *Invisible Man*, 198
Ellmann, Mary, 43
Enlightenment, and women, 32–34, 65, 147, 149, 153
Epigraphs, 97–100, 195
Epistolary narration: 26, 44–47; Austen's use of, 67, 68; "public," in *Jane Eyre*, 186–87; and women's silencing, 33, 55; women's uses of, 45–47, 141, 166, 212-13. *See also* Voice, private
Erdrich, Louise, 263
Ewbank, Inga-Stina, 177n
Extradiegesis, 16. *See also* Voice, public

Faulkner, William: *As I Lay Dying*, 21
Fauset, Jessie: *Plum Bun*, 126, 137n
"Female Ingenuity," 9–15
Female voice. *See* Voice, female
Femme, double meaning of, 148, 150, 152, 269
Ferrier, Susan, 78

Fichte, Johann, 32
Fiedler, Leslie, 102–3, 105–6
Fielding, Henry, 48, 50, 57, 67; *Amelia*, 58–59; *Tom Jones*, 52
Fielding, Sarah, 49–50, 57; *The Countess of Dellwyn*, 49–50, 57, 59, 64
Fifer, Elizabeth, 214
Flaubert, Gustave: *Madame Bovary*, 87, 240
Flint, Candyce: *Mother Love*, 261
Fortin, Nina. *See* Tuchman, Gaye
Foster, Hannah, 46
Foucault, Michel, 6n, 33
Fowler, Rowena, 246
Franklin, (Sarah) Miles: *My Brilliant Career*, 188
Free indirect discourse, 61, 73–76, 101n, 113, 116, 123, 200, 203, 206
Freeman, Janet, 183n
Friedman, Edward, 35n
Fullerton, Georgiana, 46n
Furst, Lilian, 156

Gallagher, Catherine, 86n, 98
Gaskell, Elizabeth, 91, 92, 97; "The Cage at Cranford," 245; *Cranford*, 241–47, 251
Gass, William, 190n
Gates, Henry Louis, Jr., 73n, 136n, 195–96, 198n, 200, 202n, 203, 206, 212
Genette, Gérard, 4, 16, 17, 19, 85, 250
Genlis, Stéphanie de, 64
Gilbert, Sandra, and Susan Gubar, 13, 62n, 67, 82, 98, 99, 103n, 165–67, 190n, 192n
Gilligan, Carol, 82
Gilman, Charlotte Perkins, 146, 189; *Herland*, 240–41
Godwin, William, 171–72, 235–36
Goethe, Johann Wolfgang von: *Die Leiden des jungen Werthers*, 175
Goldberg, Rita, 224n
Goldberger, Avriel, 163
Gordon, Mary, 106; *A Company of Women*, 263; *Final Payments*, 189
Governess narratives, 177–82, 184
Grafigny, Françoise de: *Lettres d'une péruvienne*, 27n
Graham, J. W., 111–12, 114
Graham, Kenneth, 87, 177n
Graham, Rosemary, 164
Grahn, Judy, 125, 208, 214, 263n
Gramsci, Antonio, 87n
Griffith, Elizabeth, 64
Gubar, Susan. *See* Gilbert, Sandra
Gutwirth, Madelyn, 162n

Halperin, John, 67n, 71n
Hamilton, Elizabeth, 46n
Harden, Elizabeth, 78n
Hardy, Barbara, 96n

Harlem Renaissance, 126
Harper, Frances E. W.: *Iola Leroy*, 123–25, 256
Harris, Jocelyn, 67, 70
Harris, Trudier, 208
Harrison, Fredric, 176–77
Hayman, David, 106
Hays, Maria, 64
Haywood, Eliza, 36, 49
Henderson, Mae G., 198n, 202n, 203–4
Hennelly, Mark M., Jr., 184n, 187
Hermann, Claudine, 52, 149
Hernton, Calvin, 122n
"Heroine's text," 27, 31–34, 226
Heterodiegesis, 16, 85–86; as strategy, 201, 227–28, 247–48, 263
Heterosexuality. *See* Lesbian sexuality; Novel; Plot; Sexuality and voice
Higdon, David Leon, 98n
History, literary. *See* Novel: histories of
Hite, Molly, 202n
Hodges, Devon, 165n, 170–71
Hogue, Lawrence, 176
Homans, Margaret, 8, 156n, 161
Honan, Park, 67n, 70, 72, 80
Hooks, Bell, 121n, 191
Hopkins, Pauline: *Contending Forces*, 123–25, 256
Humphrey, Robert, 105–6
Hurston, Zora Neale, 126, 205–6; *Their Eyes Were Watching God*, 201–6, 234, 278

Idealism, 5, 160–61
Ideology, 5, 15, 17
Imitation, 52–53, 58, 59, 182
Imperialism, 145, 160, 190, 193, 214–17, 275–76
Indirection, 61–62, 79–80, 189.
Individualism: and authorship, 6; and female authority, 29, 31, 36–37, 251–52; in narrative poetics, 21; in the novel, 36–37, 224, 231, 236–37, 269, 270, 277; and patriarchy, 32; and voice, 118, 192, 255, 279. *See also* Novel; Plot
Intradiegesis. *See* Voice, private
Irigaray, Luce, 3, 11, 55, 277

Jackson, Susan, 152n
Jacobs, Harriet: *Incidents in the Life of a Slave Girl*, 91n
Jacobus, Mary, 82, 165n, 236
Jelinek, Estelle, 196
Jewett, Sarah Orne: *Country of the Pointed Firs*, 241, 246–51, 256; *Deephaven*, 257–59
Johnson, Barbara, 165–67, 202n, 205–6
Johnson, Claudia, 62n, 67n
Johnson, James Weldon, 195, 198

Johnson, Samuel, 48, 57
Jones, Gayl, 201; *Corregidora*, 211; *Eva's Man*, 211
Jong, Erica: *Fear of Flying*, 189
Joyce, James: *Portrait of the Artist*, 104–5

Kant, Immanuel, 32–33, 149
Kaplan, Deborah, 62n, 68n
Katzenbach, Maria, 261
Kauffman, Linda, 28n, 45n, 47
Kiely, Robert, 165n
Kincaid, Jamaica: *Annie John*, 214–18, 278; *A Small Place*, 194, 214–15, 218–19
Kingston, Maxine Hong, 20
Kirkham, Margaret, 62n, 67n, 71
Kramarae, Cheris, 10–11
Kristeva, Julia, 103
Kroeber, Karl, 186
Krüdener, Barbara de, 162
Kubitschek, Missy Dehn, 203

Laclos, Pierre Choderlos de: *Les Liaisons dangereuses*, 256
Lakoff, Robin, 10, 11, 93
Landes, Joan, 40
Lansbury, Coral, 245
Lanser, Susan S.: *The Narrative Act*, 16n, 23; "Toward a Feminist Narratology," 4n, 9n; "Who Are the 'We'?", 262n; *See also* Radner, Joan N.
Larnac, Jean, 20n
Leavis, F. R., and Q. D. Leavis, 187n
Lennox, Charlotte, 48
Lesbian sexuality, 40, 189, 230, 237, 257–59. *See also* Novel; Plot
Lessing, Doris, 188
Lidoff, Joan, 116–17
Lorde, Audre, 22, 141
Lovell, Terry, 88n, 97n
Lubbock, Percy, 104

McCormick, Peter, 7n
McCredie, Wendy, 202n, 203n
McDowell, Deborah E., 120n, 126, 198n
Macherey, Pierre, 84–85
McKeon, Michael, 38n
Main, Alexander, 82–83
Male authors. *See* Voice, female: men's use of; Novel: histories of
Malmgren, Carl, 86
Manley, Delariviere, 36
Marivaux, Pierre de, 35–36, 52
Marks, Elaine, 107; and Isabelle de Courtivron, 267
Marriage: as "death," 31–35, 142–43, 150–53; and narrative voice, 31, 142–43, 149–50, 152, 189, 245–46; and plot, 53,

Marriage: and plot (*cont.*)
142–46, 148, 178, 252; and "women's
language," 11–12, 191–92
Marshall, Alice, 65n
Masson, David, 36–37
Maxims, 17; in Austen, 73–75; in *The
Countess of Dellwyn*, 50; in Eliot, 82–83,
93, 96–99; in *Les Guérillères*, 274; in
Morrison, 136; in Woolf, 108–9, 115–18
Meese, Elizabeth, 202n, 203n
Mellor, Anne, 166
Menant, Sylvain, 29n
Meriwether, Louise: *Daddy Was a Number
Runner*, 209–10
Miller, D. A., 100–101
Miller, J. Hillis, 86, 96n, 109
Miller, Nancy K., 17n, 25n, 27
Mimicry, 11; in Riccoboni, 28, 53, 55
Minow-Pinkney, Makiko, 118–19
Modernism, 102–8, 126, 255
Moers, Ellen, 35, 167n, 172, 183, 189
Monod, Sylvère, 186
Monologue, interior, 19, 211
Montagu, Elizabeth, 57
Moraga, Cherríe, 267, 275
More, Hannah: *Coelebs in Search of a Wife*,
71, 179–80
Morrison, Toni, 18, 59–60, 120–23, 126–
32, 135–36, 138; *Beloved*, 122, 130–38,
263, 278; *Bluest Eye*, 121, 130–33, 135–
38, 209–10, 257, 259–60; *Song of
Solomon*, 133–35, 137; *Sula*, 131–33, 136,
138; *Tar Baby*, 133
Muller, Herbert J., 107n
Musselwhite, David, 71
Musset, Alfred de, 174
Myers, Mitzi, 236

Naremore, James, 109n
Narratee: collective, in *Les Guérillères*, 273;
direct engagement with: in Eliot, 91–92,
in *Jane Eyre*, 185–86, in Rowson, 64–65,
in *A Small Place*, 218; effacing, 88;
private, in *Dessa Rose*, 198–99; public,
141; public and private, in *Like One of the
Family*, 208. *See also* Audience
Narration, figural, 16, 87, 88, 104, 200
Narrative poetics (Narratology), 4–6, 8, 23,
278–79
Narrator, "engaging," 91–92, 185–86
Naylor, Gloria, 264
Negation, as strategy, 11–13, 69, 136–37,
181, 210
Neumann, Anne Waldron, 74n
Newton, Judith Lowder, 62n
Nitchie, Elizabeth, 171
Nouveau roman, 267, 270
Novel: Austen's defense of, 69–70; as

commercial project, 63, 86–88;
conventions of, 7, 39, 146, 256, 261, 263;
"governess," 177–82, 185–86;
heterosexism of, 39, 256; histories of,
36–39, 71, 103, 107; individualism of,
36, 37, 223, 231, 261; marital closure in,
27, 142–43, 146, 253; and maxims, 17;
modernist, 102–4; postmodernist, 123,
126–28, 131–35; realist, 84–87, 124–25;
representations of race in, 196–98; "rise"
of, and women, 15, 25–26, 36–38, 40;
Romantic, 156–58, 161–62, 164–65, 170,
172, 175. *See also* Plot

Omniscience, 68, 86, 100, 130–36
Omolade, Barbara, 200
Overt authoriality: *See* Authoriality;
Authorial voice

Pascal, Roy, 18n, 61, 62, 73–75
Patriarchy, 26, 32–33, 225; and democracy,
26, 32, 33, 147, 149
Perry, Ruth, 29, 45n
Personal voice, 15, 18–20, 22, 278–79;
absence of, in Woolf, Austen, Eliot, 108;
avoidance of, in *Their Eyes Were Watching
God*, 201–4; as mask, in slave narrative,
197; Morrison's use of, 130; private
forms of, 26, 33–34, 141; public forms
of, 142, 177, 178, 189–90; and race, 190,
192–95; resistance to, by "singular"
communal voice, 241; traces of, in
African-American novels, 194, 201, 207.
See also Autobiography; Epistolary
narration; Voice, private
Peterson, Carla L., 184n, 187
Peterson, Linda, 184n
Piercy, Marge, 45, 59
Plath, Sylvia, 189
Plot: effects of communal voice on, 22,
237, 241; heterosexual conventions of,
224, 261; individualism of, 21, 236–37;
marital closure in, 27, 142–43, 146, 253;
marriage-death oppositions, 27, 30, 276;
narration as, 244, 247, 277; rejection of,
in *Les Guérillères*, 268; resistance to
heterosexual conventions of, 39, 53, 159,
232, 241, 246, 252
Pollock, Walter, 78n
Ponsot, Marie, and Rosemary Deen, 255,
262
Poovey, Mary, 23, 26, 40n, 62n, 88, 165,
177n, 231, 236
Postmodernism, 123, 126–29, 135–36
Pratt, Annis, 209
Prefaces (to novels), 64–65, 69, 97
Private voice. *See* Voice, private

Pryse, Marjorie, and Hortense Spillers, 121n
Pseudonyms, 18, 88, 93–94
Public voice. *See* Voice, public

Rabine, Leslie, 156n
Race, 14; and Enlightenment, in Charrière, 161; and personal voice, differences of, 190, 193–96; and realist narration, 124, 125; representations, in the novel, 196, 198; and self-division, 205–6. *See also* African-American fiction; Black English
Radcliffe, Anne, 66
Radner, Joan N., and Susan S. Lanser, 59, 62
Reader. *See* Audience; Narratee
Realism, classic: 84–90; challenged: by modernism, 103–6; by postmodernism, 131–135; by techniques of *nouveau roman*, 268, 270, 275; "feminine," 105; race and class implications of, 124–25
Redinger, Ruby, 86n
Reeve, Clara, 36, 64, 66
Rhys, Jean: *Wide Sargasso Sea*, 190, 215
Riccoboni, Marie-Jeanne, 35, 38, 40, 45, 49–51, 54–59, 143; *L'Abeille* 49, 51–56, 58–59; *Amélie*, 58–59; *Lettres de Milady Juliette Catesby*, 27–32, 34, 36, 38–41, 50, 52, 55, 224; *Lettres de Mistriss Fanni Butlerd*, 33, 34; *Suite de Marianne*, 38, 59
Rich, Adrienne, 191, 221
Richardson, Alan, 157n
Richardson, Dorothy: *Pilgrimage*, 105–6, 108–9, 188
Richardson, Samuel, 35–36, 57, 77
Rimmon-Kenan, Shlomith, 17, 72
Rodolff, Rebecca, 181
Rogers, Katharine, 47
Romanticism: and female subjectivity, 34, 156–62, 164, 166–69, 171–72, 175, 181; and *Jane Eyre*, 177, 183, 187; and masculine authority, 156–57, 161–63, "Wertherian," in Charrière, 158–60
Ross, Marlon, 156n
Rossard, Janine, 159
Rousseau, Jean-Jacques, 32–33
Rowbotham, Sheila, 25, 28
Rowson, Susanna, 64–66
Rukeyser, Muriel, 139

Said, Edward, 7
Saisselin, Rémy, 47
Sand, George, 89, 91–92, 155, 162, 172, 175; *Lélia*, 172–75
"Santiago, Danny" [Daniel James]: *Famous All Over Town*, 36
Scholes, Robert, 86
Scott, Joan, 101n

Scott, Sarah, 57, 225, 237; *Millenium Hall*, 225–31, 237, 241, 278
Scott, Walter, 36, 37, 97
Self-authorization, of women, 7, 49, 98–99, 101, 130, 226,
Self-silencing: in eighteenth-century novels, 41, 49, 54–55, 151–54, 225, 231, 235–37; and *Les Guérillères*, 276; in *Our Nig*, 199–200
Sexuality and voice, 29, 40, 47, 169–70, 172–73, 189, 191, 211. *See also* Lesbian sexuality
Shange, Ntozake, 261, 263
Shelley, Mary, 162, 167–69, 171–72; *Frankenstein*, 155, 164–72, 175; *Mathilda*, 164, 166, 168–72, 175
Sheridan, Frances, 46n
Sherwood, Mary Martha: *Caroline Mordaunt*, 177–81
Showalter, Elaine, 110, 188
Silencing (of female voice), 30–32, 34, 190, 193, 203–4, 235
Simpson, Richard, 89
Sitter, John, 34, 47
Sivert, Eileen Boyd, 173
Skerrett, Joseph T., Jr., 122n
Slave narrative, 91n, 196–99, 219
Smith, Barbara, 120n
Smith, Charlotte, 65, 66, 78; *The Old Manor House*, 74n, 162
Smith, Valerie, 122n, 131, 132
Smollett, Tobias, 37
The Spectator, 51, 55, 70
Spender, Dale, 10–11, 37, 45, 48, 121, 278
Spivak, Gayatri Chakravorty, 164n, 185n, 191
Staël, Germaine de, 64, 155, 162–63; *Corinne, ou l'Italie*, 50, 66, 162–64, 175; *Delphine*, 66
Stanley, Julia Penelope, 93, 96
Stanton, Judith Phillips, 25n
Stanzel, Franz, 16–17, 104n
Starobinski, Jean, 159
Stepto, Robert, 203
Stevenson, John Allen, 39n
Stewart, Joan Hinde, 29n, 31–32, 143n
Still, William, 124
Stoddard, Elizabeth, 188
Stoneman, Patsy, 246
Stowe, Harriet Beecher, 91–92; *Uncle Tom's Cabin*, 89, 198
Subbaraman, Sivagami, 247n
Sypher, Eileen, 112

Tan, Amy: *The Joy Luck Club*, 264
Tuchman, Gaye, and Nina Fortin, 88, 90
Tye, J. R., 98n

Utopias, 226, 240–41, 275

Vallois, Marie-Claire, 163–64
Voice, 3–6, conventional singularity of,
239, 253, 255–57; gender dichotomies,
45–46, 141–42; "generic masculine," 18;
refusal of gender dichotomies, 276. *See
also* Authorial voice; Communal voice;
Personal voice
Voice, double. *See* "Double-voiced"
discourse
Voice, female, 6–8, 11–13; men's uses of,
25, 141–42, 189, 200
Voice, male, women writers' uses of: 19n,
46n, 92; 181, 226–27, 240; in
Romanticism, 155, 157–59, 162, 164–68,
171
Voice, private, 11–15, 20, 33–34; as
resistance strategy in African-American
women's writing, 198–99, 207–8, 213. *See
also* Epistolary narration
Voice, public, 11–16, 20; in African-
American women's writing, 209, 212;
constraints, for women, 46–48, 141, 189;
importance for women, 33, 34, 40, 41,
143; limitations in eighteenth-century
women's novels, 144–45, 154, 234–35; in
nineteenth-century women's novels, 177–
78. *See also* Authoriality; Autobiography;
Narratee
Voznesenskaya, Julia: *The Women's
Decameron*, 265–66

Walker, Alice, 120n; *The Color Purple*, 212–
13
Waller, Margaret, 157n
Warhol, Robyn, 4n, 91, 94

Warner, Susan, 98
Washington, Mary Helen, 121–22, 202–3
Watt, Ian, 37
West, Cornel, 128
Wilde, Alan, 110, 117, 127–28
Williams, Raymond, 5
Williams, Sherley Anne: *Dessa Rose*, 198–99
Wilson, Harriet, 199; *Our Nig*, 123, 194–
96, 199–200
Wilson, James D., 156
Wittig, Monique: *Les Guérillères*, 267–77
Wolf, Christa: *Nachdenken über Christa T.*,
21, 139
Wolff, Maria Tai, 202n
Wollstonecraft, Mary, 53, 65, 225, 235–37;
Mary, a Fiction, 64, 232n; *The Wrongs of
Woman or, Maria*, 74, 171n, 204, 225–26,
230–37
Women's communities. *See* Community,
female
"Women's language," 5, 10–12, 89, 93, 192
Woodhull, Winifred, 269
Woolf, Virginia: *Between the Acts*, 117–19;
as critic, 37, 40, 46, 84, 102–3, 106–7,
146, 176, 187–88, 239; *Jacob's Room*,
113–17; *Mrs. Dalloway*, 113, 115, 117;
Night and Day, 111; as novelist, 18, 59–
60, 106–19, 126, 130–31, 136; "The
Pargiters," 112–13; stories, 110–11; *To
the Lighthouse*, 113, 115–17; *The Voyage
Out*, 108, 111; *The Waves*, 111–16; *The
Years*, 113

Yetman, Norman, 197n
Young, Karl, 49
Yourcenar, Marguerite, 189

Zimmerman, Bonnie, 126

Library of Congress Cataloging-in-Publication Data
Lanser, Susan Sniader, 1944–
    Fictions of authority : women writers and narrative voice / Susan Sniader Lanser.
    p. cm.
    Includes bibliographical references (p.   ) and index.
    ISBN 0–8014–2377–5 (cloth : alkaline paper); ISBN 9921–6 (paper : alkaline paper)
      1. English fiction—Women authors—History and criticism.
    2. American fiction—Women authors—History and criticism.
    3. French fiction—Women authors—History and criticism.
    4. Authorship—Sex differences. 5. Women and literature.
    6. Narration (Rhetoric) I. Title.
    PR830.W6L38 1992
    823.009'9287—dc20   91-55537